WORKBOOK FOR

The Musician's Guide to Theory and Analysis

THIRD EDITION

WORKBOOK FOR

The Musician's Guide to Theory and Analysis

THIRD EDITION

Jane Piper Clendinning
Florida State University College of Music

Elizabeth West Marvin
Eastman School of Music

W. W. NORTON & COMPANY
NEW YORK • LONDON

Copyright © 2016, 2011, 2005 by W. W. Norton & Company, Inc.

Third Edition

Manufacturing by Hess Print Solutions
Associate project editor: Michael Fauver
Production manager: Jane Searle
Book design: Rubina Yeh
Composition, layout, and music setting: David Botwinik
Copyeditor: Jodi Beder
Proofreader: Debra Nichols

ISBN 978-0-393-26462-3 (pbk.)

W. W. Norton & Company, Inc., 500 Fifth Avenue, New York, NY 10110
    www.wwnorton.com
W. W. Norton & Company, Ltd., Castle House, 75/76 Wells Street, London W1T3QT

5 6 7 8 9 0

Contents

Part IV   The Twentieth Century and Beyond

Preface

The study of music theory is not a spectator sport. To learn musical elements and how to analyze them requires action—personal engagement with compositions. This workbook is designed to accompany *The Musician's Guide to Theory and Analysis*, providing hands-on, minds-engaged assignments for students to complete outside of class or for use in class, as the teacher chooses. Assignments are arranged in chapter order, so that you will have enough information to complete the first homework assignment on a given topic even if you have only covered the first part of that chapter. Assignments include fundamental skills such as chord spelling, style composition—from melody writing to figured bass to composing music in complete small forms—and music analysis. Many chapters ask for short, prose responses to questions about the music you are studying. By practicing each new skill from a variety of perspectives, you will have a better and more well-rounded understanding.

Our text's approach to learning music theory is a "spiral" one, in which we revisit the anthology's core repertoire from chapter to chapter as new concepts are introduced; the workbook continues the spirals established in the text, revisiting anthology scores in a series of analytical explorations, as well as introducing additional compositions. We hope that by examining aspects of these works as you learn analytical methods, you will eventually be able to hear anthology pieces in your head—as you do familiar songs—and also understand why the pieces sound the way they do.

In this third edition, we have incorporated the ideas of helpful reviewers, colleagues, and students, while retaining the musicality and richness of content of the first two editions. New for this edition is Know It? Show It!, an innovative online pedagogy that helps students develop music theory fluency:

- First, students watch video tutorials that explain key concepts through animated graphics showing how to approach each task.

- Then, formative quizzes—powered by Norton InQuizitive—help students develop the skills they'll need to complete assignments. InQuizitive asks students questions—many featuring musical notation—until they demonstrate mastery, while robust feedback to incorrect responses points students back to the textbook and tutorials for review.

- Finally, students are ready to complete assignments in either the printed or online workbook. With the online workbook, students can easily hear the results of their work, and teachers can grade and return assignments electronically.

These new resources are all designed to be easily employed in any theory class and to help students succeed.

Our Thanks to . . .

A work of this size and scope is helped along the way by many people. We are especially grateful for the support of our families—Elizabeth A. Clendinning, Rachel Armstrong, and Bill Iliff; and Glenn, Russell, and Caroline West. Our work together as coauthors has been incredibly rewarding, and we are thankful for that collaboration and friendship. We also thank Joel Phillips (Westminster Choir College) for his many important contributions—pedagogical, musical, and personal—to our project, and especially for the coordinated aural skills component of this package, *The Musician's Guide to Aural Skills* with Paul Murphy (Muhlenberg College), who has become a key member of our team. While working on the project, we have received encouragement and useful ideas from our students at Florida State University and the Eastman School of Music, as well as from music theory teachers across the country. We thank these teachers for their willingness to share their years of experience with us.

We are indebted to the W. W. Norton staff for their commitment to *The Musician's Guide* series and their painstaking care in producing these volumes. Most notable among these are Justin Hoffman, who steered the entire effort with a steady hand and enthusiastic support; Susan Gaustad, whose knowledge of music and detailed, thoughtful questions made her a joy to work with; and Maribeth Payne, whose vision helped launch the series. Michael Fauver project edited the workbook, Jodi Beder copyedited the manuscript and checked the assignments, and Debra Nichols proofread it. David Botwinik set the text and Workbook, and Andy Ensor and Jane Searle oversaw the production of this multifaceted project through to completion. We are grateful for Norton's forward-thinking technology editor Steve Hoge, who coordinated the development of the online workbook, with the assistance of Stephanie Eads, Courtney Hirschey, and Meg Wilhoite. Our sincere gratitude to one and all.

Jane Piper Clendinning
Elizabeth West Marvin

WORKBOOK FOR

The Musician's Guide to Theory and Analysis

THIRD EDITION

PART I

Elements of Music

1 Pitch and Pitch Class

NAME _____

Assignment 1.1

I. Identifying letter names from the keyboard

A. Count letter names above the pitches labeled on the keyboard (e.g., 3 above C). Be sure to count the given note (C-D-E). Write the letter name of the new pitch (E) on the appropriate key and in the blank provided.

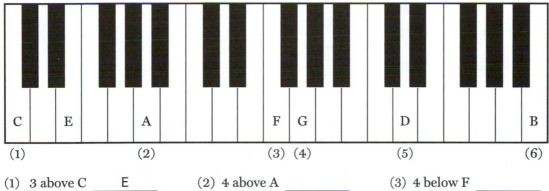

(1) 3 above C   __E__   (2) 4 above A _____   (3) 4 below F _____

(4) 6 above G _____   (5) 3 above D _____   (6) 3 below B _____

B. Write the letter name for each numbered white or black key in the blank. Choose either enharmonic name for black keys.

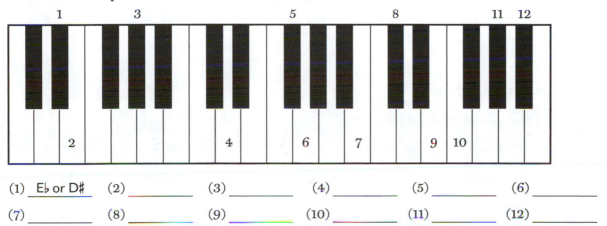

(1) __E♭ or D♯__   (2) _____   (3) _____   (4) _____   (5) _____   (6) _____

(7) _____   (8) _____   (9) _____   (10) _____   (11) _____   (12) _____

II. Identifying whole and half steps at the keyboard

Locate each pair of pitches on the keyboard below in any octave. Write their names on a white key or above a black key. Then, in the blank provided, write W (whole step), H (half step), or N (neither).

(a) A♯-B   H   (b) F-E   (c) G♭-A

(d) B♭-C   (e) G♯-G♮   (f) D♭-C♭

(g) F♯-G♯   (h) E-F♭   (i) G♭-G♮

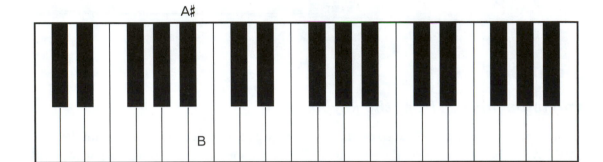

(j) B-C   (k) G-A♯   (l) C♯-D♯

(m) E♭-E♮   (n) A-B   (o) A♭-G♭

(p) B♭-C♯   (q) E♭-F   (r) A♭-A♮

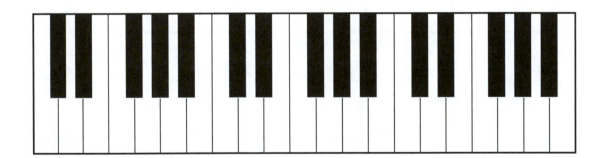

III. Enharmonic pitches

Circle any pair of pitches that are *not* enharmonic.

(a) F♯-G♭   (b) B×-C   (c) A♯-B♭   (d) C♭-B   (e) G♭♭-F   (f) D-E♭♭

(g) E♯-F♭   (h) A♭♭-G   (i) D×-E   (j) C×-D   (k) B♭-C♭♭   (l) A×-B♭

Assignment 1.2

I. Identifying whole and half steps at the keyboard

In each exercise below, start with the key indicated and move your finger along the path of half and whole steps given. In the blank, write the name of the pitch where you end.

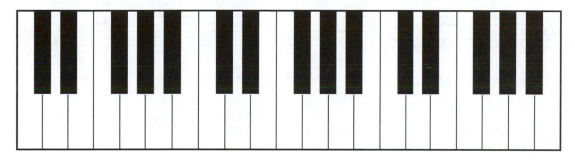

(a) Begin on C: down W, down H, down W, up H, up H = ____A____

(b) Begin on E: up W, up H, up W, down H, up W, up W = _____

(c) Begin on F♯: down W, down W, up H, down W, down H, up W = _____

(d) Begin on A♭: up W, up W, up W, down H, up W, up W = _____

(e) Begin on C♯: down W, up H, up W, up W, up H, up H = _____

(f) Begin on B: up H, up H, down W, down H, down W, down W = _____

(g) Begin on D: up H, down W, down W, down H, down H, up W = _____

(h) Begin on E♭: down W, down W, down H, down W, up H, up H = _____

II. Staff notation

Write the letter name of each pitch in the blank below.

A. Treble and bass clefs

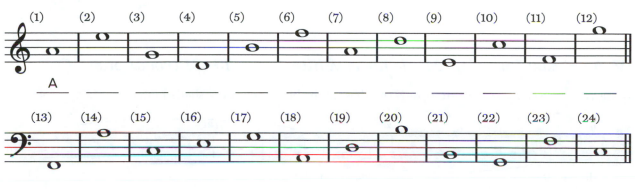

B. Alto and tenor clefs

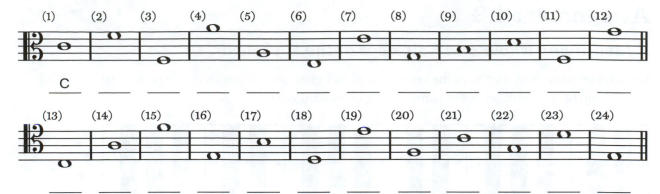

III. Half and whole steps from staff notation

For each pitch pair below, write W (whole step), H (half step), or N (neither) in the blank.

IV. Analysis: Purcell, "Music for a While," mm. 19–21 (vocal part)

Write W (whole step), H (half step), or N (neither) in the blank below the shaded pitches.

(a) H   (b) ___   (c) ___   (d) ___   (e) ___

Assignment 1.3

I. Writing whole and half steps on the staff

For each given note:

- Draw a stem to make a half note; be sure that the stem is on the correct side of the note and extends in the correct direction.
- Write a second half note a whole or half step above or below the given note, as indicated by the arrow.
- Choose a spelling for the second note that has a different letter name from the given pitch.

II. Identifying pitches with and without ledger lines

Write the letter name of each pitch in the blank provided.

III. Identifying pitches in C-clefs

For each pitch on the left, write the C-clef equivalent on the right. Then label every pitch with the correct letter name and octave number in the blank. Don't change the octave.

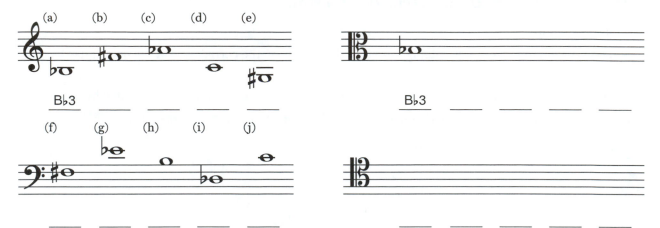

(a) (b) (c) (d) (e)

B♭3 _____ _____ _____ _____   B♭3 _____ _____ _____ _____

(f) (g) (h) (i) (j)

_____ _____ _____ _____ _____

IV. Analysis

In the following melodies, write W or H for each bracketed pair of pitches in the blank below.

A. Joel Phillips, "Blues for Norton," mm. 20-24 (bass line)

(1) W (2) ___ (3) ___ (4) ___ (5) ___ (6) ___ (7) ___

B. Mozart, *Variations on "Ah, vous dirai-je, Maman,"* mm. 164-168 (left hand)

(1) ___ (2) ___ (3) ___ (4) ___ (5) ___ (6) ___ (7) ___

C. Joplin, "Pine Apple Rag," mm. 1-4 (right hand)

(1) ___ (2) ___ (3) ___ (4) ___ (5) ___ (6) ___ (7) ___ (8) ___

D. Willie Nelson, "On the Road Again," mm. 11-14

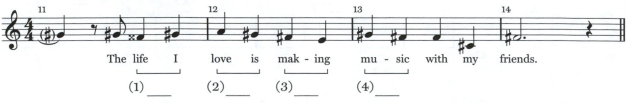

The life I love is mak-ing mu-sic with my friends.

(1) ___ (2) ___ (3) ___ (4) ___

Assignment 1.4

I. Identifying pitches in mixed clefs

Write the letter name and octave number of each pitch below.

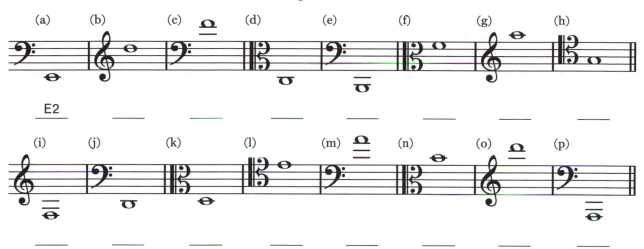

E2

II. Writing half and whole steps in mixed clefs

In the following exercises, choose a spelling that has a different letter name from the given pitch.

A. Write a whole step above each given note.

B. Write a whole step below each given note.

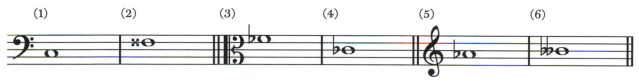

C. Write a diatonic half step above each given note (with a different letter name).

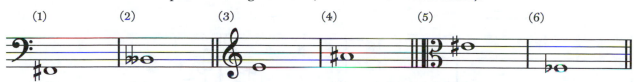

D. Write a diatonic half step below each given note (with a different letter name).

III. Identifying pitch and register in musical contexts

In the excerpts below, write the letter name and octave number of the shaded pitch in the blank that corresponds with the numbers marked on the score.

A. Haydn, String Quartet in D Minor, Op. 76, No. 2 (*Quinten*), mvt. 3, mm. 1-11

(1) ___F5___	(2) _____	(3) _____	(4) _____	(5) _____
(6) _____	(7) _____	(8) _____	(9) _____	(10) _____

B. Clara Schumann, *Drei Romanzen*, Op. 21, No. 1, mm. 5-8

(1) ___E5___	(2) _____	(3) _____	(4) _____	(5) _____	(6) _____

Assignment 1.5

I. Arranging

Rewrite each excerpt on the blank staff provided, according to the individual instructions. Use ledger lines as needed. Remember to change the stem direction where necesssary in the new octave. Copy note heads, stems, and other symbols as shown (you'll learn more about them in Chapter 2).

A. Foster, "Jeanie with the Light Brown Hair," mm. 5-8

Rewrite one octave lower in the bass clef.

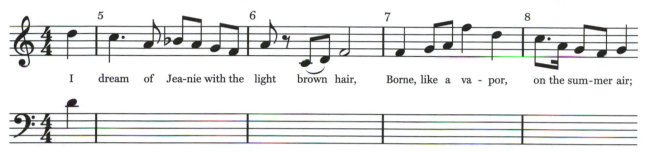

B. Purcell, "Music for a While," mm. 21-22

Rewrite this line for bassoon in the tenor clef; don't change the octave.

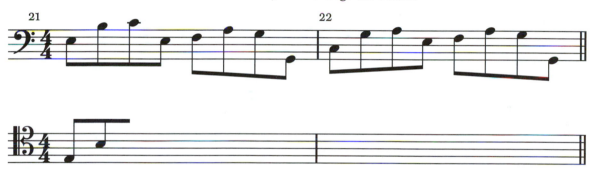

C. Mozart, Symphony No. 41 in C Major, mvt. 4, mm. 407-411 (viola)

Rewrite this viola part for violin in the treble clef; don't change the octave.

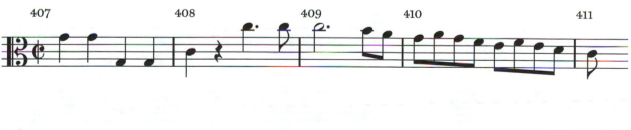

II. Composing melodies

On the staves below, compose two melodies of mostly whole and half steps in any musical style you choose.

- Choose a different "home" pitch for each melody. Begin and end on this note.
- Write at least ten pitches for each, using only adjacent letter names (e.g., B–C or G–F♯–E).
- Write two to three times as many whole steps as half steps.
- Notate all accidentals, even naturals.
- Notate your melody with rhythm if you wish, or use filled and hollow note heads as shown below (hollow note heads last twice as long as filled).

Sample melody 1

C = home

Sample melody 2

B♭ = home

A. Melody 1

B. Melody 2

2 Simple Meters

NAME _____

Assignment 2.1

I. Notation basics

A. Circle any notation errors on the left, then renotate the entire exercise correctly on the right.

B. For each rhythmic value or rest notated on the first line, notate the corresponding rest or note on the second line.

II. Identifying meter

Write the meter signatures and meter type (e.g., simple duple) for each of the following melodies.

A. Bach, Minuet II from Cello Suite No. 1 in G Major, mm. 1–8 🎧

Meter: _____   Meter type: _____

B. Clara Schumann, "Liebst du um Schönheit," mm. 3–6 🎧

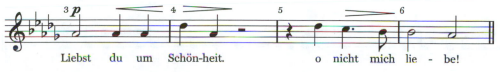

Liebst   du   um   Schön-heit.   o   nicht   mich   lie - be!

Meter: _____   Meter type: _____

C. Schubert, Waltz in B Minor, Op. 18, No. 6, mm. 1–8

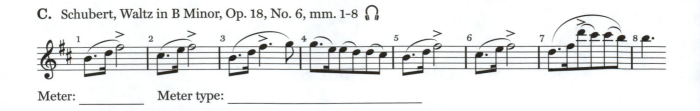

Meter: _____   Meter type: _____

III. Counting rhythms

For each rhythm provided, add the missing bar lines and write the counts below the score. Then perform the rhythm.

(1) Lionel Richie, "Three Times a Lady," mm. 11–14

Now   that we've come   to the   end   of   our   rain - bow

1   (2)   3   &

(2) Bono and U2, "Miracle Drug," mm. 29–32 (last measure is incomplete)

Free - dom   has a scent   like the   top   of   a new - born   ba - by's head._

Assignment 2.2

I. Understanding dots

Write the appropriate note value in each empty box of the chart provided.

II. Counting rhythms with beat subdivisions

A. Add the missing bar lines to each rhythm, and write the counts below. Then perform the rhythm.

(1)

1 (2)

(2)

(3)

(4)

B. At each position marked by an arrow, add one note to complete the measure in the meter indicated. If you write an eighth or sixteenth note, beam or flag it properly.

(1)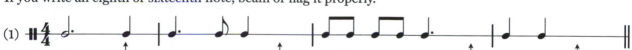

(2)

(3)

(4)

(5)

III. Counting rhythms with rests

Rewrite each rhythm and melody on the blank staff provided, supplying the missing bar lines and correcting the beaming to reflect the beat. The Schumann melody begins with an anacrusis, as shown; do not recopy the text.

(4) Schumann, "Im wunderschönen Monat Mai," mm. 5-10

Im wun - der schö - nen Mo - nat Mai, als

al - le Knos - pen sprang-en, da ist in mei - nem Her - zen

Assignment 2.3

I. Beaming to reflect the beat

Rewrite each of the following rhythms with correct beams to reflect the beat unit. Add the counts beneath the rhythm, and read the rhythm aloud.

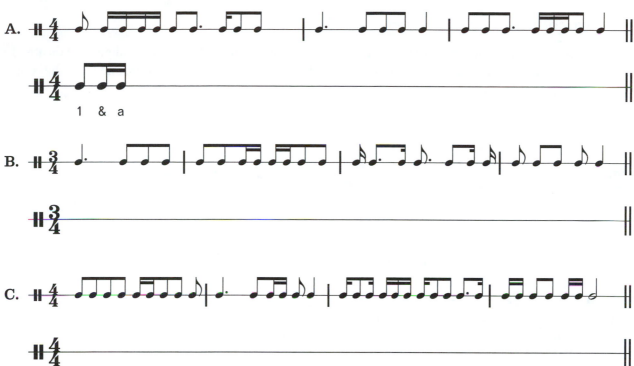

II. Counting rhythms with dots and ties

Rewrite the following rhythms with dots in place of tied notes. Be careful to beam your answers correctly. Write the counts beneath the rewritten rhythm, with the beat number in parentheses if there is no corresponding note above it.

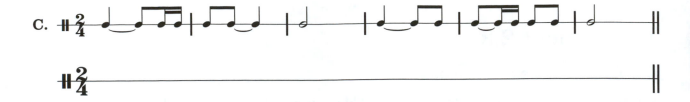

III. Syncopation

Syncopated rhythms are widespread in music written for popular songs, the movies, and musical theater. In each of the following tunes, draw an arrow above the staff that points to a syncopation, and write the counts for the entire rhythm beneath.

A. Carole King, "You've Got a Friend," mm. 4–8

B. Jonathan Larson, "Seasons of Love," mm. 41–44

C. James Horner, Barry Mann, and Cynthia Weil, "Somewhere Out There," mm. 27–28

D. Shania Twain, "You're Still the One," mm. 13–16

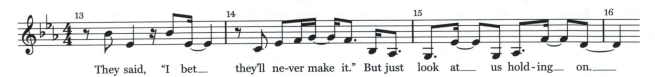

Assignment 2.4

I. Reading meter signatures

A. Fill in the empty boxes in the chart with a meter or note value.

METER TYPE	METER	BEAT UNIT	BEAT DIVISION	FULL BAR DURATION
Simple duple	2/2	♩	♩ ♩	𝅝
Simple duple			♫	
Simple triple	3/8			
Simple triple				𝅗𝅥.
Simple quadruple		♩		𝅜
Simple quadruple	4/4			

B. Write the meter signature and meter type (e.g., simple duple) for each of the given works.

(1) Corelli, Preludio, from Trio Sonata in D Minor, Op. 4, No. 8, mm. 1–7

Meter: ___3/2___   Meter type: _____

(2) Orlando Gibbons, Song 46, mm. 1–4 (last measure is incomplete)

Meter: _____   Meter type: _____

(3) Scarlatti, Sonata in G Major, L. 388, mm. 1–6

Meter: _____   Meter type: _____

II. Reading and writing in different meters

A. At each position marked by an arrow, write the appropriate note value. If you write an eighth or sixteenth note, beam or flag it properly.

B. Renotate the following rhythms with ties instead of dotted notes.

Assignment 2.5

I. Understanding meter signatures

For each meter given, write the beat unit on the staff (on any line or space), and the meter type (duple, triple, or quadruple) in the blank.

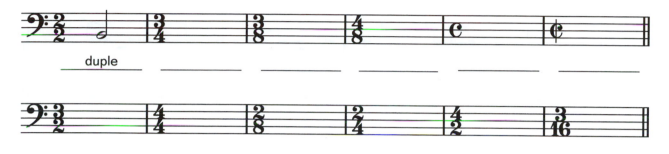

duple _____ _____ _____ _____ _____

_____ _____ _____ _____ _____ _____

II. Writing in different meters

A. Renotate Schumann's melody (not the text) on the blank staves, in ¾. When beaming the rhythms, use modern ("instrumental") style rather than vocal notation.

Schumann, "Widmung" ("Dedication"), mm. 18-25

B. Renotate the following rhythms without ties. Then perform each rhythm.

(1)

Renotated

(2)

Renotated

(3)

Renotated

C. Complete the following rhythms by adding one or two rests to complete any measure marked by an arrow. Then perform each rhythm.

(1)

(2)

(3)

(4)

(5)

(6)

Assignment 2.6

I. Anacrusis notation

Each of these melodies begins with an anacrusis. What note value (or note value plus rest) should the composer use to fill the final measure of the composition (not shown) to balance the anacrusis? Write this value in the blank provided.

A. Bach, Passacaglia in C Minor, mm. 1–7

Final note value: _____

B. Haydn, Scherzo, from Piano Sonata No. 9 in F Major, mm. 1–4

Final note value: _____

C. "Wayfaring Stranger," mm. 1–4

Final note value: _____

D. Don McLean, "American Pie," mm. 1–3

Final note value: _____

II. Composing a rhythmic canon

Compose a rhythmic canon in four parts to perform with classmates.

- Begin by performing the following canon as an example, with classmates divided into four groups. Each group starts at the beginning, entering when the preceding group reaches rehearsal number 2: Group 2 enters when Group 1 reaches rehearsal number 2, and so on—just like "Row, Row, Row Your Boat."

- For a more elaborate rhythmic composition, listen to Ernst Toch's *Geographical Fugue*, whose text is based on names of places: "Trinidad, and the big Mississippi and the town Honolulu. . . ." Try writing a similar text with the names of your classmates, buildings on campus, or countries of the world.

- Build in ties and syncopations. Use rhythms that emphasize different beats or parts of the beat, and add contrasting dynamics to each line to create an interesting and musical effect in performance.

Your composition:

3 Pitch Collections, Scales, and Major Keys

NAME _____

Assignment 3.1

I. Writing scales

A. Beginning on the pitch given, build an ascending major scale by adding flats or sharps where needed, following the correct pattern of whole and half steps.

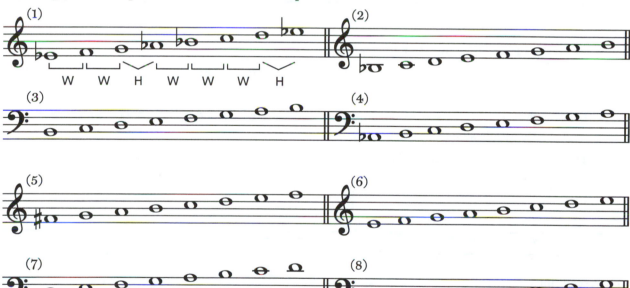

B. Write the major scales indicated, beginning with the specified pitch.

(1) D4 ascending   (2) F♯4 ascending

(3) A♭3 descending   (4) E♭3 ascending

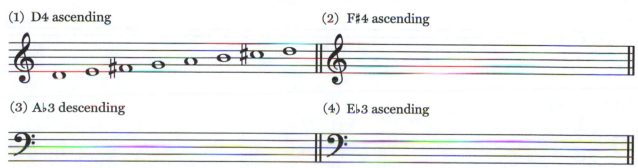

(5) B3 ascending

(6) F3 descending

(7) G5 descending

(8) E4 ascending

(9) D♭3 ascending

(10) B♭3 descending

(11) C♯4 ascending

(12) C♭4 ascending

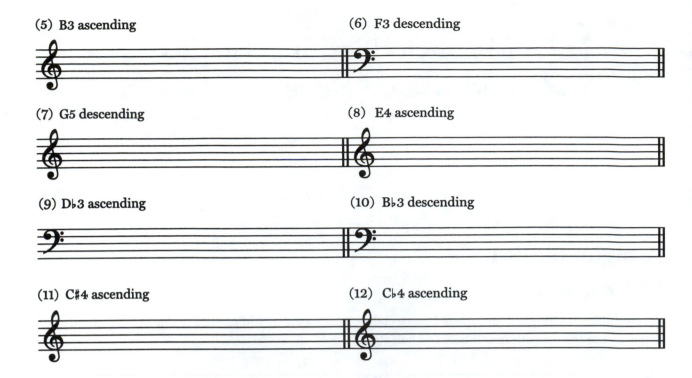

C. Write chromatic scales, using the following steps.

- Write a major scale with hollow note heads, ascending or descending as specified, starting with the given pitch.
- Label each pitch with its scale-degree number, and mark whole and half steps. Leave a space between the whole steps to add a note between.
- Then fill in half steps (with filled note heads) as needed to make a chromatic scale.

(1) Ascending

(2) Descending

(3) Descending

(4) Ascending

Assignment 3.2

I. Key signatures

A. On the following staves, write the key signature for each major key indicated. Be sure that the sharps and flats appear in the correct order and octave.

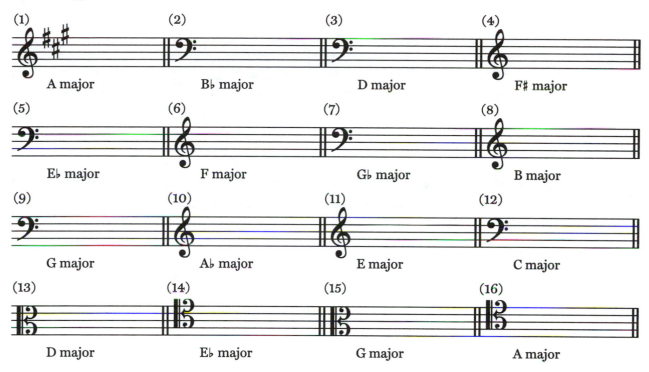

B. Identify the name of the major key associated with each of these key signatures.

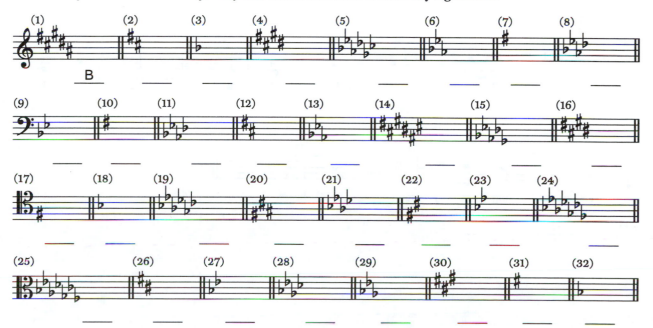

II. Scale-degree analysis of melodies

These vocal melodies include prominent scale passages or segments. For each melody, (1) mark scale segments (five notes or longer) with a bracket, (2) write the name of the key in the blank below the melody, then (3) write the appropriate scale-degree numbers or solfège syllables (first letter only) above each note. Finally, sing on scale-degree numbers or solfège.

A. "Come, Follow Me" (anonymous); perform as a round 🎧

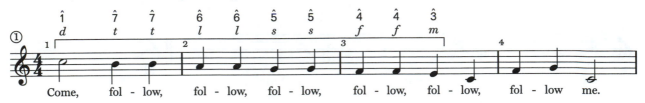

Key: _____

B. Richard Rodgers and Oscar Hammerstein, "The Sound of Music," mm. 9-15 🎧

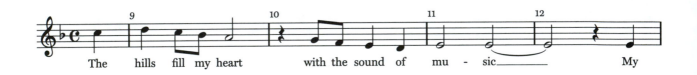

Key: _____

Assignment 3.3

I. Scale and scale degree

A. Given the scale degree notated on the left, write the major scale to which it belongs. Begin by writing whole notes on each line and space, then fill in the necessary accidentals. Write the scale-degree number or name beneath the given note in your scale, to check your answer.

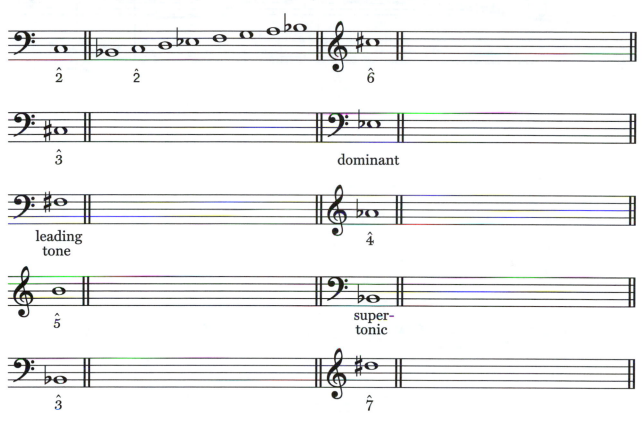

B. Complete the table by writing the requested major key, scale degree, or pitch name.

	MAJOR KEY	SCALE DEGREE	PITCH
(1)	E	$\hat{7}$	
(2)		supertonic	C♯
(3)	F♯		C♯
(4)	E♭	$\hat{3}$	
(5)		$\hat{4}$	G♭
(6)		leading tone	A

	MAJOR KEY	SCALE DEGREE	PITCH
(7)	F	subdominant	
(8)	D	leading tone	
(9)		$\hat{4}$	F♯
(10)	B	$\hat{5}$	
(11)	C	mediant	
(12)		$\hat{6}$	F

II. Scale and key analysis

Each of the following pieces features a prominent scale or scale segment. Write the scale or segment on the staff below. Is it chromatic or major? If major, name the tonic.

A. Mozart, Piano Sonata, K. 333, mvt. 1, mm. 8–10

Scale type or major key: _____

B. Joplin, "The Ragtime Dance," mm. 61–64

Scale type or major key: _____

C. Handel, Chaconne, mm. 49–51

Scale type or major key: _____

Assignment 3.4

I. Key signature review

A. Identify the major key indicated by each key signature.

(1) F# (2) ___ (3) ___ (4) ___ (5) ___ (6) ___ (7) ___ (8) ___ (9) ___ (10) ___

B. Write the key signature for each major key specified. Place sharps or flats in the correct order and octave.

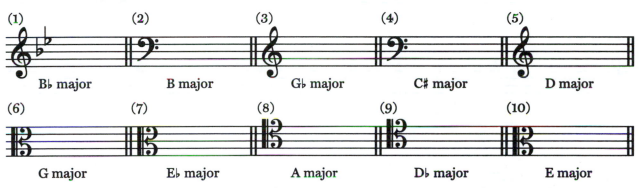

(1) Bb major (2) B major (3) Gb major (4) C# major (5) D major

(6) G major (7) Eb major (8) A major (9) Db major (10) E major

II. Identifying scale degrees

A. Write the appropriate note on the staff indicated by the major key and scale degree.

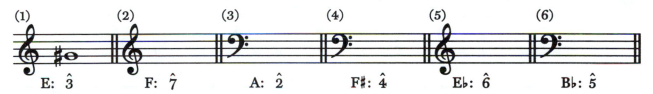

(1) E: $\hat{3}$ (2) F: $\hat{7}$ (3) A: $\hat{2}$ (4) F#: $\hat{4}$ (5) Eb: $\hat{6}$ (6) Bb: $\hat{5}$

B. Each of the following sequences of scale degrees and solfège syllables represents a well-known melody. (Solfège is notated with just the first letter of the syllable.) An underlined symbol shows a pitch below the tonic.

- On the top staff, write out the major scale specified, and label with scale degrees or solfège.
- Use these labels to write out the melody (with correct key signature) on the lower staves. (Rhythm is optional.)
- If you know the name of the tune, write it in the blank provided (optional).

(1) A major

$\hat{1}$ $\hat{2}$
d   *r*

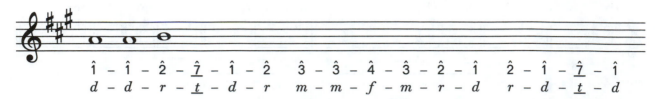

$\hat{1} - \hat{1} - \hat{2} - \underline{\hat{7}} - \hat{1} - \hat{2}$ $\hat{3} - \hat{3} - \hat{4} - \hat{3} - \hat{2} - \hat{1}$ $\hat{2} - \hat{1} - \underline{\hat{7}} - \hat{1}$
d – *d* – *r* – *t* – *d* – *r*   *m* – *m* – *f* – *m* – *r* – *d*   *r* – *d* – *t* – *d*

Name of melody: _____

(2) B♭ major

$\hat{1} - \hat{1} - \hat{2} - \hat{3} - \hat{1} - \hat{3} - \hat{2} - \underline{\hat{5}}$ $\hat{1} - \hat{1} - \hat{2} - \hat{3} - \hat{1} - \underline{\hat{7},}$
d – *d* – *r* – *m* – *d* – *m* – *r* – *s*   *d* – *d* – *r* – *m* – *d* – *t,*

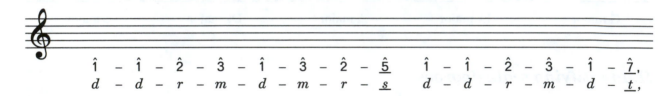

$\hat{1} - \hat{1} - \hat{2} - \hat{3} - \hat{4} - \hat{3} - \hat{2} - \hat{1} - \underline{\hat{7}} - \underline{\hat{5}} - \underline{\hat{6}} - \underline{\hat{7}} - \hat{1} - \hat{1}$
d – *d* – *r* – *m* – *f* – *m* – *r* – *d* – *t* – *s* – *l* – *t* – *d* – *d*

Name of melody: _____

III. Pentatonic scale

Write the following major pentatonic scales ($\hat{1}$-$\hat{2}$-$\hat{3}$-$\hat{5}$-$\hat{6}$, or *do-re-mi-sol-la*).

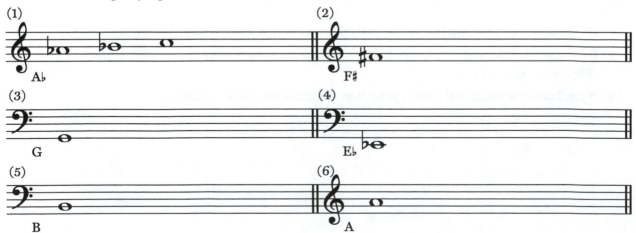

(1)   (2)

A♭   F♯

(3)   (4)

G   E♭

(5)   (6)

B   A

Assignment 3.5

I. Scale review

Write the scales requested, beginning with the given pitch. Add accidentals before each note as needed, rather than using a key signature.

A. Scales ascending and descending

(1) Major

(2) Chromatic

(3) Major

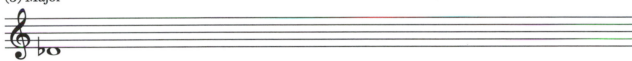

(4) Chromatic

(5) Major

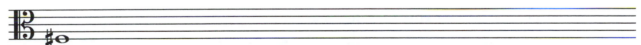

B. Scales either ascending or descending

(1) Major pentatonic, ascending

(2) Major, descending

(3) Major pentatonic, ascending

(4) Major pentatonic, ascending

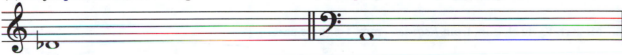

(5) Major, ascending

(6) Major, descending

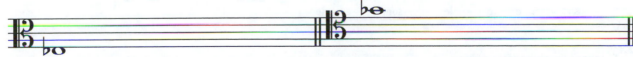

II. Analysis of scale type

Look at the key signature and melodic cues from the beginning and end of each given melody to determine the key. Write the name of the major key (or "not major") in the blank. If major, label the scale degrees of each note below the staff to confirm that they fit well in the key you have chosen.

A. "Hush, Little Baby," mm. 1-8

Hush, lit-tle ba-by, don't say a word. Ma-ma's going to buy you a mock-ing bird.

Key: _____

B. Schubert, "Der Lindenbaum," mm. 9-12

Am Brun - nen vor dem Tho - re da steht ein Lin - den - baum;

Translation: By the fountain in front of the gate, there stands a linden tree.

Key: _____

C. "Masters in the Hall" (carol), mm. 5-8

Brought from o - ver sea,____ And ev - er I you pray:

Key: _____

D. H. Worthington Loomis, "The Frog in the Bog," mm. 1-5

There once was a frog who lived in a bog and played a fid-dle in the

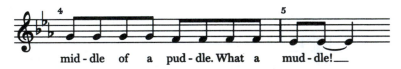

mid-dle of a pud-dle. What a mud-dle!___

Key: _____

E. Mozart, Kyrie eleison, from *Requiem*, mm. 1-5 (bass part)

Ky - ri-e e - le - i-son, e - le - - - - i - son

Key: _____

4 Compound Meters

NAME _____

Assignment 4.1

I. Understanding simple and compound meter signatures

A. From the information given, complete the following chart.

METER TYPE	METER	BEAT UNIT	BEAT DIVISION	FULL BAR DURATION
Compound duple	$\frac{6}{4}$	𝅗𝅥.	♩ ♩ ♩	𝅝.
Compound duple			♫♫	
Simple triple				𝅗𝅥.
Compound triple	$\frac{9}{4}$			𝅝⌣𝅗𝅥.
Simple quadruple		♪		
Compound quadruple	$\frac{12}{16}$			

B. Each of these melodies is taken from a keyboard prelude in Bach's *Well-Tempered Clavier*, Book I. Provide the correct simple or compound meter signature, then write the meter type (e.g., compound triple) and beat unit (e.g., ♪.) in the blanks provided. (The final measure of the excerpt may be incomplete.)

(1) Prelude in A Minor, mm. 1–4 (left hand, m. 4 is incomplete) 𝆓

Meter: ___$\frac{9}{8}$___   Meter type: _____   Beat unit: _____

(2) Prelude in A♭ Major, mm. 1–5 (right hand) 𝆓

Meter: _____   Meter type: _____   Beat unit: _____

(3) Prelude in G♯ Minor, mm. 1-4 (right hand)

Meter: _____ Meter type: _____ Beat unit: _____

(4) Prelude in C♯ Minor, mm. 1-4 (right hand)

Meter: _____ Meter type: _____ Beat unit: _____

(5) Prelude in E♭ Minor, mm. 1-4 (right hand)

Meter: _____ Meter type: _____ Beat unit: _____

(6) Prelude in E Major, mm. 1-3 (left hand)

Meter: _____ Meter type: _____ Beat unit: _____

(7) Prelude in C♯ Major, mm. 1-7 (right hand)

Meter: _____ Meter type: _____ Beat unit: _____

(8) Prelude in F Major, mm. 1-2 (left hand)

Meter: _____ Meter type: _____ Beat unit: _____

Assignment 4.2

I. Understanding simple and compound meter signatures

For each meter signature given, fill in the missing information.

METER	METER TYPE	BEAT UNIT	BEAT DIVISION	BEAT SUBDIVISION
$\frac{9}{8}$	Compound triple	♩.	♫♫	♬♬♬
$\frac{6}{4}$				
$\frac{12}{16}$				
$\frac{3}{2}$				
$\frac{9}{4}$				

II. Compound meters with ♩. beat units

A. At each position marked by an arrow, add one note value that completes the measure in the meter indicated. Then write the counts below the staff.

(1)

1   li   (2)

(2)

(3)

(4)

(5)

B. Rewrite the following rhythms with correct beaming to reflect the beat. Practice the rhythms on "ta" or counting syllables. Be prepared to perform them in class.

(1)

(2)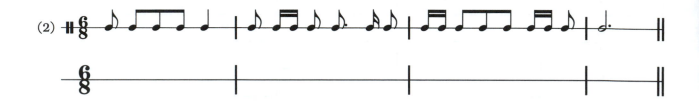

(3)

(4)

(5)

(6)

Assignment 4.3

I. Understanding compound meters

For each melody, provide the missing bar lines that correspond with the meter signature given. The final measure may be incomplete.

A. Beethoven, String Quartet in F Major, Op. 18, No. 1, mvt. 2 (cello part, adapted)

B. Hensel, "Schwanenlied" (adapted)

C. Bartók, String Quartet No. 2, mvt. 1 (cello)

II. Understanding rests

At each position marked with an arrow, add one rest to complete the measure in the meter indicated. Write the counts below the rhythm; enclose counts in parentheses if they fall on a rest.

III. Beaming to reflect the meter

Vocal music, especially in older editions, is often written with flags that correspond to syllables of the sung text. Copy the vocal lines on the blank staves (without text), replacing flags with beams to reflect the meter and beat unit instead. Copy the rests exactly.

A. Handel, "How beautiful are the feet of them," from *Messiah*, mm. 5-9 🎧

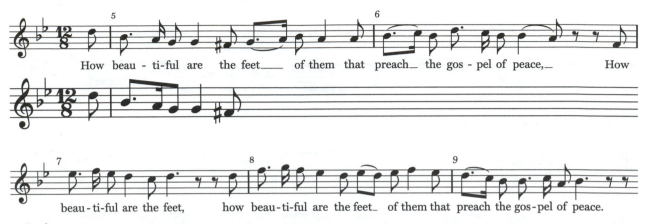

B. Mozart, "Lacrimosa," from *Requiem*, mm. 9-10 (soprano part) 🎧

C. Schumann, "Ich hab' im Traum geweinet," from *Dichterliebe*, mm. 10-13 🎧

Assignment 4.4

I. Compound meters with 𝅗𝅥. and ♪. beat units

A. Write counts beneath each melody. Then rewrite the melody (not the words) in the meters indicated. Use proper beaming and stem direction.

(1) "Agincourt Song," mm. 1-4

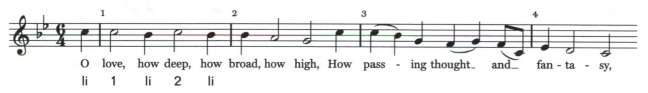

(2) "The Pretty Girl Milking Her Cow," mm. 3-4

(3) "When Johnny Comes Marching Home," mm. 1-4

(4) Ralph Vaughan Williams, "The Call," mm. 2-6

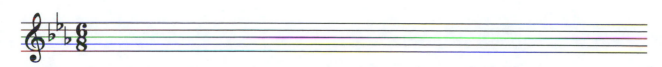

B. At each position marked by an arrow, add one note value to complete the measure in the meter indicated. Remember to subtract the value of an anacrusis from the final bar.

II. Rhythmic duets

Compose a second line to go with each of the following rhythms. Write notes and rests that complement (and don't overpower) the first line. Make sure that each measure is complete. Prepare your duet for performance with a classmate.

Assignment 4.5

I. Reading and writing triplets

A. In each of these rhythms, provide the missing bar lines that correspond with the meter signature given.

B. Renotate each of these rhythms, and insert a triplet in place of the bracketed beat. Write the rhythm counts beneath your answer. Then perform the rhythm you have written.

1 (2 3) 4   1 la li

II. Syncopations

A. Rewrite each rhythm, adding ties or accent marks to create syncopations. Be prepared to perform each syncopated rhythm.

B. Compose a syncopated compound-meter rhythmic canon for performance with classmates. Begin by performing the following three-part canon as an example. Divide into three groups; each new group begins when the previous group has reached ②. In your composition:

- Make the three lines distinctive, including rhythms that emphasize different beats or offbeats for contrast.
- Add a text and contrasting dynamics and accents in each line to create an interesting and musical effect in performance.
- Circle each syncopated pattern.

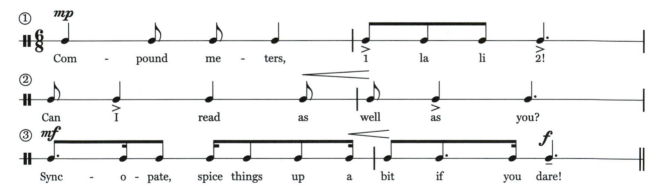

Your composition:

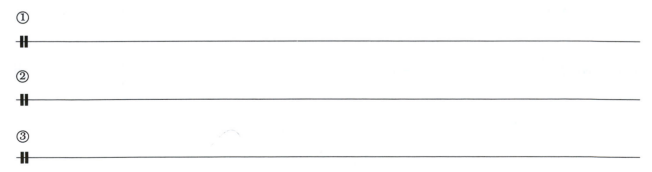

Assignment 4.6

I. Analysis

Name the meter type for each excerpt. Then, below the staff write the counts where indicated. Finally, answer the question below the excerpt with one or two sentences.

A. Handel, "Rejoice greatly" (soprano part, alternate version), mm. 9-14

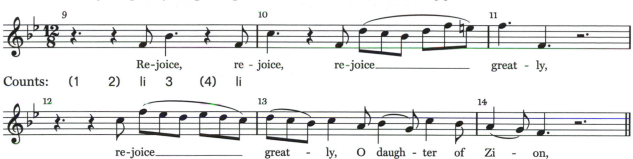

Counts: (1   2) li 3   (4) li

Counts:

Meter type: _____

How does this setting differ from the one in your anthology? Which version do you think is simpler to sing, and why?

B. Schubert, "Erlkönig," mm. 15-19

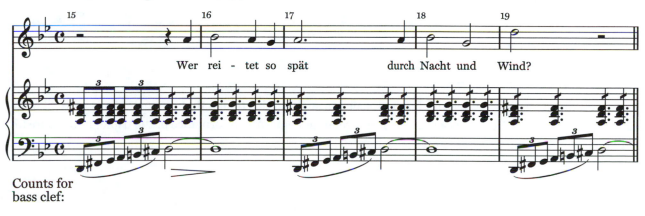

Counts for
bass clef:

Meter type: _____

With so many triplets, Schubert might have chosen to write the piano accompaniment in what compound meter?

Meter: _____

On the staff, write the vocal part for measures 15-19 in that compound meter.

C. Andrew Lloyd Webber and Tim Rice, "Don't Cry for Me Argentina," mm. 3-8 🎧

Write the counts for the melody line above the staff, as though in $\frac{2}{2}$ meter (cut time).

Meter type: _____

Some popular songs are notated in $\frac{4}{4}$ but performed in such a quick tempo that the meter feels more like cut time (alla breve), or $\frac{2}{2}$. How does a cut-time interpretation help with performance of the triplet in measure 8? What other notational features suggest cut time?

5 Minor Keys and the Diatonic Modes

NAME _____

Assignment 5.1

I. Writing minor scales

A. For each major key requested, write the key signature and major scale in the left column. Circle scale degree $\hat{6}$. Then, in the right column, write its relative natural minor and name it, as shown.

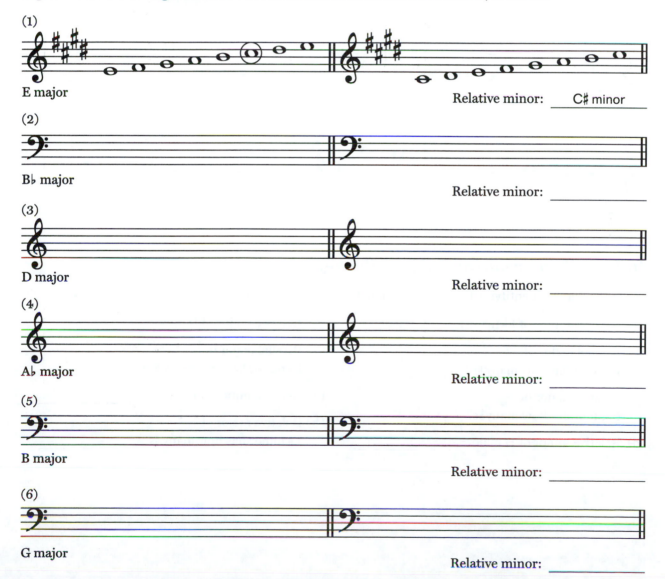

(1)

E major

Relative minor: _____ C♯ minor _____

(2)

B♭ major

Relative minor: _____

(3)

D major

Relative minor: _____

(4)

A♭ major

Relative minor: _____

(5)

B major

Relative minor: _____

(6)

G major

Relative minor: _____

B. On the left, build the ascending natural minor scale specified by adding flats or sharps in front of the pitches given. On the right, write the key signature of the relative major, and name the key. Then write the complete major scale.

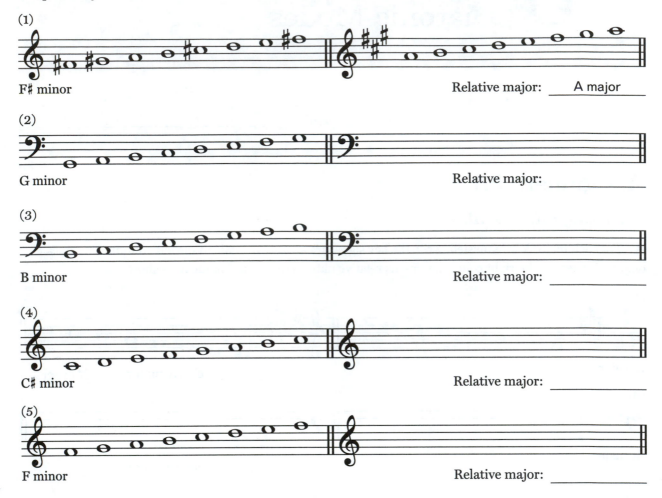

(1)

F♯ minor

Relative major: A major

(2)

G minor

Relative major: _____

(3)

B minor

Relative major: _____

(4)

C♯ minor

Relative major: _____

(5)

F minor

Relative major: _____

II. Identifying relative and parallel keys

Fill in the blanks, identifying the key or key signature.

(a) Relative minor of E♭ major: C minor

(b) Parallel major of
E minor has how many ♯s? _____

(c) Relative major of
F minor has how many ♭s? _____

(d) Relative minor of D major: _____

(e) Relative major of D minor: _____

(f) Parallel major of
F♯ minor has how many ♯s? _____

(g) Relative minor of B♭ major: _____

(h) Relative major of
F♯ minor has how many ♯s? _____

Assignment 5.2

I. Key signatures

A. For each signature given, identify its major key in the top row of blanks and its relative minor key in the bottom row, as shown. Use a lowercase letter for minor keys.

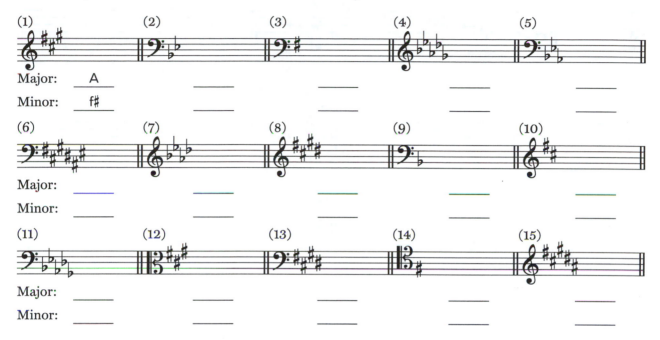

(1) (2) (3) (4) (5)

Major: A   _____   _____   _____   _____

Minor: f♯   _____   _____   _____   _____

(6) (7) (8) (9) (10)

Major: _____ _____ _____ _____ _____

Minor: _____ _____ _____ _____ _____

(11) (12) (13) (14) (15)

Major: _____ _____ _____ _____ _____

Minor: _____ _____ _____ _____ _____

B. Write the requested key signature.

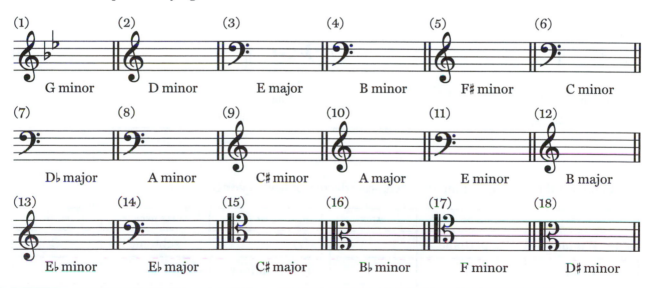

(1) G minor   (2) D minor   (3) E major   (4) B minor   (5) F♯ minor   (6) C minor

(7) D♭ major   (8) A minor   (9) C♯ minor   (10) A major   (11) E minor   (12) B major

(13) E♭ minor   (14) E♭ major   (15) C♯ major   (16) B♭ minor   (17) F minor   (18) D♯ minor

II. Scale degrees in minor

A. Given the scale degree labeled on the left, write the minor scale to which that pitch belongs, labeling the given scale degree in the scale you have written.. Use natural minor, unless the raised submediant or leading tone is requested (indicating melodic or harmonic minor); in these two cases, indicate in the blank which scale type you've written. Begin by writing whole notes on the lines and spaces, then fill in the necessary accidentals.

(1) mediant   mediant

(2) leading tone   Scale type: _____

(3) subdominant

(4) dominant

(5) raised submediant   Scale type: _____

(6) subtonic

(7) supertonic

(8) submediant

(9) raised submediant   Scale type: _____

(10) leading tone   Scale type: _____

B. Complete the table by writing the pitch, scale degree, or key requested.

	KEY	SCALE DEGREE	PITCH
(1)	B minor	supertonic	
(2)	E minor	♭$\hat{3}$	
(3)		♭$\hat{6}$	D♭
(4)		leading tone	G♯
(5)	F♯ minor		A
(6)	C♯ minor	subdominant	

	KEY	SCALE DEGREE	PITCH
(7)		subtonic	C
(8)	E♭ minor	$\hat{4}$	
(9)		raised submediant	C♯
(10)	C♯ minor	leading tone	
(11)	B minor		F♯
(12)		subtonic	E♭

Assignment 5.3

I. Forms of the minor scale

On the blank staves provided, write the correct key signature for each minor key indicated. Then write the scale requested, ascending and descending, altering scale degrees $\hat{6}$ and $\hat{7}$ as needed. Provide accidentals both ascending and descending.

(1) C♯ harmonic minor

(2) F melodic minor

(3) G♯ harmonic minor

(4) E melodic minor

(5) B♭ natural minor

(6) D melodic minor

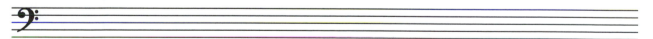

(7) G harmonic minor

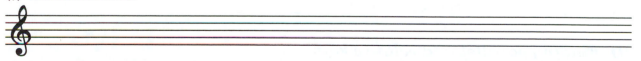

(8) D♯ natural minor

II. Scale and scale-degree analysis

Each of the following excerpts features a prominent scale or scale segment. Name the major or minor key. If minor, specify the type of minor scale (e.g., melodic minor).

A. Jean Baptiste Loeillet, Sonata, Op. 3, No. 10, mvt. 4, mm. 1-4

Key: _____   Scale type (if minor): _____

B. Handel, Chaconne, mm. 53-56

Key: _____   Scale type (if minor): _____

C. Mozart, String Quartet, K. 421, mvt. 1, mm. 5-8

Key: _____   Scale type (if minor): _____

D. Alan Menken and Tim Rice, "A Whole New World," from *Aladdin*, mm. 34-37

Key: _____   Scale type (if minor): _____

E. Corelli, Sarabanda, from Sonata, Op. 5, No. 8, mm. 21-24

Key: _____   Scale type (if minor): _____

III. Finding parallel and relative keys

For each pair of excerpts in the previous exercise, circle the appropriate relationship.

(1) Handel and Corelli   relative keys   parallel keys

(2) Loeillet and Menken & Rice   relative keys   parallel keys

(3) Mozart and Menken & Rice   relative keys   parallel keys

Assignment 5.4

I. Writing melodies from scale degrees

Each sequence of solfège syllables and scale-degree numbers given represents a minor-key melody. An underlined syllable or number indicates a pitch *below* the tonic. On the first staff, write the scale specified (along with the key signature), and label it with solfège and scale-degree numbers. Then use these to write the melody on the second staff (rhythm is optional). If you know the name of the tune, write it in the blank.

A. D natural minor

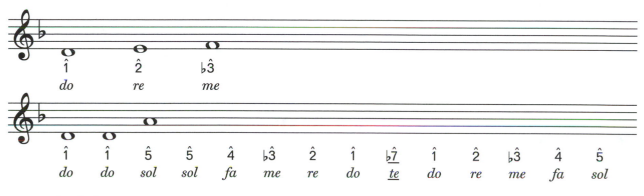

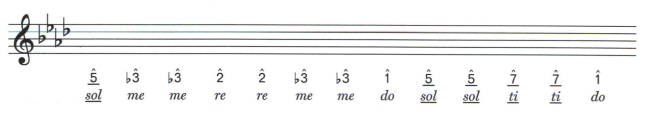

Name of melody: _____

B. F harmonic minor

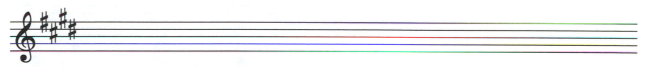

Name of melody: _____

C. C♯ natural minor

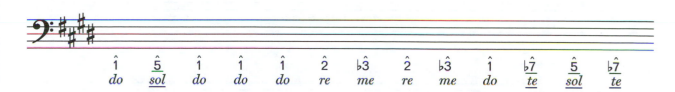

$\hat{1}$ $\underline{\hat{5}}$ $\hat{1}$ $\hat{1}$ $\hat{1}$ $\hat{2}$ $\flat\hat{3}$ $\hat{2}$ $\flat\hat{3}$ $\hat{4}$ $\hat{5}$ $\flat\hat{3}$ $\hat{5}$

do   *sol*   *do*   *do*   *do*   *re*   *me*   *re*   *me*   *fa*   *sol*   *me*   *sol*

Name of melody: _____

II. Writing pentatonic scales

Write the pentatonic scales requested (ascending form only).

A. F minor pentatonic

B. A♭ major pentatonic

C. B♭ major pentatonic

D. G minor pentatonic

E. E♭ minor pentatonic

F. C minor pentatonic

G. D major pentatonic

H. F♯ major pentatonic

III. Composing a melody

On your own paper or on these staves, compose a folk-like melody in a minor or minor pentatonic key, taking the melodies in the chapter as examples. Notate your tune in treble or bass clef, simple or compound meter. For a minor melody, use a key signature with accidentals for $\hat{6}$ and $\hat{7}$ as needed. Use scale segments where possible, keeping the melody simple enough that you can sing it.

Assignment 5.5

I. Writing mixed types of scales

Write the following scales as specified, starting from the given pitch. Write accidentals before each note (rather than key signatures).

A. Major, ascending

B. Natural minor, descending

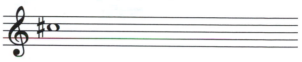

C. Melodic minor, ascending and descending

D. Harmonic minor, ascending

E. Harmonic minor, descending

F. Chromatic, ascending and descending (use context of a C♯ major scale)

G. Major, descending

H. Harmonic minor, descending

I. Natural minor, descending

J. Major pentatonic, ascending

K. Minor pentatonic, ascending

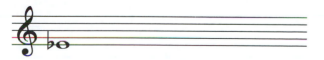

L. Minor pentatonic, ascending

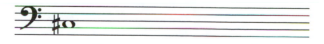

II. Analyzing keys in musical contexts

For each Bach invention:

- Write the key in the blank provided.
- For each bracketed portion of the melody, write the scale type suggested by the melodic line.

A. Bach, Invention No. 2, mm. 1-2

Key: _____

B. Bach, Invention No. 11, mm. 1-3

Key: _____

C. Bach, Invention No. 13, mm. 1-3

Key: _____

D Bach, Invention No. 7, mm. 1-3

Key: _____

E. In a sentence or two, explain how the melody for Invention No. 7 does not conform to the scale types considered in this chapter.

Assignment 5.6

I. Writing the diatonic modes

A. As scales: Beginning on the given pitch, write the mode requested, adding accidentals before the pitches as needed.

(1) C Phrygian

(2) F♯ Dorian

(3) F Mixolydian

(4) B♭ Lydian

(5) E Dorian

(6) A Phrygian

(7) A♭ Lydian

(8) D Mixolydian

(9) C♯ Dorian

(10) B Lydian

B. With key signatures: Write the correct key signature for the mode requested.

(1) B Phrygian

(2) G Dorian

(3) E♭ Mixolydian

(4) A Lydian

(5) B♭ Mixolydian

(6) C Dorian

(7) E Phrygian

(8) G Lydian

(9) B Dorian

(10) G Mixolydian

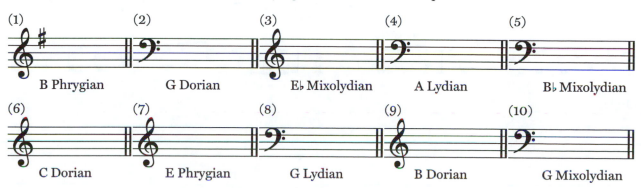

II. Analyzing modal melodies

Play or sing each of these melodies. Then, on the blank provided, indicate the mode (e.g., G Phrygian).

A. "Scarborough Fair"

Mode: _____

B. "Pange Lingua" (Sarum plainchant, abridged)

Mode: _____

C. Tomás Luis de Victoria, "O magnum mysterium," mm. 5-9

Mode: _____

D. "Swallowtail Jig," mm. 1-8

Mode: _____

6 Intervals

NAME _____

Assignment 6.1

I. Identifying interval size

A. Write the number that represents the size of each interval in the blank below.

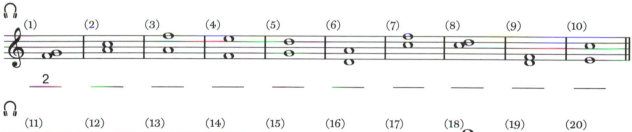

B. In the numbered blanks that correspond with each circled melodic interval, write the interval size.

Mozart, Sonata in C Major, K. 545, mvt. 1, mm. 1–4

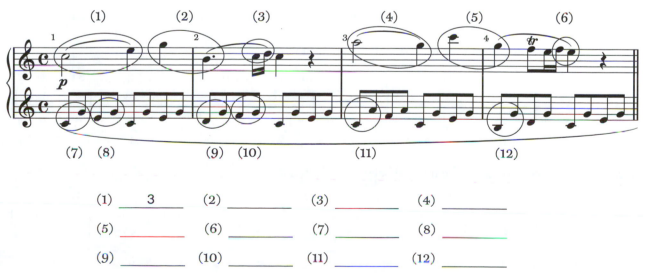

(1) ___3___   (2) _____   (3) _____   (4) _____

(5) _____   (6) _____   (7) _____   (8) _____

(9) _____   (10) _____   (11) _____   (12) _____

C. The circled intervals given may be simple or compound. In the first row of blanks, write the simple interval size (e.g., 3 not 10). In the second row, write a C for any compound interval and an S for any simple interval.

Anonymous, Minuet in D Minor, from the *Anna Magdalena Bach Notebook*, mm. 9-16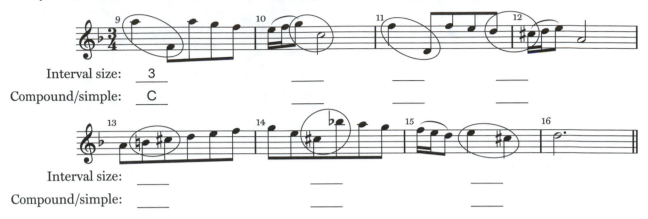

Interval size: 3   ____   ____   ____

Compound/simple: C   ____   ____   ____

Interval size: ____   ____   ____

Compound/simple: ____   ____   ____

II. Writing interval sizes

Write a whole note on the correct line or space to make each interval size specified. Don't add sharps or flats.

A. Write the specified melodic interval above the given note.

B. Write the specified melodic interval below the given note.

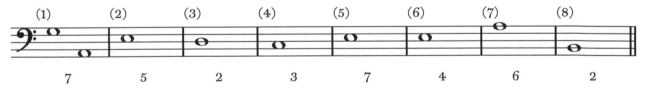

C. Write the specified harmonic interval above the given note.

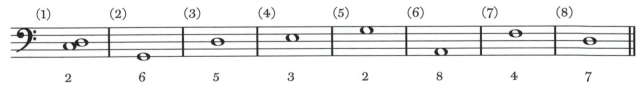

D. Write the specified harmonic interval below the given note.

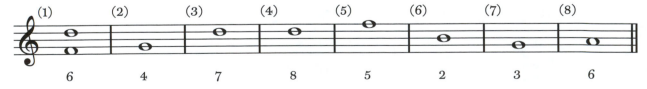

Assignment 6.2

I. Identifying intervals

A. For each harmonic interval, write the size and quality.

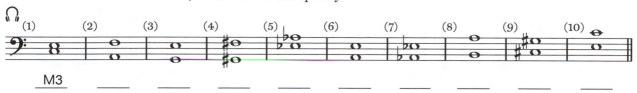

M3 ___ ___ ___ ___ ___ ___ ___ ___ ___

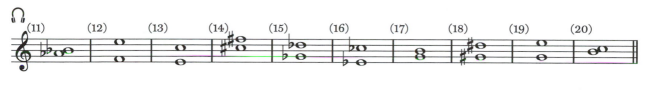

___ ___ ___ ___ ___ ___ ___ ___ ___ ___

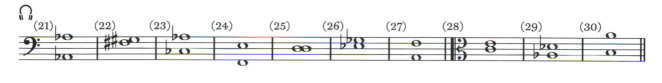

___ ___ ___ ___ ___ ___ ___ ___ ___ ___

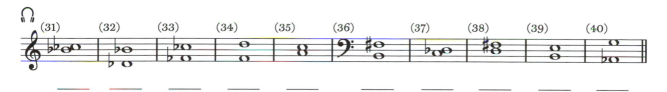

___ ___ ___ ___ ___ ___ ___ ___ ___ ___

B. For each circled interval, write the size and quality in the corresponding blank. (You identified the size of these intervals in Assignment 6.1.)

Mozart, Sonata in C Major, K. 545, mvt. 1, mm. 1–4

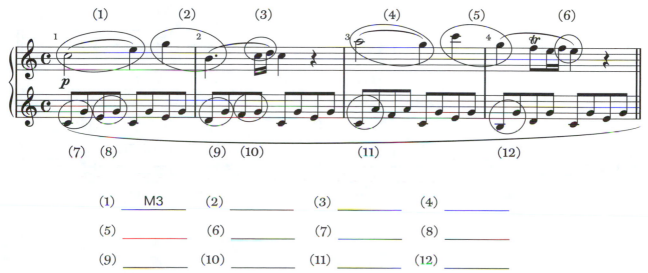

(1) ___M3___ (2) _____ (3) _____ (4) _____

(5) _____ (6) _____ (7) _____ (8) _____

(9) _____ (10) _____ (11) _____ (12) _____

C. In the blanks provided below the staff, write the size and quality of the melodic intervals indicated.

Webern, "Dies ist ein Leid," from *Fünf Lieder aus "Der siebente Ring,"* Op. 3, No. 1, mm. 1-5 (melody only)

Translation: Of pious tears . . . Through the morning garden it sounds, lightly lifting. Only for you alone.

II. Writing intervals

A. Write the following harmonic intervals, as whole notes, above the given pitch.

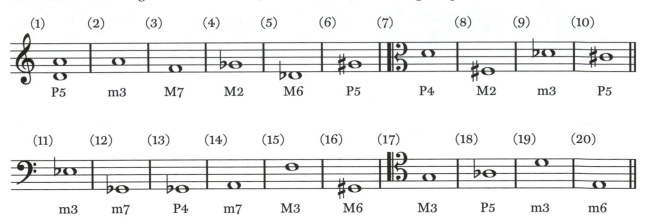

B. Write the following melodic intervals, as whole notes, above the given pitch.

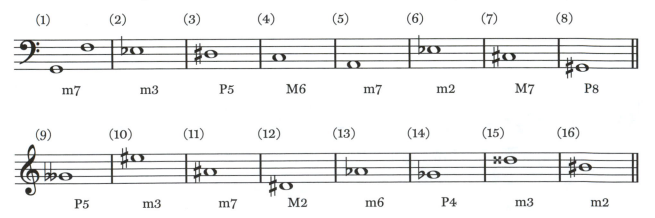

Assignment 6.3

I. Writing major, minor, and perfect melodic intervals

A. Write the melodic intervals, as whole notes, above the given pitch.

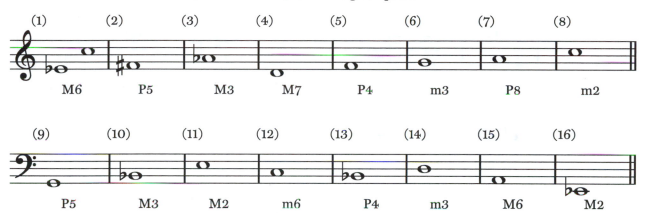

II. Writing major, minor, and perfect harmonic intervals

A. Write the harmonic intervals, as whole notes, above the given pitch.

B. Write the melodic intervals, as whole notes, below the given pitch.

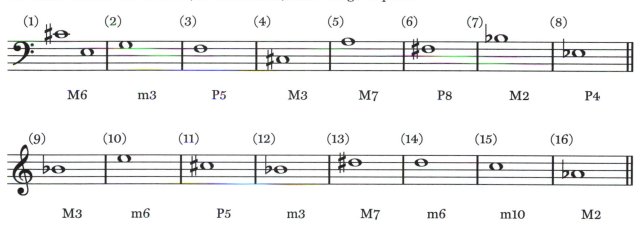

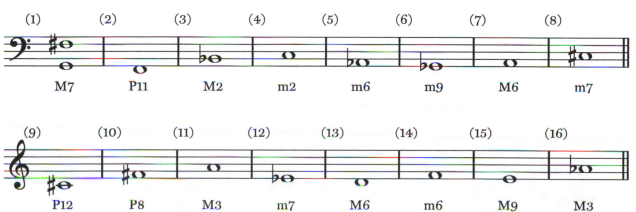

B. Write the following harmonic intervals, as whole notes, below the given pitch.

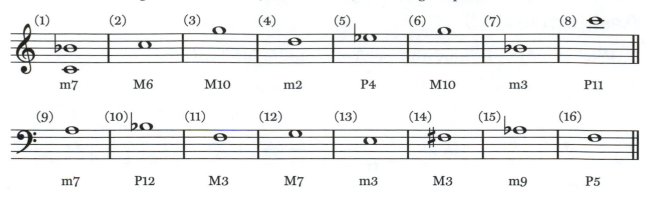

III. Writing melodies from intervals

Starting with the given pitch, write the following series of melodic intervals. The labels and arrows above the staff indicate the interval and whether it should be written above or below the previous note. When finished, play or sing the pitches to determine which song you have notated. Write the name of the song (if you know it) in the blank.

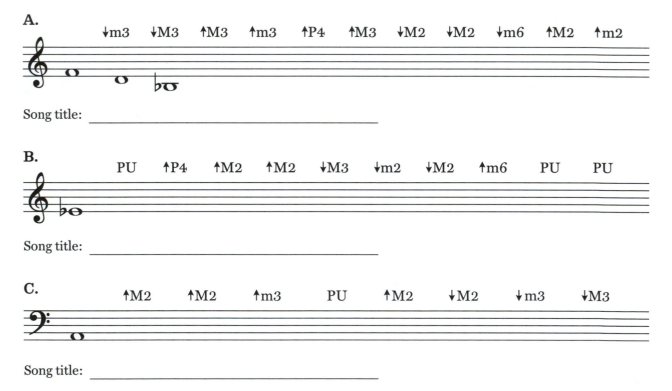

A.

Song title: _____

B.

Song title: _____

C.

Song title: _____

Assignment 6.4

I. Interval inversion

A. For each given interval, rewrite the second pitch, then write the first pitch up an octave. Label both intervals.

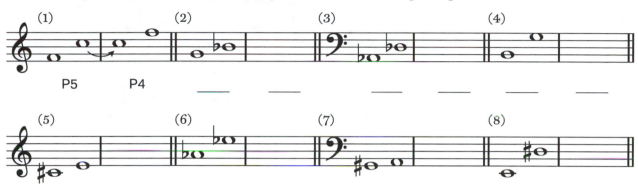

B. Invert each given interval as in part A, but this time rewrite the second pitch, then write the first pitch *down* an octave. Label both intervals.

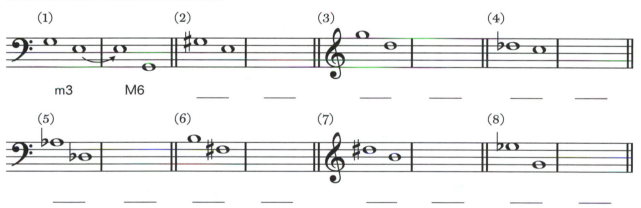

II. Writing augmented and diminished intervals

A. First write the major, minor, or perfect interval requested, above the given note. Then copy the bottom note in the blank measure, and raise or lower the top note to create the interval specified.

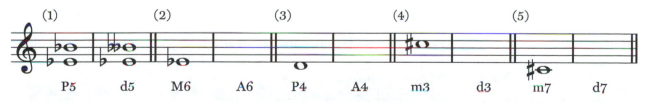

B. First write the major, minor, or perfect melodic interval requested, below the given note. Then copy the top note in the blank measure, and raise or lower the bottom note to create the melodic interval specified.

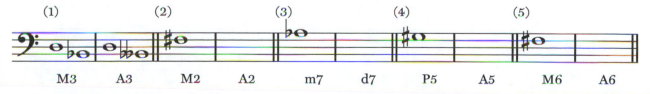

III. Identifying intervals

A. Listen to this melody. Then write the size and quality of each melodic interval below the staff in the blanks provided. Don't forget to check the flats from the key signature.

Beethoven, Piano Sonata in C Minor, Op. 13 (*Pathétique*), mvt. 2, mm. 1-8

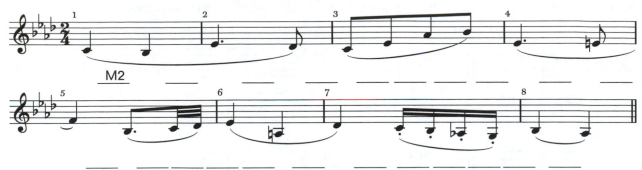

B. Listen to the following passages. Identify the harmonic intervals between the soprano and bass voices (circled in the Bach example). Change any compound interval to a simple one. In the second row of blanks label the interval type by writing P (perfect consonance), I (imperfect consonance), or D (dissonance).

(1) Beethoven, *Pathétique* Sonata, mvt. 2, mm. 1-8

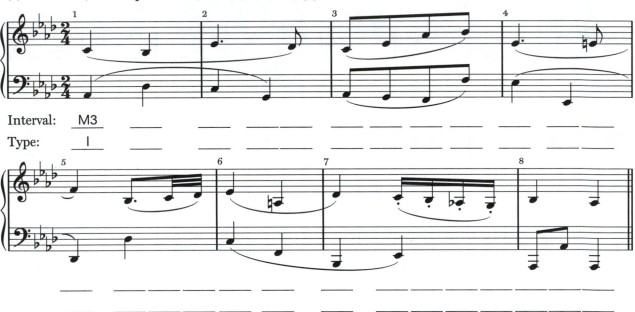

(2) Bach, Chaconne, from Violin Partita No. 2 in D Minor, mm. 112-119

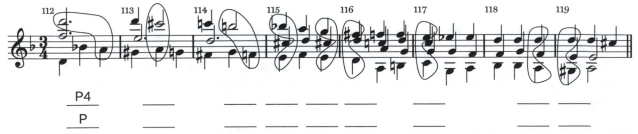

Assignment 6.5

I. Writing diminished and augmented intervals

A. Write the specified harmonic interval above the given note.

II. Writing enharmonically equivalent intervals

For each given interval, write two intervals beside it that sound the same but are spelled differently. Label each interval in the blank provided.

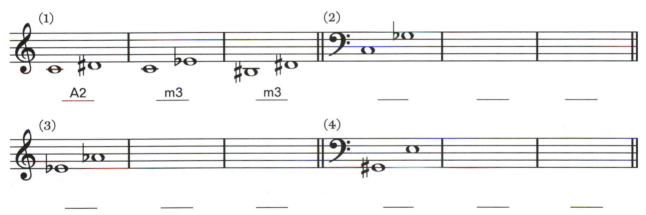

III. Writing all interval types

A. Write the specified melodic interval above the given note.

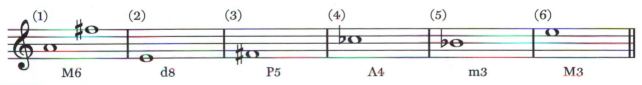

B. Write the specified melodic interval below the given note.

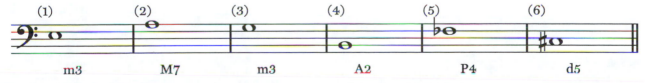

C. Write the specified melodic interval above and below the given note.

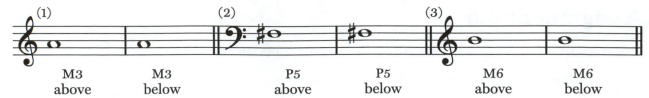

| M3 above | M3 below | P5 above | P5 below | M6 above | M6 below |

IV. Identifying intervals in a key context

A. For each circled and numbered harmonic interval, write its size and quality (e.g., m6) in the corresponding blank. Remember to include sharps from the key signature.

Bach, "Aus meines Herzens Grunde," mm. 1–4

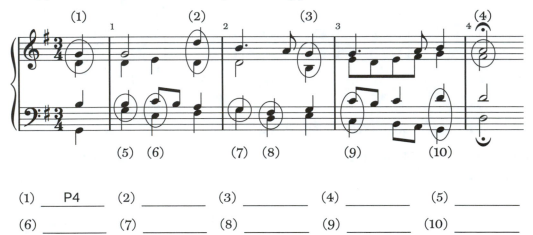

(1) ___P4___ (2) _____ (3) _____ (4) _____ (5) _____

(6) _____ (7) _____ (8) _____ (9) _____ (10) _____

B. For each melodic interval, write its size and quality in the blank below the staves. Remember to include sharps from the key signature.

Schoenberg, "Traumleben," from *Acht Lieder*, Op. 6, No. 1, mm. 1–9

Translation: Around my neck is draped a bloom-white arm, it rests upon my mouth [like] a spring young and warm.

Assignment 6.6

I. Identifying all interval types

Identify the size and quality of the following intervals. In the second row of blanks, label each interval P (perfect consonance), I (imperfect consonance), or D (dissonance).

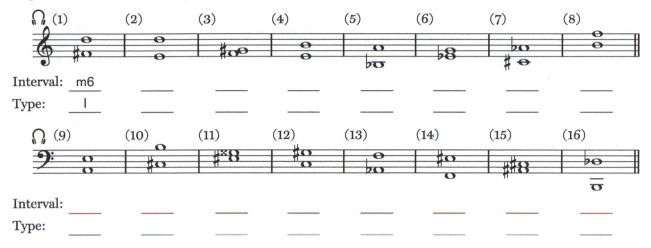

Interval: m6   ____   ____   ____   ____   ____   ____   ____

Type: I   ____   ____   ____   ____   ____   ____   ____

II. Writing all intervals

A. Write the following harmonic intervals, as whole notes, below the given pitch.

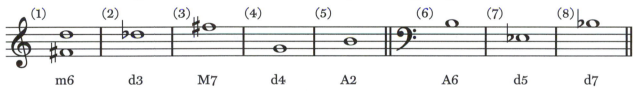

m6   d3   M7   d4   A2   A6   d5   d7

B. Write the following harmonic intervals, as whole notes, above the given pitch.

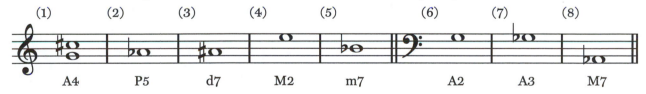

A4   P5   d7   M2   m7   A2   A3   M7

C. Write the inversion of each given harmonic interval, as whole notes, on the staff beneath. Write the name of each interval in the blank provided.

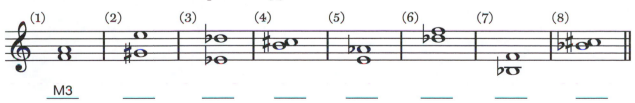

M3   ____   ____   ____   ____   ____   ____   ____

Inversion:

m6   ____   ____   ____   ____   ____   ____   ____

III. Melodic analysis

A. Begin by playing the melody notes, either on the piano or on your own instrument. Then (1) label each melodic interval in the blanks below the staff; (2) circle any pitch pairs that are compound intervals. Label chromatic half steps as AU (augmented unison).

Webern, "In Windesweben," from *Fünf Lieder aus Der siebente Ring*," Op. 3, No. 2, mm. 3–9 (melody only)

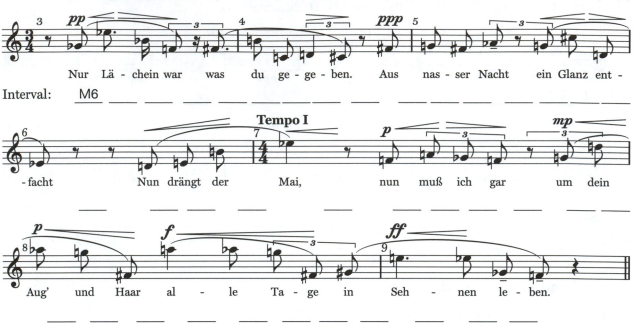

Translation: Only a smile was your reply. A wet night kindled a glow. Now it pushes toward May, and I must live for your eyes and hair all the days in longing.

B. For class discussion or in a paragraph, as assigned by your teacher, consider Webern's vocal writing style. What types of melodic intervals do you find? How wide is the range and what are the highest and lowest pitches? What challenges would a singer face in preparing this melody for performance?

7 Triads

NAME _____

Assignment 7.1

I. Writing scale-degree triads

Notate the requested scale in whole notes (ascending only), adding any needed accidentals. Above each scale degree, write a triad, again adding the necessary accidentals. In minor keys, use the leading tone from harmonic minor to spell the chords built on $\hat{5}$ and $\hat{7}$. Then in the blank, identify each triad's quality as M (major), m (minor), d (diminished), or A (augmented).

A. Major scales

D: M   ____   ____   ____   ____   ____   ____

E♭:   ____   ____   ____   ____   ____   ____   ____

B. Harmonic minor scales

g: m   ____   ____   ____   ____   ____   ____

e: ____   ____   ____   ____   ____   ____   ____

II. Triad quality

Identify the quality of each triad as M (major), m (minor), d (diminished), or A (augmented) in the blank.

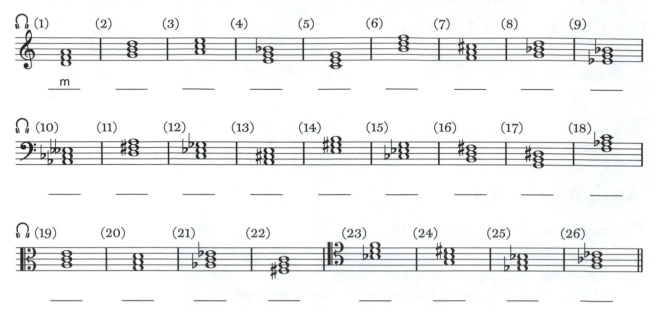

(1) m (2) ___ (3) ___ (4) ___ (5) ___ (6) ___ (7) ___ (8) ___ (9) ___

(10) ___ (11) ___ (12) ___ (13) ___ (14) ___ (15) ___ (16) ___ (17) ___ (18) ___

(19) ___ (20) ___ (21) ___ (22) ___ (23) ___ (24) ___ (25) ___ (26) ___

III. Identifying triads in a musical context

For each quarter-, dotted-quarter-, or half-note chord, write the triad in root position on the treble-clef staff in whole notes. Then label the root and quality for each chord in the blanks beneath.

"St. Prisca," mm. 1-4

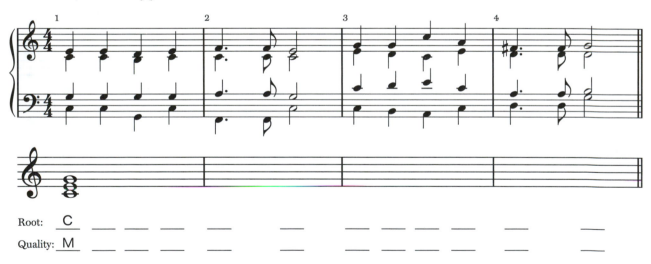

Root: C   ___   ___   ___   ___   ___   ___   ___

Quality: M   ___   ___   ___   ___   ___   ___   ___

Assignment 7.2

I. Identifying major and minor triads

Identify the root and quality of each given triad. Write capital letters for major triads (F♯) and lowercase for minor triads (f♯).

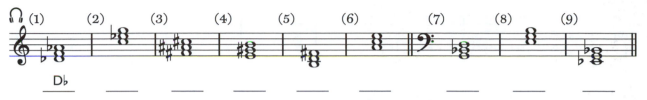

Db ___ ___ ___ ___ ___ ___ ___ ___ ___

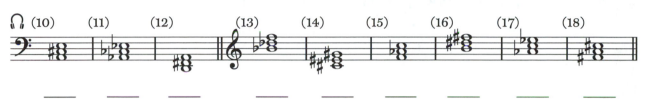

___ ___ ___ ___ ___ ___ ___ ___

II. Spelling all triad types

A. Rewrite each major triad, adding or subtracting accidentals to create the chord quality specified.

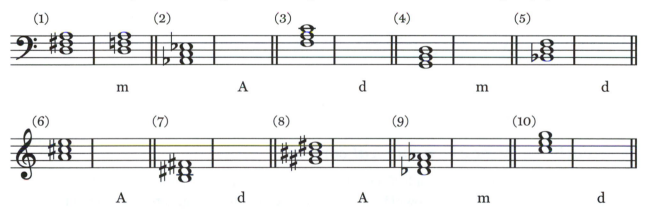

(1)   (2)   (3)   (4)   (5)
       m   A   d   m   d

(6)   (7)   (8)   (9)   (10)
A   d   A   m   d

B. Consider each given pitch to be the root of a triad. Write the remaing pitches to create the quality specified.

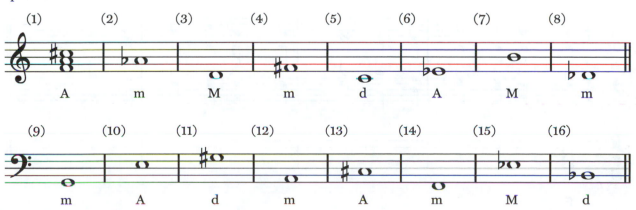

(1)   (2)   (3)   (4)   (5)   (6)   (7)   (8)
A   m   M   m   d   A   M   m

(9)   (10) (11) (12) (13) (14) (15) (16)
m   A   d   m   A   m   M   d

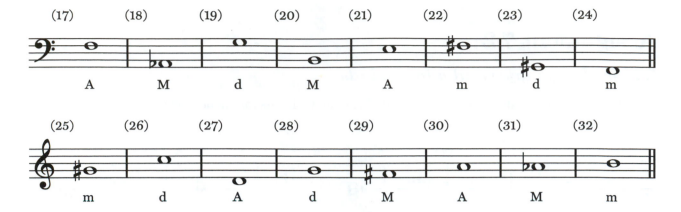

III. Identifying triad root, quality, and inversion

In the top row of blanks, identify the chord root and quality (e.g., D or d). In the second row, identify the position or inversion (root, 1st, or 2nd).

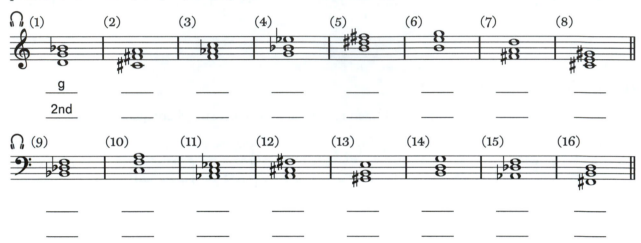

IV. Identifying triads in a musical context

For each quarter-, dotted-quarter-, or half-note chord, write the triad in root position on the treble-clef staff (using whole notes). In the top row of blanks, write each chord root and quality. In the second row, identify the position or inversion (root, 1st, or 2nd) of that chord in the musical excerpt.

"St. George's Windsor," mm. 1-4

Assignment 7.3

I. Writing triads in a key

Write triads in root position above the given roots, using whole notes. Don't write accidentals except in minor keys, where you should use the leading tone to spell the chords built on $\hat{5}$ and $\hat{7}$. In the blanks, identify the triads, using upper- or lowercase Roman numerals and the symbols ° and + to show their quality and position in the scale.

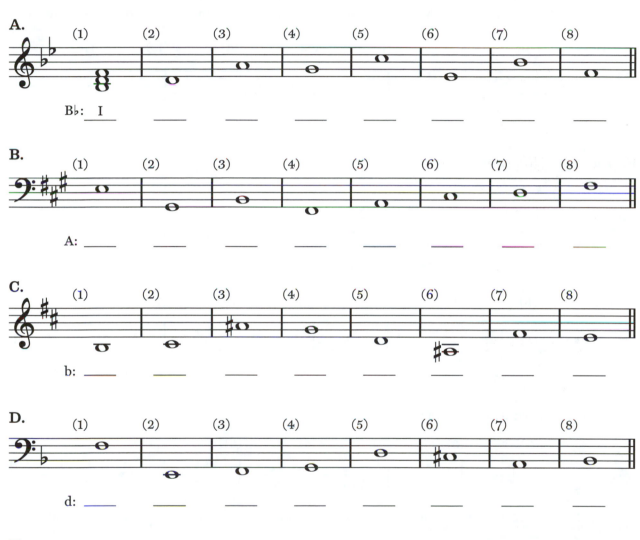

II. Spelling isolated triads

Fill in the other notes of each triad, adding accidentals as needed to make the correct quality. Don't change the given pitch.

A. Each given pitch is the root of a triad.

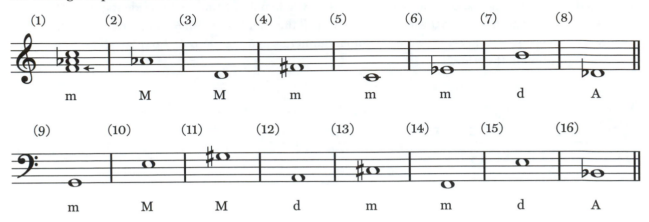

B. Each given pitch is the third of a triad.

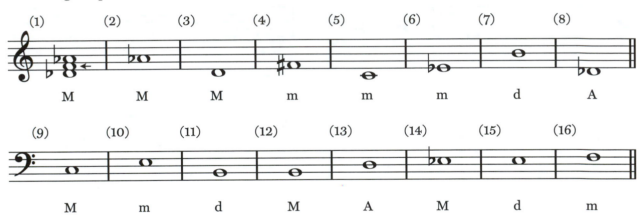

C. Each given pitch is the fifth of a triad.

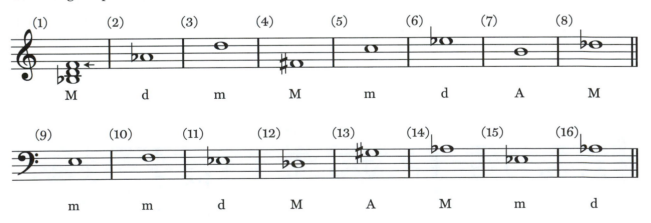

Assignment 7.4

I. Writing triads from chord symbols

Write the triads indicated in root position, in whole notes. Include all needed accidentals for the correct triad quality.

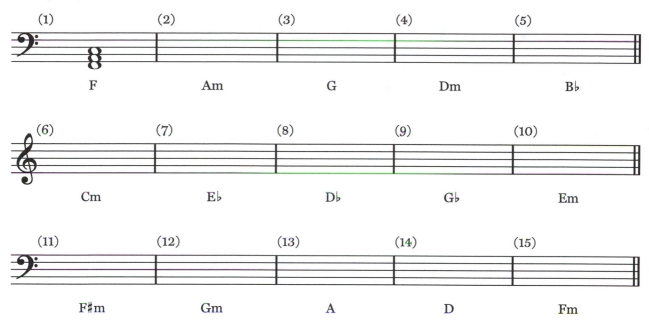

II. Identifying triads

Identify the quality and root of each triad using chord symbols (e.g., Gm, F). Don't specify any inversion.

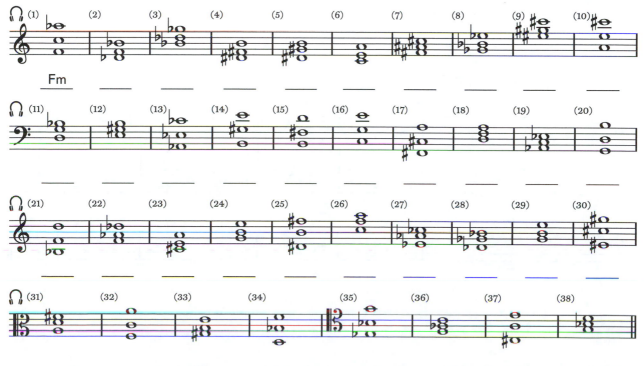

III. Identifying triads in musical contexts

For each chord, write the triad in root position (whole notes) on the blank staff. Ignore any circled notes. In the blanks beneath, identify the triad with an upper- or lowercase Roman numeral to show its quality and position in the key. You need not specify inversions.

A. Johann Pachelbel, Canon in D Major, mm. 3-4

D: I   ___   ___   ___   ___   ___   ___

B. Johann Crüger, "Nun danket alle Gott," mm. 1-4

E♭: ___   ___   ___   ___   ___   ___   ___   ___

C. "Old Hundredth," mm. 1-6

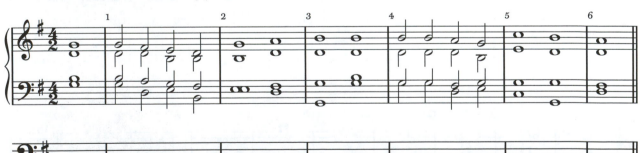

G: ___   ___   ___   ___   ___   ___   ___   ___   ___   ___   ___   ___

Assignment 7.5

I. Identifying triads from figured bass

On the treble-clef staff, write the triad indicated by the bass and figures. Use whole notes stacked in thirds. In the blank below the staff, write the Roman numeral reflecting the triad's position and quality in the given key. For inverted triads, also write the inversion (e.g., IV⁶).

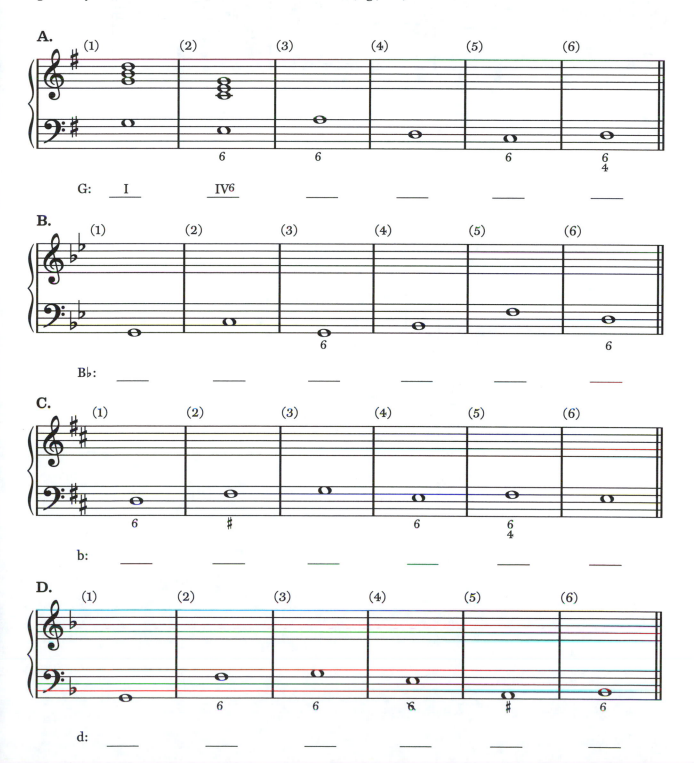

II. Identifying triads in musical contexts

For these excerpts, in the positions indicated by the blanks, write the triads in root position (whole notes). Ignore any circled notes. Identify the triad with an upper- or lowercase Roman numeral (to show its quality and position in the key) and figures (to show its inversion) in the blank below the staff.

A. Schumann, "Wilder Reiter," mm. 1–3

B. "Chartres," mm. 1–4

NAME _____

Assignment 8.1

I. Writing seventh chords above a scale

Notate the requested scale in whole notes (ascending only), adding any needed accidentals. Above each note, write a seventh chord with the necessary accidentals for that key. In minor keys, use the leading tone for the chords on $\hat{5}$ and $\hat{7}$. In the first row of blanks, identify the seventh-chord quality as MM7, Mm7, mm7, $\varnothing$7 (half-diminished), or $^{\circ}$7 (fully diminished). In the second row of blanks, write the Roman numeral.

A.

F: MM7   mm7   mm7   ____   ____   ____   ____

I7   ii7   iii7   ____   ____   ____   ____

B.

a: ____   ____   ____   ____   ____   ____   ____

____   ____   ____   ____   ____   ____   ____

C.

f♯: ____   ____   ____   ____   ____   ____   ____

____   ____   ____   ____   ____   ____   ____

D.

G: ____   ____   ____   ____   ____   ____   ____

____   ____   ____   ____   ____   ____   ____

II. Identifying scale-degree seventh chords

A. Root-position chords

In the first row of blanks, provide a Roman numeral that reflects the correct seventh-chord quality in the given key. In the second row, write the chord quality (e.g., Mm7, ⌀7).

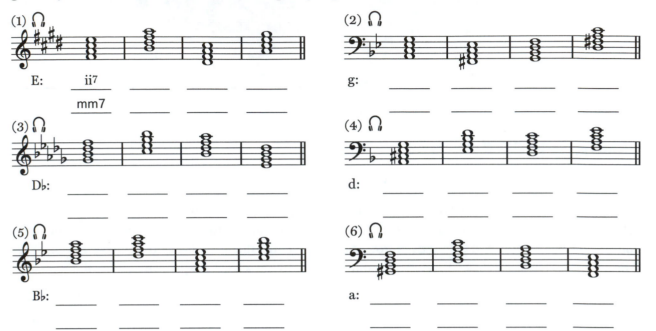

(1) E: _____ ii7 _____ _____ _____ _____
     _____ mm7 _____ _____ _____ _____

(2) g: _____ _____ _____ _____ _____

(3) D♭: _____ _____ _____ _____ _____
     _____ _____ _____ _____ _____

(4) d: _____ _____ _____ _____ _____
     _____ _____ _____ _____ _____

(5) B♭: _____ _____ _____ _____ _____
     _____ _____ _____ _____ _____

(6) a: _____ _____ _____ _____ _____
     _____ _____ _____ _____ _____

B. Chords in inversion

Provide a Roman numeral and figures ⁶₅, ⁴₃, or ⁴₂ for each given seventh chord.

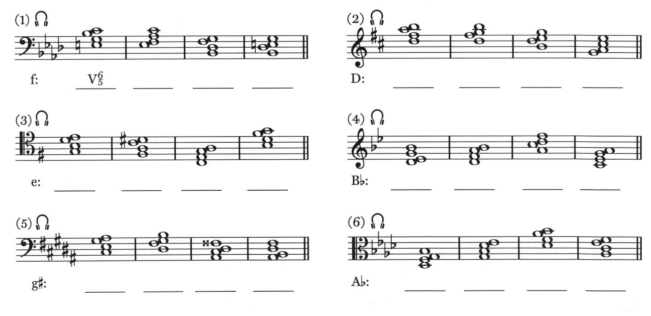

(1) f: _____ V⁶₅ _____ _____ _____

(2) D: _____ _____ _____ _____

(3) e: _____ _____ _____ _____

(4) B♭: _____ _____ _____ _____

(5) g♯: _____ _____ _____ _____

(6) A♭: _____ _____ _____ _____

Assignment 8.2

I. Writing scale-degree seventh chords from Roman numerals

A. Write each of the following root-position seventh chords. Provide the key signature, and add accidentals to make the correct quality. For minor keys, use the leading tone for the chords on $\hat{5}$ and $\hat{7}$.

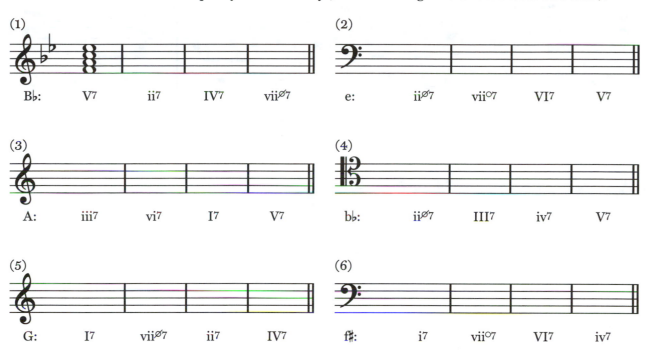

(1)

Bb: V7 ii7 IV7 vii⊘7

(2)

e: ii⊘7 vii°7 VI7 V7

(3)

A: iii7 vi7 I7 V7

(4)

bb: ii⊘7 III7 iv7 V7

(5)

G: I7 vii⊘7 ii7 IV7

(6)

f#: i7 vii°7 VI7 iv7

B. Write each seventh chord in the key and inversion specified. Provide the key signature, and add accidentals to make the correct quality. For minor keys, use the leading tone for the chords on $\hat{5}$ and $\hat{7}$.

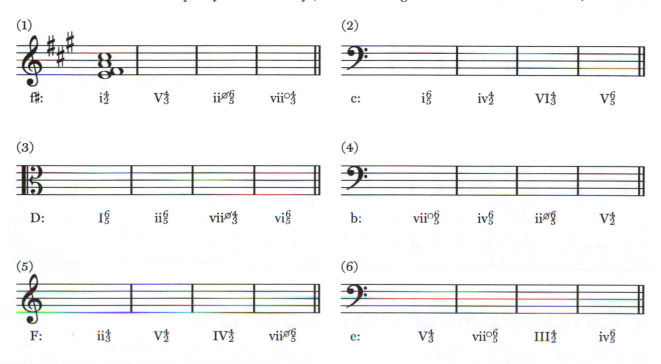

(1)

f#: i^4_2 V^4_3 $ii⊘^6_5$ $vii°^4_3$

(2)

c: i^6_5 iv^4_2 VI^4_3 V^6_5

(3)

D: I^6_5 ii^6_5 $vii⊘^4_3$ vi^6_5

(4)

b: $vii°^6_5$ iv^6_5 $ii⊘^6_5$ V^4_2

(5)

F: ii^4_3 V^4_2 IV^4_2 $vii⊘^6_5$

(6)

e: V^4_3 $vii°^6_5$ III^4_2 iv^6_5

II. Analyzing seventh chords in musical contexts

In the excerpts provided, write the name of each circled seventh chord (e.g., Mm7, $\varnothing^6_5$) in the blank underneath. When identifying chord quality, be sure to check the key signature and any accidentals. For chords in inversion, give the appropriate figures (e.g., Mm $^6_5$).

A. Brahms, Ballade in G Minor, Op. 118, No. 3, mm. 15-19 🎧

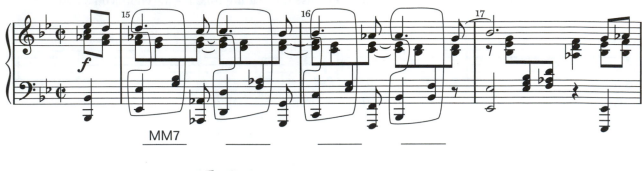

MM7 ____ ____

____

B. Felix Mendelssohn, "Aber der Herr sieht es nicht," from *Elijah*, No. 5, mm. 68-79 🎧

Denn ich der Herr dein Gott ich bin ein eif - ri - ger Gott,

____ ____

der da heim - sucht der Vä - ter Mis - se - that

____

Translation: For I, the Lord your God, am a jealous God, who visits the sins of your fathers.

Assignment 8.3

I. Identifying isolated seventh chords

A. Roman numerals

Write the appropriate Roman numeral and figures for each seventh chord in the given key.

(1)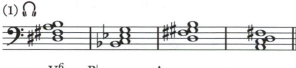

e: V^6_5 B♭: _____   A: _____   g: _____

(2)

d: _____   B♭: _____   d: _____   F: _____

(3)

G: _____   b: _____   E: _____   g♯: _____

(4)

c: _____   A♭: _____   f♯: _____   f: _____

(5)

b♭: _____   D♭: _____   B: _____   E♭: _____

(6)

a: _____   D: _____   c♯: _____   G♭: _____

B. Chord quality

Write the chord quality (e.g., mm7, °7) for each seventh chord.

(1)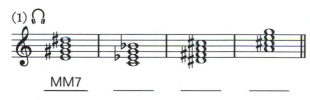

MM7   _____   _____   _____

(2)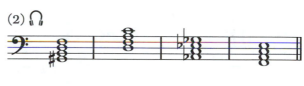

_____   _____   _____   _____

(3)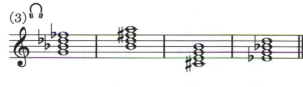

_____   _____   _____   _____

(4)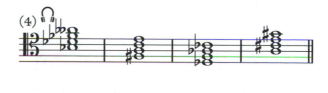

_____   _____   _____   _____

(5)

_____   _____   _____   _____

(6)

_____   _____   _____   _____

II. Writing isolated seventh chords

Write the seventh chords specified, (A) given the key and Roman numeral or (B) the chord type. Spell with accidentals rather than key signatures.

A. Roman numerals

(1)

G: viiº$^6_5$ b: V7   a: viiº$^4_3$ E: IV$^6_5$

(2)

c#: iiø$^6_5$ Bb: iii7   F: vi$^6_5$ bb: V7

(3)

f#: iv$^6_5$ D: viiø$^6_5$ c: VI7   Eb: ii$^6_5$

(4)

Db: I$^4_2$ g#: III$^6_5$ eb: i$^4_3$ A: viiø$^4_3$

(5)

d#: V$^6_5$ Gb: viiø$^6_5$ B: V$^4_2$ d: i$^6_5$

(6)

a#: VI$^6_5$ Db: V$^4_3$ A: iii$^6_5$ e: V$^4_3$

B. Chord qualities (root is given)

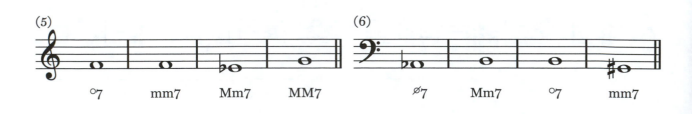

(1)

º7   MM7   Mm7   mm7

(2)

Mm7   ø7   º7   MM7

(3)

Mm7   ø7   mm7   º7

(4)

MM7   mm7   ø7   Mm7

(5)

º7   mm7   Mm7   MM7

(6)

ø7   Mm7   º7   mm7

Assignment 8.4

I. Writing chords from a lead sheet

"Rich and Rare" (traditional Irish melody), arranged by Joel Phillips

Examine each chord symbol in the following lead sheet. Write the chords on the staff underneath each measure, using dotted-half, half, and quarter notes, in the correct inversion.

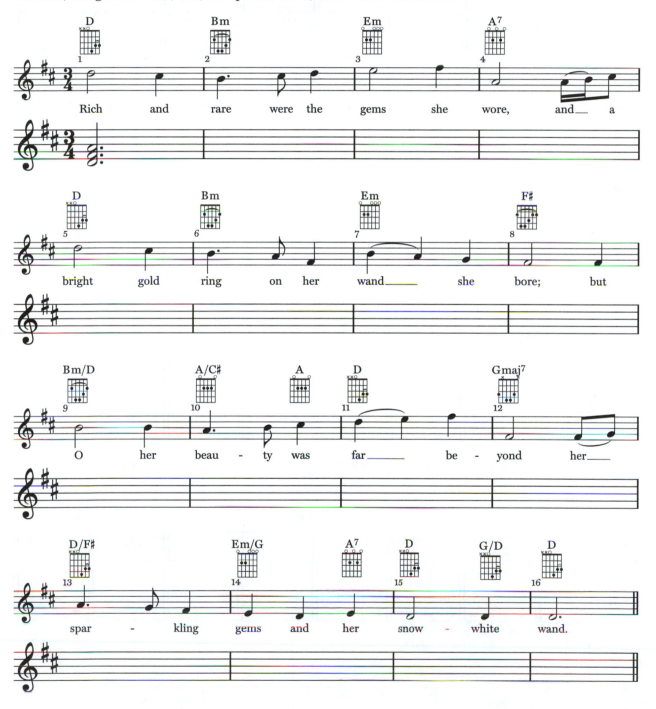

II. Triads and seventh chords from lead-sheet symbols

Write each chord requested in four parts in keyboard style (in quarter notes)—three parts in the right hand and one part in the left. Include any accidentals needed to make the correct chord quality. If slash notation is used (e.g., F/A), put the proper chord member in the bass. Check that each seventh-chord member is present; for triads, double the bass note.

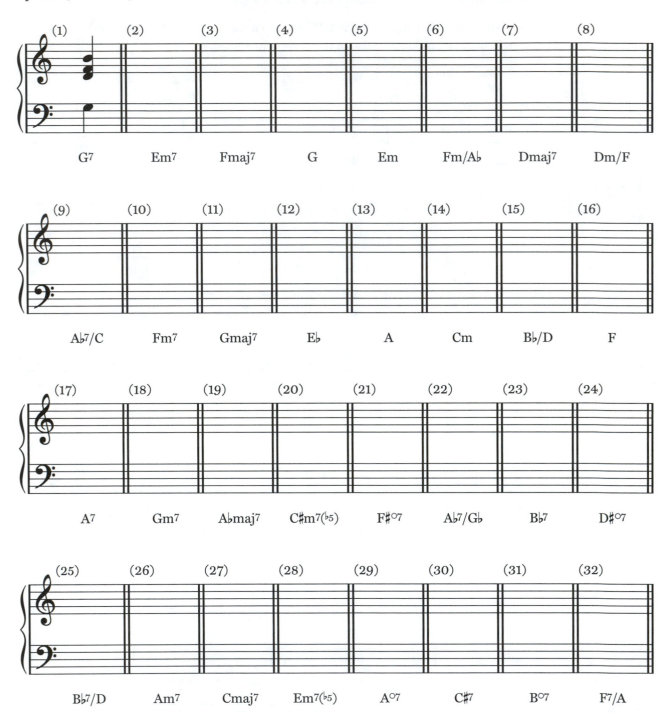

(1) G7 (2) Em7 (3) Fmaj7 (4) G (5) Em (6) Fm/A♭ (7) Dmaj7 (8) Dm/F

(9) A♭7/C (10) Fm7 (11) Gmaj7 (12) E♭ (13) A (14) Cm (15) B♭/D (16) F

(17) A7 (18) Gm7 (19) A♭maj7 (20) C♯m7(♭5) (21) F♯°7 (22) A♭7/G♭ (23) B♭7 (24) D♯°7

(25) B♭7/D (26) Am7 (27) Cmaj7 (28) Em7(♭5) (29) A°7 (30) C♯7 (31) B°7 (32) F7/A

Assignment 8.5

I. Spelling isolated seventh chords

Fill in the other notes of each seventh chord, adding accidentals as needed to make the correct quality. Don't change the given pitch.

A. Each given pitch is the root of a seventh chord.

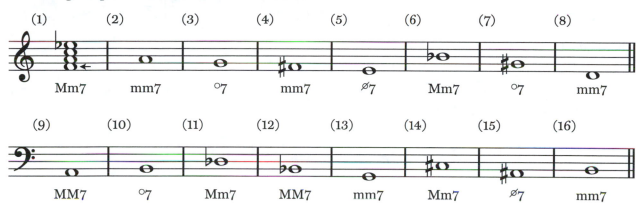

B. Each given pitch is the third of a seventh chord.

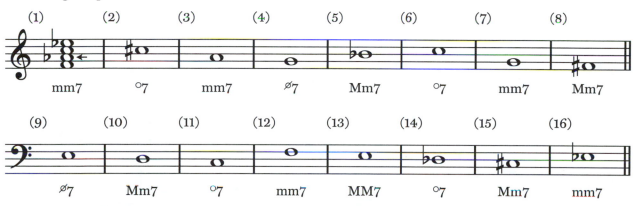

C. Each given pitch is the fifth of a seventh chord.

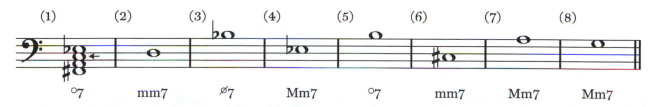

D. Each given pitch is the seventh of a seventh chord.

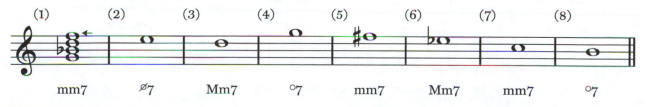

II. Analyzing seventh chords in musical contexts

A. John Lennon and Paul McCartney, "You Never Give Me Your Money," mm. 1-8 🎧

Identify the chord quality and inversion of each circled chord.

Chord quality: __mm7__   _____

_____

B. Brahms, "Tageweis von einer schönen Frauen," from *28 Deutsche Volkslieder*, mm. 5-8 🎧

Identify each circled chord in the blank underneath, with Roman numerals and figures.

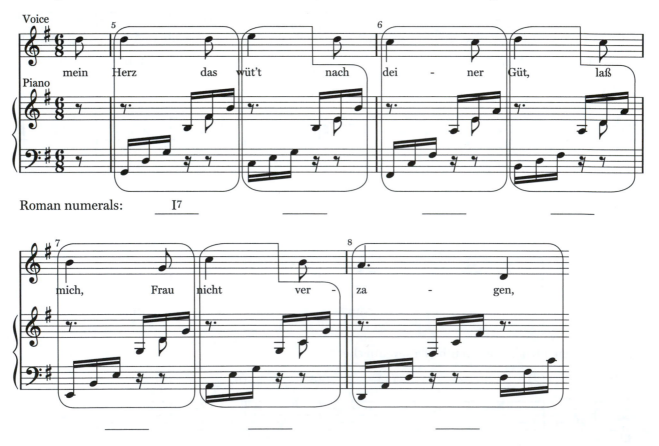

Roman numerals: __I7__   _____   _____

_____   _____   _____

Translation: My heart is raging for your charms; don't drive me to despair my lady.

Assignment 8.6

I. Analysis: Chord quality and Roman numerals

A. Identify the chord quality of the circled chords in the blanks below the staff.

Marc Shaiman and Scott Wittman, "Good Morning Baltimore," from *Hairspray*, mm. 5-12 (ignore Gs in m. 12)

B. Identify the circled chords using Roman numerals and figures.

Frédéric Chopin, Étude, Op. 10, No. 1, mm. 39-44

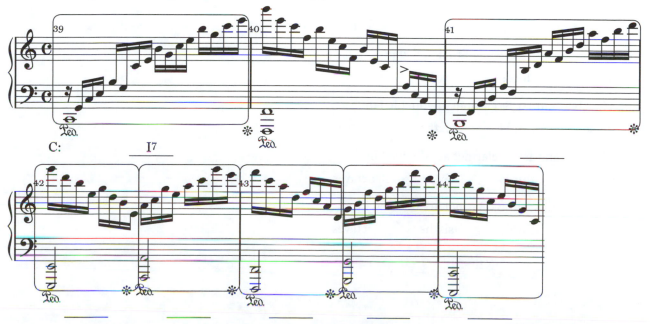

II. Instrumentation and score reading

Listen to the recording of this excerpt, paying attention to the instruments that are playing or doubling the melody.

Holst, Second Suite in F for Military Band, mvt. 4, mm. 41-44 🎧

For each of the following pairs of instruments, circle the interval at which the melody is doubled in measures 42-44.

A. The piccolo and oboe are doubled in

     thirds   sixths   octaves   double octaves

B. The oboe and E♭ clarinet are doubled in

     unison   thirds   sixths   octaves

C. The oboe and 1st B♭ clarinet are doubled in

     unison   thirds   sixths   octaves

D. The flute and 1st B♭ clarinet are doubled in

     unison   thirds   sixths   octaves

E. The oboe and 2nd B♭ clarinet are doubled in

     unison   thirds   sixths   octaves

Connecting Intervals in Note-to-Note Counterpoint

NAME _____

Common Counterpoint Errors Checklist

Keep this page in your notebook or workbook to use for Assignment 9.4 and to check your work for errors. Your teacher may also identify errors in your part writing with the letters given here.

Opening:

    A. Opening harmonic interval is not PU, P8, or P5.

    B. Opening does not establish the tonic harmony.

Closing:

    C. Closing harmonic interval is not P8 or PU.

    D. There is an incorrect interval approaching the close (must be 6-8, 10-8, or 3-U in strict style) or a missing leading tone.

    E. Leading tone does not resolve to the tonic.

Harmonic intervals:

    F. Parallel octaves, or parallel octaves by contrary motion (this also includes P8-PU, PU-P8, and PU-PU).

    G. Parallel fifths, or parallel fifths by contrary motion.

    H. Too many parallel imperfect consonances (3 or 6).

    I. Too many perfect consonances.

    J. Dissonant interval not allowed in strict species.

Soprano or bass line:

    K. Melodic line is static: repeats notes or circles around one note.

    L. Leap or skip is not set with a step in the other part.

    M. Melodic leap not preceded and followed by stepwise contrary motion.

    N. Dissonant melodic interval (e.g., leap of m7, M7, d5, A4, or A2).

    O. Leap or skip in the upper part into an octave or a fifth (may also create hidden octaves or fifths).

    P. Too little contrary motion.

    Q. Counterpoint line lacks a single high (or low) point.

Traditional Cantus Firmus Lines

Use these cantus lines for practice in class and as assigned by your teacher for additional homework for Chapters 9 and 10. Each can serve as the upper or lower part.

Try writing your own cantus firmus, starting on $\hat{1}$ and ending with $\hat{2}$-$\hat{1}$. Make a pleasing contour, using mostly steps, but also include some skips or one leap for interest and to make the cantus more challenging for those composing a counterpoint.

Assignment 9.1

I. Melodic and harmonic intervals in counterpoint

In each of the following completed first-species settings:

- Label the harmonic intervals between the staves.
- Mark with a bracket any skip or leap in the counterpoint or cantus.

In the chart below the counterpoint:

- Indicate where (measure numbers) and in which part each skip and leap appears.
- Indicate whether there is a step, skip, leap, or repeated pitch in the other part at that point.
- Label the type of motion between parts at that point.

A. Cantus firmus 5 (Kirnberger) in a first-species setting

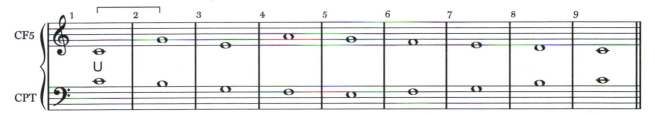

MEASURES	PART	SKIP OR LEAP?	SKIP/STEP/LEAP IN OTHER PART?	TYPE OF MOTION
1–2	cantus	leap	step	contrary

B. Cantus firmus 5 (Kirnberger) in another first-species setting

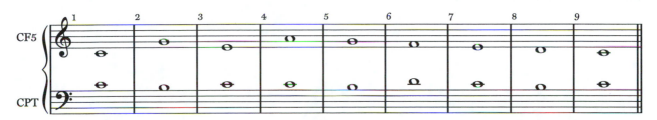

MEASURES	PART	SKIP OR LEAP?	SKIP/STEP/LEAP IN OTHER PART?	TYPE OF MOTION

C. Cantus firmus 5 (Kirnberger) in a first-species setting 🎧

MEASURES	PART	SKIP OR LEAP?	SKIP/STEP/LEAP IN OTHER PART?	TYPE OF MOTION

II. Evaluating Counterpoint

Answer the following questions about the three cantus settings provided in part I, or be prepared to discuss them in class.

A. What challenges are presented by the first half of the cantus? What about the second half? What considerations are important to keep in mind in setting this cantus?

B. Listen carefully to each setting. Name at least two strengths and two weaknesses of each. Which do you think is the best setting? Explain.

C. What are other ways this cantus may be set? Be prepared to discuss other options for setting notes 1–4 and 5–9.

Assignment 9.2

I. Opening a counterpoint

Set each of the following cantus firmus openings (the first four notes) in two different ways. Write in the harmonic interval numbers, and label any skips or leaps. If you like, use the tables to identify letter names of the possible consonant intervals. At the beginning of A, for example, the consonances below the first note C4 are C (8), A (3), F (5), and E (6), shown in the column below that note; since this first note should be set with an octave, C (bold) has been chosen. You may eliminate other potential intervals as you make selections, by marking any that would make parallel octaves or fifths; also cross out any d5s.

A. Cantus as upper part

(1) CF5

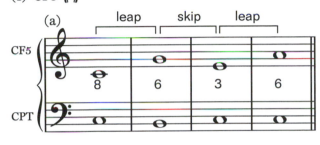

(b)

8	C	G	E	A
3	A			
5	F			
6	E			

8	C	G	E	A
3				
5				
6				

(2) CF6

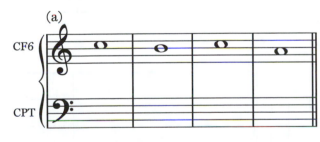

(b)

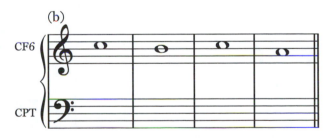

8	C	B	C	A
3				
5				
6				

8	C	B	C	A
3				
5				
6				

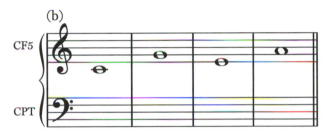

(3) CF7

(a)

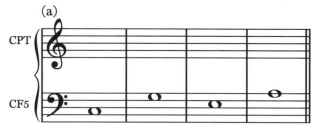

8	C	E	F	G
3				
5				
6				

(b)

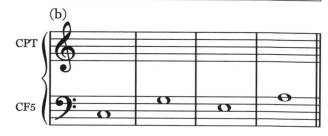

8	C	E	F	G
3				
5				
6				

B. Cantus as lower part

(1) CF5

6				
5				
3				
8	C	G	E	A

(a)

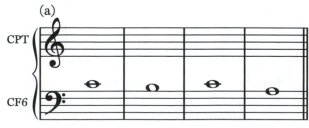

6				
5				
3				
8	C	G	E	A

(b)

(2) CF6

6				
5				
3				
8	C	B	C	A

(a)

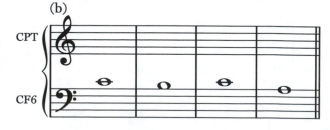

6				
5				
3				
8	C	B	C	A

(b)

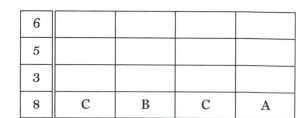

Assignment 9.3

I. Closing a counterpoint

Set each of the following cantus firmus closings (last four notes) in two different ways. Write in the harmonic interval numbers, and label any skips or leaps.

A. Cantus as upper part

(1) CF1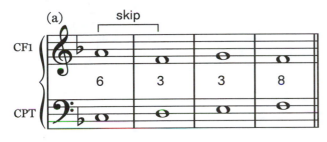

(a)

8	A	F	G	F
3	F			
5	D			
6	C			

(b)

8	A	F	G	F
3				
5				
6				

(2) CF3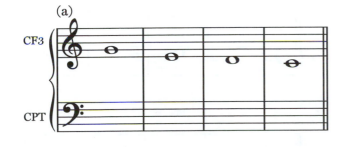

(a)

8	G	E	D	C
3				
5				
6				

(b)

8	G	E	D	C
3				
5				
6				

(3) CF2 (Remember to use the leading tone in the approach to the cadence in minor counterpoint.)

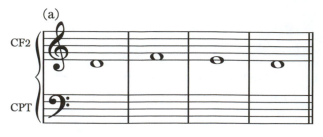

(a)

8	D	F	E	D
3				
5				
6				

(b)

8	D	F	E	D
3				
5				
6				

B. Cantus as lower part

(1) CF1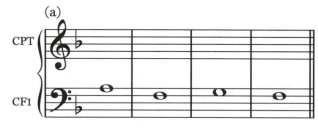

6				
5				
3				
8	A	F	G	F

6				
5				
3				
8	A	F	G	F

(a)

(b)

(2) CF3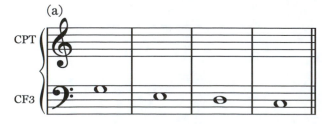

6				
5				
3				
8	G	E	D	C

6				
5				
3				
8	G	E	D	C

(a)

(b)

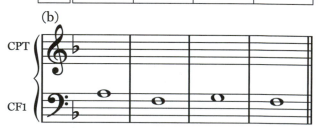

NAME _____

Assignment 9.4

I. Evaluating strict counterpoint

Identify the errors in the following settings. First write the harmonic intervals between the staves, then examine the counterpoint. Circle each mistake, list the measures and voice part where the mistake occurs, then label it in the blank boxes with a letter code from the Errors Checklist on page 93. There may be more than one mistake in a location.

A. Find seven errors in six locations.

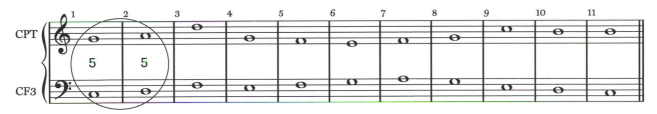

	MEASURE(S)	ERROR CODE(S)	PART (CPT, CF, BOTH)
1	1–2	G	both
2	2–3	L, M	both
3			

	MEASURE(S)	ERROR CODE(S)	PART (CPT, CF, BOTH)
4			
5			
6			

B. Find three errors in specific locations and one overall.

(transposed)

	MEASURE(S)	ERROR CODE(S)	PART (CPT, CF, BOTH)
1	2	J	both
2			
3			

Error overall: _____

C. Find eight errors in six locations and one overall. 🎧

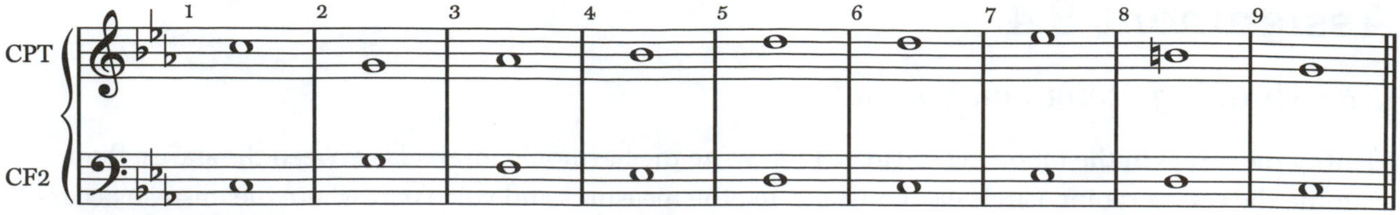

(transposed)

	MEASURE(S)	ERROR CODE(S)	PART (CPT, CF, BOTH)
1			
2			
3			

	MEASURE(S)	ERROR CODE(S)	PART (CPT, CF, BOTH)
4			
5			
6			

Error overall: _____

D. Find three errors in two locations and two overall. 🎧

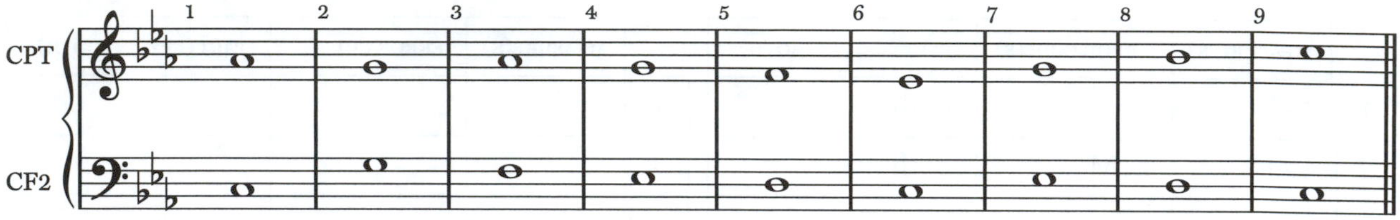

(transposed)

	MEASURE(S)	ERROR CODE(S)	PART (CPT, CF, BOTH)
1			
2			

Errors overall: _____

E. Find three errors in the opening (three locations), four in the closing (three locations), and one overall. Both voices are free counterpoint (no cantus); indicate upper or lower part or both. 🎧

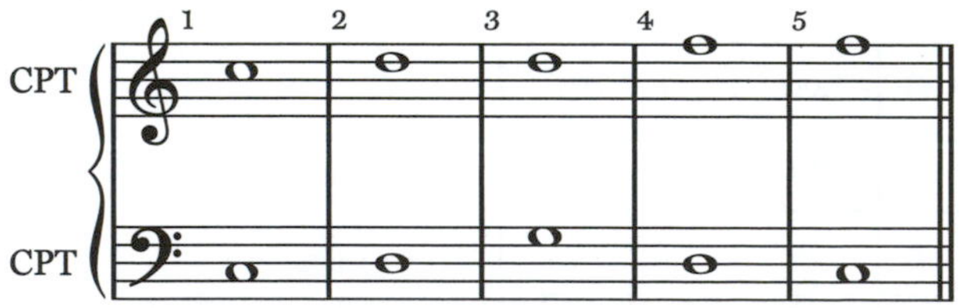

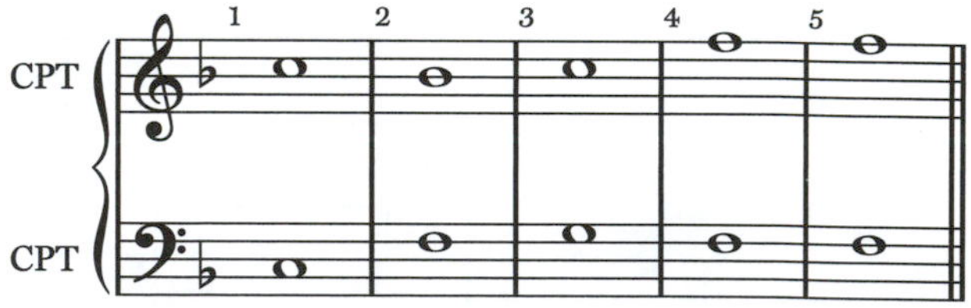

Opening:

	MEASURE(S)	ERROR CODE(S)	PART (CPT, CF, BOTH)
1			
2			
3			

Closing:

	MEASURE(S)	ERROR CODE(S)	PART (CPT, CF, BOTH)
1			
2			
3			

Error overall: _____

NAME _____

Assignment 9.5

I. Writing a note-to-note counterpoint

Write a note-to-note counterpoint for each given cantus firmus in strict style, in whole notes. Write the harmonic interval numbers between the staves, and indicate above the CPT line if the motion between the parts is contrary (C), similar (S), oblique (O), or parallel (P). If it helps, fill in the table with letter names of the possible consonant pitches.

A. Above a given line

(1)

6	A♭							
5	G							
3	E♭							
8	C							

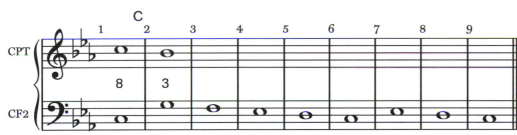

(transposed)

(2)

6										
5										
3										
8										

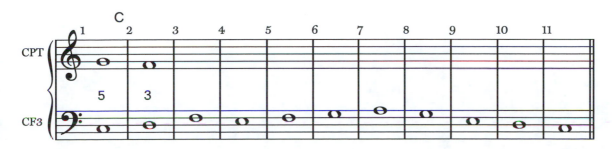

B. Below a given line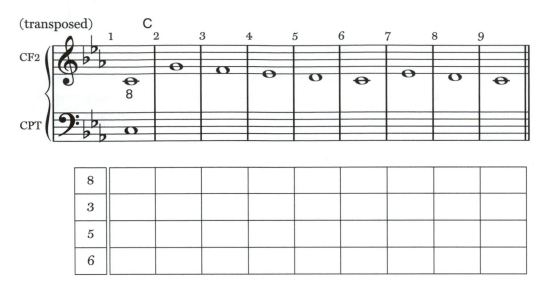

(transposed)

8								
3								
5								
6								

Assignment 9.6

I. Writing a note-to-note counterpoint

Write a note-to-note counterpoint for each of the given cantus firmus lines in strict style, with whole notes. Write the harmonic interval numbers between the staves, and indicate above the CPT line if the motion between the parts is contrary (C), similar (S), oblique (O), or parallel (P).

A. Above a given line

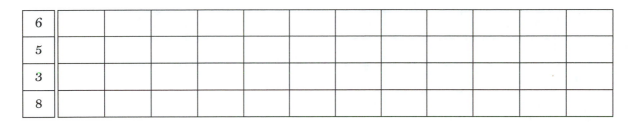

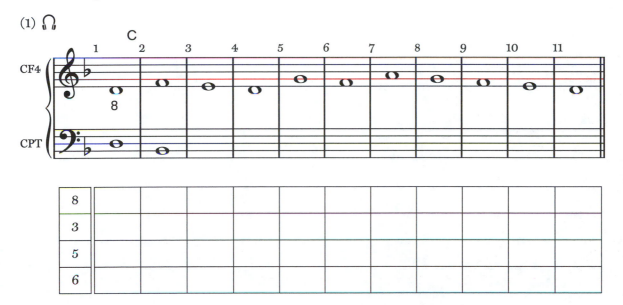

B. Below a given line

(1)

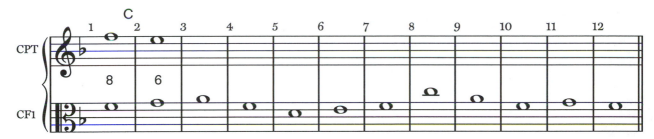

(2)

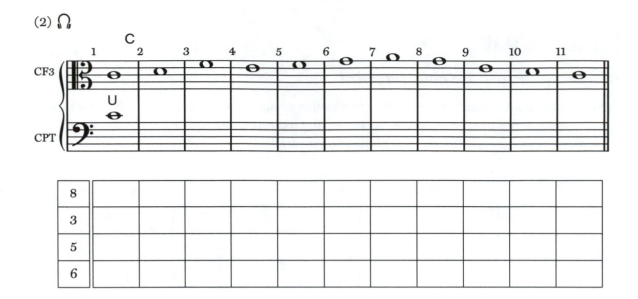

8											
3											
5											
6											

10 Melodic and Rhythmic Embellishment in Two-Voice Composition

Checkpoints for Students and Teachers

When writing second-species (2:1) counterpoint, we suggest two passes to check your work:

1. Check the harmonic intervals first.
   - The first and last intervals should be either 8 or U. The first can be 5 only if the counterpoint is above the cantus.
   - Each cantus note should be paired with a consonance (the first half note in the measure, falling "on the beat"). A dissonance written on this beat is an error.
   - If there is an 8 or 5 on the beat, check the first half note in the next measure for parallel octaves or fifths; also look back at the approach to the 8 or 5, which should be by step in the upper part (check for hidden fifths or octaves) and not from another interval of the same size.
   - The second half note ("offbeat") of each measure may include a dissonant passing or neighbor tone. Make sure any 2, 4, 7, or 9 is prepared and resolved as a passing or neighbor tone, and mark it P or N. An A4 or d5 must be treated as a passing or neighbor tone, and must resolve to the correct interval.
   - The offbeat may be another consonance, approached by step, skip, or leap, in oblique motion with the cantus note. You can leap or skip into octaves or fifths on the offbeats; octaves or fifths on consecutive offbeats are also acceptable, unless they draw attention to themselves. If the offbeat note is an 8 or 5, check the connection to the next beat for parallels.
   - The unison (U) should only appear at the beginning or end of the counterpoint (some teachers allow it on the second half of the measure if the voices are close together).
   - The close in strict style should be 3-U (10-8) or 6-8, with the parts approaching the final note in contrary motion by step over the bar line. The next-to-last cantus note may be set 2:1 or 1:1; the final note is 1:1. Raise $\flat\hat{7}$ in minor to make a leading tone, and $\flat\hat{6}$ if necessary, but only approaching at the close.
2. Examine the contour and melodic intervals of the counterpoint line.
   - There should be one high or low point, with perhaps a subsidiary high or low point.
   - If the cantus includes a skip or leap, the counterpoint should balance it, ideally with steps in the opposite direction.
   - Any leaps in the counterpoint line should be prepared by an approach contrary to the direction of the leap, and followed by steps contrary to the direction of the leap.

- Dissonant melodic intervals (7, d5, A4, A2) are not allowed.
- There should be a mix of perfect consonances, imperfect consonances, and dissonances (treated correctly as passing or neighbor tones). A second-species exercise must include some dissonant passing or neighbor tones; complete lack of them is an error!

When writing third-species counterpoint (4:1), check for the following elements:

1. Check the harmonic intervals first.
   - The first and last intervals should be either 8 or U. The first can be 5 only if the counterpoint is above the cantus.
   - Each cantus note should be paired with a consonance (the first quarter note in the measure, falling "on the beat"). A dissonance written on the downbeat is an error.
   - There should be some diversity of intervals on the downbeats—ideally no more than three 3 or three 6 in a row, and at least one 8 or 5 in the middle of the exercise (two if it is a long cantus) in addition to the opening and closing intervals—to mix the "sweetness" of the imperfect consonances with the "hollowness" of the perfect consonances.
   - If there is an 8 or 5 on the downbeat, check the first quarter note in the next measure for parallel octaves or fifths; also look back at the approach to the 8 or 5, which should be by step in the upper part (check for hidden fifths or octaves) and not from another interval of the same size.
   - If the third quarter note in a measure is an 8 or 5, check the next downbeat, which should not be the same interval (creating parallel octaves or fifths).
   - The intervals 8 or 5 on consecutive offbeats are acceptable unless they draw attention to themselves, through contour or repetition. The intervals 8 and 5 from the second quarter note to the following downbeat, or from the second, third, or fourth quarter to any beat other than the downbeat of the next measure, are acceptable.
   - The unison should only appear at the beginning or end of the counterpoint (some teachers, including Fux, allow it on the second, third, or fourth quarter note if the voices are close together).
   - The second, third, and fourth notes of each measure may include a dissonant passing or neighbor tone or may be a consonance. A consonance may be approached by step, skip, or leap. Make sure any 2, 4, 7, or 9 is prepared and resolved as a passing or neighbor tone, and mark it P or N.
   - An A4 or d5 must be treated as a passing or neighbor tone, and must resolve to the correct interval. In third species, these intervals normally appear on the final quarter note of the measure so as to resolve immediately. To identify places to include them, look for scale degrees $\hat{4}$-$\hat{3}$ or $\hat{7}$-$\hat{1}$ in the cantus (without both together the resolution is not possible).
   - The closing intervals should be 3-U (10-8) or 6-8, with the parts approaching the final note in contrary motion by step over the bar line. Raise $\flat\hat{6}$ and $\flat\hat{7}$ in minor only when approaching $\hat{1}$ at the close.

2. Examine the contour and melodic intervals of the counterpoint line.
   - Examine the melody in units of five quarter notes (downbeat to the downbeat of the following measure) for local continuity. Each five-note unit should make a pleasing contour, with a melodic step crossing the bar line. Avoid repeating the same melodic shape in consecutive measures.

- Avoid a static line—circling around a few pitches or repeating a pitch more than three times in a span of two measures—by using a wider range than in second species. Do not immediately repeat any notes, whether within the bar or across the bar line.
- The counterpoint may span up to an octave and a fifth in overall range, but do not move more than an octave in one direction without a change of direction.
- Leaps and skips in the counterpoint line should be placed within the measure (not over the bar line). Leaps are prepared by an approach contrary to the direction of the leap and followed by steps contrary to the direction of the leap. Skips normally involve a change of direction as well and should not follow a series of steps in the same direction.
- Dissonant melodic intervals (7, d5, A4, A2) are not allowed.
- There should be one high or low point, with a subsidiary high or low point. The contour of an upper counterpoint should be like mountains in the distance. A lower counterpoint should be like the mountains reflected in a lake.
- A well-crafted third-species counterpoint creates the feeling of soaring—like a raptor floating on the thermals, swooping downward, then soaring upward. This effect is made from primarily stepwise motion enlivened by judiciously placed skips and employment of a properly placed and prepared leap. Counterpoint melodies that are too conservative—occupying a narrow range or exclusively stepwise—will not soar.

When writing fourth-species counterpoint, check for the following elements:
- The first and last intervals should be either 8 or U. The counterpoint can begin with 5 if it is above the cantus.
- The counterpoint begins with a half rest, followed by a half note (preferably tied over the bar line), and ends with a whole note. The second half note in the penultimate measure is not tied over.
- If the counterpoint is below the cantus, the last two measures will end with a 2-3 suspension to an 8 or U; if the counterpoint is above the cantus, it will close with a 7-6 suspension to 8. Because the closing suspension must be prepared, the last two and a half measures will be $\hat{1}$ tied over and then resolved to $\hat{7}$, followed by $\hat{1}$.
- The second half note in each measure (on the offbeat) should be tied over to the same note on the downbeat of the following measure wherever possible.
- Where possible, the tied-over note should create a dissonant suspension, prepared by a consonance on the offbeat of the previous measure, and resolving down by step on the offbeat.
- When you break species, the second half note is not tied over to the following downbeat. The resulting half notes follow the guidelines for second-species counterpoint.
- Acceptable dissonant suspensions are 4-3, 7-6, and 9-8 when the counterpoint is in the upper voice, and 2-3 when the counterpoint is in the lower part. The consonant suspensions 5-6 and 6-5 may be used when the counterpoint is in either voice.
- The only suspensions that may be used in a chain are 7-6 and 4-3 in the upper part, and 2-3 in the lower. Chains should be broken, either by a change in the suspension type or by breaking species, to avoid more than three repetitions of the same intervallic pattern.

- The suspensions 9-8 and 6-5 may not be used in chains, as this creates the sound of parallel octaves or fifths.
- If it is not possible to create a dissonant suspension, a consonant note on the offbeat may be tied across the bar to form a consonant interval with the following cantus note. When consonance is tied across to consonance, there is no need for resolution on the offbeat downward or by step; instead the counterpoint may step, skip, or leap upward or downward to prepare the next suspension.
- Contour is less of a concern in fourth species (counterpoints tend to move downward), but be careful to avoid excessive use of any one note and to keep the counterpoint and cantus lines from crossing or overlapping. It will occasionally be necessary to leap or skip upward within a bar (from one consonant interval to another) to allow the counterpoint room to continue to descend.
- Breaking species should be reserved for the following situations:
  (a) when dissonant suspensions are not available and there is no consonance that can be tied over;
  (b) to reestablish the proper distance between the parts when they are about to cross or to make a more interesting line;
  (c) to break off a chain of suspensions;
  (d) to prevent counterpoint errors and to solve difficult places in the cantus.

Assignment 10.1

I. Writing 2:1 counterpoint openings

Write a 2:1 counterpoint opening for each given cantus firmus line in strict style. Start with either a half rest and a half note or two half notes in measure 1, then continue with two half notes for each remaining measure. Include passing tones, neighbor tones, and consonant skips, and write the harmonic interval numbers between the staves. Circle the interval number for any harmonic dissonance, and check that it forms a correct P or N.

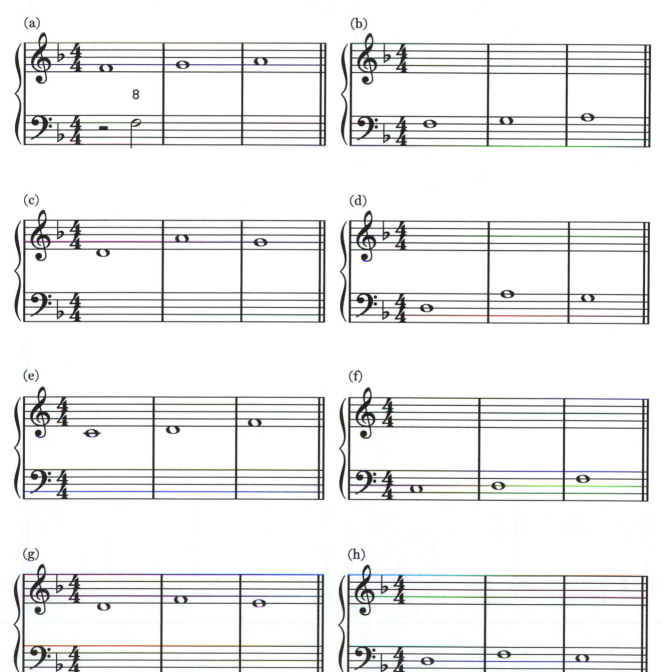

II. Writing 2:1 counterpoint closings

Write a 2:1 counterpoint closing for each given cantus firmus in strict style, two half notes per each whole note except for the last (and possibly penultimate) measure. Use passing tones, neighbor tones, and consonant skips, and write the harmonic interval numbers between the staves. Circle the number for any harmonic dissonance, and check that it forms a correct P or N.

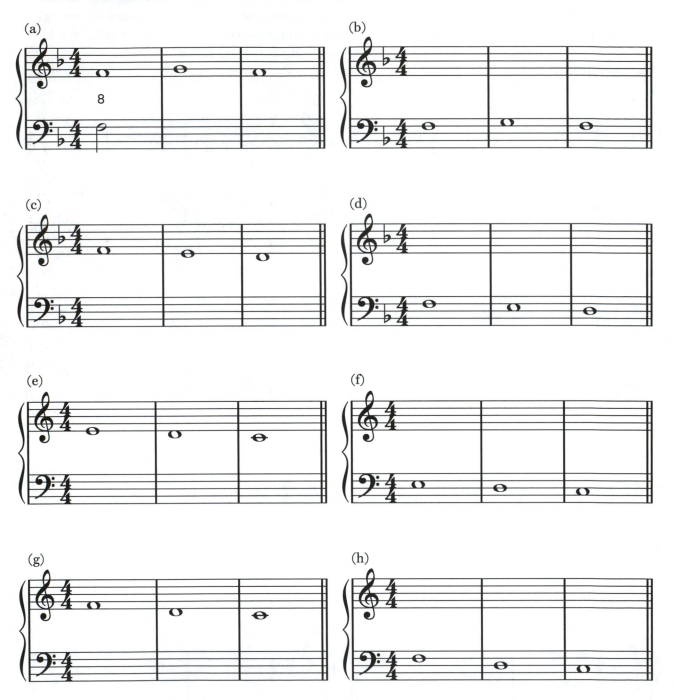

Assignment 10.2

I. Writing a 2:1 counterpoint

Write a 2:1 counterpoint for each given cantus firmus in strict style, using two half notes for each cantus whole note. Include passing tones, neighbor tones, and consonant skips, and write the harmonic interval numbers between the staves. Circle the number for each harmonic dissonance.

A. Above a given line

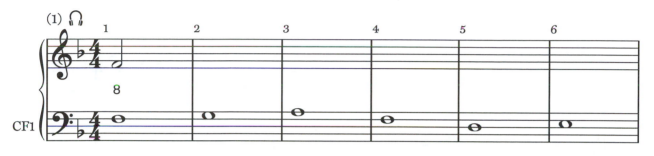

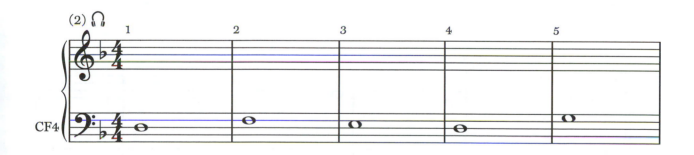

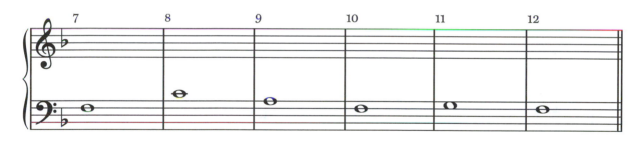

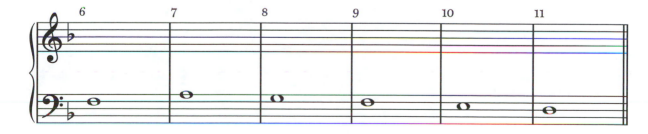

B. Below a given line

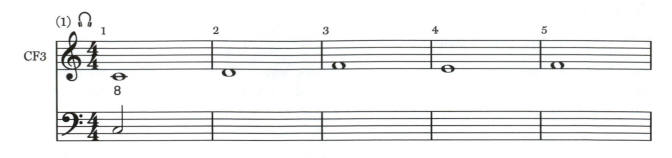

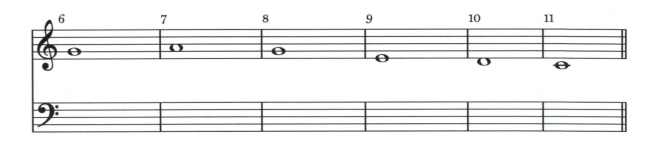

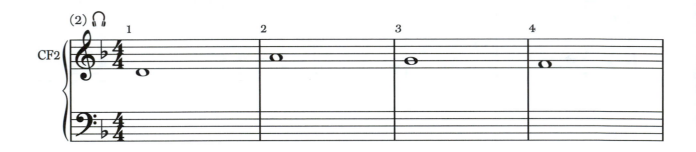

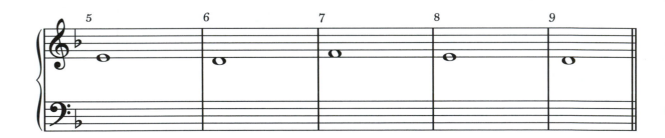

Assignment 10.3

I. Writing a 2:1 counterpoint

Write a 2:1 counterpoint in strict style for each given cantus firmus, as for Assignment 10.2.

A. Below a given line

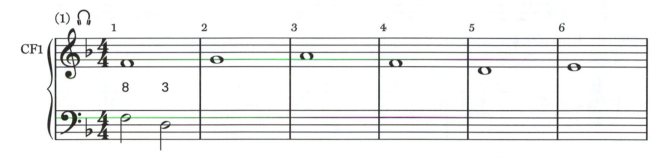

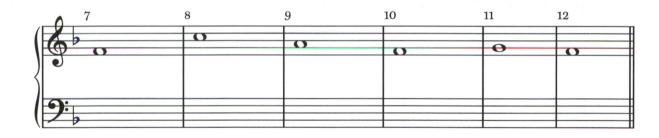

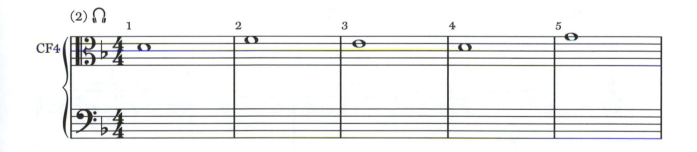

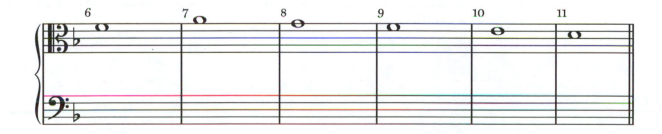

B. Above a given line

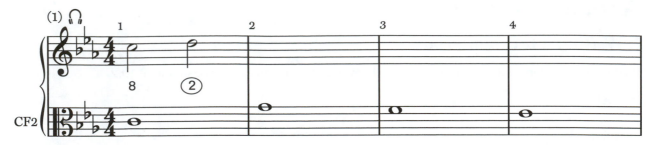

CF2

(transposed)

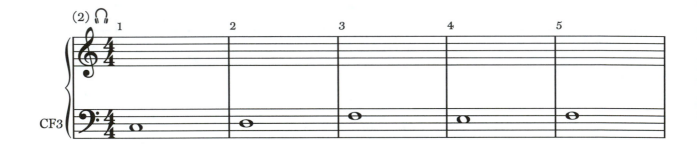

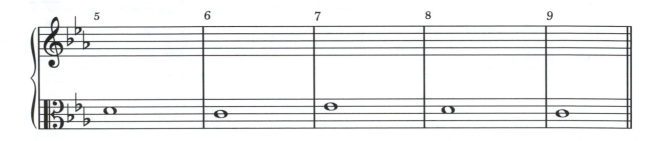

CF3

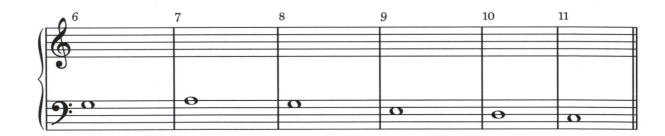

Assignment 10.4

I. Writing a 4:1 counterpoint

Write a 4:1 counterpoint for each given cantus firmus in strict style, using four quarter notes for each cantus whole note, starting either with a quarter rest followed by three quarter notes or a full measure of quarter notes in the counterpoint. Include passing tones, neighbor tones, and consonant skips, and write the harmonic interval numbers between the staves. You may include a cambiata or double neighbor pattern; if so, bracket and label it (both patterns extend a whole measure plus the next downbeat). Circle the number for each harmonic dissonance, and label it as passing (P) or neighboring (N).

A. Below a given line.

(1)

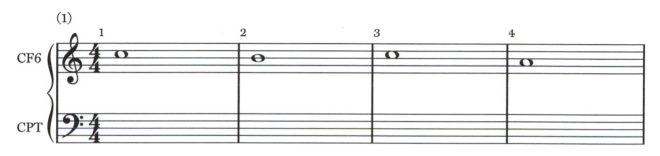

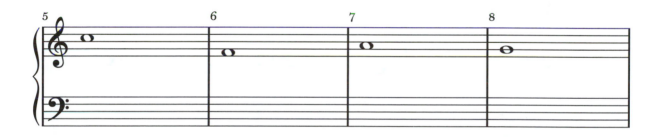

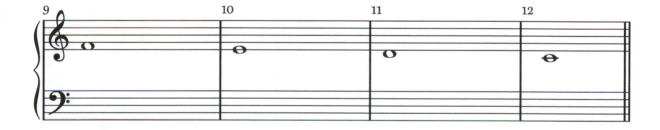

(2)

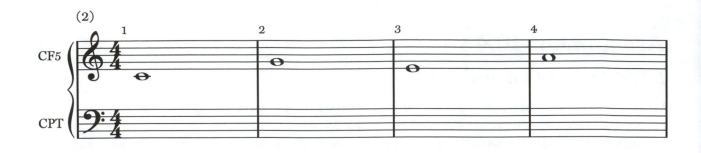

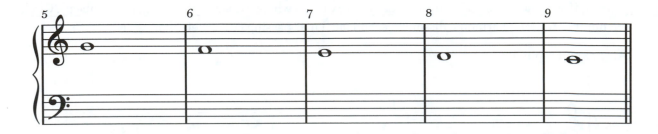

B. Above a given line.

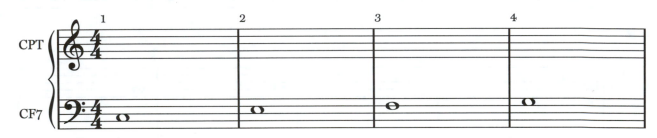

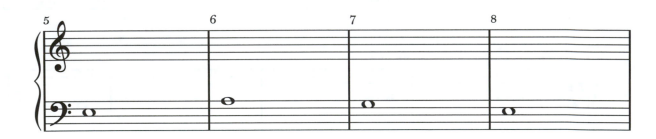

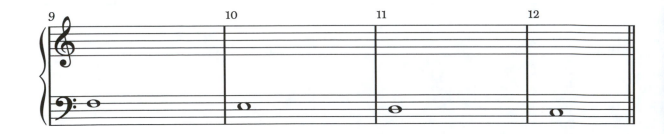

Assignment 10.5

I. Suspensions in note-to-note counterpoint

For each note-to-note framework, make a dissonant suspension as shown. Between the staves, write the interval numbers for both the framework and your suspension. Above the staff, label the three parts of the suspension: preparation (prep), dissonant suspension (S), and resolution (res). Include at least one bass suspension.

(a)

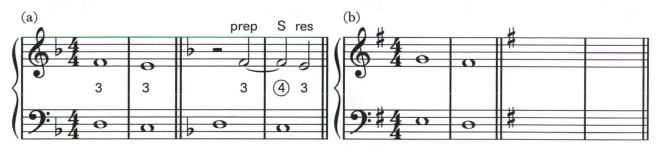

(b)

(c)

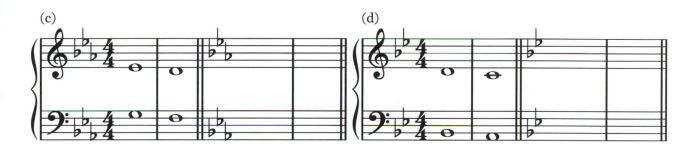

(d)

(e)

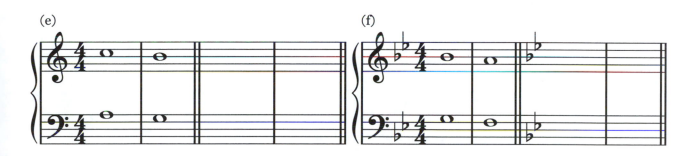

(f)

(g)

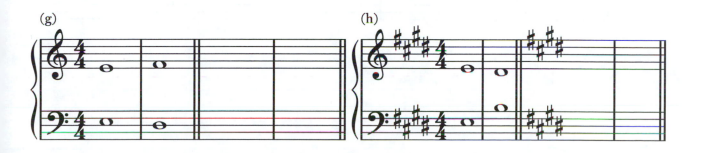

(h)

II. Writing chains of suspensions

Use rhythmic displacement to make chains of suspensions from the given parallel thirds or sixths. In (d) and (e), write your own suspension chains, using a different type of suspension in each. Play your chains at a keyboard, or sing or play them as a duet with a partner.

(a) Write suspensions in the upper part.

3   ④   3

(b) Write suspensions in the lower part.

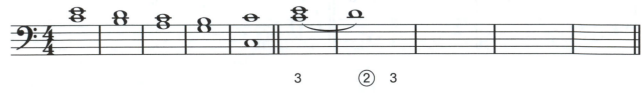

3   ②   3

(c) Write suspensions in the upper part.

6

(d) Write a chain of suspensions.

(e) Write another chain, using a suspension type other than the one in (d).

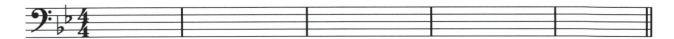

Assignment 10.6

I. Writing fourth-species counterpoint

Write a fourth-species counterpoint in strict style for each given cantus firmus with two half notes tied over the bar line for each whole note. Write the harmonic interval numbers between the staves, and circle the number for any harmonic dissonance.

A. Above a given line

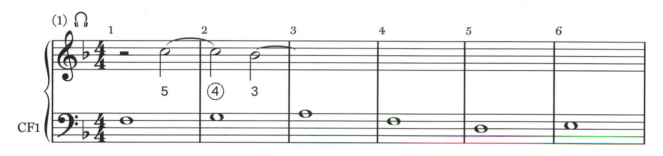

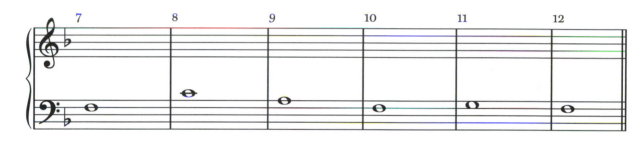

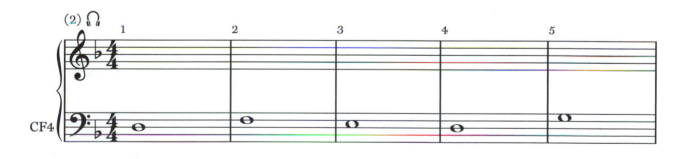

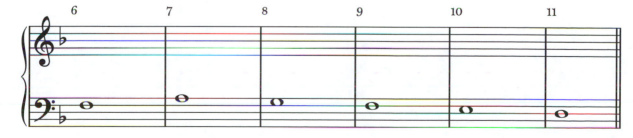

B. Below a given line

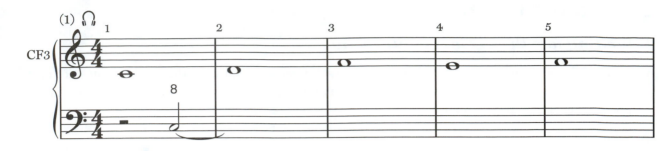

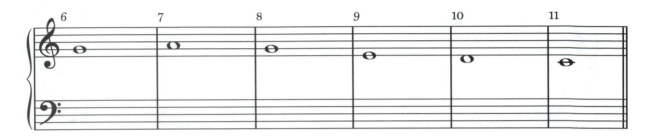

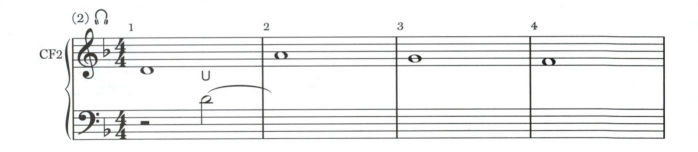

Assignment 10.7

I. Writing fourth-species counterpoint

Write a fourth-species counterpoint in strict style for each given cantus firmus, as in Assignment 10.6.

A. Below a given line

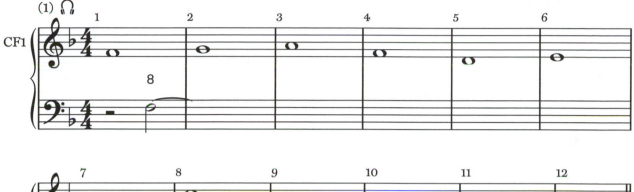

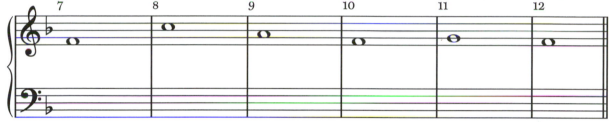

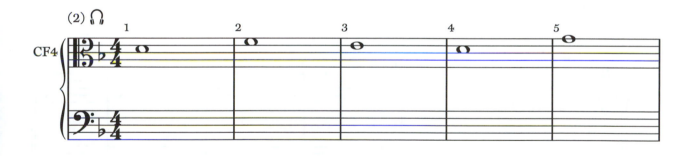

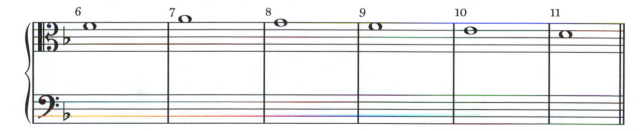

B. Above a given line

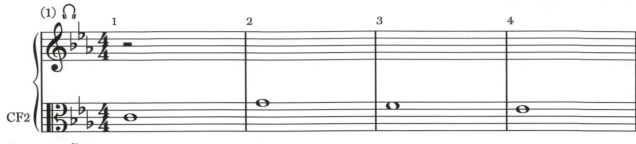

(transposed)

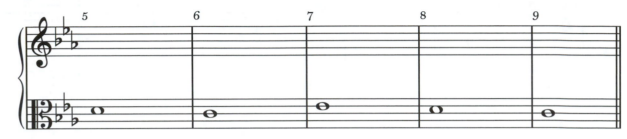

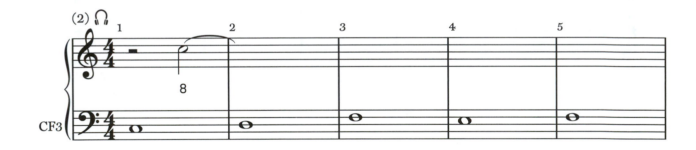

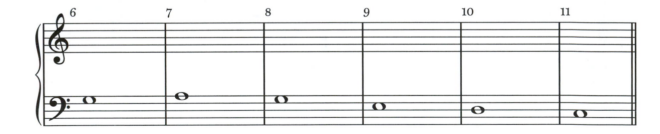

Assignment 10.8

Evaluating second, third, and fifth species

A. Shown are two examples of second-species counterpoint by Jeppesen. Write in the harmonic interval numbers between the staves. Circle each dissonance, and identify as a passing tone (P) or neighbor tone (N).

(1)

(2)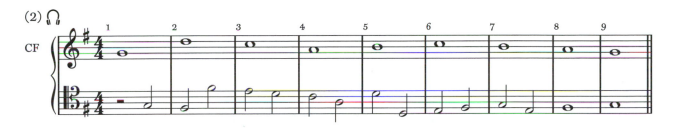

B. In this example of third-species counterpoint by Fux, write the harmonic interval numbers between the staves. Circle each dissonance, and identify as P or N.

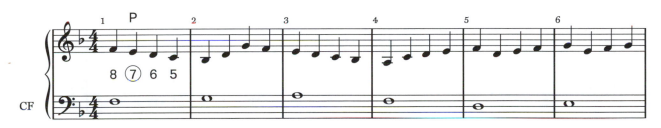

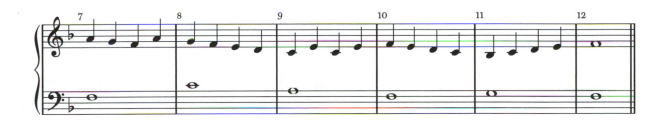

C. In these examples of fifth-species counterpoint, write the harmonic intervals between the staves. Circle each dissonance, and identify as a passing tone (P), neighbor tone (N), suspension (sus), or combination.

PART II

Diatonic Harmony
and Tonicization

From Species to Chorale Style: Soprano and Bass Lines

NAME _____

Assignment 11.1

I. Chorale melody settings

Here are the soprano and bass parts for four settings by J. S. Bach of the first phrase of an anonymous chorale melody (composed in 1539), each set to a different text. Write the scale degrees for the melody above the first setting (A), then sing or play each of these. Label the harmonic intervals between the staves, circling any that are dissoant, then examine the counterpoint. In the blanks above the staff, mark the type of motion from beat to beat: contrary (C), oblique (O), similar (S), or parallel (P). Circle and label any dissonant passing (P) or neighbor (N) tones.

As your teacher assigns: Write a paragraph summarizing the similarities and differences in these settings, or be prepared to compare them in class discussion.

A. Chorale No. 50, from *St. Matthew Passion* ("O Welt, sieh hier dein Leben"; "O World, Behold Your Life") 🎧

B. Chorale No. 275 ("O Welt, ich muß dich lassen"; "O World, I Must Leave You") 🎧

C. Chorale No. 289 ("Nun ruhen alle Wälder"; "Now All the Woods Are Peaceful") 🎧

D. Chorale No. 355, from Cantata No. 44 ("In allen meinen Taten"; "In All My Actions") 🎧

II. Resolving chordal dissonances

For each pair of intervals:

1. Write scale-degree numbers for each note in the specified key.

2. Identify each dissonant interval (d5, A4, or 7).

3. Add notes to resolve the dissonance correctly:

   d5 → 3: both voices move in by step.

   A4 → 6: both voices move out by step.

   7 → 3: the lower voice skips up a P4 or down a P5; the upper voice moves down by step.

4. Identify the scale degree of the notes you added in step 3.

5. Write Roman numerals and figures underneath (V7, V⁶₅, V⁴₂; I, I⁶, i, or i⁶) for each implied chord.

Assignment 11.2

I. Opening patterns in eighteenth-century style note-to-note counterpoint

For each pattern:

1. Write scale-degree numbers for each given note in the specified key.

2. Add a note to complete the pair of intervals. In minor, add an accidental for the leading tone.

3. Label both intervals, circling dissonant intervals, and write the new note's scale-degree number.

4. Label each chord with Roman numerals and figures, selecting from I, i, I⁶, i⁶, V, V⁶, V⁷, V⁶₅, and V⁴₃.

A. Without an anacrusis

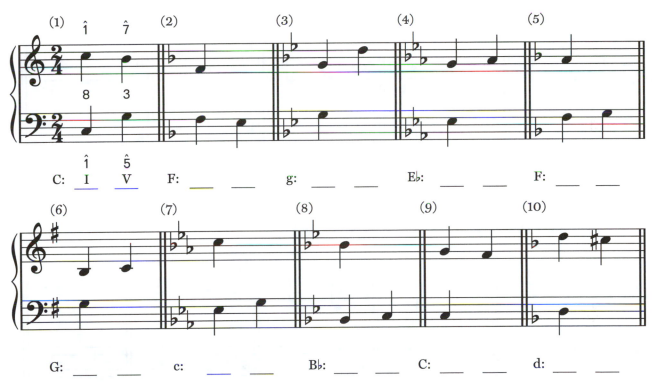

B. With an anacrusis

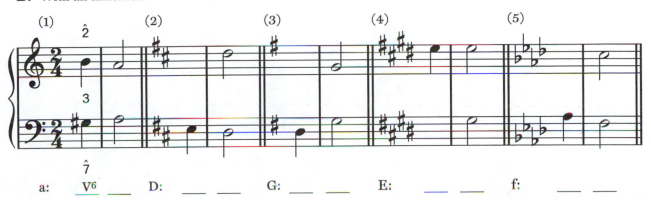

II. Closing patterns in eighteenth-century style note-to-note counterpoint

Follow the instructions for part I.

A. Conclusive closes

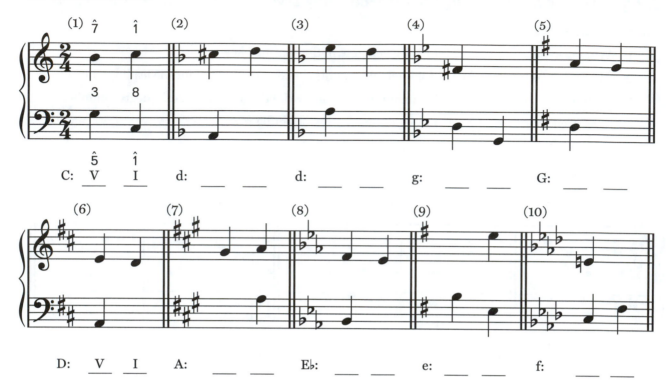

C: $\underline{V}$ $\underline{I}$ d: $\underline{\hspace{1em}}$ $\underline{\hspace{1em}}$ d: $\underline{\hspace{1em}}$ $\underline{\hspace{1em}}$ g: $\underline{\hspace{1em}}$ $\underline{\hspace{1em}}$ G: $\underline{\hspace{1em}}$ $\underline{\hspace{1em}}$

D: $\underline{V}$ $\underline{I}$ A: $\underline{\hspace{1em}}$ $\underline{\hspace{1em}}$ E♭: $\underline{\hspace{1em}}$ $\underline{\hspace{1em}}$ e: $\underline{\hspace{1em}}$ $\underline{\hspace{1em}}$ f: $\underline{\hspace{1em}}$ $\underline{\hspace{1em}}$

B. Less conclusive closes

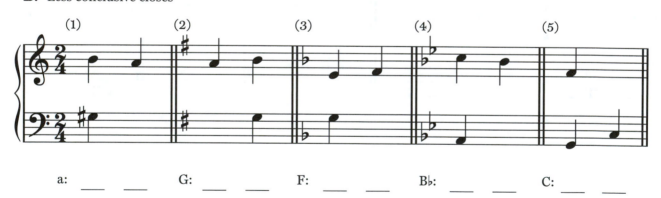

a: $\underline{\hspace{1em}}$ $\underline{\hspace{1em}}$ G: $\underline{\hspace{1em}}$ $\underline{\hspace{1em}}$ F: $\underline{\hspace{1em}}$ $\underline{\hspace{1em}}$ B♭: $\underline{\hspace{1em}}$ $\underline{\hspace{1em}}$ C: $\underline{\hspace{1em}}$ $\underline{\hspace{1em}}$

Assignment 11.3

Writing a note-to-note counterpoint in eighteenth-century style

A. Above a given bass line

1. Examine the bass line to identify the key and mode, then determine which chords (selecting from I, i, I^6, i^6, V, V^6, V^7, V^6_5, and V^4_3) are implied at the beginning and end, and write those Roman numerals in the blanks.

2. Write the opening and closing counterpoint, then provide one soprano note for each of the other bass notes.

3. You may use chordal dissonances (d5, A4, m7) if they can be resolved correctly; approach these intervals by common tone or step.

4. Label the harmonic intervals between the staves, and circle chordal dissonances.

(1)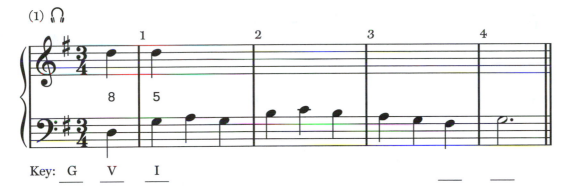

Key: <u>G</u>   <u>V</u>   <u>I</u>   <u>   </u> <u>   </u>

(2)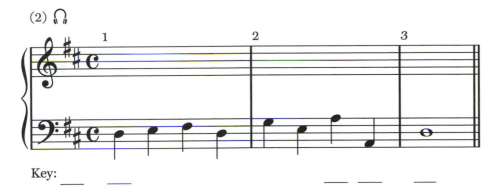

Key: <u>   </u> <u>   </u>   <u>   </u> <u>   </u>   <u>   </u>

(3)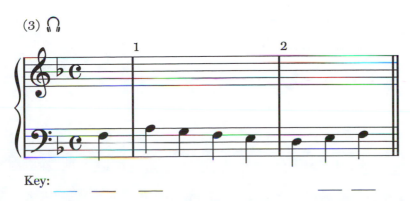

Key: <u>   </u> <u>   </u> <u>   </u>   <u>   </u> <u>   </u>

B. Below a given chorale melody

1. Identify the key, and determine which chords (selecting from I, i, I⁶, i⁶, V, V⁶, V⁷, V⁶₅, and V⁴₃) are implied at the beginning and end, as for part A.

2. Write the opening and closing counterpoint, then provide one bass note per quarter-note beat.

3. You may use chordal dissonances (d5, A4, m7) if they can be resolved correctly; approach these intervals by common tone or step.

4. Label the harmonic intervals between the staves, and circle chordal dissonances.

(1) "Ich muss meine Abendswerk tun" ("I Must Perform My Evening's Work")

Key: d   V   i

(2) "Heut ist, o Mensch, ein grosser Trauentag" ("Today Is, O Man, a Day of Great Sadness")

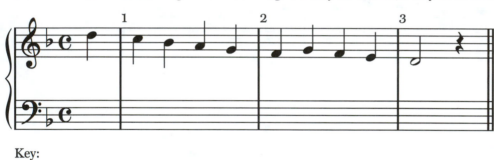

Key: __ __   __ __

(3) "In allen meinen Taten" ("In All My Actions")

Key: __ __ __   __ __

Assignment 11.4

I. Analysis of 2:1 counterpoint in eighteenth-century style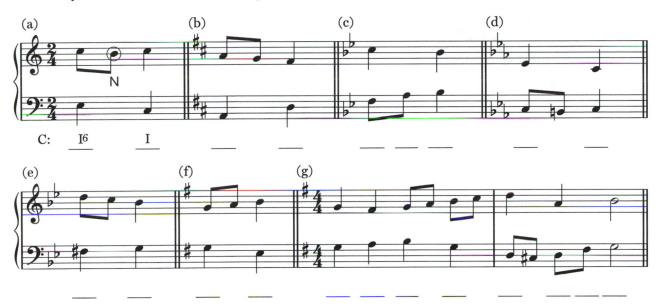

Circle each embellishing tone in each measure, and label as P (passing), N (neighbor), or CS (consonant or chordal skip). Indicate the key and mode for each example, and label the implied harmonies (dominant or tonic only) with Roman numerals and figures.

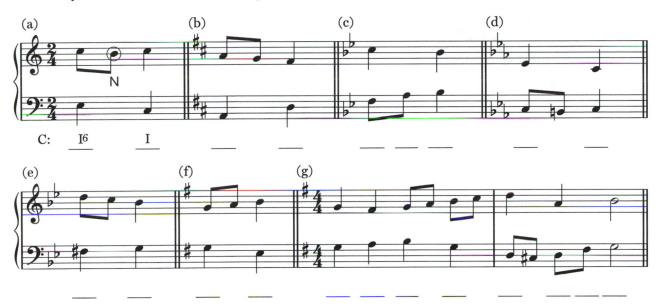

II. Analysis of suspensions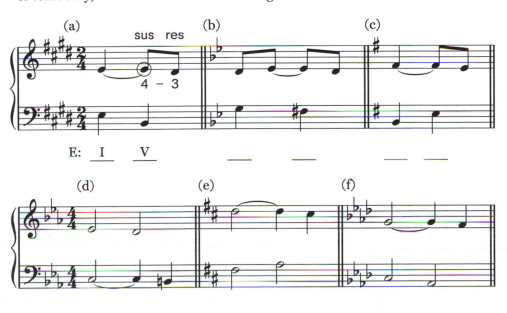

Circle and label each suspension, and indicate its type (e.g., 4–3). Also label the preparation (prep) and resolution (res). Indicate the key and mode for each example, and label the implied harmonies (dominant or tonic only) with Roman numerals and figures.

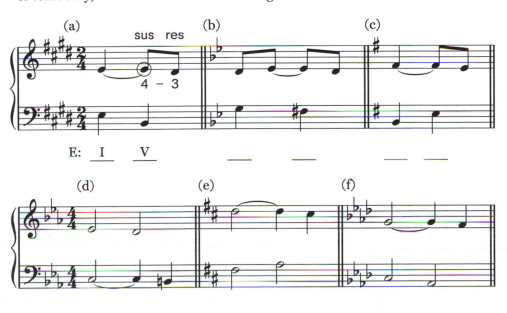

III. Analyzing suspensions in musical contexts

Listen to the opening of this aria, then label the intervals between the soprano and bass lines. For each suspension, write 4-3, 2-3, or 7-6 between the staves and "sus" above the staff.

Handel, "Rejoice greatly"

A. Mm. 7-8 🎧

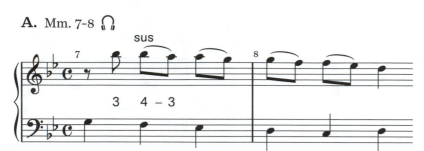

B. Mm. 20-22 🎧

C. Mm. 34-35 🎧

Assignment 11.5

I. Analysis of chorale-style counterpoint

Given are four settings of the opening phrase of the tune "Nun danket alle Gott" ("Now Thank We All Our God"), a chorale melody composed by Johann Crüger (1648): two settings are by J. S. Bach, one is by Felix Mendelssohn (1840), and one is by the authors.

Write the scale degrees for the melody above the first setting, then sing or play each one. Label the harmonic intervals between the staves, and examine the counterpoint. In the blanks below the staff, identify any implied I or V chords, and indicate inversions. Circle and label any dissonant passing or neighbor tones.

As your teacher assigns: Write a paragraph summarizing the similarities and differences in these settings, or be prepared to compare them in class discussion.

A. Bach, Chorale No. 32

B. Bach, Chorale No. 330

C. Mendelssohn, from Episcopal Hymnal 1940

D. Clendinning and Marvin

II. Writing chorale-style counterpoint from a given bass line

Write a chorale-style counterpoint for each given line. Combine note-to-note and 2:1 patterns, using 2:1 where possible; you may include suspensions, but don't change the given line. Write the harmonic interval numbers between the staves, circle any dissonant intervals, and label any passing tones, neighbor tones, or suspensions. Identify the key and mode, and write Roman numerals and figures for the opening and closing chords in the blanks, using only I and V(7).

A.

Key: F ___ I ___ I⁶ ___

B.

Key: ___ ___ ___ ___ ___

C.

Key: ___ ___ ___ ___

Assignment 11.6

I. Writing chorale-style counterpoint from a chorale melody

Write a chorale-style counterpoint for each given line. Combine note-to-note and 2:1 patterns, using 2:1 where possible; you may include suspensions, but don't change the given line. Write the harmonic interval numbers between the staves, circle any dissonant intervals, and label any passing tones, neighbor tones, or suspensions. Identify the key and mode, and write Roman numerals and figures for the opening and closing chords in the blanks, using only I and V(7) and their inversions. Write scale-degree numbers above each melody.

A. "Nun danket," mm. 1-4

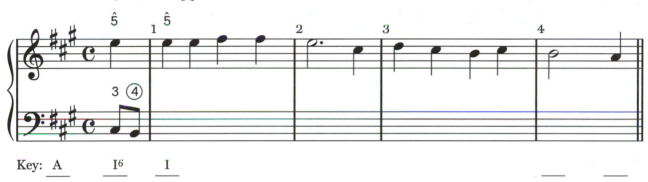

Key: A   I⁶   I   ___   ___

B. "Heut ist, o Mensch, ein grosser Trauentag," mm. 1-3

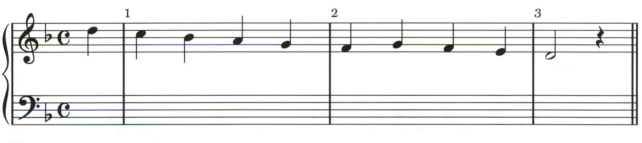

Key: ___ ___   ___ ___

C. "In allen meinen Taten," mm. 1-2

Key: ___ ___   ___   ___   ___

II. Bach, Chorale No. 168, mm. 4–6 (adapted)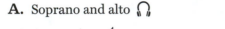

This chorale melody by Matthäus Apelles von Löwenstern (1633) is known as "Heut ist, o Mensch, ein grosser Trauertag." From Bach's four-part setting, pairs of voices have been isolated in A–C. Consider each pair a two-part counterpoint: write the harmonic interval numbers below the staff (A) or between the staves (B and C), circle any dissonant intervals, and label any passing tones, neighbor tones, or suspensions. (Hint: Watch out for rearticulated suspensions.) For B and C, provide Roman numerals in the blanks. When there is a chordal skip in the bass, calculate the inversion from the lowest bass note. Then compare these two-part counterpoints to the four-voice setting in D, and circle and label any dissonance not found in A–C.

A. Soprano and alto

B. Soprano and bass

C. Alto and bass

D. Full chorale setting

12 The Basic Phrase in SATB Style

NAME _____

Assignment 12.1

I. Analyzing cadence types

Identify the key of each excerpt, and write Roman numerals for the two chords that end each phrase. Circle the abbreviation that represents the cadence type. If cadence is IAC, circle "strong" or "contrapuntal."

A. Bach, "O Haupt voll Blut und Wunden," mm. 11-12

Key: __F__

                    ___   ___

             HC   IAC   PAC

If IAC: strong   contrapuntal

B. Schubert, "Der Lindenbaum," mm. 29-32

Ich musst'   auch heu - te wan - dern   vor - bei   in tie - fer Nacht,

Key: ___

                    ___   ___

             HC   IAC   PAC

If IAC: strong   contrapuntal

Key: ___

HC   IAC   PAC

If IAC: strong   contrapuntal

II. SATB doubling in triads

Write the triads requested in four parts (SATB), using half notes and adding any accidentals needed to make the correct chord quality. Carefully check the stem direction, voice range, doubling, and spacing.

A. Root position

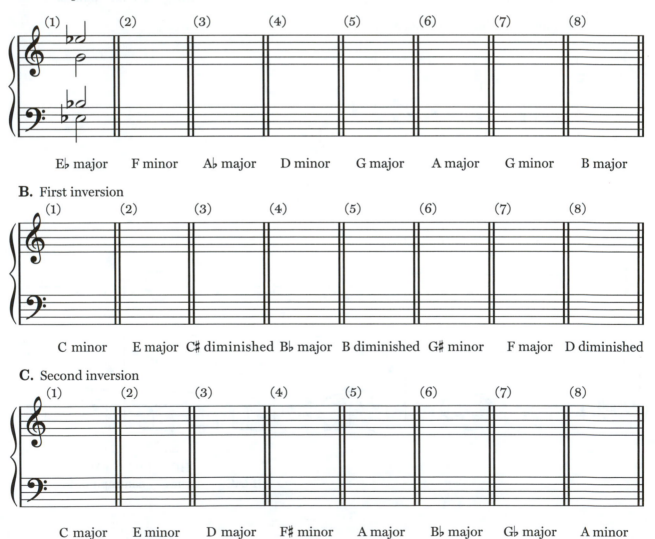

(1) E♭ major   (2) F minor   (3) A♭ major   (4) D minor   (5) G major   (6) A major   (7) G minor   (8) B major

B. First inversion

(1) C minor   (2) E major   (3) C♯ diminished   (4) B♭ major   (5) B diminished   (6) G♯ minor   (7) F major   (8) D diminished

C. Second inversion

(1) C major   (2) E minor   (3) D major   (4) F♯ minor   (5) A major   (6) B♭ major   (7) G♭ major   (8) A minor

Assignment 12.2

I. Error detection in chord spacing

Write the root, quality, and inversion ($\frac{5}{3}$, $\frac{6}{3}$, or $\frac{6}{4}$) for each SATB chord. Then choose from the following list the type of error that applies to the chord, and write the letter in the blank. Rewrite the chord in the measure to the right, with the error corrected.

A. Incorrect doubling

B. Spacing more than an octave between soprano and alto

C. Spacing more than an octave between alto and tenor

D. Voice part out of suggested range

E. Crossed voices

F. Incorrect chord spelling

Root: A   _____   _____   _____   _____

Quality: maj   _____   _____   _____   _____

Inversion: $\frac{5}{3}$ _____   _____   _____   _____

Error: C   _____   _____   _____   _____

Root: _____   _____   _____   _____   _____

Quality: _____   _____   _____   _____   _____

Inversion: _____   _____   _____   _____   _____

Error: _____   _____   _____   _____   _____

II. Analyzing basic phrases

For each basic phrase given, label the key and provide a Roman numeral analysis. Circle the correct label for each cadence. Finally, complete a contextual analysis (T-D-T) that shows the positions of the tonic and dominant areas in each phrase.

A. Friedrich Kuhlau, Sonatina, Op. 55, No. 1, mvt. 1, mm. 1-4

C: I
T

HC   IAC   PAC

B. Jeremiah Clarke, *Trumpet Voluntary*, mm. 49-52

HC   IAC   PAC

C. Johann Kuhnau, *Biblical Sonata* No. 1, "The Fight between David and Goliath," closing section, mvt. 2, mm. 1-8

HC   IAC   PAC   HC   IAC   PAC

Assignment 12.3

I. Scale-degree triads in inversion

For each of the Roman numerals in the keys indicated, notate the triads in quarter notes on the grand staff, in the specified inversion. Use proper SATB voicing, stem direction, doubling, and spacing. In minor keys, use the leading tone to spell the chords built on $\hat{5}$ and $\hat{7}$.

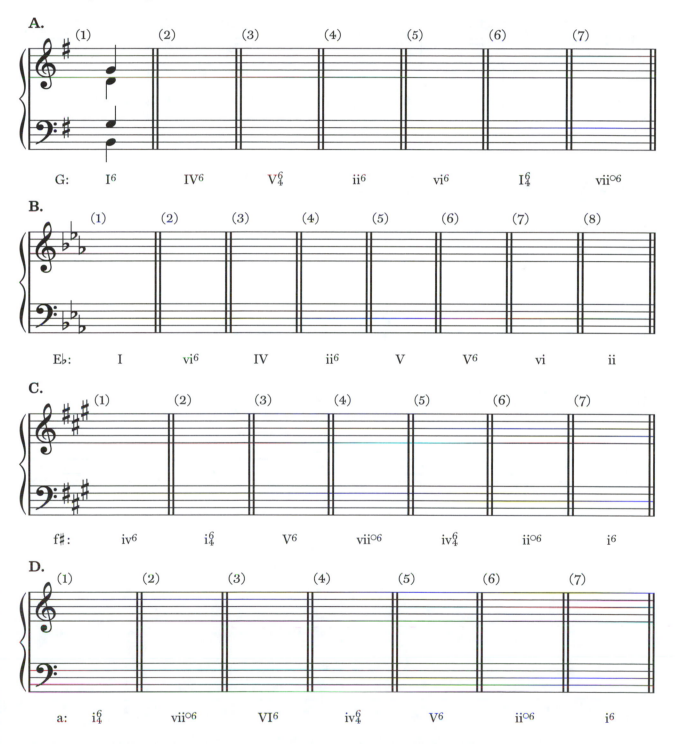

A.

G: I6 (1)   IV6 (2)   V$^6_4$ (3)   ii6 (4)   vi6 (5)   I$^6_4$ (6)   vii°6 (7)

B.

E♭: I (1)   vi6 (2)   IV (3)   ii6 (4)   V (5)   V6 (6)   vi (7)   ii (8)

C.

f♯: iv6 (1)   i$^6_4$ (2)   V6 (3)   vii°6 (4)   iv$^6_4$ (5)   ii°6 (6)   i6 (7)

D.

a: i$^6_4$ (1)   vii°6 (2)   VI6 (3)   iv$^6_4$ (4)   V6 (5)   ii°6 (6)   i6 (7)

II. Analyzing SATB voicing and spacing

(1) Listen to the following piece, or sing it with your class. (2) Write the chords in root position on the staff below the example, and label each chord and quality in the blanks (maj, min, Mm7, etc). Disregard the circled pitches. (3) Evaluate the spacing; write an asterisk (*) above any chord that diverges from the doubling guidelines, and be prepared to discuss in class. (4) Circle any spots where voices cross.

William Billings, "Chester," mm. 1-12

Root: C   A   G   __   __ __ __   __   __   __ __   __ __

Quality: maj   min maj   __   __ __ __   __   __   __ __   __ __

Root: __ __ __ __   __ __ __   __ __ __   __ __ __   __ __

Quality: __ __ __ __   __ __ __   __ __ __   __ __ __   __ __

Assignment 12.4

I. Writing triads from figured bass

Write the triad indicated above each given bass note. Use half notes, in SATB style, making sure the stem direction is correct. In the blank, write the Roman numeral and inversion symbol for each chord in the key indicated.

A. SATB spacing and voicing

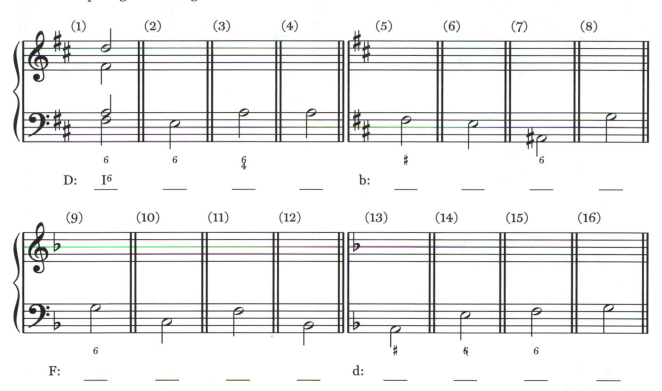

B. Keyboard spacing and voicing (three notes in the right hand and one in the left)

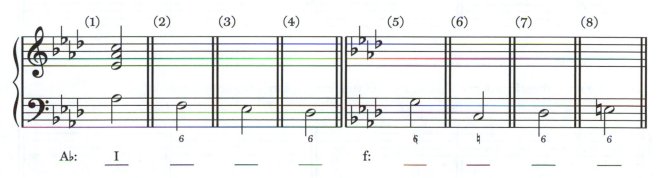

II. Writing cadences with I and V

Write the following cadences in SATB voicing, with half notes. Provide the appropriate key signatures, and add accidentals as needed in minor keys. Keep a common tone between chords. Draw arrows to show the upward resolution of leading tones.

A. Write a PAC.

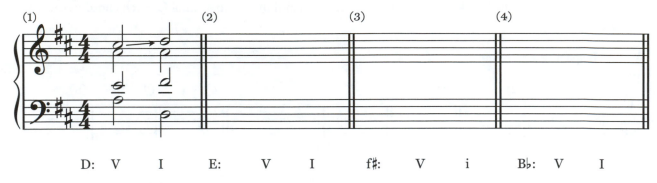

D:	V	I	E:	V	I	f#:	V	i	B♭:	V	I

B. Write a strong IAC (root-position triads).

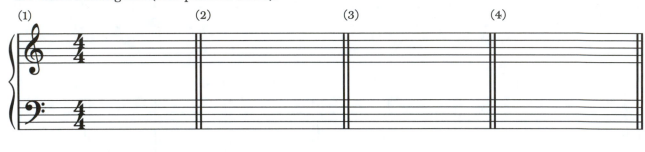

C:	V	I	b:	V	i	F:	V	I	A♭:	V	I

C. Write a HC.

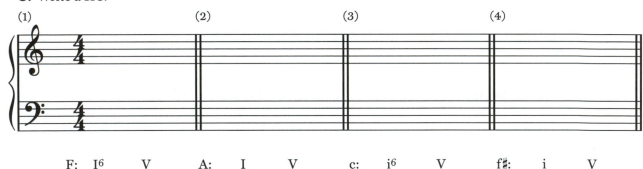

F:	I⁶	V	A:	I	V	c:	i⁶	V	f#:	i	V

F: I^6 V   A: I V   c: i^6 V   f#: i V

D. Write an authentic cadence (PAC or IAC) of your choice. Circle the appropriate label.

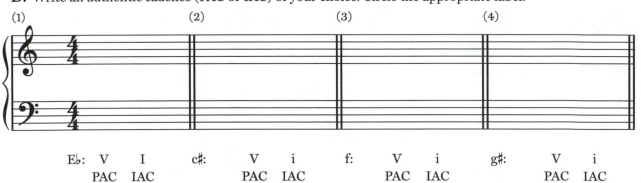

E♭: V   I   c#:   V   i   f: V   i   g#:   V   i
    PAC IAC   PAC IAC   PAC IAC   PAC IAC

Assignment 12.5

I. Writing basic phrases

Write the following progressions in SATB voicing in the meter indicated, one chord per measure. Provide the appropriate key signatures, and add a contextual analysis beneath the Roman numerals. Where a chord is repeated, change the spacing. Finally, label the cadence type.

A.   **B.**

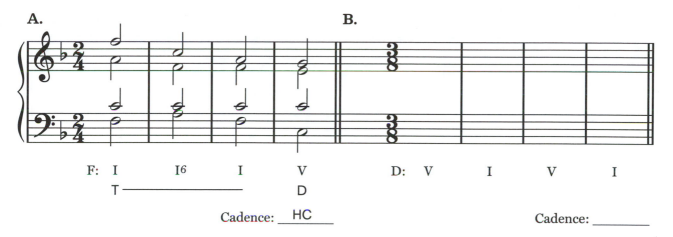

F: I   I6   I   V   D: V   I   V   I
T ——————————————   D

Cadence: __HC__   Cadence: _____

C.   **D.**

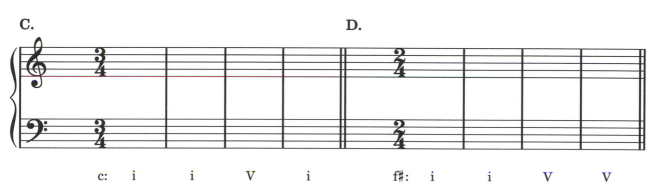

c: i   i   V   i   f#:   i   i   V   V

Cadence: _____   Cadence: _____

E.   **F.**

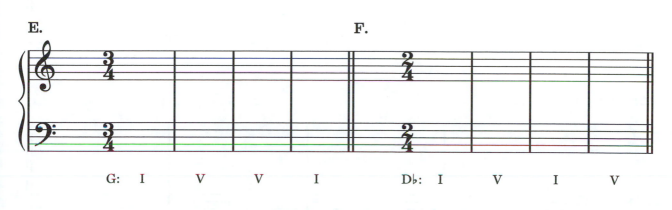

G: I   V   V   I   Db: I   V   I   V

Cadence: _____   Cadence: _____

II. Keyboard settings

Below the empty staves are Roman numerals for the progressions you wrote in part I, exercises B and E. On the first staff, write a keyboard setting with arpeggiation, Alberti bass, or another figuration shown in the chapter; follow the voice-leading from your SATB part-writing. On the second staff, convert the major setting into the parallel minor by changing the key signature and adding appropriate accidentals (without changing the part-writing or figuration).

A.

(1) Keyboard setting of I B

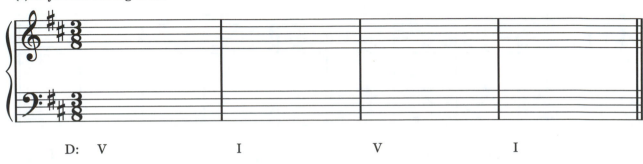

D: V   I   V   I

(2) Minor setting of I B

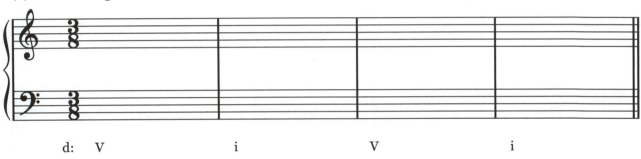

d: V   i   V   i

B.

(1) Keyboard setting of I E

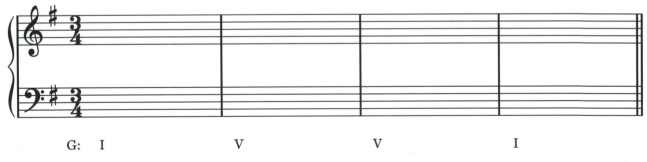

G: I   V   V   I

(2) Minor setting of I E

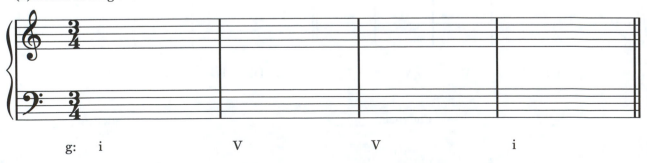

g: i   V   V   i

Assignment 12.6

I. Folk melody harmonization

Sing each melody on scale degrees or solfège, or play it on an instrument. Use the scale degrees (and your ears) to harmonize each measure: pick either I or V. You may wish to play the bass and melody at the keyboard. For melody B, use the leading tone for a major V chord, and harmonize measure 6 with i (instead of minor v). Circled notes are embellishing tones, which may be ignored in choosing harmonies.

A. "Hush, Little Baby," mm. 1-8

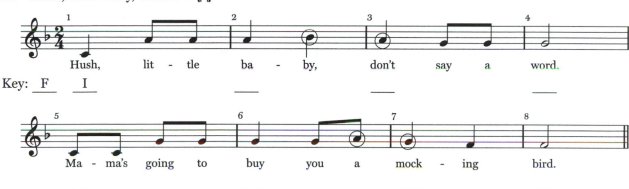

Hush, lit – tle ba – by, don't say a word.

Key: F   I   ___   ___   ___

Ma – ma's going to buy you a mock – ing bird.

___   ___   ___   ___

B. "Peter Gray," mm. 1-8

Once on a time there lived a man, his name was Pe – ter Gray.___ He

Key: ___   ___   ___   ___

lived way down in that here town, called Penn – syl – va – ni – a.

___   ___   ___   ___

C. "The More We Get Together," mm. 1-8

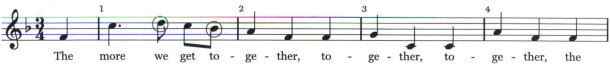

The more we get to – ge – ther, to – ge – ther, to – ge – ther, the

Key: ___   ___   ___   ___

more we get to – ge – ther the hap – pier we'll be.

___   ___   ___   ___

D. Waltz tune, mm. 1-8

Key: ___ ___ ___ ___

II. Writing in freer textures

Write a keyboard accompaniment to one of the melodies in part I. Write the melody on the top staff, and align the accompaniment on the grand staff below it.

Dominant Sevenths, the Predominant Area, and Chorale Harmonization

NAME _____

Assignment 13.1

I. Writing root-position V⁷–I and V⁷–i from soprano-bass pairs in SATB style

For each two-chord progression, provide a key signature and write the inner voices in quarter notes. If a harmony is marked with an asterisk, write an incomplete chord. Use the leading tone in minor. Label the leading tone (LT) and chordal seventh (7), and draw arrows to show the resolution of the leading tone up and the chordal seventh down. In the blanks below each example, write "I" or "C" to designate which chords are incomplete and complete.

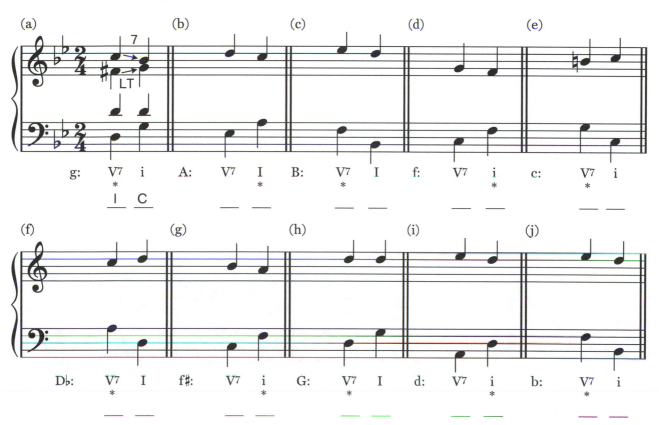

II. Analysis

Write the key and provide Roman numerals below the staff, disregarding any circled embellishing tones; assume a harmonic rhythm of one chord every one or two measures. Write a contextual analysis below the Roman numerals, assuming two four-bar phrases in each example; label all cadences.

A. Mozart, "In quegli anni" ("In Those Years"), from *The Marriage of Figaro*, Act 4, No. 2, mm. 42-49

Translation: While I silently gaze at that gift.

B. Schubert, Dance, Op. 9, No. 23, mm. 1-8

Assignment 13.2

I. Error detection 🎧

In each cadence pattern, locate three voice-leading errors, and mark them on the score. In the blank underneath, write the number of each error type found in that measure.

1. missing/incorrect chord tone
2. parallel fifths or octaves
3. unresolved chordal 7th
4. doubled leading tone
5. unresolved leading tone
6. incorrect Roman numeral or figure

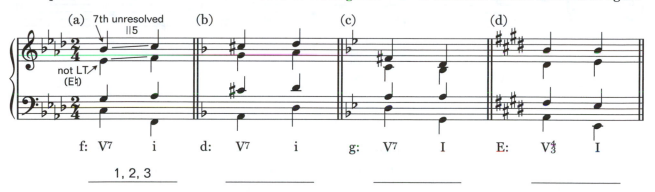

f: V⁷ i   d: V⁷ i   g: V⁷ I   E: V⁴₃ I

  1, 2, 3 _____   _____   _____   _____

II. Resolving V⁷ and its inversions

Write the following progressions in SATB voicing, with half notes. Provide the appropriate key signatures, and add accidentals as needed. Draw arrows to show the resolution of leading tones up and chordal sevenths down. For root-position V⁷–I, make one chord incomplete.

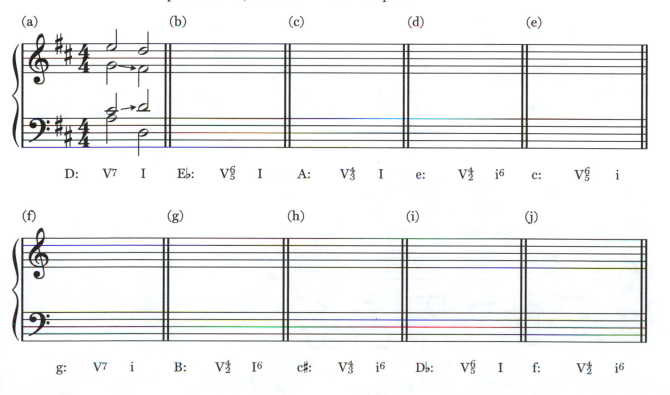

D: V⁷ I   E♭: V⁶₅ I   A: V⁴₃ I   e: V⁴₂ i⁶   c: V⁶₅ i

g: V⁷ i   B: V⁴₂ I⁶   c#: V⁴₃ i⁶   D♭: V⁶₅ I   f: V⁴₂ i⁶

III. Figured bass

A. Part-write the following figured-bass progressions in quarter notes. In the blanks, write the key and a Roman numeral analysis.

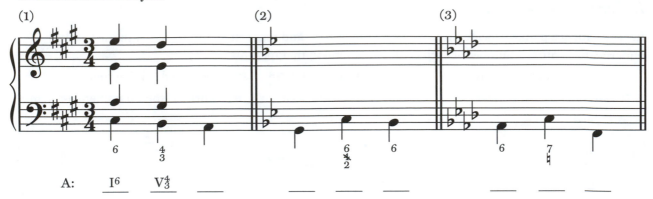

B. Analysis: Antonio Vivaldi, *Gloria*, sixth movement, mm. 7-11 🎧

Realize the figured bass given to accompany the soprano solo. Use keyboard spacing: a three-note chord in the right hand for each dotted-quarter beat. When a triad is repeated, you may change the right-hand voicing to create musical interest. (Don't worry about parallel unisons or octaves with the voice, if you temporarily double that part.) Write the key, Roman numerals, and cadence type below the staff. Then provide a contextual analysis for the phrase beginning in measure 9.

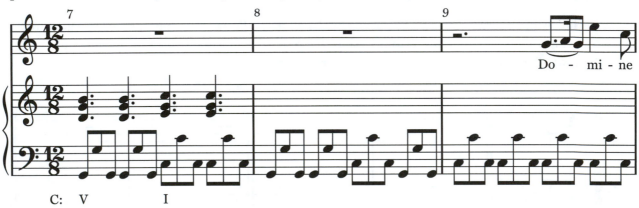

Translation: Lord God, heavenly king.

Assignment 13.3

I. Three-chord progressions in SATB style

For each progression, provide a key signature and part-write in quarter notes. Use the leading tone in minor. Where V appears between two tonic chords, write parallel tenths between the soprano and bass.

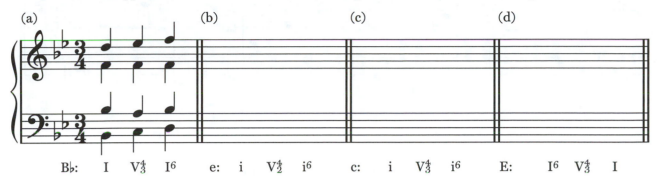

(a) (b) (c) (d)

Bb: I V$_3^4$ I^6 e: i V$_2^4$ i^6 c: i V$_3^4$ i^6 E: I^6 V$_3^4$ I

II. Writing basic phrases

Write the following progressions in SATB voicing in the meter indicated. (Bar lines are indicated with the Roman numerals.) Provide the appropriate key signatures, and add accidentals as needed. Write a contextual analysis beneath the Roman numerals.

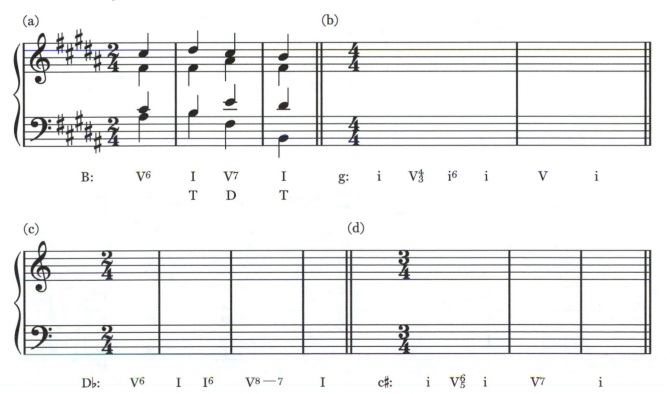

(a) (b)

B: V^6 I V^7 I   g: i V$_3^4$ i^6 i V i
     T D T

(c) (d)

Db: V^6 I I^6 V$^{8-7}$ I   c#: i V$_5^6$ i V^7 i

III. Analysis

For each excerpt, write the key and provide Roman numerals below the staff, disregarding any circled embellishing tones. Each excerpt consists of two phrases; label each cadence. Below the Roman numerals, provide a contextual analysis.

A. Schubert, Waltz in B Minor, Op. 18, No. 6, mm. 1–8

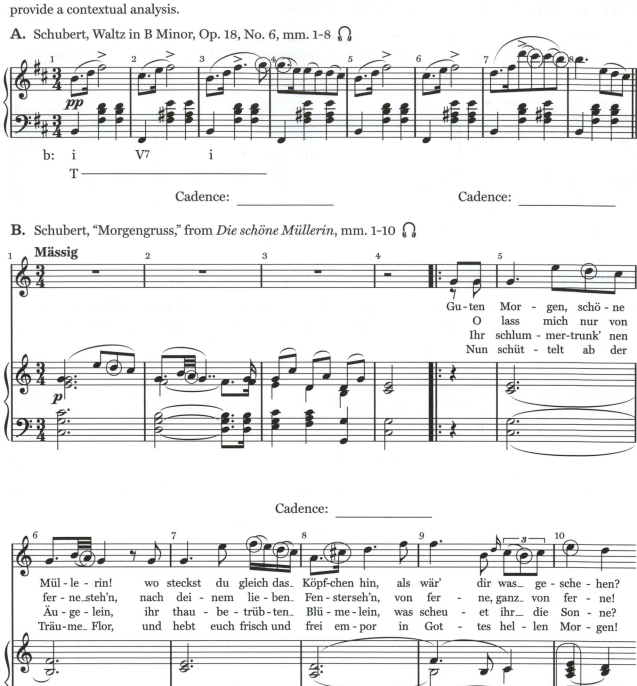

Cadence: _____ Cadence: _____

B. Schubert, "Morgengruss," from *Die schöne Müllerin*, mm. 1–10

Assignment 13.4

I. Connecting predominant and dominant harmonies

Write the following progressions in SATB voicing with half notes. Provide the appropriate key signatures, and add accidentals as needed.

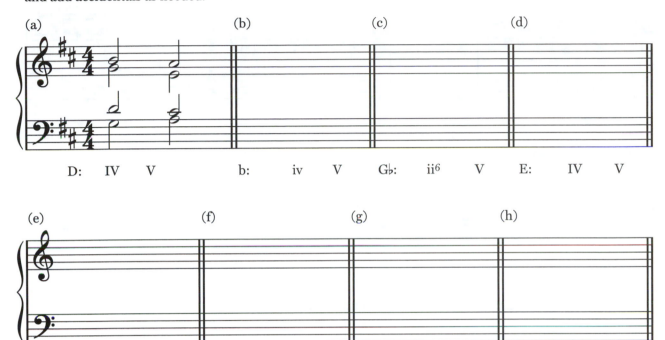

II. Writing predominant and dominant harmonies in short phrases

Write the following phrases from Roman numerals and melody in SATB voicing. In the blank under each measure, label the cadence type (HC, PAC, IAC).

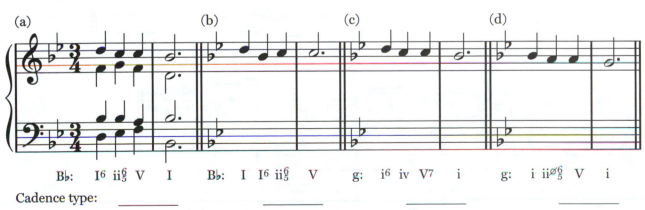

Cadence type: _____   _____   _____   _____

III. Analysis

Write the key, and provide Roman numerals in the blanks below the staff; these should indicate a harmonic rhythm of one or two chords per measure. When a single harmony spans more than one bass note, choose the lowest note to calculate the position/inversion. Write a contextual analysis below the Roman numerals, and label any cadence types.

A. Beethoven, Piano Sonata, Op. 2, No. 3, mvt. 1, mm. 1-8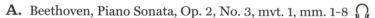

B. Haydn, String Quartet, Op. 20, No. 5, mvt. 1, mm. 1-5

Assignment 13.5

I. Writing basic phrases with predominants

Write the following progressions in SATB voicing in the meter indicated. In minor, raise $\flat\hat{7}$ to make a leading tone. Provide a contextual analysis below the Roman numerals.

(a)

(b)

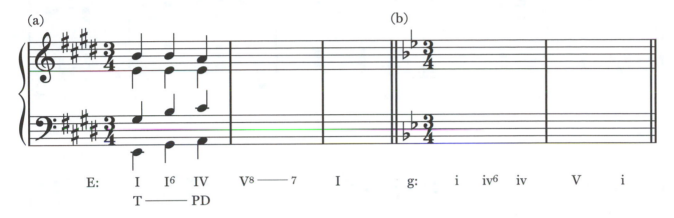

E: I I⁶ IV V⁸——7 I   g: i iv⁶ iv V i

T ——— PD

(c)

(d)

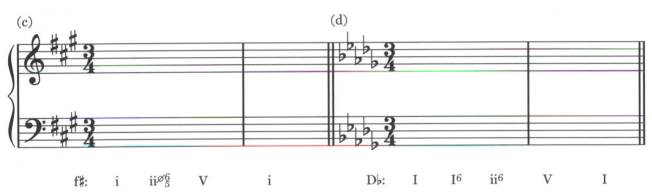

f♯: i ii⌀⁶₅ V i   D♭: I I⁶ ii⁶ V I

(e)

(f)

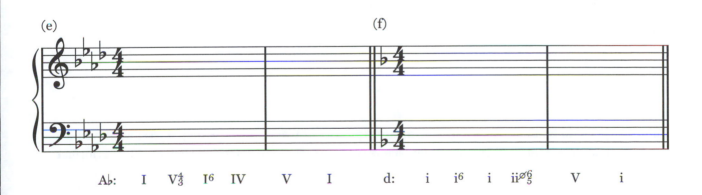

A♭: I V⁴₃ I⁶ IV V I   d: i i⁶ i ii⌀⁶₅ V i

II. Analysis: Chopin, Mazurka, Op. 33, No. 2, mm. 1–16 🎧

Provide Roman numerals in the blanks below the staff, disregarding any passing or neighbor tones. Indicate the entrance of a chordal seventh off the beat by the figures 8-7 where appropriate. Write a contextual analysis below the Roman numerals, and label each cadence.

This excerpt could be analyzed as four four-measure phrases or two eight-measure phrases; what would be the cadence labels for each phrase? What factors support each interpretation? How might a performer make the phrases clear?

Assignment 13.6

I. Analysis

Write the key, and provide a Roman numeral and contextual analysis for each chorale phrase, ignoring any circled embellishing tones. Indicate the entrance of a chordal seventh off the beat by the figures ⁸⁻⁷ where appropriate. Label each cadence type. For class discussion: How does the placement of the embellishments and the choice of inversions add to the interest of each harmonization?

A. Bach, "Lass, o Herr, dein Ohr sich neigen" ("Incline Your Ear, O Lord," Chorale No. 218), mm. 1–3

B. Bach, "Lobt Gott, ihr Christen allzugleich" ("Praise God, Christians, All Together," Chorale No. 342), mm. 1–2

II. Chorale melody harmonization

Harmonize each melody in SATB style, following phrase-model progressions. Remember to consider the counterpoint between the soprano and bass, while also evaluating the harmonies supplied by the melody. Use only triads and sevenths studied thus far (I, ii, IV, V and their inversions), in primarily quarter-note rhythm. Write a predominant harmony at the positions marked by an asterisk. Write the key, Roman numerals, and cadence type below each staff.

A. Bach, "O Haupt voll Blut und Wunden," phrase 6, mm. 11–12

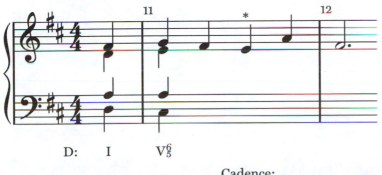

D: I   V$^6_5$

Cadence: _____

B. Bach, "Liebster Jesu" ("Blessed Jesus," Chorale No. 131), phrases 1 and 2, mm. 1-5

Cadence: _____   Cadence: _____

C. Bach, "Herz liebster Jesu, was hast du verbrochen" ("Dearest Jesus, What Have You Done," Chorale No. 111), phrase 1, mm. 1-3

Cadence: _____

D. Bach, "Christus, der ist mein Leben" ("Christ, Who Is My Life," Chorale No. 6), phrase 1, mm. 1-4

Cadence: _____   Cadence: _____

14 Expanding the Basic Phrase

NAME _____

Assignment 14.1

I. Writing cadential $^6_4$s from Roman numerals

A. Write the following cadence patterns in SATB voicing, with quarter and half notes in the meter indicated. Add accidentals as needed. Circle the cadence type: HC, IAC, or PAC.

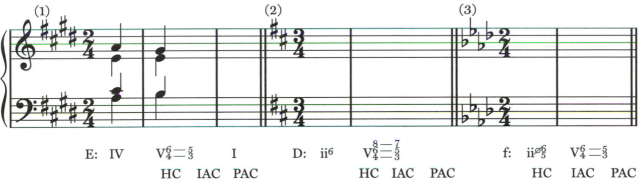

(1) E: IV V^6_4—$^5_3$ I

HC IAC PAC

(2) D: ii^6 $V^6_4$$\overset{8—7}{}$$^5_3$

HC IAC PAC

(3) f: ii$^{\o6}_5$ V^6_4—$^5_3$

HC IAC PAC

B. Write the following longer progressions in SATB voicing, with rhythms appropriate to the meter indicated. Add accidentals as needed, and a contextual analysis beneath.

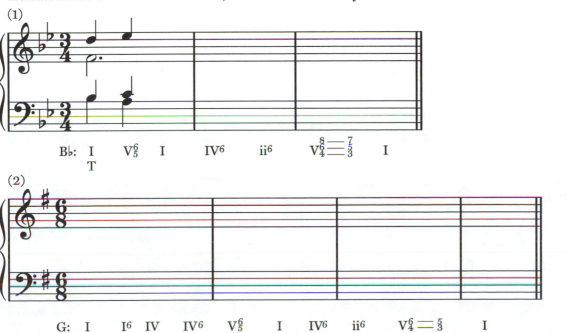

(1) B♭: I V^6_5 I IV^6 ii^6 $V^6_4$$\overset{8—7}{}$$^5_3$ I
      T

(2) G: I I^6 IV IV^6 V^6_3 I IV^6 ii^6 V^6_4—$^5_3$ I

II. Brief analysis

Identify the key of each excerpt, and provide a Roman numeral and contextual analysis. Disregard any circled notes.

- Where a triad is arpeggiated, choose the lowest note to determine its inversion.
- Where the tonic area is expanded by V, draw a horizontal line after the "T."
- Circle the correct cadence type.

A. Hensel, "Neue Liebe, neues Leben," mm. 52-56

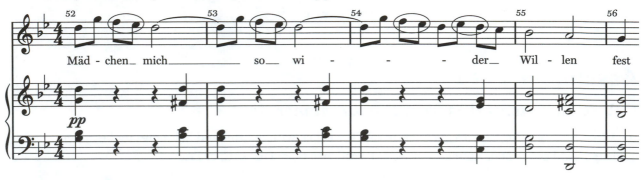

Translation: [The sweet, mischievous] maiden holds me so tightly against my will.

HC   IAC   PAC

B. Mozart, Piano Sonata, K. 570, mvt. 3, mm. 1-4

HC   IAC   PAC

C. Schubert, Sonata for Violin and Piano, Op. 137, No. 3, mvt. 2, mm. 1-4

HC   IAC   PAC

Assignment 14.2

I. Writing cadential $^6_4$s from figured bass

A. Write the following cadence patterns in SATB voicing, with quarter and half notes in the meter indicated. Add accidentals as needed, and analyze with Roman numerals. Circle the cadence type.

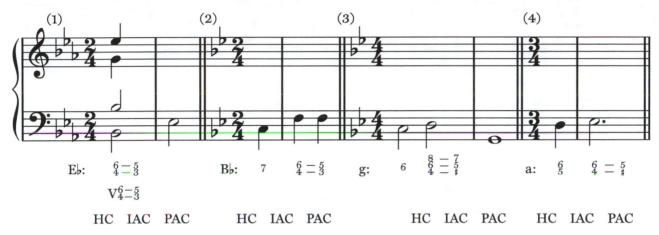

(1)   (2)   (3)   (4)

Eb: $^6_4 - ^5_3$ Bb: 7 $^6_4 - ^5_3$ g: 6 $^8_6 = ^7_5$ a: $^6_5$ $^6_4 - ^5_\sharp$

V$^{6-5}_{4-3}$

HC IAC PAC   HC IAC PAC   HC IAC PAC   HC IAC PAC

B. Write the following longer progressions in SATB voicing, with rhythms appropriate to the meter indicated. Add accidentals as needed, and provide a Roman numeral and contextual analysis.

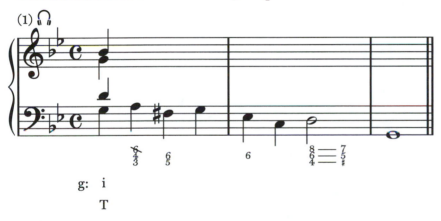

(1)

$^6_{4-3}$ $^6_5$ 6 $^8_6 \underline{\quad} ^7_5$
      $^6_4 \quad ^7_5 \sharp$

g: i

T

(2)

$^6_5$ 6   ♮   6   6 $^6_4 \underline{\quad\quad} ^5_\natural$

II. Analysis: Recognizing $^6_4$ chords

In these excerpts, circle at least one $^6_4$ chord, then circle its type: pedal (neighboring), cadential, or arpeggiating.

A. Handel, Chaconne in G Major, mm. 29-32 🎧

pedal (neighboring) $^6_4$ cadential $^6_4$ arpeggiating $^6_4$

B. Schumann, "Wilder Reiter," mm. 1-4 🎧

pedal (neighboring) $^6_4$ cadential $^6_4$ arpeggiating $^6_4$

C. Mozart, String Quartet in D Minor, K. 421, third movement, mm. 44-47 🎧

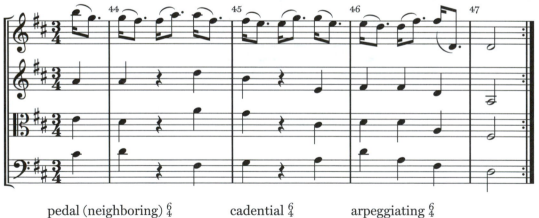

pedal (neighboring) $^6_4$ cadential $^6_4$ arpeggiating $^6_4$

Assignment 14.3

I. Writing pedal (or neighboring) $^6_4$s

Write the following $^6_4$ patterns in SATB voicing, using primarily quarter notes, in the indicated meter. Add accidentals as needed. Write (ped $^6_4$) or (N$^6_4$) to show the type.

A. From Roman numerals: add a contextual analysis.

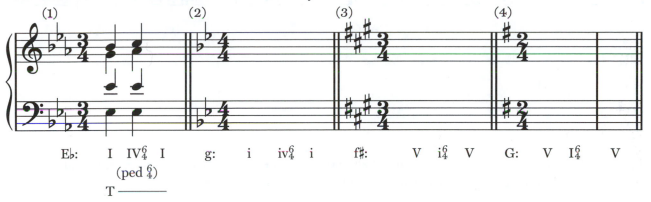

B. From figured bass: provide Roman numeral and contextual analyses.

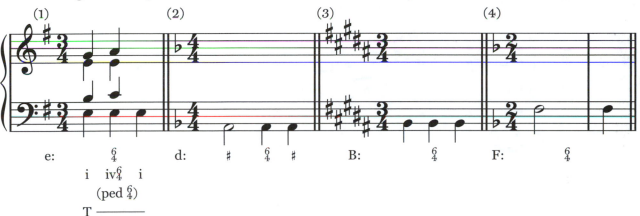

II. Writing arpeggiating $^6_4$s

Write the following $^6_4$ patterns in SATB voicing, using primarily quarter notes, in the indicated meter. Add accidentals as needed, and write (arp $^6_4$) to show the $^6_4$ type.

A. From Roman numerals: add a contextual analysis.

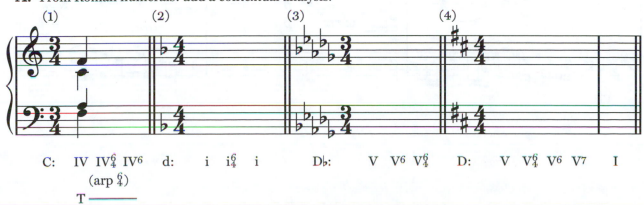

B. From figured bass: provide Roman numeral and contextual analyses.

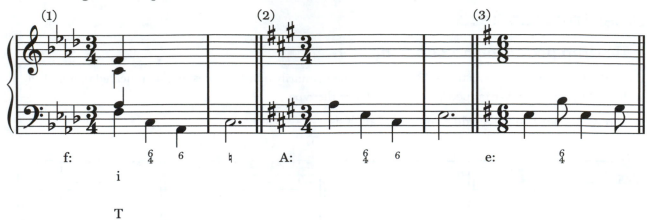

III. Analysis

Label the key, then analyze with Roman numerals and specify the $^6_4$ chord type, if applicable. Provide a contextual analysis under the Roman numerals and identify the cadence type.

A. Bach, "O Haupt voll Blut und Wunden," mm. 3-4 🎧

(Hint: Measure 3 begins with a 9-8 suspension.)

Translation: Full of sorrow, full of scorn.

B. Mozart, Piano Sonata, K. 457, mvt. 2, mm. 1-3 🎧

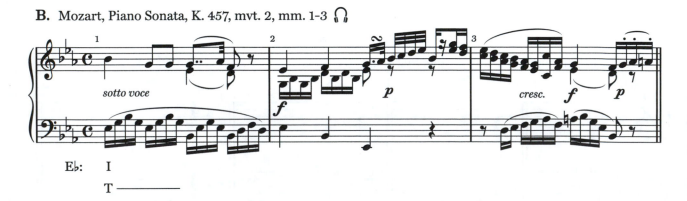

Assignment 14.4

I. Passing $^6_4$ chords

Write each example in SATB style, using quarter notes. Provide two levels of Roman numerals to show which harmony is expanded.

A. From Roman numerals

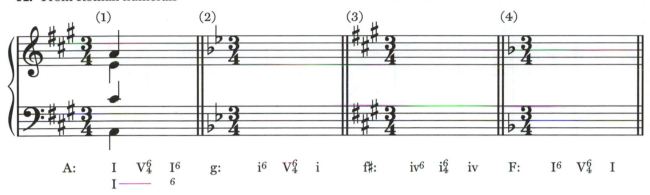

A: I   V$^6_4$ I^6 g: i^6 V$^6_4$ i   f♯:   iv^6 i$^6_4$ iv   F: I^6 V$^6_4$ I

I ——— 6

B. From figured bass

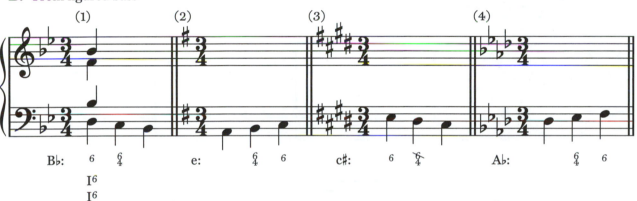

B♭:   6 $^6_4$ e: $^6_4$ 6   c♯:   6 $^6_4$ A♭: $^6_4$ 6

I^6

I^6

II. Melody harmonization 🎧

A. Harmonize the given melody in an SATB setting, with a harmonic rhythm of one chord per beat. In each position marked by an asterisk, write a $^6_4$ chord. Analyze with Roman numerals, label each $^6_4$ chord type, and provide a contextual analysis.

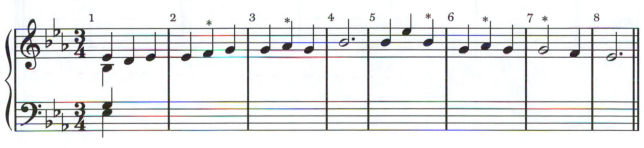

E♭:   I

T

B. Brahms, "Lullaby" (Although this melody was composed by Brahms, it is now so well known that some consider it a folk tune.)

Write a simple piano accompaniment to this melody, following the model given in the first measure and using a harmonic rhythm of one chord per measure. Use a $^6_4$ chord in the spots marked by an asterisk (mm. 2, 9, and 11) and specify the $^6_4$ chord type. Provide a Roman numeral analysis below.

Assignment 14.5

I. Writing $^6_4$ chords from figured bass

Write the following phrases in SATB voicing, with quarter, half, and dotted-half notes in the meter indicated. Add accidentals as needed and analyze with Roman numerals. Provide a contextual analysis underneath.

A.

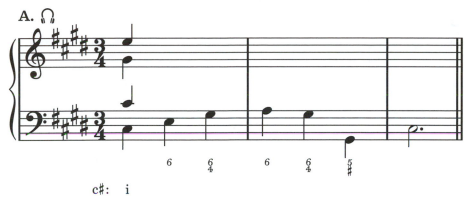

B.

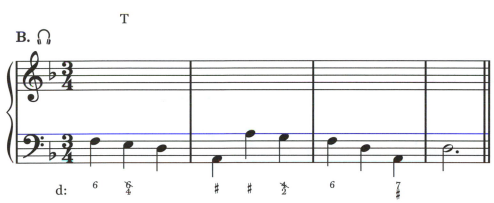

II. Figured bass: Rule-of-the-octave harmonization

The "rule of the octave" was an eighteenth-century keyboard exercise with a bass line that spanned an octave by step (like the one shown). Musicians memorized and transposed them to every key. Part-write the progression from figured bass, then write the key and a Roman numeral analysis below the staff. Because this is a keyboard exercise, write in keyboard style, with three notes in the right hand. Specify each $^6_4$ type.

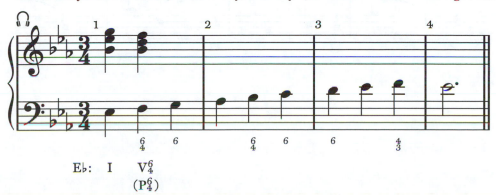

III. Analysis

Label the key, then analyze with Roman numerals and specify the chord type, if applicable. Provide a contextual analysis under the Roman numerals, and identify the cadence type.

A. "St. Anne" chorale, mm. 1–2

B. Schubert, "Du bist die Ruh," mm. 8–11

C. Hy Zaret and Alex North, "Unchained Melody," mm. 13–17

Assignment 14.6

I. Part-writing with the submediant

Write each example in SATB style, using quarter notes.

A. From Roman numerals

After writing the harmonic progression, add a contextual analysis below the Roman numerals.

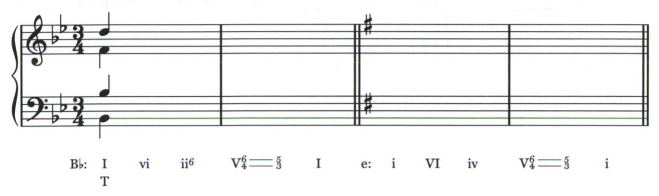

Bb: I   vi   ii⁶   V⁶₄ ─ ⁵₃   I   e: i   VI   iv   V⁶₄ ─ ⁵₃   i
      T

B. From figured bass

Provide a Roman numeral and contextual analysis that shows how the tonic area is expanded.

(1)

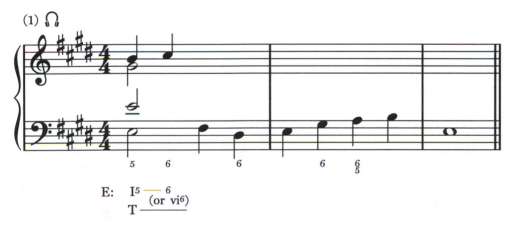

          5   6   6   6   ⁶₅

E: I⁵ ── 6
         (or vi⁶)
    T ─────

(2)

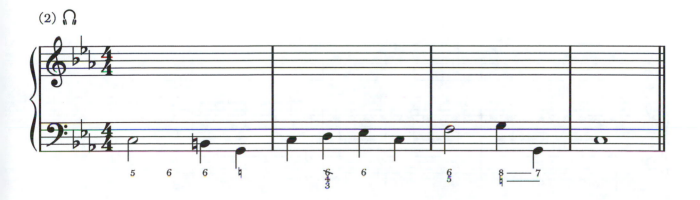

      5   6   6   ♮   ⁶₄₃   6   ⁶₅   8 ── 7

II. Analysis with $\frac{6}{4}$ chords

For each excerpt, supply Roman numerals in the blanks provided, then add a contextual analysis below. Disregard the circled notes. For each $\frac{6}{4}$ chord, label its type. For the minuet, base your analysis on the chords implied by the two voices.

A. Anonymous, Minuet in D Minor, mm. 1-4

(1) Mm. 1-4

d: i

T

(2) Mm. 13-16

B. Mozart, Sonata for Violin and Piano, K. 296, mvt. 3, mm. 9-16

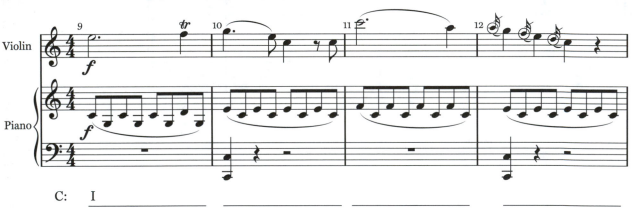

C: I

T

15 New Cadence Types and Diatonic Root Progressions

NAME _____

Assignment 15.1

I. Writing deceptive, plagal, and Phrygian cadences

Write the following cadence patterns in SATB voicing, with half notes. Identify each cadence pattern as deceptive, plagal, or Phrygian.

A. From Roman numerals: Provide the appropriate key signature, and add accidentals as needed.

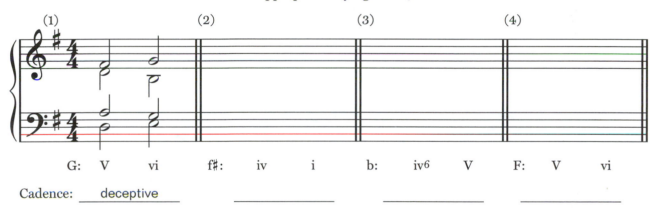

(1)   (2)   (3)   (4)

G: V vi   f♯: iv i   b: iv6 V   F: V vi

Cadence: ____deceptive____   _____   _____   _____

B. From figured bass: Provide a Roman numeral analysis under the figures.

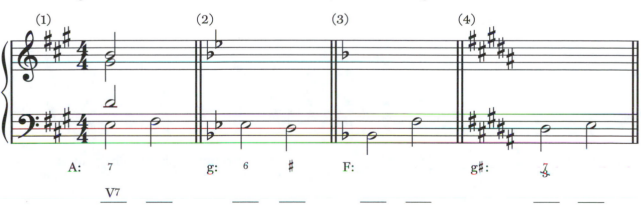

(1)   (2)   (3)   (4)

A: 7   g: 6 ♯   F: g♯: 7

  V7   ____   ____   ____

Cadence: _____   _____   _____   _____

II. Cadences in SATB settings

Identify each cadence by circling the correct label. In each example, circle one spacing or voice-leading irregularity, and write its type in the blank.

A. Praetorius, "Rosa Mystica," mm. 1–5

Voice-leading: _____   HC   IAC   PAC

B. Bach, "O Mensch, schau Jesum Christum an" ("O Mankind, Look on Jesus Christ," Chorale No. 203), mm. 8–11

This example uses a Baroque key signature: one flat in the signature and E♭s written in as needed. Analyze this passage in G minor.

Voice-leading: _____   deceptive   plagal   Phrygian

C. John Henry Hopkins Jr., "We Three Kings," mm. 26–33

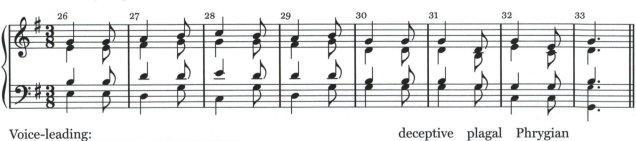

Voice-leading: _____   deceptive   plagal   Phrygian

Assignment 15.2

I. Writing deceptive, plagal, and Phrygian cadences

Write the following cadence patterns from Roman numerals and identify them, as in Assignment 15.1, I.A.

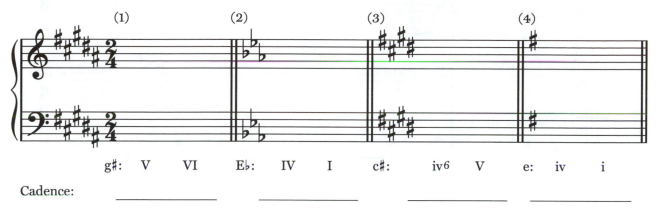

g#:   V   VI   Eb: IV   I   c#:   iv6   V   e: iv   i

Cadence: _____   _____   _____   _____

II. Realizing figured bass: Corelli, Allemanda, from Trio Sonata in A Minor, Op. 4, No. 5

Realize the figured bass in keyboard style (add two or three pitches in the right hand, treble clef). Write a Roman numeral and contextual analysis beneath the staff, and label the cadence type.

A. Mm. 10-12: The figures $\frac{5}{4}$ and ^{6} in measures 10-11 indicate the 4-3 suspension in violin 1, with a change of bass (to a first-inversion triad) as the suspension resolves.

a: i

T _____

Cadence: _____

B. Mm. 27–28: The figures ^{9} and ^{6} in measure 27 indicate the 9–8 suspension in the violin 2 that resolves with a change of bass.

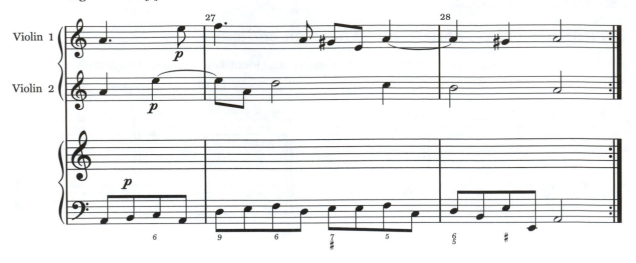

A deceptive resolution appears in measure _____ .

Cadence: _____

III. Analysis

Corelli, Sarabanda, from Sonata for Violin and Continuo, Op. 5, No. 8, mm. 5–8

Provide a Roman numeral and contextual analysis for the excerpt, and identify the cadence type.

e: VI⁷
    (PD

Cadence: _____

This progression features (circle any that apply):

asc. 2nds root progression   desc. 3rds root progression   parallel $^6_3$ chords   minor v

Assignment 15.3

I. Analysis

In the space below each excerpt, circle the name of the root progression that governs the passage. In these popular-music pieces, some chords are enriched with additional tones. Look for the underlying triads or seventh chords—usually one per measure—to find the root progression.

A. Nino Oliviero, Riz Ortolani, and Norman Newell, "More," mm. 9-12

Root progression: descending thirds   descending fifths   ascending seconds

B. Earl Edwards, Eugene Dixon, and Bernie Williams, "Duke of Earl," mm. 1-4

Root progression: descending thirds   descending fifths   ascending seconds

C. Rodgers and Hammerstein, "My Favorite Things," from *The Sound of Music*, mm. 27-30

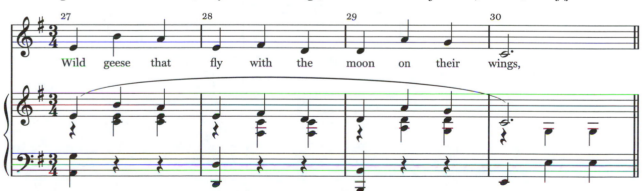

Root progression: descending thirds   descending fifths   ascending seconds

II. Writing music with root progressions

Write the following progressions in SATB voicing, with quarter and half notes, in the meter indicated. Above the staff, bracket and label any chord pair with roots related by ascending second (asc. 2), descending fifth (desc. 5), or descending third (desc. 3).

A. From Roman numerals

(1)

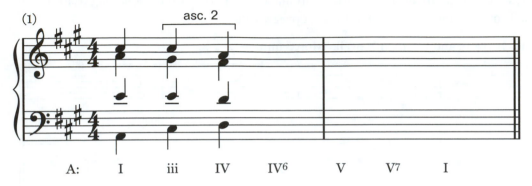

A: I   iii   IV   IV⁶   V   V⁷   I

(2)

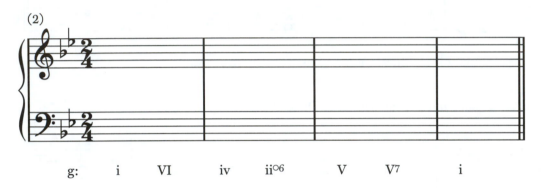

g: i   VI   iv   ii°⁶   V   V⁷   i

B. From figured bass. Provide a Roman numeral analysis.

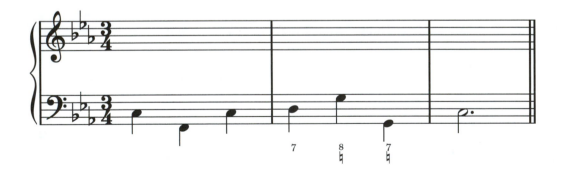

Assignment 15.4

I. Writing chords from Roman numerals

In each key specified, write the harmonies indicated by the Roman numerals.

A. Descending fifths

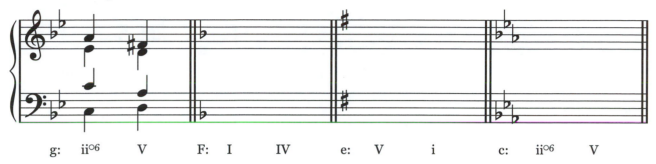

g: ii°6   V   F: I   IV   e: V   i   c: ii°6   V

B. Descending thirds

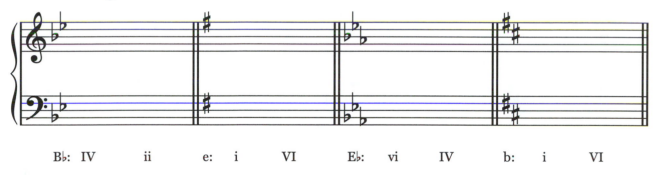

B♭: IV   ii   e: i   VI   E♭: vi   IV   b: i   VI

C. Ascending seconds

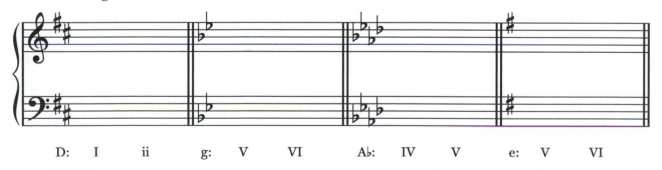

D: I   ii   g: V   VI   A♭: IV   V   e: V   VI

D. Longer progressions

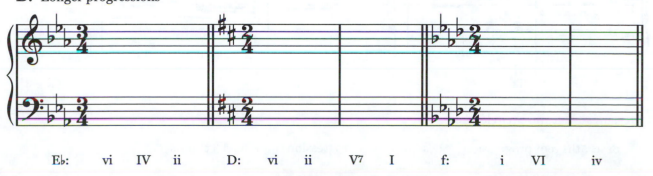

E♭: vi   IV   ii   D: vi   ii   V7   I   f: i   VI   iv

II. Melody harmonization

Write an accompaniment for this modal melody, including the minor v. First write Roman numerals for your harmonic choices under the melody note, then complete the accompaniment, selecting an appropriate keyboard pattern and using correct voice-leading. Don't worry about doubling the vocal part. Perform as an accompanied round in class, comparing different settings of the tune.

"Hey, Ho, Nobody Home"

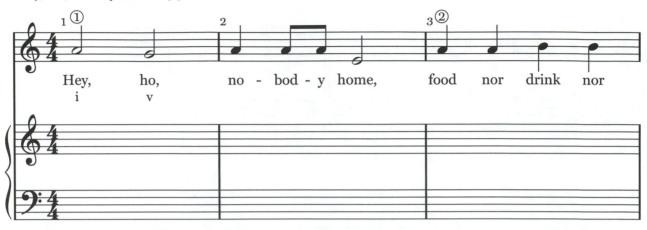

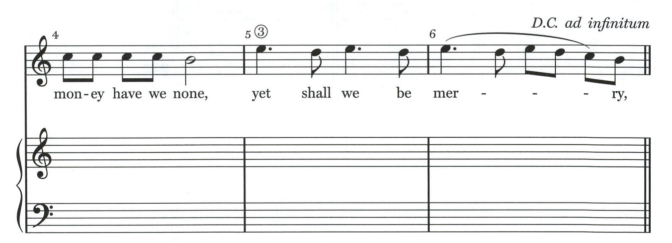

III. Analysis: Mozart, Piano Sonata in C Major, mvt. 3, mm. 1–4

Provide a Roman numeral and contextual analysis for this excerpt, and identify the cadence type.

Measures 1–2 feature (circle one):

desc. 5ths root progression   desc. 3rds root progression   parallel § chords

Assignment 15.5

I. Figured bass: Rule-of-the-octave harmonization

Part-write the progression from the figured bass given, then write the key and a Roman numeral analysis below the staff. Because this is a keyboard exercise, write in keyboard style, with three notes in the right hand. Begin with $\hat{1}$ in the highest voice.

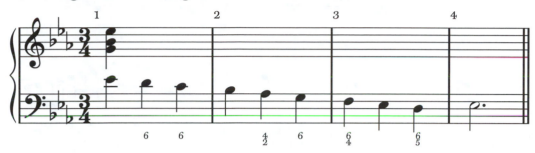

This progression features (circle any that apply):

cadential $^6_4$ passing $^6_4$ asc. 2nds root progression   desc. 3rds root progression   parallel $^6_3$ chords

II. Analysis

Provide Roman numerals and figures for the following excerpts, and answer the questions below each. Write a contextual analysis underneath the Roman numerals.

A. Mozart, Piano Sonata in G Major, K. 283, mvt. 1, mm. 112-114

Hint: In writing the Roman numeral analysis, consider each rhythmically displaced note as part of the chord that began on the beat. Circled pitches are embellishing, and not part of the chord.

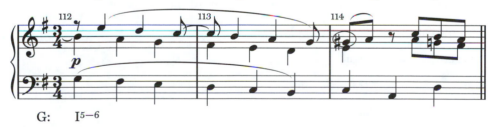

G: I 5—6

(1) This progression is embellished with suspensions in the top part, introduced by a 5-6 motion.

What type are they? (circle one):   7-6   4-3   9-8   2-3

(2) This progression features (circle any that apply):

cadential $^6_4$ passing $^6_4$ desc. 5ths root progression   desc. 3rds root progression   parallel $^6_3$ chords

(3) With which type of cadence does this example end? (circle one)

PAC   IAC   HC   Phrygian   DC   Plagal

B. Mozart, Piano Sonata in C Major, K. 545, mvt. 1, mm. 63-73

Hint: Measure 68 includes chromaticism that we will study in Chapter 20. Ignore that measure for now.

C: I⁶

[ignore for now]

(1) The harmonic rhythm in this example is primarily (choose one)

   one chord per measure   two chords per measure   three or more chords per measure

(2) What is the cadence type in measures 69-71? (circle one)

   PAC   IAC   HC   Phrygian   DC   Plagal

(3) What is the cadence type in measures 72-73? (circle one)

   PAC   IAC   HC   Phrygian   DC   Plagal

(4) Measures 71-73 are called a _____

(5) This passage features (circle any that apply):

   cadential $^6_4$ passing $^6_4$ desc. 5ths root progression   desc. 3rds root progression   parallel $^6_3$ chords

16 Embellishing Tones

NAME _____

Assignment 16.1

I. Writing embellishments

Add passing or neighbor tones as specified, using eighth notes on the offbeat between the given chords.

- Don't change the voicing or spacing.
- There are multiple correct answers; play the progressions with the passing or neighbor tones you have added to check that they sound good and do not create voice-leading problems.
- Provide a Roman numeral analysis.

A. Add passing tones.

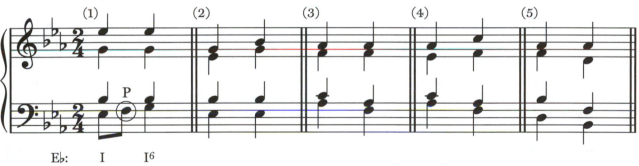

B. Add neighbor tones.

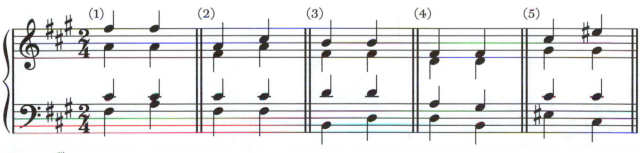

C. Add simultaneous passing tones.

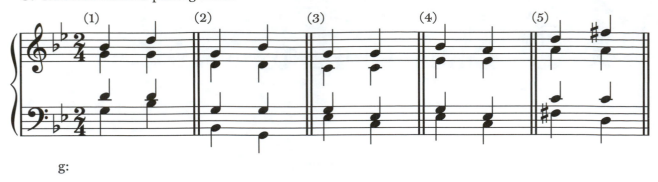

g:

D. Add simultaneous passing and neighbor tones.

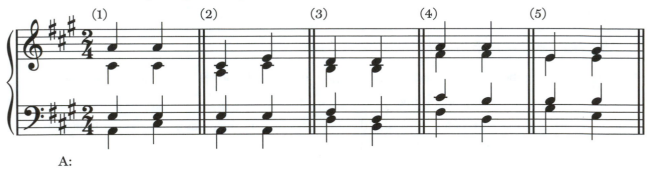

A:

II. Part-writing

Write the following progressions in SATB voicing, including the specified embellishing tones. Write a soprano line that makes an interesting melody and good counterpoint with the bass. Include passing tones, neighbor tones, and at least one pair of simultaneous passing or neighbor tones, and use eighth-note motion in at least one part on each beat except the last measure. When a chord is repeated, you may change the voicing of the upper three parts to incorporate passing tones. Circle and label each embellishing tone in your setting.

A.

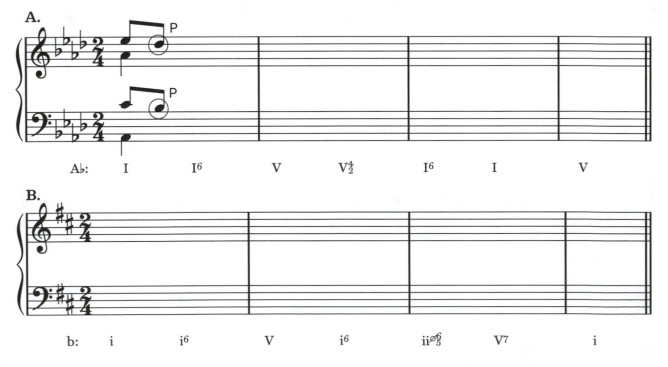

A♭:   I   I⁶   V   V⁴₂   I⁶   I   V

B.

b: i   i⁶   V   i⁶   ii°⁶₅   V⁷   i

Assignment 16.2

I. Writing suspensions and retardations in four parts from Roman numerals

Write the following progressions with SATB voicing and durations appropriate for the given meter. Include suspensions or retardations where specified, with the proper preparation and resolution. Provide a contextual analysis below the Roman numerals, and label the cadence type.

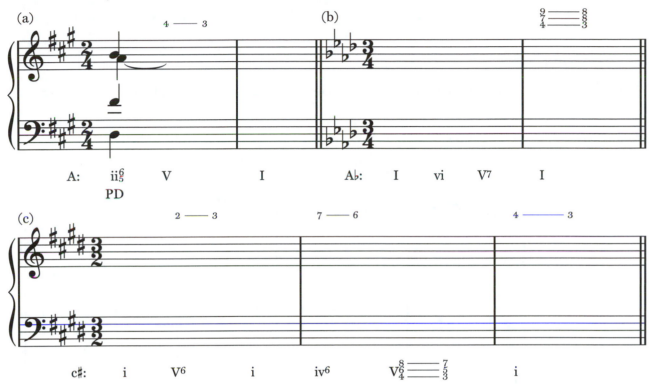

II. Part-writing

Write the following progressions in SATB voicing, including the specified embellishing tones. Write a soprano line that makes an interesting melody and good counterpoint with the bass. Circle and label each embellishing tone in your setting.

A. Include passing tones, neighbor tones, and a suspension.

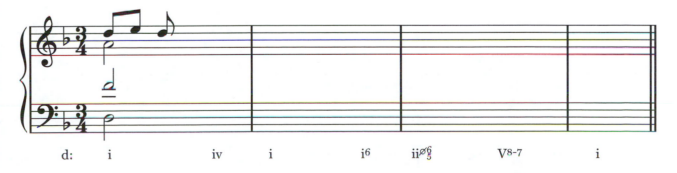

B. Include one set of simultaneous passing or neighbor tones and two suspensions.

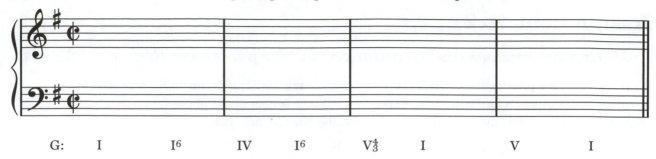

G: I   I⁶   IV   I⁶   V⁴₃   I   V   I

III. Analysis

Write a Roman numeral under each chord. Circle and label each embellishing tone. Provide a contextual analysis.

Mozart, String Quartet in D Minor, K. 421, mvt. 4, mm. 1–4

A blank staff has been included in case you want to make a reduction to help you identify the chords.

Assignment 16.3

I. Writing anticipations

Add an anticipation in the soprano part to each short progression, using a ♪♫ or ♩♪ rhythm. Provide a
Roman numeral analysis.

Eb: V7

II. Analysis: Purcell, "Dido's Lament," from Dido and Aeneas, mm. 38–44

Provide a Roman numeral analysis, and circle and label each embellishing tone in the vocal melody.
In measure 39, label a new chord on beat 2, with a tonic pedal point. In measure 41, analyze with a
downbeat 7-6 suspension, as shown. In measure 42 consider beat 2 to be a passing chord.

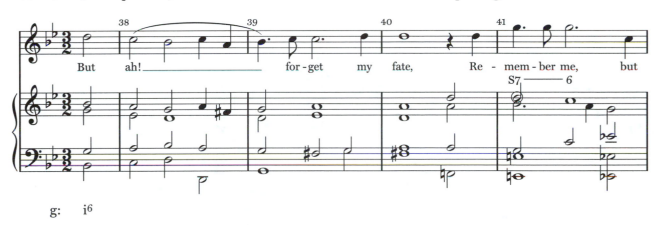

g: i6

III. Analysis

Circle and label the embellishing tones in following excerpts. Provide a Roman numeral analysis in the blanks. Bracket and label any passages with pedal points as "tonic pedal" or "dominant pedal." Provide a contextual analysis.

A. Beethoven, Sonatina in F Major, mvt. 2, mm. 1-8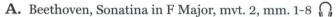

F: I

tonic pedal

B. Beethoven, Sonatina in F Major, mvt. 2, mm. 17-29

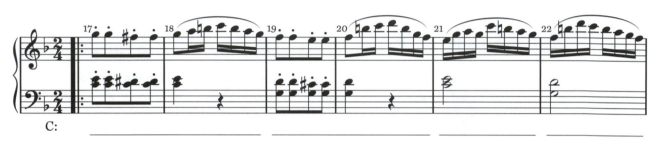

C:

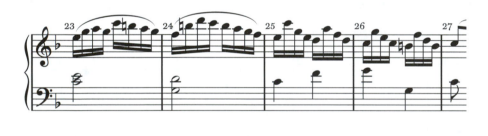

C. Schumann, "Ich grolle nicht," mm. 32-36

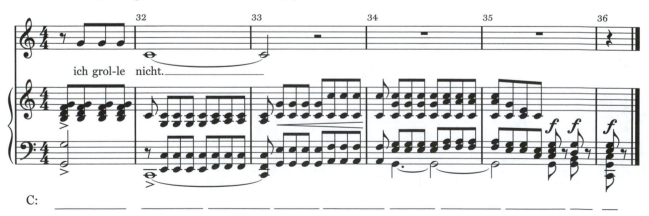

ich grol-le nicht.

C:

Assignment 16.4

Analyzing mixed embellishing tones

The embellishing tones in the following excerpts are circled.

- Examine the immediate harmonic context and label each with the abbreviation P, N, IN, ANT, R, or S in the score.
- A composer's choices of embellishments are a marker of style. Complete the table below each passage by circling P, N, IN, ANT, R, or S in the table for each embellishing-tone type found in that measure to summarize the types of embellishments found.
- In the blanks to the right, specify the type of suspension if present, and write "chromatic" if the P, N, or IN embellishment is chromatic (do not consider the leading tone in minor to be chromatic).
- We will then use this table to compare Joplin's embellishing tones with Bach's (on the next page).

A. Joplin, "Pine Apple Rag," mm. 5-12

Measure 5:	P	N	IN	ANT	R	S	_____
Measure 6:	P	N	IN	ANT	R	S	_____
Measure 7:	P	N	IN	ANT	R	S	_____
Measure 9:	P	N	IN	ANT	R	S	_____
Measure 10:	P	N	IN	ANT	R	S	_____
Measure 11:	P	N	IN	ANT	R	S	_____
Measure 12:	P	N	IN	ANT	R	S	_____

B. Bach, "Jesu, meine Freude" ("Jesus My Joy," Chorale No. 138), mm. 1–13 🎧

Measure 1:	P	N	IN	ANT	R	S	_____
Measure 2:	P	N	IN	ANT	R	S	_____
Measure 3:	P	N	IN	ANT	R	S	_____
Measure 5:	P	N	IN	ANT	R	S	_____
Measure 7:	P	N	IN	ANT	R	S	_____
Measure 8:	P	N	IN	ANT	R	S	_____
Measure 9:	P	N	IN	ANT	R	S	_____
Measure 10:	P	N	IN	ANT	R	S	_____
Measure 11:	P	N	IN	ANT	R	S	_____
Measure 12:	P	N	IN	ANT	R	S	_____

In a sentence or two, summarize how Bach's use of embellishing tones is similar to or different from Joplin's.

Assignment 16.5

I. Embellishing tones in popular music

Examine the embellishing tones in the passages that follow and answer the questions.

A. Taylor Swift, "Back to December," mm. 33-37

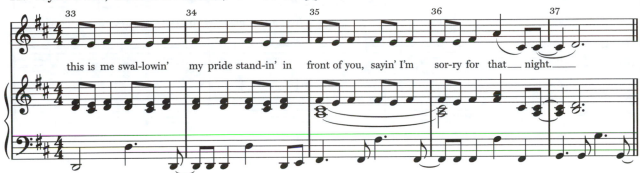

(1) Measures 33-35 feature repeated   P   N   IN   ANT   R   S

(2) The cadence in measure 37 includes   P   N   IN   ANT   R   S

B. Bono, The Edge, and U2, "Stuck in a Moment You Can't Get Out Of," mm. 5-7

(1) Measure 6, beats 1-2 feature   P   N   IN   ANT   R   S

(2) The dissonance over the bar line between measures 6-7 is:

        P   N   IN   ANT   R   S

C. John Deacon, "You're My Best Friend," mm. 5-8

(1) The accompaniment features   IN   ANT   PED   R   S

(2) The end of each vocal subphrase ("make me live" and "give to me") features

        P   N   IN   ANT   R   S

II. Analysis of a jazz standard

Jerry Gray and Eddie de Lange, "A String of Pearls," mm. 5–11 🎧

Despite its complicated sound, this piece has a fairly simple harmonic plan, with one main type of embellishment. Examine and label the circled embellishing tones, and answer the questions that follow.

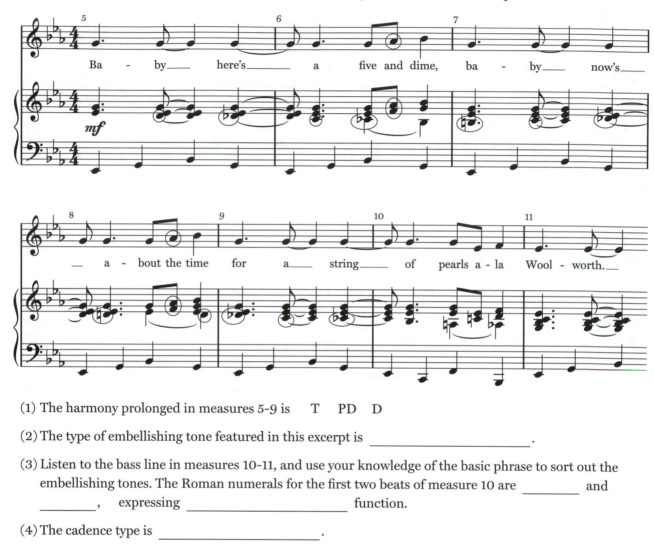

(1) The harmony prolonged in measures 5–9 is   T   PD   D

(2) The type of embellishing tone featured in this excerpt is _____.

(3) Listen to the bass line in measures 10–11, and use your knowledge of the basic phrase to sort out the embellishing tones. The Roman numerals for the first two beats of measure 10 are _____ and _____,   expressing _____ function.

(4) The cadence type is _____.

(5) In the last chord (m. 11), there is an added interval above the bass that does not alter its harmonic function, but gives it a jazzy sound. What is it? _____

Assignment 16.6

Embellishing tones in variation sets

In parts A and B, first listen to the theme while following the anthology score. Then examine the variations shown here. Circle and label embellishing tones (N, IN, DN [double neighbor], P, and include suspension types, e.g., S4-3), and indicate what types are employed in each variation.

A. Mozart, Piano Sonata in D Major, K. 284, mvt. 3

(1) Variation 4, mm. 69-72

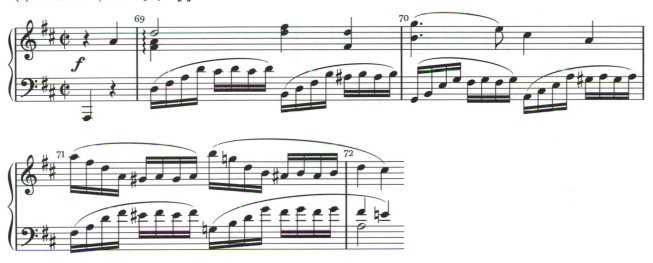

Embellishment type(s): _____

(2) Variation 11, mm. 188-191

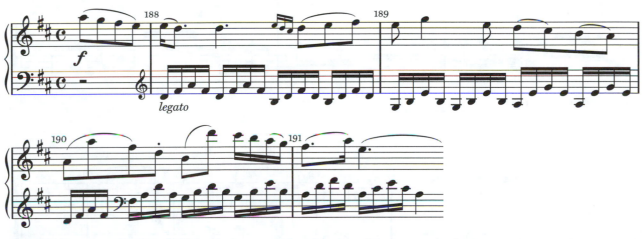

Embellishment type(s): _____

B. Mozart, Variations on "Ah, vous dirai-je Maman"

(1) Variation 3, mm. 73-80 (in mm. 76-79, align the notes in the right hand as a chord to identify the embellishments) 🎧

Embellishment type(s): _____

(2) Variation 6, mm. 145-152 (in mm. 147-150, there are embellishing tones in both hand parts) 🎧

Embellishment type(s): _____

(3) Variation 9, mm. 217-224 🎧

Embellishment type(s): _____

17

Voice-Leading Chords: vii°6, vii°7, viiø7, and Others

NAME _____

Assignment 17.1

I. Chorale analysis with vii°6: Bach, "Aus meines Herzens Grunde"

Listen to this chorale, then provide a Roman numeral analysis for these chorale phrases. Circle and label all embellishing tones, and label the cadences. For suspensions, label the type (e.g., S7-6). Each phrase begins with a substantial tonic prolongation prior to the cadence. Below the Roman numerals, add a two-level contextual analysis that shows how the tonic area is expanded with embedded PD-D-T in the first level, and the overall basic phrase T-PD-D-T progression in the second level.

A. Mm. 1-7

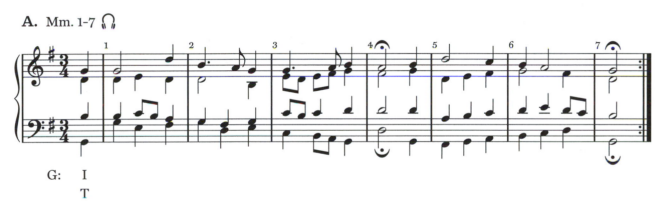

G: I
       T
       T

B. Mm. 15-21

II. Analysis: Clementi, Sonatina in G Major, Op. 36, No. 5, mvt. 3, mm. 1–16 🎧

Write Roman numerals under the staff, circle and label all embellishing tones, and label the cadences.

Write a few sentences explaining the function of the vii°7 chords.

Assignment 17.2

I. Writing and resolving vii°6

Write the following SATB progressions, in quarter notes, from the given Roman numerals. Provide the key signature and any needed accidentals. Draw an arrow to show the correct resolution of the leading tone.

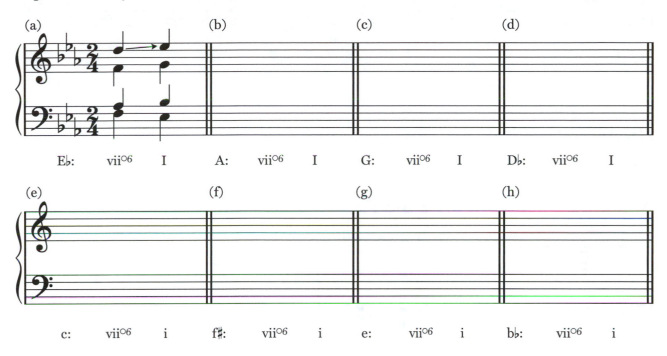

(a)		(b)		(c)		(d)					
Eb:	vii°6 I	A:	vii°6 I	G:	vii°6 I	Db:	vii°6 I				

(e)		(f)		(g)		(h)	
c:	vii°6 i	f#:	vii°6 i	e:	vii°6 i	bb:	vii°6 i

II. Expanding the tonic area with passing vii°6 or V^6_4 chords

Write the following SATB progressions from the Roman numerals or figured bass. In part A, provide the key signature. In both A and B, write a second level of Roman numerals to show the tonic expansion. Use a voice exchange [as shown by the crossed lines in example A(1)] in each progression.

A. From Roman numerals

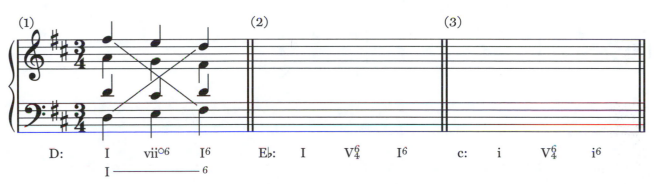

(1)				(2)				(3)		
D:	I	vii°6	I6	Eb:	I	V^6_4	I6	c:	i	V^6_4 i6
	I ——————— 6									

B. From figured bass

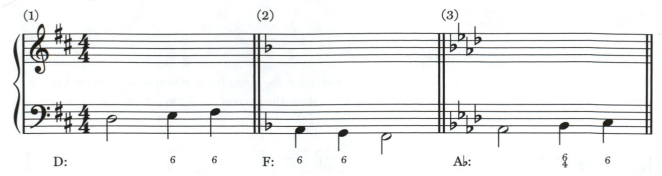

(1)   (2)   (3)

D: 6   6   F: 6   6   A♭: $^6_4$ 6

III. Analysis with vii°6

For each passage, write a Roman numeral analysis in the blanks provided. Add a contextual analysis beneath.

A. Handel, Chaconne in G Major, mm. 13-16

B. Bach, "O Haupt voll Blut und Wunden," mm. 1-2

Assignment 17.3

I. Resolving vii⌀⁷ and vii°⁷

Part-write the following SATB progressions, in quarter notes, from the Roman numerals. Provide the key signatures and needed accidentals, and draw arrows to show the resolution of leading tones and chordal sevenths.

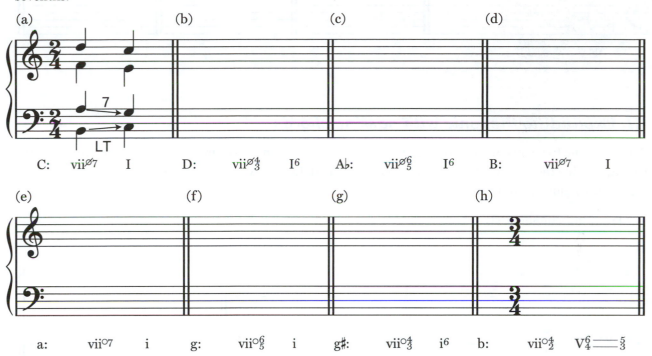

(a)	(b)	(c)	(d)
C: vii⌀⁷ I	D: vii⌀⁴₃ I⁶	A♭: vii⌀⁶₅ I⁶	B: vii⌀⁷ I

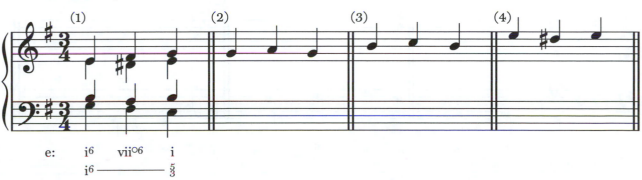

(e)	(f)	(g)	(h)
a: vii°⁷ i	g: vii°⁶₅ i	g♯: vii°⁴₃ i⁶	b: vii°⁴₂ V⁶₄——⁵₃

II. Harmonizing melody fragments with leading-tone seventh chords

For each melody fragment, expand the tonic area using vii°⁶ or vii°⁶₅. Provide Roman numerals on two levels to show the tonic expansion.

A. In a minor key

(1)	(2)	(3)	(4)
e: i⁶ vii°⁶ i			
i⁶ ——————— ⁵₃			

B. In a major key

Write a vii°$^6_5$: add an accidental to lower the chordal seventh.

A♭:

III. Expanding the tonic with passing chords

Part-write the following SATB progressions, in quarter notes, from the Roman numerals or figured bass. In part A, provide the key signatures and accidentals needed. In both A and B, write a second level of Roman numerals to show the tonic expansion.

A. From Roman numerals

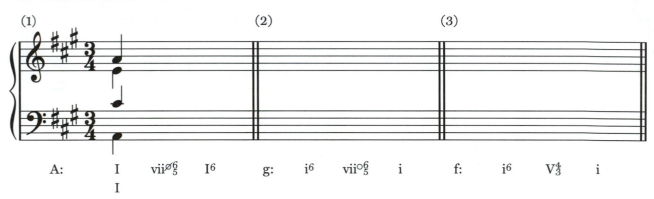

B. From figured bass

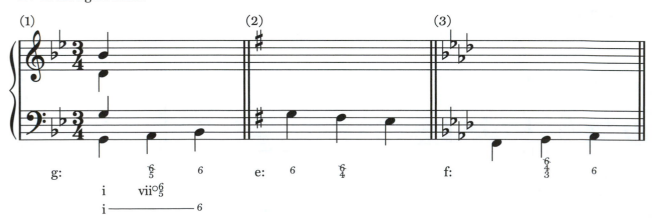

Assignment 17.4

I. Writing passing and neighboring $\frac{4}{2}$ chords

Write the following progressions from Roman numerals in SATB voicing.

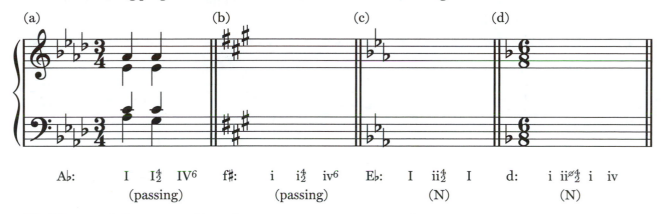

(a)				(b)				(c)				(d)			

A♭:   I   I$\frac{4}{2}$ IV⁶   f♯:   i   i$\frac{4}{2}$ iv⁶   E♭:   I   ii$\frac{4}{2}$ I   d: i   ii°$\frac{4}{2}$ i   iv
        (passing)   (passing)   (N)   (N)

II. Figured-bass realization

Realize these figured bass excerpt in keyboard spacing. Provide a Roman numeral analysis; write "passing" for each passing $\frac{4}{2}$ chord.

Bach, Cantata No. 140, mvt. 1, mm. 1-5 𝄐

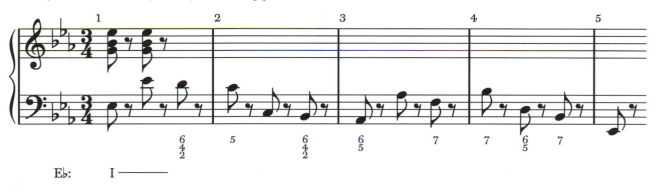

E♭:   I ————

III. Analysis

Write a Roman numeral analysis and circle and label all embellishing tones. This excerpt contains parallel $\frac{6}{3}$ chords; provide a Roman numeral for each sonority and then bracket and label the parallel $\frac{6}{3}$ passage.

Handel, "Rejoice greatly," mm. 3-7 𝄐

B♭:   I⁶   V$\frac{6}{5}$

IV. Melody harmonization

Set the following melody with one chord per half or whole note. (This melody, "Old Hundredth," appears in the anthology; write a *different* harmonization here.)

- First locate the places where there should be strong cadences, and select appropriate chords.
- Then examine the beginnings of the phrases to select a progression that makes a tonic expansion, using inversions of V, leading-tone chords, or an embedded PD-D-T.
- Complete the remaining voices using the progressions you have selected, and add a contextual analysis.

G: I
      T

Assignment 17.5

I. Setting scalar bass lines (rule-of-the-octave harmonization)

The rule of the octave was an eighteenth-century musician's keyboard exercise, memorized and transposed to every key. In A (1) and B (1), realize the figured bass in keyboard spacing, then write a Roman numeral analysis below the staff. In A (2) and B (2), revise these harmonizations using substitute chords vii°6 and vii°7 or their inversions for V$^6_4$ and V$^4_3$. You may also substitute other harmonies, such as vi for I, I$^6_2$ for V6 with a descending $\hat{7}$, or ii$^4_3$ for IV6. Play both solutions to hear the difference.

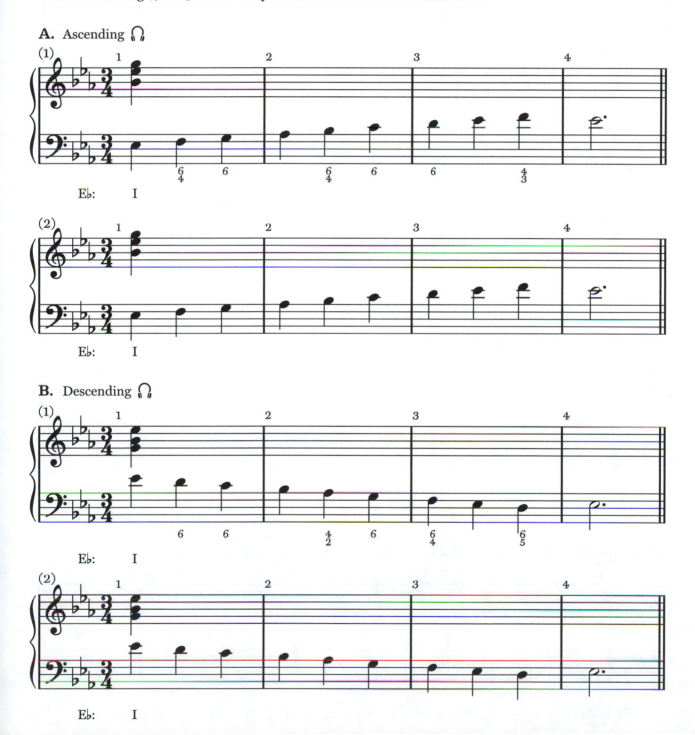

A. Ascending

B. Descending

II. Harmonizing scalar melodies

Choose a harmonization for these melodies, incorporating passing chords and phrase-model progressions. Include at least one leading-tone triad or seventh chord. Where possible, aim for a bass line in stepwise contrary motion to the soprano. Write in SATB style, and provide a Roman numeral analysis below the staff.

A. Ascending, major key

D: I⁶

B. Descending, major key

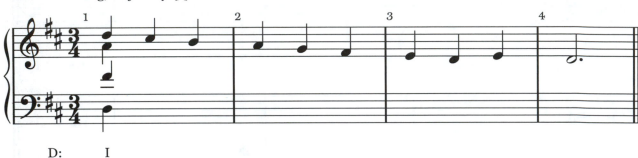

D: I

C. Ascending, minor key

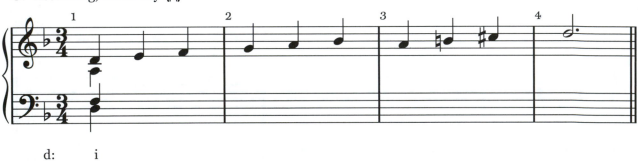

d: i

D. Descending, minor key (Hint: Use minor v to set the subtonic scale degree.)

d: i

18 Phrase Structure and Motivic Analysis

NAME _____

Assignment 18.1

I. Analyzing phrases

A. Hensel, "Neue Liebe, neues Leben," mm. 1-8 (anthology) 🎧

Listen to the opening of this song while following your anthology score.

(1) Draw a diagram that represents the phrase structure. Include the number of measures in each phrase, letters to show whether the phrases are parallel or contrasting, and cadence types.

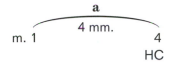

(2) Circle the term that best describes this passage:

    (a) parallel period   (b) contrasting period   (c) repeated phrase   (d) two independent phrases

B. Schubert, "Der Lindenbaum," mm. 9-24 (anthology) 🎧

Start by listening to the introduction and first stanza of this song (to m. 24), while following your anthology score.

(1) Draw a phrase diagram of measures 9-24. Include the number of measures in each phrase, letters to show whether the phrases are parallel or contrasting, and cadence types.

(2) Circle the term that best describes measures 9-16:

    (a) parallel period   (b) contrasting period   (c) repeated phrase   (d) two independent phrases

(3) Circle the term that best describes measures 17-24:

    (a) parallel period   (b) contrasting period   (c) repeated phrase   (d) two independent phrases

C. Beethoven, *Für Elise*, mm. 1-8 (anthology)

Listen to the opening of this piano piece while following your anthology score.

(1) Draw a diagram that accurately represents the phrase structure. Include the number of measures in each phrase, letters to show whether the phrases are parallel or contrasting, and cadence types.

(2) Circle the term that best describes this passage:

    (a) parallel period   (b) contrasting period   (c) repeated phrase   (d) two independent phrases

II. Motivic transformations

These motives are from the first movement of Clementi's Sonatina in F Major, Op. 36, No. 4. Listen to each one, then write its inversion. For the inversion, invert the contour and retain the interval size (don't attempt to match the interval quality). Play your solutions and alter them if necessary to "make sense" in the key and meter (there may be more than one possible solution). A first note is suggested.

A. From mm. 1-2

Motive

Inversion

B. From m. 13

Motive

Inversion

C. From mm. 9-10

Motive

Inversion

D. From m. 15

Motive

Inversion

E. From mm. 18-19

Motive

Inversion

Assignment 18.2

Analyzing phrase structure and motives

A. Mozart, Piano Sonata in C Major, K. 545, mvt. 3, mm. 1-8

Listen to this movement while following your anthology score.

(1) Write a Roman numeral analysis below the staff, and label each cadence type.

C: (I)   vi

(2) Circle the term that best describes measures 1-4:

    (a) parallel period   (b) contrasting period   (c) sentence   (d) subphrase

(3) Circle the term that best describes measures 1-8:

    (a) parallel period   (b) contrasting period   (c) sentence   (d) subphrase

(4) Listen to the movement again. In the score provided, identify two motives in the first eight measures that appear later in the piece. In the following table, list measure numbers where they reappear, and indicate how they are transformed.

Motive 1 (from mm. 1-8): mm. _____

Motive 2: mm. _____

MOTIVE 1 RETURNS	HOW TRANSFORMED?	MOTIVE 2 RETURNS	HOW TRANSFORMED?

B. Mozart, Piano Sonata in B♭ Major, K. 333, mvt. 3, mm. 1-16

Listen to this excerpt, then draw a phrase diagram of all sixteen measures. Include the number of measures in each phrase, letters to show whether the phrases are parallel or contrasting, and cadence types. Indicate how many phrases and periods are in this excerpt, and of what type. Circle on the score two different motives and their repetition in an altered form. Draw an arrow from each motive to its transformation.

Phrase diagram:

Assignment 18.3

I. Writing consequent phrases

Here, you will write antecedent-consequent phrases in Classical style, based on major-key melodies from Mozart piano sonatas. Sing through the antecedent phrases (ending on a HC), then write two possible consequent phrases, each ending on a PAC. For your first solution, write a parallel period; for your second, write a contrasting period. The slurs are Mozart's markings; slurs are optional in your answer. (If you like, find a score and compare your consequent phrase with Mozart's!)

A. Sonata in B♭ Major, K. 281, mvt. 3, mm. 1-4

Antecedent:

Consequent 1 (parallel):

Consequent 2 (contrasting):

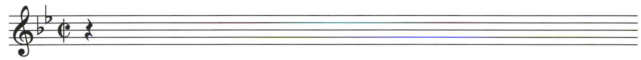

B. Sonata in D Major, K. 284, mvt. 3, mm. 1-4

Antecedent:

Consequent 1 (parallel):

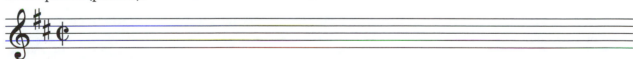

Consequent 2 (contrasting):

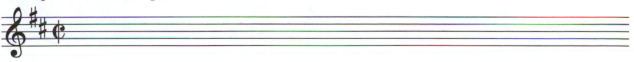

C. Sonata in D Major, K. 311, mvt. 3, mm. 1–4

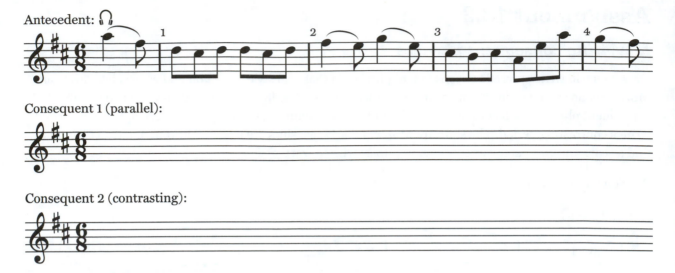

Consequent 1 (parallel):

Consequent 2 (contrasting):

II. Composing complete parallel periods

In this exercise, you will write a harmonic progression and two melodies that fit with it. Each melody should be an eight-measure parallel period, with each parallel period consisting of two phrases. You will need to work on your own staff paper, or use notation software to prepare your score. We strongly recommend that you work at a keyboard, to be able to hear the progression you have written while composing your melodies.

- Start by preparing your score. You will want three staves—one for your melody, and two below it connected with a grand staff for your keyboard harmonization.

- Write a four-part harmonic progression of your choice, in keyboard style, that follows an antecedent-consequent model (T-PD-D, T-PD-D-T). Use a slow harmonic rhythm, with one or two chords per measure. The tonic harmony may last for one or more measures at the beginning of each phrase, with an acceleration at the cadence.

- Play your progression at a keyboard, or listen to it using notation software, and sing improvised melodies to go with the progression. Use parallel structure: the first part of each phrase should have the same melody.

- When you have composed a melody you like, write it out on the top stave above the harmonization.

- Prepare a second (different) melody following the same procedure, using the same harmonic progression.

Extra challenge: Make a piano setting from your harmonization to accompany one of your melodies.

Assignment 18.4

Analyzing phrase structure

A. Haydn, Piano Sonata No. 13 in E Major, mvt. 2, mm. 1–8 🎧

(1) This example is the opening section of a short movement. Write a Roman numeral analysis, and label each cadence type.

E: I

(2) Measures 1–4 are best described as a subphrase because:

    (a) its motives are not developed.   (b) it has no cadence.   (c) it is short.

(3) Circle the term that best describes measures 1–8:

    (a) parallel period   (b) contrasting period   (c) single phrase   (d) subphrase

B. Mozart, String Quartet in D Minor, K. 421, mvt. 3 🎧

The opening phrase of both the minuet and the trio are shown for comparison. Listen to each, focusing on cadences and phrase structure (you need not analyze every chord). Then answer the questions that follow.

Minuet, mm. 1–10 🎧

Trio, mm. 40-47

(1) Draw a diagram that represents the phrase structure of the Trio (the second excerpt shown). Include the number of measures in each phrase, letters to show whether the phrases are parallel or contrasting, and cadence types.

(2) Circle all terms that apply to the Trio's phrase structure.

    (a) parallel period   (b) contrasting period   (c) modulating period   (d) sentence

(3) The first phrase of the Minuet is 10 measures in length; it is expanded by

    (a) internal expansion   (b) external expansion   (c) cadential extension

(4) On the scores provided, circle one motive in each passage. Then circle a repetition or transformation (transposition, inversion, etc.) of each.

Assignment 18.5

Phrase analysis: Beethoven, Sonata for Violin and Piano in C Minor, Op. 30, No. 2, mvt. 1, mm. 1–23

Listen to the first twenty-four measures of this sonata movement.

(1) The opening of this movement is characterized by short motives and subphrases separated by rests. Remember to look for cadences as you determine the phrase structure.

Provide a phrase diagram for the first sixteen measures. Include the number of measures in each phrase, letters to show whether the phrases are parallel or contrasting, and cadence types.

(2) Circle the term that best describes measures 1-16:

    (a) parallel period   (b) contrasting period   (c) two independent phrases   (d) sentence

(3) Circle the term that best describes measures 9-16:

    (a) parallel period   (b) contrasting period   (c) two independent phrases   (d) sentence

(4) Find two lead-ins, and give their measure numbers: m. _____; m. _____

(5) For class discussion or a short essay (on your own paper): Consider the relationship between the violin and piano in this section. What might contribute to the idea that the first eight measures are introductory? What is the source of the thematic material in measures 17-23?

Assignment 18.6

I. Phrase analysis and hypermeter: Haydn, Piano Sonata No. 13 in E Major, mvt. 2 🎧

Listen to or play through this movement.

We examined the first phrase of this movement in Assignment 18.4. We look now at the remainder of the movement.

(1)   Following the opening phrase (measures 1-8), measures 9-14 comprise a six-bar phrase. The phrase expansion occurs at the (circle one)

    beginning   middle   end

(2) Cite two places in measures 8-14 that relate motivically to phrase 1. Give measure numbers and the type of motivic transformation.

MEASURE NUMBER	TRANSFORMATION	LOCATION OF ORIGINAL MOTIVE

(3) Measures 15-24 comprise a ten-bar phrase. Compare with measures 1-8. The phrase expansion occurs at the (circle one)

beginning   middle   end

(4) Name two ways that this final phrase differs from that in measures 1-8.

(a)

(b)

(5) How are the motives in the phrase expansion related to what has been heard previously?

II. Composing a sentence from a motive

Given the two-measure basic idea from Beethoven's Bagatelle Op. 119, No. 1, compose a sentence with the following guidelines:

- Use 2 + 2 + 4 measure groupings.
- Answer the harmonic motion of the basic idea (i to V) with a variant of the basic idea that moves from V to i.
- Develop the motive further in the final four measures with accelerated motion toward a PAC.

19 Diatonic Sequences

NAME _____

Assignment 19.1

I. Completing sequences

Each of the following exercises provides a two-chord sequence pattern and the first chord of its transposition.

- Examine the given pattern, then complete the sequence so that it connects to the harmonic conclusion shown. Remember to maintain the exact voice-leading and doubling in the transpositions.
- Bracket the sequence pattern and each of its transpositions, and use arrows with numbers above to show the interval of transposition.
- Write the LIP (linear intervallic pattern) interval numbers between the staves, and fill in the name of the sequence type and LIP in the blanks provided.
- Complete the Roman numeral analysis.

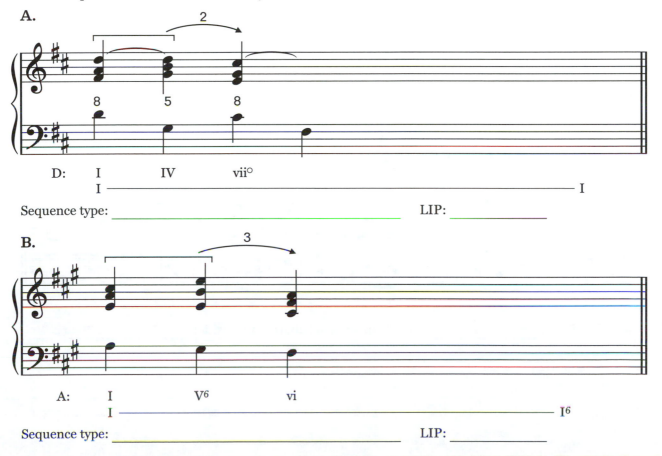

A.

D: I   IV   vii°   I
      I ——— I

Sequence type: _____   LIP: _____

B.

A: I   V⁶   vi
      I —————————————————————————————— I⁶

Sequence type: _____   LIP: _____

C.

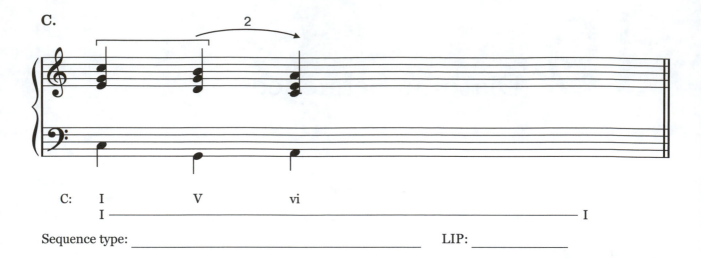

C: I   V   vi

I ——————————————————————————————————— I

Sequence type: _____   LIP: _____

II. Analysis of sequences

Locate the sequence in each short excerpt. Below the staff, write the root of each chord (using capital letters). Mark the sequence pattern with a bracket above the staff and add an arrow with the interval of transpositions, then identify the pattern length in beats, interval of transposition, and sequence type.

A. Mozart, Rondo, K. 494, mm. 95–98

Roots:

Pattern length: _____   Interval of pattern transposition: _____

Sequence type: _____

B. Bach, Invention in F Major, mm. 21–24

Roots:

Pattern length: _____   Interval of pattern transposition: _____

Sequence type: _____

Assignment 19.2

I. Writing three-voice sequences

Each of the exercises provides an incomplete sequence, which appears in three parts to avoid the parallels that would occur with the usual doublings in four parts.

- Examine the given pattern, then complete the sequence so that it connects to the harmonic conclusion shown.
- Write the LIP (linear intervallic pattern) interval numbers between the staves, and fill in the name of the sequence type and LIP in the blank.

A.

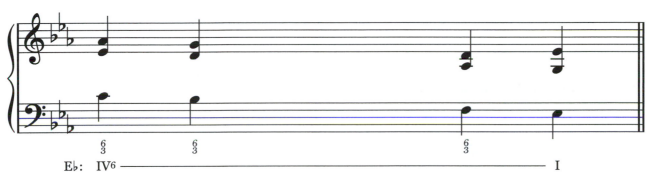

E♭:   IV⁶ ———————————————————— I

Sequence type: _____   LIP: _____

B.

F: I⁶ ———————————————————— I

Sequence type: _____   LIP: _____

C.

B♭:   I ———————————————————— V

Sequence type: _____   LIP: _____

II. Analysis of sequences

Locate the sequence in each short excerpt. Mark the pattern with a bracket above the staff and add an arrow with the interval of transposition. Then, in the blanks, identify the pattern length in beats or measures, interval of transposition, and sequence type.

A. Domenico Scarlatti, Sonata in G Major, L. 388, mm. 72-78 🎧

Pattern length: _____   Interval of pattern transposition: _____

Sequence type: _____

B. Beethoven, *Für Elise*, from *Albumblatt*, mm. 17-20 🎧

Pattern length: _____   Interval of pattern transposition: _____

Sequence type: _____

C. Bach, Chaconne, from Violin Partita No. 2 in D Minor, mm. 56-59 🎧

Pattern length: _____   Interval of pattern transposition: _____

Sequence type: _____

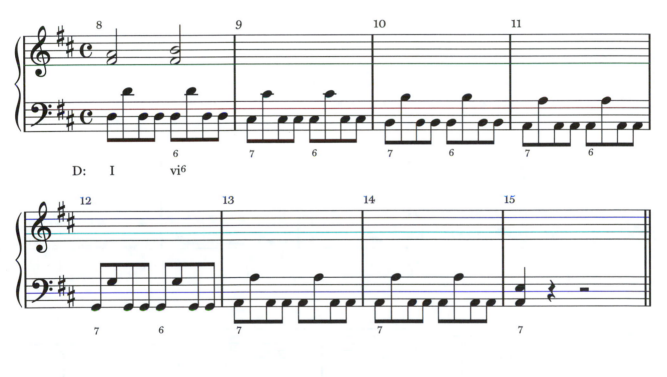

Assignment 19.3

Figured-bass realization

Realize these figured basses. For each:

- Use keyboard spacing (two or three voices in the right hand).
- Provide a Roman numeral analysis.
- Mark the sequence pattern with a bracket above the staff, and add an arrow with the interval of transposition.
- Identify the sequence type.
- Identify the LIP with interval numbers (e.g., 10-10-10).
- Follow any specific instructions given with the individual exercises.

A. Antonio Vivaldi, *Gloria*, mvt. 1, mm. 8-15

This type of sequence is usually voiced with two upper parts instead of three; use a half-note harmonic rhythm. Change to three voices after the sequence, at the cadence.

Sequence type: _____   LIP: _____

Cadence type (mm. 12–13): _____

B. Vivaldi, Violin Concerto Op. 8, No. 4 ("L'inverno" ["Winter"]), from *Le quattro stagioni* (*The Four Seasons*), second movement (adapted), mm. 10–13.

Use quarter note chords, with two or three parts in the right hand.

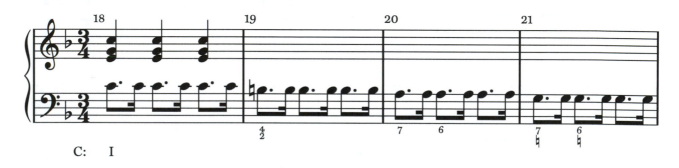

E♭:

For measures 10–11

Pattern length: _____   Interval of transposition: _____

For measures 12–13

Pattern length: _____   Sequence type: _____

C. Vivaldi, Gloria, mvt. 7, mm. 18–26

Despite the key signature, this excerpt is in C major. Change to a three-voice texture (two voices in the right-hand part) when the sequence begins in measure 20.

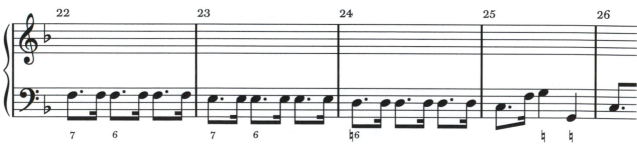

C: I

Sequence type: _____   LIP: _____

Cadence type (mm. 25–26): _____

Assignment 19.4

Analysis

A. Mozart, Sonata in C Major, K. 545, mvt. 1

Listen to the opening of this movement, following your anthology score.

(1) Bracket the pattern of the sequence above the treble staff and add an arrow with the interval of transposition. Then make a chordal reduction of measures 5–9 on the grand staff, with one whole-note chord per measure. (Although scales are prominent in this excerpt, don't show them in the reduction. They simply decorate the underlying sequence framework; focus on the downbeats.) Identify the sequence type and LIP.

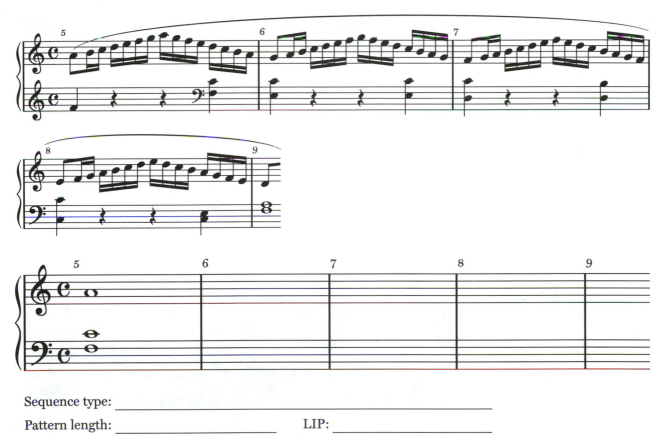

Sequence type: _____

Pattern length: _____   LIP: _____

(2) Bracket the sequence pattern and add an arrow with the interval of transposition, then make a two-voice reduction of measures 18–21 on the grand staff, with two half notes per measure. (Again, use the strong beat and harmonic rhythm to guide your reduction.) This passage is in G major. Label each chord with Roman numerals that represent the entire harmony. Bracket the pattern and its transpositions in your reduction.

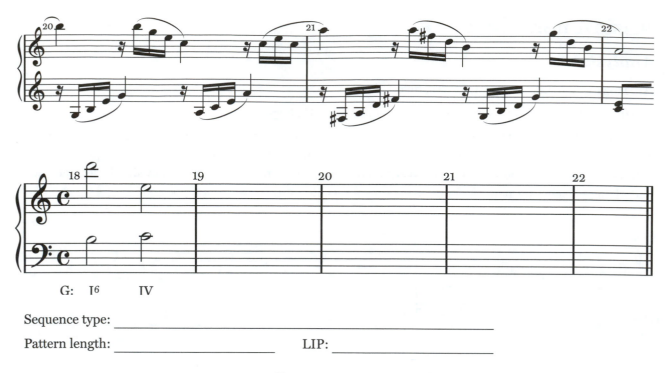

G: I⁶   IV

Sequence type: _____

Pattern length: _____   LIP: _____

B. Bach, Invention in B♭ Major, mm. 4–5 🎧

Bracket the sequence pattern and label the interval of transposition, then make a two-voice reduction of measures 4–5 (through beat 3) on the grand staff. The harmony changes on each beat. In the reduction, show only the highest and lowest note in each chord, but label each chord with a Roman numeral that represents the entire harmony (the fifth is omitted in most of the chords). Bracket the pattern and its transpositions in your reduction.

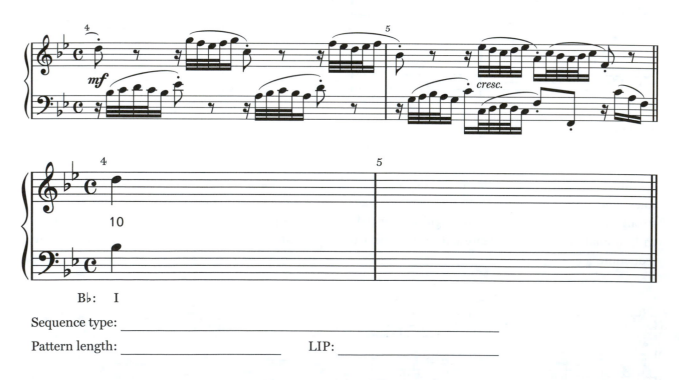

B♭:   I

Sequence type: _____

Pattern length: _____   LIP: _____

Assignment 19.5

I. Analysis

Bracket the pattern of the sequence above the treble staff and add an arrow with the interval of transposition. Provide Roman numerals for each chord and then identify the sequence type.

A. Handel, Chaconne in G Major, Variation 13, mm. 105-108 🎧

g: i ——————— iv

Sequence type: _____

B. Bach, Prelude, from Cello Suite No. 2 in D Minor, mm. 4-8 🎧

For this sequence, analyze one Roman numeral per measure (watch for seventh chords).

Sequence type: _____

II. Figured bass

Corelli, Allemanda, from Trio Sonata in A Minor, Op. 4, No. 5, mm. 23-24 🎧

Realize the figured bass in keyboard style (three notes in the right hand). Provide Roman numerals and a contextual analysis that includes a sequence label. (Reminder: 9 6 in the figures of the final measure denotes a 9-8 suspension with change of bass.)

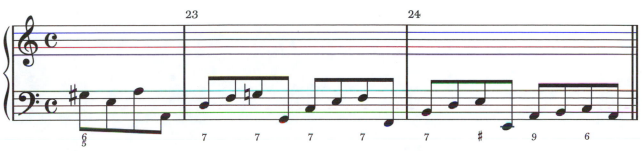

a:

III. Completing sequences with seventh chords

Continue the two-chord pattern of measure 2 as a descending-fifth sequence with seventh chords.

- Prepare all sevenths by common tone and resolve down by step.
- For sequences with all root-position seventh chords, alternate complete and incomplete chords (to avoid parallels).
- Bracket the two-chord pattern above the staff and add an arrow with the interval of transposition.

A. Use alternating seventh chords in the sequence.

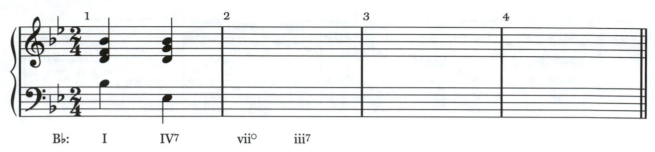

B. Use all seventh chords in the sequence.

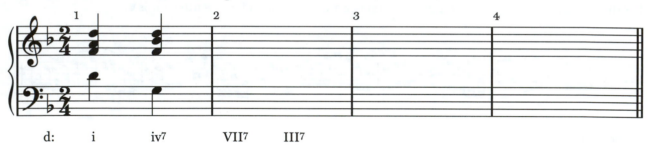

Assignment 19.6

Creative writing

Write your own sequence-based composition. First decide what combination of instruments you will use.

A. *Song or solo with keyboard accompaniment*: Set up the score with three staff lines—the top line for the solo part (choose either bass or treble clef), and the lower two for the keyboard part in a grand staff. If you are writing for a vocalist, select a text, and make sure the vocal line falls within an appropriate range for the singer (soprano, alto, tenor, or bass). A good model is Hensel's "Neue Liebe," measures 1-8. If writing for an instrument, make sure your solo falls within the range for that instrument. For transposing instruments, prepare both a score for the accompanist and the transposed part for the soloist.

B. *Unaccompanied solo*: For unaccompanied vocalist or solo instrument, set up the staff with the appropriate clef for the instrument you have chosen. This assignment is more difficult, because the solo line will need to capture the sense of the sequence framework through arpeggiation or compound melody, while making a playable/singable line.

C. *Keyboard solo*: Use a grand staff, and make sure right- and left-hand parts are playable (not too wide a reach) and are idiomatic for the keyboard. There are many models of keyboard sequences in the chapter.

Choose a sequence framework that you like (from examples or assignments), then follow this procedure:

- Select a key and mode. Write in the key signature.
- Sketch an opening progression that establishes the tonic harmony in measures 1-2; perhaps use one of the tonic expansion progressions.
- Sketch in the cadences: use a half cadence in measures 7-8 and a PAC in 15-16.
- Transpose the sequence framework you have selected to the key and mode you have chosen. Sketch it in measures 3-6.
- Embellish the sequence framework by adding passing or neighbor tones, or arpeggiate it to create the accompaniment or solo part, or apply a melodic or rhythmic motive to make an interesting sequence. Any of the voice-leading strands of the sequence (S, A, or I in the chapter or workbook examples) can serve as the highest part, as long as the entire strand is in the same part and there is one of each strand. The bass lines of these frameworks need to stay in the bass.
- Copy measures 1-6 in 9-14 to start the second phrase of a parallel period.

Part II Diatonic Harmony and Tonicization

20 Secondary Dominant and Leading-Tone Chords to V

NAME _____

Assignment 20.1

I. Spelling root-position secondary dominants to V

Write the triad or seventh chord in each key requested, in whole notes. Provide the key signature, and then add any necessary accidentals to adjust the chord quality.

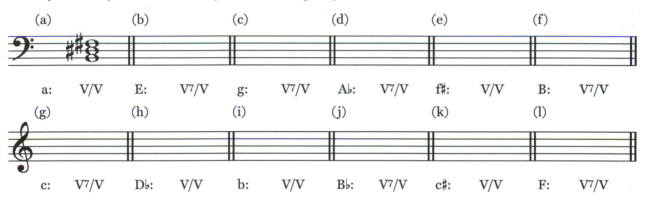

(a)	(b)	(c)	(d)	(e)	(f)

a: V/V   E: V7/V   g: V7/V   A♭:   V7/V   f♯:   V/V   B: V7/V

(g)	(h)	(i)	(j)	(k)	(l)

c: V7/V   D♭:   V/V   b: V/V   B♭:   V7/V   c♯:   V/V   F: V7/V

II. Resolving root-position secondary dominants to V

Write the two- and three-chord patterns in the keys specified, using SATB voicing and quarter notes.

- Draw arrows to show temporary leading tones resolving up and chordal sevenths down.
- For V7/V to V, make one chord complete and the other incomplete.
- For V7/V to V7, move the temporary leading tone down to the chordal seventh of V7.
- In minor keys, add an accidental to the V chord to make it major.

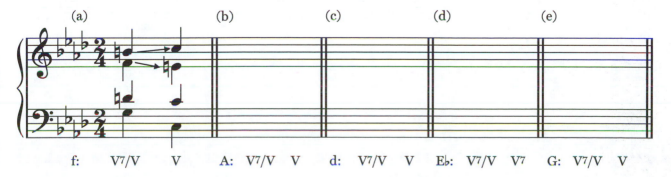

(a)	(b)	(c)	(d)	(e)

f: V7/V   V   A: V7/V   V   d: V7/V   V   E♭:   V7/V   V7   G: V7/V   V

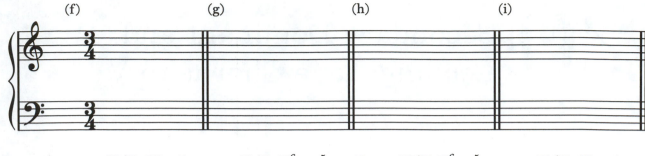

Ab: V7/V V7 I   e: V7/V V$^6_4$ = $^5_3$ B: V7/V V$^6_4$ = $^5_3$ c: V7/V V7 i

III. Analysis

Provide a Roman numeral and figures analysis.

A. Foster, "I Dream of Jeanie," mm. 5-8 🎧

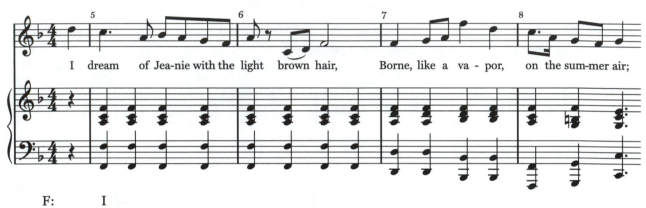

I dream of Jea-nie with the light brown hair, Borne, like a va-por, on the sum-mer air;

F: I

B. Billy Joel, "Piano Man," mm. 18-25 🎧

Hint: This excerpt features passing $^6_4$ and $^4_2$ chords for the stepwise bass.

Paul is a real es-tate nov-el-ist, Who nev-er had time for a___ wife_____

C: I   I$^4_2$

Assignment 20.2

I. Spelling secondary dominants to V with inversions

Write the secondary dominant in each key requested, in whole notes. Provide the key signature, and then add any necessary accidentals to adjust the chord quality.

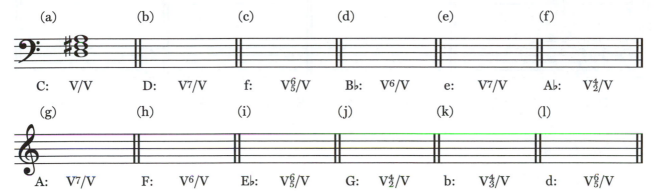

(a)   (b)   (c)   (d)   (e)   (f)

C: V/V   D: V⁷/V   f: V⁶₅/V   B♭: V⁶/V   e: V⁷/V   A♭: V⁴₂/V

(g)   (h)   (i)   (j)   (k)   (l)

A: V⁷/V   F: V⁶/V   E♭: V⁶₅/V   G: V⁴₂/V   b: V⁴₃/V   d: V⁶₅/V

II. Resolving secondary dominants to V

Write the two-chord pairs in the specified keys, using SATB voicing and half notes. Draw arrows to show resolutions of leading tones up and chordal sevenths down. Compare with Assignment 13.2, part II. How are the progressions there related to these?

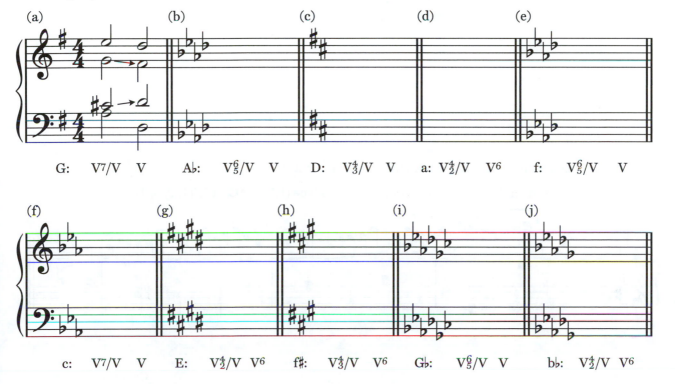

(a)   (b)   (c)   (d)   (e)

G: V⁷/V V   A♭: V⁶₅/V V   D: V⁴₃/V V   a: V⁴₂/V V⁶   f: V⁶₅/V V

(f)   (g)   (h)   (i)   (j)

c: V⁷/V V   E: V⁴₂/V V⁶   f♯: V⁴₃/V V⁶   G♭: V⁶₅/V V   b♭: V⁴₂/V V⁶

III. Resolving secondary dominants to V⁷

Write the two-chord pairs in the specified keys, using SATB voicing and quarter notes. Draw arrows to show resolutions of the chordal seventh down; resolve #4̂ to ♮4̂, the chordal seventh of the dominant.

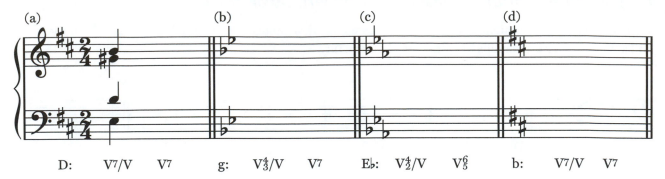

D: V⁷/V   V⁷   g: V⁴₃/V   V⁷   Eb: V⁴₂/V   V⁶₅   b: V⁷/V   V⁷

IV. Analysis

A. Mozart, Piano Sonata in C Major, K. 545, mvt. 3, mm. 10-12

Provide a Roman numeral and contextual analysis, and label the cadence type (PAC, IAC, HC, THC, or DC).

G: V⁶

Cadence: _____

B. Mozart, Piano Sonata in D Major, K. 284, mvt. 3, mm. 22-25

Provide a Roman numeral analysis and label the cadence type (PAC, IAC, HC, THC, or DC).

D: I⁶

Cadence: _____

Assignment 20.3

I. Preparing and resolving secondary dominants

Write the chords in SATB style in the keys specified.

- For (a)-(c) approach the chromatic tone by half step to avoid cross relations.
- For (d)-(f) write a chromatic voice exchange and mark it with an X.
- For (e) and (f), add a passing chord (in eighth notes) between the first two chords.

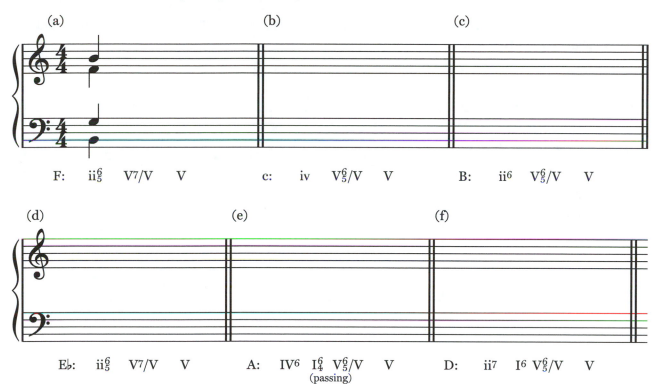

(a) F: ii$^6_5$ V7/V V (b) c: iv V$^6_5$/V V (c) B: ii^6 V$^6_5$/V V

(d) E♭: ii$^6_5$ V7/V V (e) A: IV^6 I$^6_4$ V$^6_5$/V V (passing) (f) D: ii7 I^6 V$^6_5$/V V

II. Writing secondary dominants in a phrase

A. From Roman numerals: Write the progressions in the keys and meters indicated, with SATB voicing. Remember to approach the chromatic tone in the secondary dominant by half step to avoid cross relations. Add a contextual analysis below the Roman numerals.

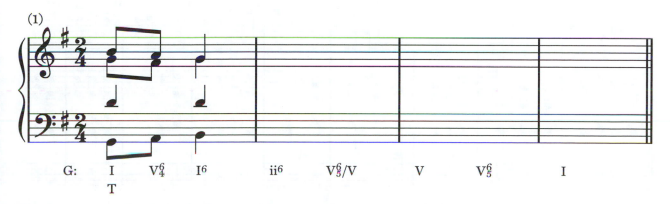

(1) G: I T V$^6_4$ I^6 ii^6 V$^6_5$/V V V$^6_5$ I

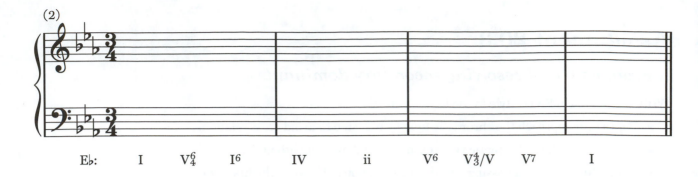

(2)

Eb: I   V$^6_4$ I^6 IV   ii   V^6 V$^4_3$/V   V^7 I

B. From figured bass: Realize the following figured bass in keyboard style. Provide Roman numeral and contextual analyses in D major.

Corelli, Preludio, from Sonata in D Minor, Op. 4, No. 4, mm. 1-5

D: I

(T ——

T ——

III. Analysis: Mozart, String Quartet in D Minor, K. 421, mvt. 3, mm. 48–55

Listen to the example, and analyze the measures reproduced here. Provide one Roman numeral per measure; use the downbeat of the measure to determine the inversion. Circle and label embellishing tones.

D: V^7

Assignment 20.4

I. Spelling secondary leading-tone chords to V

Write the secondary diminished seventh chord in whole notes, in each key requested. Provide the key signature, and add any necessary accidentals to adjust the chord quality.

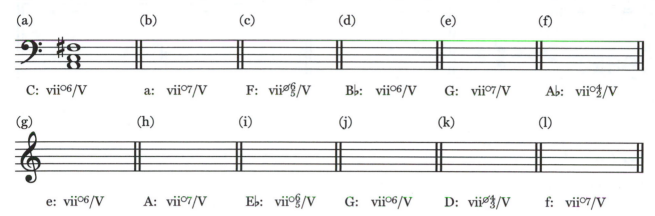

(a)   (b)   (c)   (d)   (e)   (f)

C: vii°6/V   a: vii°7/V   F: vii⌀6/5/V   B♭: vii°6/V   G: vii°7/V   A♭: vii°4/2/V

(g)   (h)   (i)   (j)   (k)   (l)

e: vii°6/V   A: vii°7/V   E♭: vii°6/5/V   G: vii°6/V   D: vii⌀4/3/V   f: vii°7/V

II. Resolving secondary leading-tone chords to V

Write the two-chord pairs in the specified keys, using SATB voicing and half notes. Provide the key signature, and draw arrows to show the resolution of leading tones up and chordal sevenths down.

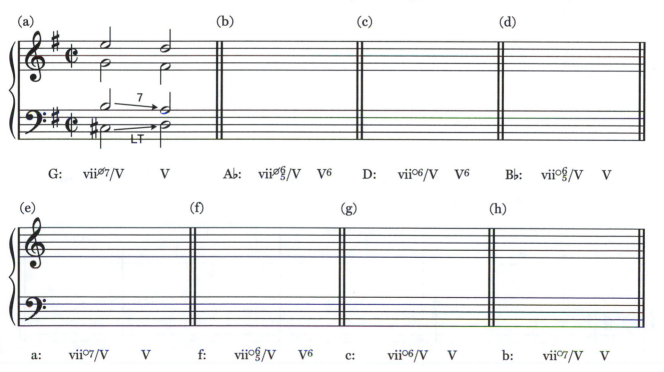

(a)   (b)   (c)   (d)

G: vii⌀7/V   V   A♭: vii⌀6/5/V   V6   D: vii°6/V   V6   B♭: vii°6/5/V   V

(e)   (f)   (g)   (h)

a: vii°7/V   V   f: vii°6/5/V   V6   c: vii°6/V   V   b: vii°7/V   V

III. Resolving secondary leading-tone chords to V⁷

Write the two-chord pairs in the specified keys, using SATB voicing and quarter notes. Provide the key signature, and resolve ♯4̂ to ♮4̂, the chordal seventh of the dominant.

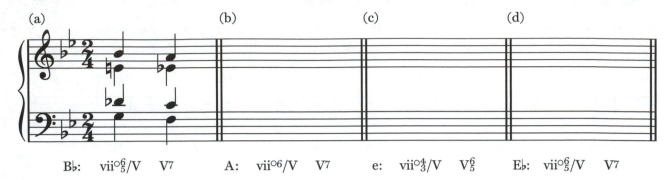

(a)   (b)   (c)   (d)

B♭: vii°⁶₅/V V⁷   A: vii°⁶/V V⁷   e: vii°⁴₃/V V⁶₅   E♭: vii°⁶₅/V V⁷

IV. Melody harmonization 🎧

Harmonize the following melodies in SATB voicing, with a harmonic rhythm of one chord per beat. Write a secondary-function chord to harmonize ♯4̂ in each melody. Provide a Roman numeral and contextual analysis underneath.

A. Harmonize with a secondary dominant and use one pedal ⁶₄ chord.

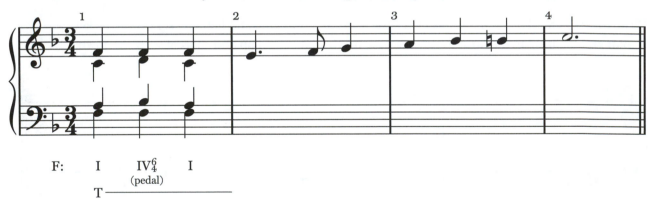

F: I   IV⁶₄   I
                  (pedal)
T ——————————————————

B. Harmonize with at least one secondary dominant and one secondary leading-tone seventh chord. The harmonic rhythm moves by eighth note, so include passing chords or pedal ⁶₄s as needed.

G:

Assignment 20.5

I. Spelling review

Spell each of the secondary-function chords, in whole notes. Provide the key signature, and then add any necessary accidentals to adjust the chord quality.

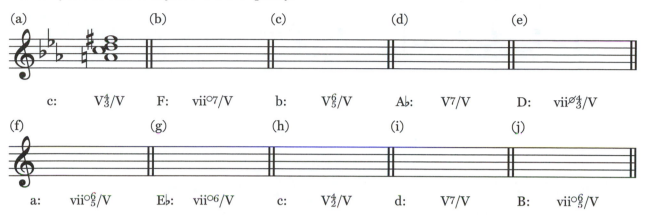

(a)	(b)	(c)	(d)	(e)
c: V_3^4/V	F: $vii°7/V$	b: V_5^6/V	A♭: $V7/V$	D: $vii°_3^4/V$

(f)	(g)	(h)	(i)	(j)
a: $vii°_5^6/V$	E♭: $vii°6/V$	c: V_2^4/V	d: $V7/V$	B: $vii°_5^6/V$

II. Writing dominant expansions

Write the dominant expansion progressions in the specified keys, using SATB voicing and quarter notes. Draw arrows to show the resolution of leading tones up and chordal sevenths down.

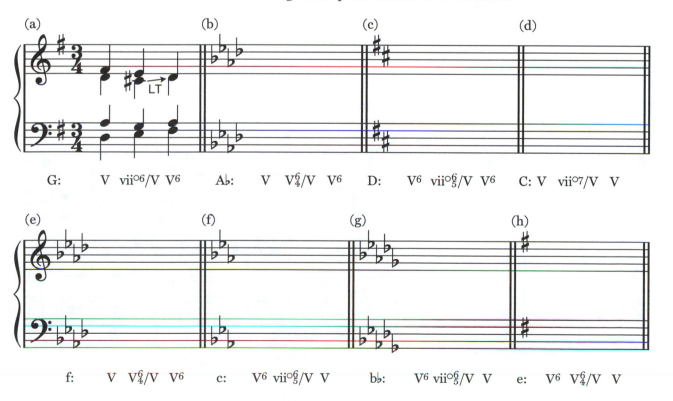

(a)	(b)	(c)	(d)
G: V vii°6/V V6	A♭: V V_4^6/V V6	D: V6 $vii°_5^6/V$ V6	C: V vii°7/V V

(e)	(f)	(g)	(h)
f: V V_4^6/V V6	c: V6 $vii°_5^6/V$ V	b♭: V6 $vii°_5^6/V$ V	e: V6 V_4^6/V V

III. Analysis

Identify the key, then provide a Roman numeral and contextual analysis for the following excerpts.

A. Bach, "Wie bist du, Seele, in mir so gar betrübt?" ("Why art Thou, Soul, so troubled?"), mm. 1-2

e: i

        T

B. Handel, "Rejoice greatly," mm. 9-11

Re-joice,   re - joice,   re - joice_____ great - ly,

C. Brahms, *Variations on a Theme by Haydn*, mm. 11-18

21 Tonicizing Scale Degrees Other Than V

NAME _____

Assignment 21.1

I. Spelling secondary dominant chords

Write the chords requested, in whole notes. Provide the key signature, then add any necessary accidentals to adjust the chord quality. It might also be helpful to provide the chord of resolution as a block chord, as shown in (a); space is provided for you to do this. Don't worry about voice-leading for now.

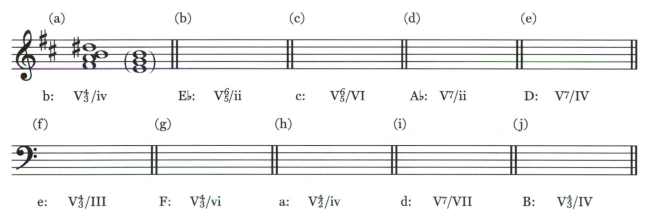

(a)   (b)   (c)   (d)   (e)

b: V^4_3/iv   Eb: V^6_5/ii   c: V^6_5/VI   Ab: V^7/ii   D: V^7/IV

(f)   (g)   (h)   (i)   (j)

e: V^4_3/III   F: V^4_3/vi   a: V^4_2/iv   d: V^7/VII   B: V^4_3/IV

II. Resolving secondary dominants

Write the two-chord pairs in the specified keys, using SATB voicing and quarter notes. Provide the key signature, and draw arrows to show the resolution of leading tones up and chordal sevenths down. For root-position chords, remember to make one complete and one incomplete.

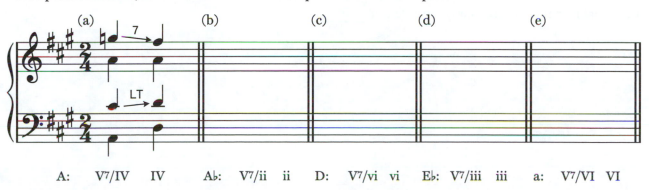

(a)   (b)   (c)   (d)   (e)

A: V^7/IV   IV   Ab: V^7/ii   ii   D: V^7/vi   vi   Eb: V^7/iii   iii   a: V^7/VI   VI

III. Analysis: Corelli, Preludio, from Sonata in D Minor, Op. 4, No. 8, mm. 25-38 🎧

Provide a Roman numeral analysis for the passage, then answer the questions that follow. (The Roman numerals need not include the many suspensions indicated by the figures).

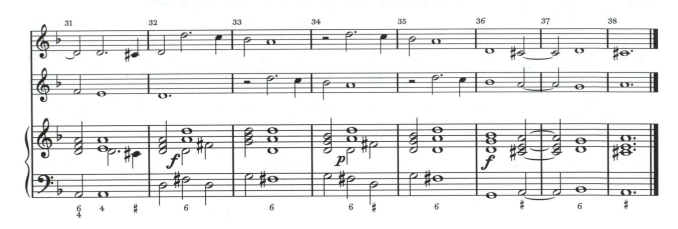

(a) This passage tonicizes just one triad repeatedly. What is it? _____

(b) This tonicization prolongs what function within the basic phrase? _____

(c) What type of cadence does it prepare? _____

(d) What rhythmic device marks the cadence? _____

Assignment 21.2

I. Resolving secondary dominants

Write the two-chord pairs in the specified keys, using SATB voicing and quarter notes. Provide the key signature, and draw arrows to show the resolution of leading tones up and chordal sevenths down.

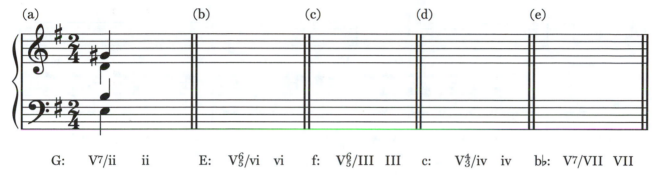

(a)　　　　　　(b)　　　　　(c)　　　　(d)　　　　(e)

G:　V7/ii　ii　　　E:　V$^6_5$/vi　vi　　f:　V$^6_5$/III　III　　c:　V$^4_3$/iv　iv　　b♭:　V7/VII　VII

II. Writing secondary dominants

Write the progressions in the keys and meters indicated, using SATB voicing. When the temporary leading tone requires an accidental, prepare and resolve it stepwise in a single voice to avoid cross relations. Add a contextual analysis below each.

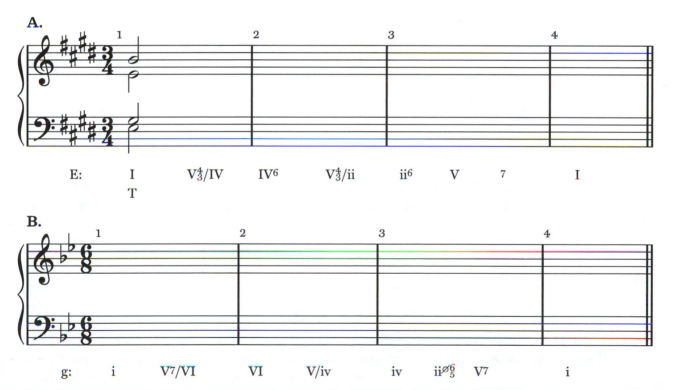

A.

E:　I　V$^4_3$/IV　IV6　V$^4_3$/ii　ii6　V　7　I
　　T

B.

g:　i　V7/VI　VI　V/iv　iv　ii$^{Ø6}_5$　V7　i

III. Analysis: Schubert, "Erlkönig"

This song tells the story of a sick boy and his father, who are riding through a stormy night on horseback. The son hears the calls of the Elf King (a mythic creature associated with darkness and doom), who eventually woos the boy to his death. The passages below are sung by the Elf King.

A. Provide a Roman numeral and contextual analysis for measures 66 to 72. Begin the basic phrase with T in measure 67.

B. Now look at the passage from measures 86 to 96 in your anthology. Provide Roman numerals and measure numbers for two different secondary dominants that are found in this passage. Do they resolve as you would expect?

	ROMAN NUMERAL	MEASURES	REGULAR RESOLUTION?
(1)	_____	_____	_____
(2)	_____	_____	_____

C. Optional: Listen to the entire song with the score to put this verse (mm. 86–96) into perspective. Then either (1) prepare for a class discussion, or (2) write a short essay, to answer the following questions: What is the mood of this verse? How do the accompaniment pattern, melodic embellishment, and harmonic choices correspond to the text? What interpretive choices by the performers would help bring out the mood?

Assignment 21.3

I. Identifying secondary dominants and leading-tone chords

For each secondary-function triad or seventh chord notated, provide a Roman numeral in the key specified.

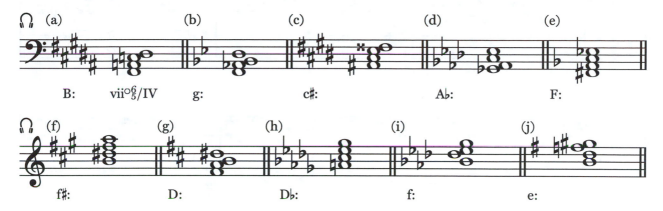

B: vii°⁶₅/IV   g: c#:   Ab: F:

f#:   D: Db: f: e:

II. Resolving secondary leading-tone chords

Write the two-chord pairs in the specified keys, using SATB voicing and quarter notes. Provide the key signature, and draw arrows to show the resolution of leading tones up and chordal sevenths down.

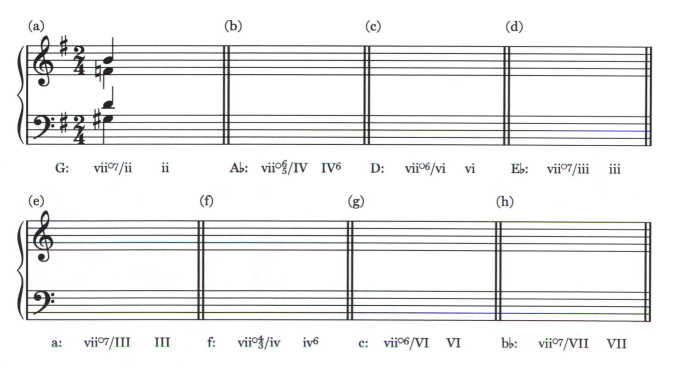

G: vii°7/ii   ii   Ab: vii°⁶₅/IV   IV⁶   D: vii°⁶/vi   vi   Eb: vii°7/iii   iii

a: vii°7/III   III   f: vii°⁴₃/iv   iv⁶   c: vii°⁶/VI   VI   bb: vii°7/VII   VII

III. Analysis

Provide a Roman numeral analysis for each passage.

A. Bach, Prelude in C Major, mm. 18-24

C: V7

In which measures does a secondary dominant resolve irregularly? What is irregular about it?

B. Queen, "Killer Queen," mm. 12-14

Hint: This excerpt ends on a minor dominant.

Cav - i - ar and cig - a - rettes,   well versed   in   et - i - quette, ex - tr'or - di - nar - i - ly nice.

Assignment 21.4

I. Analysis: Mozart, "Voi, che sapete," from The Marriage of Figaro, mm. 21-28 🎧

Provide a Roman numeral analysis.

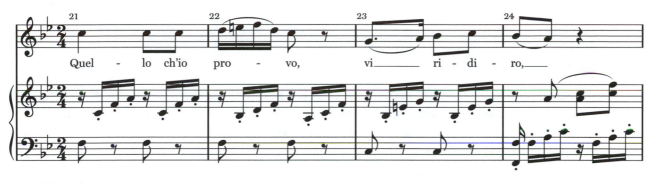

F: I

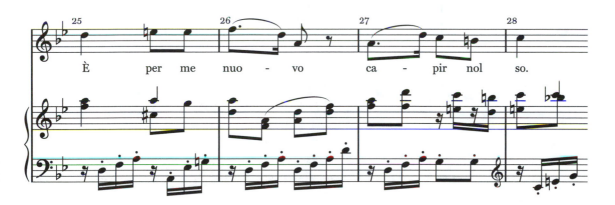

II. Preparing and resolving secondary chords

Write the three-chord progressions in the specified keys, using SATB voicing and quarter notes. Provide the key signature, then prepare the temporary tonic with stepwise motion and resolve the tendency tones properly.

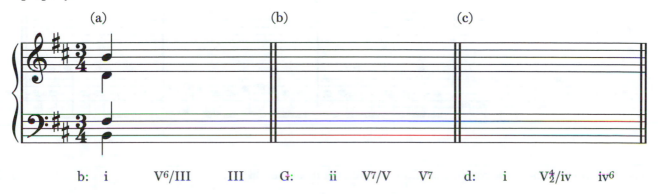

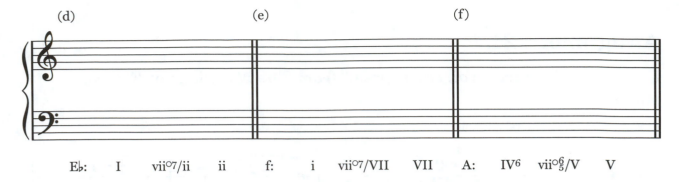

(d)   (e)   (f)

Eb: I   vii°7/ii   ii   f: i   vii°7/VII   VII   A: IV⁶   vii°⁶₅/V   V

III. Figured bass

Realize the figured-bass continuo part on the grand staff. Use keyboard voicing (three voices in the right hand, the bass line provided in the left) and a whole-note harmonic rhythm (half notes in m. 57). If necessary for proper voice-leading, you may temporarily reduce the texture to two voices in the right hand. Write a Roman numeral analysis beneath the bass line.

Antonio Vivaldi, *Gloria*, mvt. 1, mm. 50-61

What is unusual about the resolution of the harmony in measures 54-55?

Assignment 21.5

I. Figured bass: Vivaldi, "Qui tollis," from Gloria, mm. 8–15 🎧

Realize the following figured bass in keyboard style. The soprano line of the choral part is shown; don't worry about doubling keyboard voices with the soprano. This excerpt is in E minor; provide a Roman numeral analysis underneath.

Translation: Hear us now, as we make our prayers to thee.

II. Analysis

Write the key and Roman numerals for each excerpt, then answer the questions that follow.

A. Bach, Chaconne, from Violin Partita No. 2 in D minor, mm. 92–96 🎧

B. Joplin, "Solace," mm. 57-60

(1) Which diatonic triad is tonicized in this phrase? _____

(2) Is this a common choice for a phrase ending in a major key? _____

C. Brahms, *Variations on a Theme by Haydn*, mm. 1-5

Add a contextual analysis below the Roman numerals.

(1) What is the cadence type? _____

(2) What chords are tonicized in this passage? _____

(3) Are these commonly tonicized chords in a major-key piece? _____

Assignment 21.6

I. Chorale harmonization: Bach, "Jesu, meine Freude" ("Jesus, My Joy")

Harmonize this chorale tune, without modulating from E minor (although you may include tonicized half cadences). Set each melody pitch marked with an asterisk with either a secondary dominant or secondary leading-tone chord. In Baroque style, you may use a minor v in positions other than at the cadence. After completing and checking your harmonization for part-writing errors, add embellishing tones to make a typical chordal texture. Provide a Roman numeral analysis.

Bach set this melody many times. Compare your setting with one of his (for example, Chorale Nos. 96, 263, 283, 324, or 356), as well as with those of your classmates.

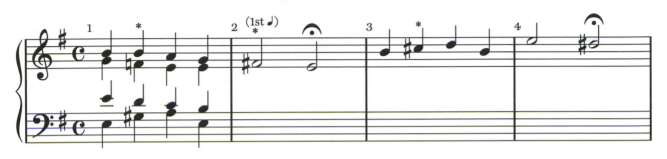

e: i   vii°7/iv iv   i

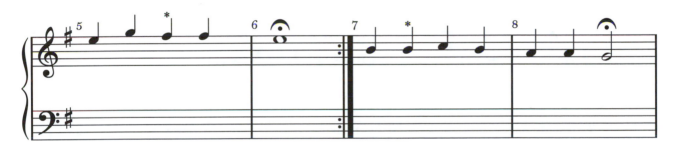

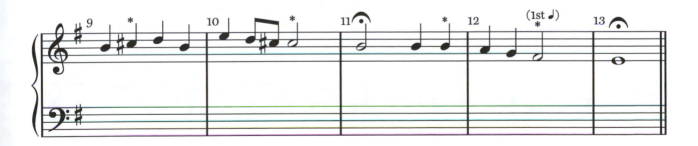

II. Analysis

For each excerpt, determine the key and provide Roman numerals with inversions. Circle the Roman numerals for any secondary dominant or leading-tone chord with an irregular resolution. Ignore any circled pitches.

A. Bach, "Er kommt," from Cantata 140 ("Wachet auf"), mm. 11–13

B. Beethoven, *Pathétique* Sonata, 3rd mvt., mm. 48–51

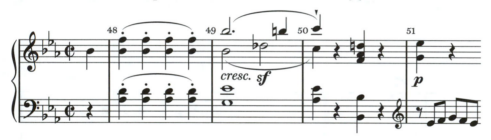

C. Brahms, "Die Mainacht," mm. 15–19 (Note that both hands of the piano are notated in treble clef.)

Translation: Veiled by leaves, a pair of doves coo their delight in front of me.

PART III

Chromatic Harmony and Form

22 Modulation to Closely Related Keys

NAME _____

Assignment 22.1

I. Triad functions

In the following charts, four triads are given in the top row. For each Roman numeral in the left-hand column, and for each triad given, fill in the appropriate key. For example, in which key would an E major triad function as III?

A.

	C MAJOR TRIAD	E MAJOR TRIAD	G MAJOR TRIAD	A♭ MAJOR TRIAD
I	C major			
III	A minor			
IV	G major			
V				
VI				
VII				

B.

	A MINOR TRIAD	D MINOR TRIAD	F MINOR TRIAD	B MINOR TRIAD
i	A minor			
ii	G major			
iii	F major			
iv				
v				
vi				

II. Identifying pivot chords

On the top staff, write the diatonic triads for each scale degree of the first key. On the given staff, copy those same chords, but add the necessary accidentals for the new key. Label all chords with Roman numerals. Draw a box around each of the possible pivot-chord pairs. In minor keys, write the triads on $\hat{5}$ and $\hat{7}$ twice: once in natural minor and once with the leading tone.

A. Modulation from G major to D major (I to V)

G major   I   ii

D major   IV   V

B. Modulation from E minor to B minor (i to v)

E minor

B minor

C. Modulation from G minor to B♭ major (i to III)

G minor

B♭ major

Assignment 22.2

I. Modulating phrases with pivot chords

Write a six-chord progression that modulates between the keys specified, using SATB voicing. The first three chords should establish the first key. Choose an appropriate pivot chord (you may refer back to Assignment 22.1, II), and write its Roman numeral in both keys; continue the analysis to the end. Remember to include accidentals needed for the cadence in the new key, and resolve all leading tones and sevenths.

A. Modulation from G major to D major (I to V)

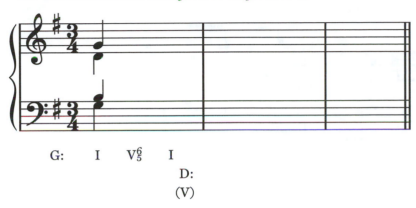

G: I   V$^6_5$ I
                       D:
                       (V)

B. Modulation from E minor to B minor (i to v)

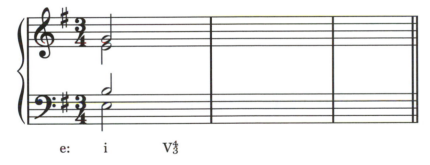

e: i   V$^4_3$

C. Modulation from G minor to B♭ major (i to III)

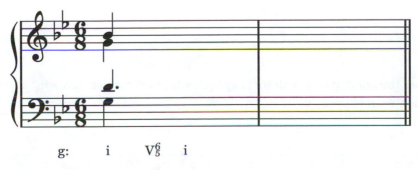

g: i   V$^6_5$ i

II. Analysis: Joplin, "Pine Apple Rag," mm. 53-60 🎧

Provide a Roman numeral analysis for this passage. The harmonic rhythm is one or two chords per measure. Be prepared to answer the questions that follow for class discussion.

(a) If the harmonic rhythm is one or two chords per measure, how do you label the syncopated eighth-note "chord" in measures 53, 54, and 57? If considered an actual chord, does it resolve as expected?

(b) What type of cadence appears in measures 59-60? Is this modulation to a key you would expect?

(c) Where and what is the pivot chord?

(d) How is the new key established? Does the music continue in that key? (Consult the complete score in your anthology.) If so, for how long? If not, what happens next?

Assignment 22.3

I. Writing modulating phrases from Roman numerals

Write the two-phrase progressions in the keys and meters indicated, using keyboard spacing (three notes in the right hand within the span of an octave, and one note in the left hand).

A. D major

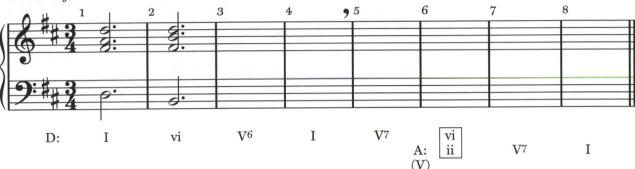

D: I   vi   V6   I   V7   A: [vi / ii]   V7   I   (V)

B. G minor

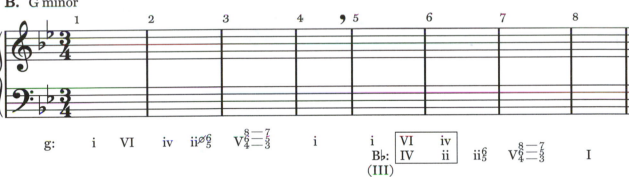

g: i VI iv ii°6/5 V8—7/4—3/6—5 i i / B♭: [VI / IV] [iv / ii] ii6/5 V8—7/4—3/6—5 I (III)

C. Write a keyboard elaboration of the progression in exercise A. (Hint: Use a Classical-style Alberti bass; embellish the melody slightly to add interest.

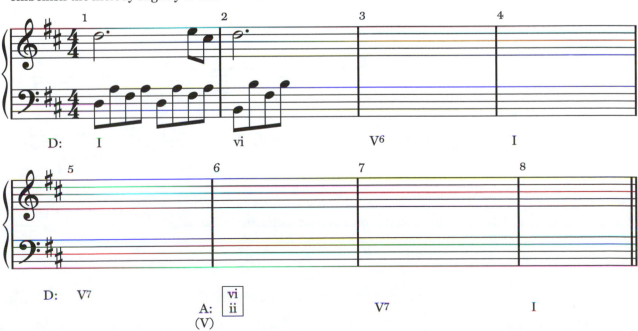

D: I   vi   V6   I

D: V7   A: [vi / ii]   V7   I (V)

II. Analysis: Bach, Prelude in E♭ Major, from *The Well-Tempered Clavier, Book II, mm. 1–12*

Listen to this prelude, or play through it at the keyboard, and analyze with Roman numerals. This excerpt includes both a tonicization and modulation. Label each. You may wish to circle and label the embellishing tones in the score to help you identify the chords.

E♭:   I

How do you distinguish between the tonicization and modulation in this passage?

Assignment 22.4

Melody harmonization

A. Melodic fragments

Each of the one-measure fragments, taken from the end of a chorale phrase, may be harmonized in at least two different keys.

- Set each fragment twice in SATB voicing: once in the major or minor key associated with the key signature and once in another, closely related key.
- Label each key, and write an analysis with Roman numerals.
- Fragments may end with half or authentic cadences.
- You may write accidentals in the lower voices, but don't change the given pitches.

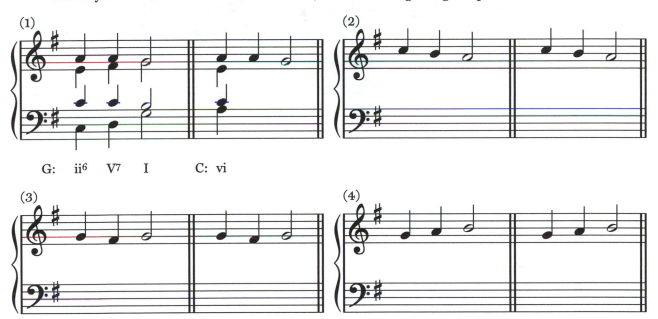

B. Mozart, Sonata for Piano and Violin, K. 6, Menuetto I, mm. 1–8 (piano melody only)

Write a keyboard accompaniment for this melody by Mozart. There are several chromatic tones in the melody; circle and label those that are embellishing tones.

- The first phrase (mm. 1–4) should confirm the initial key; the second (mm. 5–8) should modulate to the key indicated by the pitches and accidentals.
- Provide a Roman numeral analysis of your harmonization, and indicate cadence types and pivot chord(s).
- Start by writing the progression you have chosen in block chords, keyboard style, to check the voice-leading, then choose an accompaniment pattern similar to those described in Chapter 12.

Cadence type: _____

Cadence type: _____

Assignment 22.5

I. Figured bass: Bach, "Erhalt uns, Herr, bei deinem Wort" ("Keep Us in Thy Word," Chorale No. 72) 🎧

Of this chorale's four phrases (indicated by the fermatas), the first establishes the tonic, the second tonicizes (but does not modulate to) the relative major, the third modulates to the relative major, and the final phrase returns to the tonic key by means of a direct (or phrase) modulation.

Realize the figured bass with SATB spacing, as shown in measure 1, and one chord on each beat. Provide a Roman numeral analysis, identify each cadence type, and show pivot chords by drawing a box around the pivot Roman numerals in each key. If possible, arrange for a performance in class.

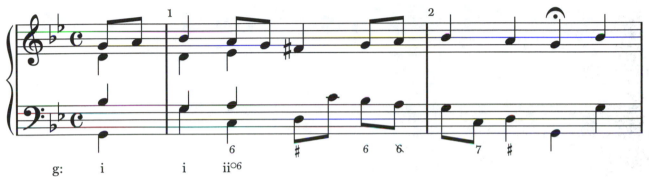

g: i   i   ii°6

Cadence type: _____

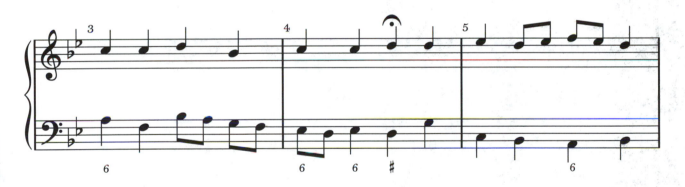

Cadence type: _____

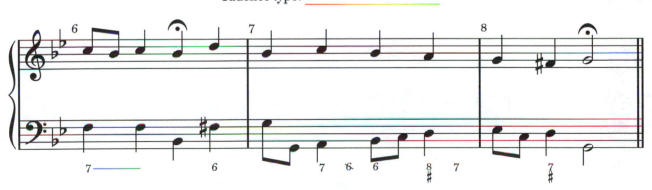

Cadence type: _____   Cadence type: _____

II. Analysis: Richard Rodgers and Lorenz Hart, "My Funny Valentine," mm. 29–36

This entire song is in C minor, except for the final four measures. The excerpt shows the end of the song, preceded by the cadence in measures 30–31 in C minor. Provide a Roman numeral analysis, beginning on the second beat of measure 30, as shown.

Is there something in the text that might motivate the modulation?

Assignment 22.6

I. Analysis: Johann Phillip Kirnberger, "La Lutine" 🎧

Provide a Roman numeral analysis for this piece, and label the phrases and cadence types. Most measures have a harmonic rhythm of one or two chords per measure, but those approaching a cadence may have three to four harmonies suggested by the counterpoint. This piece includes a modulation to a closely related key and two sequences; locate and label the pattern and level of transposition for each sequence.

(1) Where does the modulation take place? Is it a pivot-chord modulation or a direct modulation? What evidence supports each point of view?

(2) What types of sequences are employed?

(3) The music from the beginning returns in measure 17; how has it been changed?

II. Figured bass: Jean-Baptiste Loeillet, Sonata in B Minor, Op. 3, No. 10, mvt. 3, mm. 1-8 🎧

Prepare a keyboard realization of the given figured bass to accompany the flute melody. Use keyboard spacing, as shown in measure 1, and half notes (with the exception of m. 7, beat 1). Provide a Roman numeral analysis.

Cadence type: _____

Cadence type: _____

23 Binary and Ternary Forms

NAME _____

Assignment 23.1

Analyzing binary forms

Listen to each movement. Write uppercase letters above the score to represent the large sections and lowercase to show phrase structure. Label cadences, and be sure to indicate any changes of key. Provide a Roman numeral analysis.

A. Mozart, Minuet in F Major, K. 2 🎧

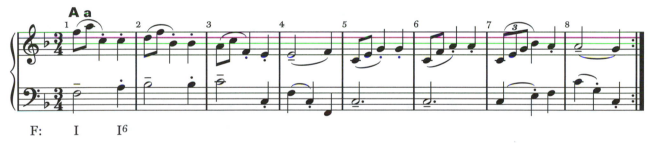

Circle any labels that apply to the form:

    rounded   simple   continuous   sectional   balanced   binary

B. Haydn, Scherzo, from Sonata No. 9 in F Major, mm. 1-25

F: I

Circle any labels that apply:

    rounded   simple   continuous   sectional   balanced   binary

Assignment 23.2

Figured bass: Corelli, Sarabanda, from Sonata in E Minor for Violin and Continuo, Op. 5, No. 8 🎧

Realize this figured bass to accompany the violin melody. Use keyboard spacing, with one chord per beat. (The $\frac{7}{4}$ in mm. 9, 11, 17, and 19 indicates that the bass note on beat 3 is a passing tone; the note on the "and" of beat 3 is the chord tone.) Provide a Roman numeral analysis, label any cadences; identify any sequences with brackets and arrows above the staff and label the sequence type below the Roman numerals.

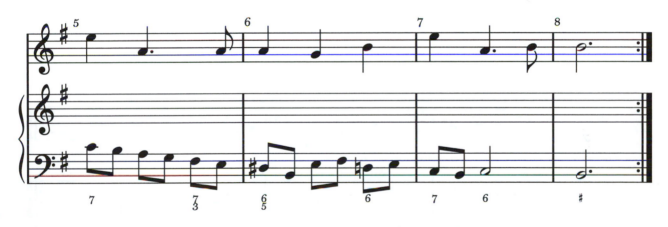

Cadence type: _____

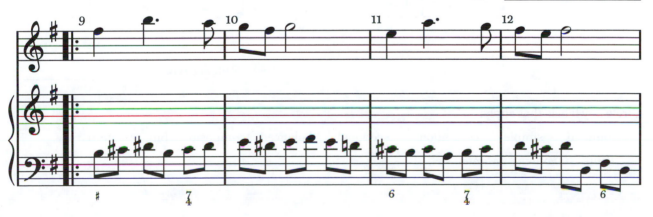

Cadence type: _____

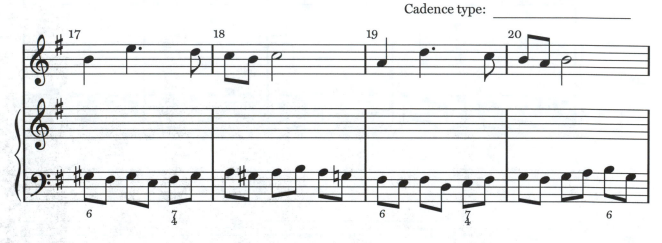

Cadence type: _____

Circle any labels that apply:

    rounded   simple   continuous   sectional   balanced   composite   binary   ternary

    Ponte   *Fonte*   *Monte*

Assignment 23.3

I. Part-writing: Binary form B section

In Assignment 22.3, you wrote two-phrase progressions that, when elaborated, could serve as the first section (A) of a binary form. Now write the harmonic progression for a second section (B) to complete the harmonic progressions for a small binary composition. Use keyboard spacing.

A. **B** section of binary piece in D major (with *Monte*)

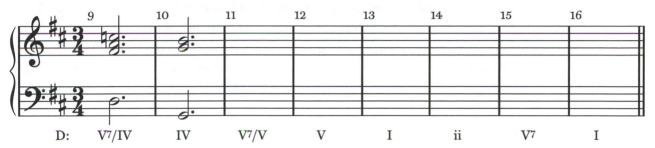

D: V⁷/IV IV V⁷/V V I ii V⁷ I

B. **B** section of binary piece in G minor (with sequence)

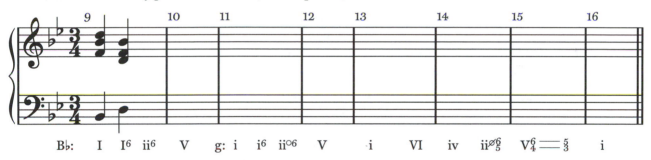

B♭: I I⁶ ii⁶ V g: i i⁶ ii°⁶ V ·i VI iv ii⌀⁶₅ V⁶₄ — ⁵₃ i

II. Writing a minuet

Write a minuet in Classical style following the guidelines presented next. The goal of this project is to write a piece you will be proud to have performed in class and, in the process, to learn more about Classical style. Aim to make sure all aspects of the composition are stylistically correct and musical.

A. Requirements

- Your minuet should be 16 measures long in $\frac{3}{4}$ meter.
  - The first section should be 8 measures long, with two 4-measure phrases *or* a sentence structure;
  - The second section should be 8 measures long, with a 4-measure harmonic disturbance followed by a 4-measure phrase that re-establishes the tonic and ends with an authentic cadence.
- Write repeat signs at the beginning and end of the sections. You may write a first and second ending if you like at the end of the first section, to make the connection smoother from measure 8 back to the beginning and from measure 8 into the second section.
- During the Classical period, major or minor keys with up to two flats or sharps were common, along with C major, C minor, and A minor. Use one of these keys.
- You may compose your own harmonic progression following the models in this chapter, or you may refer back to Assignment 22.3, Part I (p. 261) and choose the D major or G minor progression there for your **A** section, and then choose the corresponding progression in Part I of this assignment for your second section.

- This composition may be scored for keyboard, keyboard and a melodic instrument, or string quartet, as shown in the following models. It will not be written in SATB block chords, but you can sketch in block chords to plan your progression and voice-leading prior to preparing a stylistic texture based on the models.

- If possible, arrange for a performance in class.

B. Some tips to help you get started

- Make a plan for your model composition, based on information provided in Chapters 22-23. Decide which of the harmonic plans you wish to use from Key Concept boxes on pp. 476-477.

  - The minuet may be sectional (first section does not modulate) or continuous; Assignment 22.3 provides guidance on writing periods with a modulation in the second phrase.

  - The second half will start with a harmonic disturbance. You may use sequential *Monte* or *Fonte* progressions or another sequence pattern (see Chapter 19 for options), or use *Ponte* to prolong the dominant harmony. The harmonic disturbance area of the section normally ends harmonically open—on a half cadence or without a clear cadence.

  - The last four measures of the second half return to the tonic and may feature a return of the opening material (rounded) or not (simple).

- Your chord choices, voice-leading, and part-writing must follow appropriate guidelines for tonal composition. It will not be four-part SATB block chord style, but will follow an embellished style as demonstrated in the models, using accompaniment patterns in two, three, or four parts, or two-part counterpoint. If you need to review how to construct cadences in two parts, see Chapter 11; for cadences in four parts and accompaniment patterns, see Chapters 12-13; for embellishing patterns, see Chapter 16.

- One way to begin is by laying out the measures and repeat signs for each section on a piece of manuscript paper, prior to entering your score in a music notation software program.

  - Write a tonic chord in measure 1 and the last measure.

  - Write in phrase and section labels above the staff for the formal plan you have chosen, indicate the cadence types, then sketch in the cadences.

  - Study the models for the type of binary form you are writing to see how the melodic and bass lines are constructed in regard to intervals, melodic contour, and rhythm, and the type of chords that are used. Then sketch in the chords you want to use or write a melody or bass line for the opening period or sentence structure.

  - Sketch in the chords for the harmonic disturbance you have selected.

- Your composition is meant to model Classical style. The style is conveyed through texture, harmonic choices, location and type of cadences, melodic design, and other features. Closely observe the compositions you are modeling to create your own composition in that style.

Here are some models to emulate for a Classical-style composition besides those in the chapter:

- Mozart, Minuetto K. 2 (Assignment 23.1)

- Haydn, Scherzo (Assignment 23.1; also anthology)

- Haydn, String Quartet in D Minor, Op. 76, No. 2 (anthology; has Baroque characteristics as well, such as imitation)

- Mozart, K. 284, mvt. 3 Theme (anthology)

- Mozart, Variations on "Ah, vous dirai-je Maman," Theme (anthology)

- Kirnberger, "La Lutine" (Assignment 22.6)

When these steps are completed, you will be well on your way to writing the composition.

Assignment 23.4

Analyzing Binary and Ternary Forms

Listen to the following pieces to determine whether they are binary or ternary. Write uppercase letters in the score to represent the large sections and lowercase to show phrase structure. Label cadences, and be sure to indicate any changes of key.

A. Schumann, "Wilder Reiter"

Provide a Roman numeral analysis.

(1) Circle the best term for the form of measures 1–8:

    (a) parallel period   (b) contrasting period   (c) sentence structure

(2) Compare measures 9-16 with 1-8. What is the same? What is different?

(3) Which of the following best applies to the entire piece?

‖: A :‖ A′ ‖   ‖: A :‖ B ‖   ‖: A :‖ B A′ ‖   ‖: A :‖ B A ‖

(4) Circle any labels that apply to the form of the entire piece:

rounded   simple   continuous   sectional   balanced   composite   binary   ternary

B. Brahms, *Variations on a Theme by Haydn*, theme (two pianos) 🎧

Use your anthology score to answer the following questions by circling the correct answer or filling in a brief response.

(1) The cadence in measures 4-5 is best described as

  (a) an IAC in the tonic key   (b) a HC in the tonic key   (c) a DC in the tonic key

  (d) a PAC in the dominant key   (e) not a cadence

(2) The cadence in measures 9-10 is best described as

  (a) a PAC in the tonic key   (b) a PAC in the dominant key   (c) a DC in the tonic key

  (d) a plagal cadence   (e) not a cadence

(3) The phrase form in measures 1-10 is

  (a) one phrase, 10 measures long   (b) a parallel period: **a a′**   (c) a contrasting period: **a b**

  (d) a repeated phrase: **a a** (same cadence type)

(4) This theme doesn't stray far from the tonic key, but it does move away from it briefly. Where? How does this move fit into the expected harmonic plan in this type of form? What else appears here that is typical of this type of form?

(5) Measures 19-23 present music that should be familiar from earlier in the piece, but there are some changes throughout and a significant change in measure 23. Indicate the measures where this passage appeared before, and briefly describe what has changed.

(6) Briefly describe the formal function of measures 23 to the end of the piece. What is the function of measures 19-29?

(7) Circle any labels that apply to the form of the entire piece:

rounded   simple   continuous   sectional   balanced   composite   binary   ternary

Assignment 23.5

Analyzing binary and composite ternary forms

This exercise focuses on the phrase structure, tonal structure, and overall form of a piece; it is not necessary to prepare a complete Roman numeral analysis.

- Listen for the overall formal plan. Look at the score for clues, such as repeat signs. Determine whether the piece is a binary or ternary design. Write uppercase letters in your anthology score to represent the large sections.
- Listen carefully to locate and label each phrase and cadence. Be sure to indicate any changes of key.

Fill in the given charts, and prepare the questions that follow for class discussion (they also provide hints for the analysis). The optional Comments column is a place to write any observations that don't fit in the other spaces.

Mozart, String Quartet in D Minor, K. 421, mvt. 3 🎧

A. Menuetto (mm. 1–39)

SECTION	MEASURES	PHRASE	CADENCE TYPE	COMMENTS
A	1–10	**a**	PAC	

Circle any labels that apply to the Menuetto:

    rounded   simple   continuous   sectional   balanced   composite   binary   ternary

(1) What is unusual about the phrase structure in measures 1–10?

(2) Indicate the cadence type in measures 28–29, and describe what you hear in measures 11–29. What is the function of these measures, and where do they fit in the formal design?

B. Trio (mm. 40-63)

Use letters **A** and **B** for the Trio sections in this chart; when you make a graph below (part C) for the entire movement, use **C** and **D** for the Trio sections.

SECTION	MEASURES	PHRASE	CADENCE TYPE	COMMENTS
A	40–43	**a**	HC	I to V

Circle any labels that apply to the Trio:

    rounded   simple   continuous   sectional   balanced   composite   binary   ternary

C. Menuetto and Trio together

Make a graph showing the overall form of the movement, including the *da capo*. Include section labels for the large form, internal forms, and repeat signs. Then answer the questions that follow.

(1) Compare the texture of the Menuetto with that of the Trio. How do they differ? How are they similar?

(2) What is the key relationship between the Menuetto and Trio?

(3) Circle any labels that apply to the entire movement:

    rounded   simple   continuous   sectional   balanced   composite   binary   ternary

Assignment 23.6

Analyzing rags and marches

These examples focus on the phrase structure, tonal structure, and overall form of a piece; it is not necessary to prepare a complete Roman numeral analysis. For each piece:

- Listen for the overall formal plan. Look at the score for clues, such as repeat signs. Determine whether the piece is a binary or ternary design. Write uppercase letters in your anthology score to represent the large sections. Identify the composite form and the smaller forms encompassed.

- Listen carefully to locate and label each phrase and cadence. Be sure to indicate any changes of key.

A. Joplin, "Pine Apple Rag" 🎧

In the following chart, include large sections, phrases and cadences, location of modulations, and other information about the piece. (If you analyze the chords, you will find a new harmony in mm. 69-78: ♭VI, substituting for the submediant.) Use the optional Comments column for any information that does not fit elsewhere in the chart.

SECTION	MEASURES	PHRASE	KEY	CADENCE TYPE	COMMENTS
Introduction	1–4		B♭ major	HC	Melody doubled in octaves
A	5–12	**a**		HC	Tonicizes V

(1) The form of measures 5-52 is _____.

(2) The form of measures 53-84 is _____.

B. Sousa, "The Washington Post March" 🎧

Complete the following graph. Include large section labels, the measures spanned, and the overall harmonic motion of each section. You do not need to include phrase and cadence information. Indicate which sections are part of the March and which of the Trio.

             March (mm. 1–40)   Trio (mm. 41–80)

    Intro   **A**   :‖

mm. 1–7   8–

    V   G major →

For the March section, circle any labels that apply:

    rounded   simple   continuous   sectional   balanced   composite   binary   ternary

For the Trio section, circle any labels that apply:

    rounded   simple   continuous   sectional   balanced   composite   binary   ternary

Prepare the following questions for class discussion (or your teacher may ask you to write a brief essay on one or more of them).

(1) What is the relationship of the different key areas?

(2) The texture is markedly different in measures 57-63. How does that passage fit into the overall scheme of that portion of the march?

(3) How do the melodic ideas of the chromatic introduction return in the following strains?

(4) At the time it was composed (1889), this march was frequently performed at dances, to accompany the two-step, a wildly popular dance of the day. Which rhythmic elements contribute to its dance-like character?

(5) If possible, listen to several recordings of this march. In some performances, it sounds quite dramatic; in others, dance-like; and in still others, like a routine march (meant for actual marching). How are the repeated sections treated in the various performances? Do all of them follow the notated dynamic markings? Would you make the repeats distinctive if you were conducting this march, or would you play them the same? What would the dramatic character be for each section in your ideal performance?

24 Invention, Fugue, and Baroque Counterpoint

NAME _____

Assignment 24.1

Baroque melody

A. Bach, Prelude, from Cello Suite No. 2 in D Minor

Listen to measures 1–31 while following the score in your anthology. The passage begins and ends in D minor, but its *Fortspinnung* melody passes through a number of keys. Annotate each given excerpt as specified.

(1) Mm. 13–17 🎧

Measures 1–13 end with a cadence to the relative major (F), followed by a sequence. Provide a Roman numeral analysis in D minor in the blanks, and circle the type of sequence. Identify the melodic pattern with brackets above the staff.

d: III   _____   _____   _____   _____

Circle one: *Ponte*   *Monte*   *Fonte*

(2) Mm. 18–20 🎧

A new sequence pattern is introduced in measure 18. Mark the pattern with brackets, provide Roman numerals in the blanks, and label the stepwise progression of the lowest and highest "voices" with an arrow.

d: _____   _____   _____

(3) Mm. 21-22

In this compound melody, the upper voice is sequential but the bass line is not. Mark the upper-voice sequence with brackets, and the bass line with arrows.

(4) Mm. 26-30

Mark the sequence pattern with brackets. The bass voice of this compound melody moves up an entire octave by step; mark its step progression with arrows.

Circle the interval by which the sequential pattern is transposed:

ascending step   ascending third   ascending fifth

B. Handel, "Rejoice greatly," mm. 21-23

Listen to the excerpt, then provide Roman numerals and label the cadence type. Mark the melodic sequence with brackets and the step progression (in the melody) with arrows.

B♭:   V$^4_2$/V

Circle the sequence type.

descending fifth   descending second   ascending fifth

Assignment 24.2

Real and tonal answers

These subjects and answers are from Bach's *Well-Tempered Clavier*, Book I. Play or listen to each subject and answer. (1) Indicate whether each answer is real or tonal, and explain what aspect of the subject indicates that it will take a real or tonal answer. (2) Write the interval numbers between the subject and accompanying counterpoint, circling the dissonant intervals. (3) Explain how the rhythm and melody of the accompanying counterpoint contrast with the subject.

A. Bach, Fugue in A♭ Major, mm. 1-3 🎧

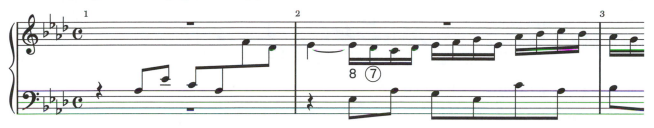

Circle one: real answer   tonal answer

Why?

How does the accompanying counterpoint contrast with the subject?

B. Bach, Fugue in B♭ Minor, mm. 1-6 🎧

Circle one: real answer   tonal answer

Why?

How does the accompanying counterpoint contrast with the subject?

C. Bach, Fugue in F♯ Minor, mm. 1-7

Circle one: real answer   tonal answer

Why?

How does the accompanying counterpoint contrast with the subject?

D. Bach, Fugue in G Major, mm. 1-9

Circle one: real answer   tonal answer

Why?

How does the accompanying counterpoint contrast with the subject?

Assignment 24.3

I. Real and tonal answers

Play or listen to each given subject and answer, from Bach's *Well-Tempered Clavier*, Book I. Analyze the intervals between the two voices and circle any dissonances. Then answer the questions that follow.

A. Bach, Fugue in F♯ Major, mm. 1-5

Circle one: real answer   tonal answer

Why?

How does the accompanying counterpoint contrast with the subject?

B. Bach, Fugue in E Minor, mm. 1-5

Circle one: real answer   tonal answer

Why?

How does the accompanying counterpoint contrast with the subject?

II. Invention analysis: Bach, Invention in F Major

A. Mm. 1-3 🎧

Begin by listening to the invention while following your anthology score. Mark the first two appearances of the subject in measures 1-3, and draw a box around two motives in these measures that appear later in the invention.

B. Mm. 10-14 🎧

In these measures, circle an example of compound melody; identify the cadence to the second key area of the invention; and bracket the entrances of the subject in the new key area.

C. Mm. 30-34 🎧

Compare the approach to the final cadence in this passage with the cadence in the previous example (B). What is the relationship between them?

Optional: As your teacher directs, write an essay addressing the following questions, or prepare these questions for class discussion.

(1) Trace the reappearances of the motives you identified in the first three measures throughout the invention. How are they varied?

(2) Does Bach feature period structures or *Fortspinnung* in this piece? Support your answer by citing specific measure numbers and examples.

Assignment 24.4

Fugue analysis: Bach, Fugue in G Minor, from The Well-Tempered Clavier, *Book 1*

A. Exposition, mm. 1–8 🎧

Mark on the score the entry of the subject (S) or answer (A) in each of the four voices and the entry of the countersubject (CS), if present. Label the bridge if present. Then answer the questions that follow.

This answer is a (circle one):   real answer   tonal answer

Is there a countersubject?   yes   no, only free counterpoint

If there is a countersubject, is it presented in invertible counterpoint?   yes   no

If there is a countersubject, are motives derived from the subject?   yes   no

　　If so, how?   augmentation   diminution   inversion   no CS

Is there a link or bridge between the second and third entries?   yes   no

　　If so, mark it on the score.

Identify and circle two significant motives introduced in the exposition.

B. On the back of this page, make a graph (like that in the chapter) for the entire fugue, starting with the entries you have marked on the score in part A.

- Enter measure numbers and beat (using a, b, c, d for beats 1, 2, 3, 4) at the top of the graph for the beginning and ending of subject and answer entries, and for sections. Draw vertical lines as needed between events in the fugue, as shown, and write in the top space of the graph exposition (and its key), episode, cadence types (e.g., PAC), and coda (if present).

- Within the expositions, show what musical materials are present in each voice, including subsequent subject or answer entries (write "subject" and "answer" or S and A), and countersubject entries (CS) if appropriate; indicate any voices with "free counterpoint" (cpt), and leave the space blank for any voices not present in the texture.

- For episodes, you do not have to account for each voice, but indicate if there is a sequence, and if so, which type, as well as listing the key to which it modulates.

MM.	1–2c	2c–4a	4a–5a		
	Exposition I (G minor)				
S		answer	bridge		
A	subject	CS	bridge		
T					
B					

MM.	
S	
A	
T	
B	

MM.	
S	
A	
T	
B	

Assignment 24.5

Analysis: Bach, Fugue in D♯ Minor

Review the discussion of this fugue in the chapter, and listen while following your anthology score. Then locate the subject and answer entries in the measures specified: the first passage (A) features unaltered (transposed) presentations of the subject and answer; the middle section (B) includes inverted subjects or answers; and the final passage (C) features augmentations and rhythmically altered subjects and answers. Also indicate for each entry, in the last column, whether it overlaps with another in stretto.

A. Mm. 12–26 🎧

Indicate each presentation of the subject or answer in the following chart. One statement appears in a rhythmic variant; note this variant in the subject/answer column.

MEASURE	BEAT	VOICE PART	STARTING PITCH	SUBJECT OR ANSWER?	COMPLETE OR INCOMPLETE?	STRETTO?
12	1	bass	A♯2	answer	complete	no

B. Mm. 34–47 🎧

Indicate inversions of the subject or answer in the following chart.

MEASURE	BEAT	VOICE PART	STARTING PITCH	SUBJECT OR ANSWER?	COMPLETE OR INCOMPLETE?	STRETTO?
36	1	alto	G♯4	answer	complete	no

C. Mm. 67-87 🎧

Indicate presentations of the subject or answer in the following chart. Some are rhythmically varied or stated in augmentation. If so, note this information in the subject/answer column.

MEASURE	BEAT	VOICE PART	STARTING PITCH	SUBJECT OR ANSWER?	COMPLETE OR INCOMPLETE?	STRETTO?

Assignment 24.6

Form analysis: Bach, Fugue in E♭ Major (St. Anne) ⊓

Analyze the expositions for subjects 1 and 2 of this triple fugue, using the score in your anthology and the following graphs. Indicate each subject and answer entry (specify whether real or tonal). Neither exposition has a CS that recurs consistently with each subject/answer entry, but the accompanying counterpoint features recurring motives. Label this counterpoint with letters: motive A, motive B, and so forth. For linking passages, write "cpt" unless the counterpoint has exact statements of motive A or B. Then answer the questions regarding the music that follows each exposition.

Exposition: Subject 1

MM.	1-2	3-4	5-6	7-8	9-10	11-13	14-15
Function	exposition	———————					
Sop. 1							
Sop. 2							
Alto	subject	motive A					
Tenor		answer (tonal)					
Bass							

An episode (mm. 16-21) cadences on the dominant. Describe the subject or answer entries in measures 21-24. In what voices do they appear, and how are they varied from the original subject? Compare them with entries in measures 31-33.

Exposition: Subject 2

MM.	37-38	39-40	41-42	43-44	45-46
Function	exposition				
Sop. 1					
Sop. 2					
Alto					
Tenor	subject				
Bass					

(1) Write a few sentences that describe how the exposition for subject 2 differs from that of subject 1. Consider number of voices, type of subject, and type of answer.

(2) On what material is the episode that begins in measure 47 based? What type of sequence appears here?

(3) Consider the role of the pedal from this point in the fugue to the very end. How does its presence or absence contribute to the dramatic reentry of the "St. Anne" theme?

25 Variation

NAME _____

Assignment 25.1

Analysis: Bach, Chaconne, from Violin Partita No. 2 in D Minor 🎧

A. Listen to the Chaconne in its entirety, following along in your anthology score. Mark each repetition of the four-measure-long theme (shown here, extending from the anacrusis before measure 1 to the first beat of measure 4). You may observe that some variations of the theme are paired (as shown) or are in groups of threes; also some are elided, with the figuration of the following variation beginning as the one before ends on beat 1. Also make notes in your score when you hear changes of texture, mode, figuration, character, and so on.

B. Harmonic Variations

Provide a harmonic analysis in the blanks for each of the following variations, and answer the questions provided with each. To calculate inversions, use the lowest-sounding chord tone in each beat or group of beats (as indicated by the blanks) as the bass note.

(1) Variation 5, mm. 16-20 🎧

_____ ___ _____ _____ _____

Examine the bass line (lowest notes) and write its name here _____

Find two other variations on the first page of the score with this same bass line, and write their variation number here: Var. _____ and Var. _____

(2) Variation 10, mm. 36-40

_____ _____ _____ _____

_____ _____ _____

(3) Variation 15, mm. 56-60

_____ _____ _____ _____

What type of sequence is represented in this variation? _____

(4) Variations 24-25, mm. 92-100

For measures 92-96 use the downbeats as the bass for inversions; these strong beats outline the lament bass, D-C-B♭-A.

_____ _____ _____ _____

(5) Variation 34, mm. 132-136

_____ _____ _____ _____ _____

This is the first presentation of the theme in major: compare the progression to the initial theme, and describe briefly what has changed.

Assignment 25.1 *(continued)*

C. Sectional shaping in the **A** section (Variations 1–33)

As is typical for continuous variations, this movement features rhythmic acceleration as a part of the overall form. Trace its progress in the first large section, measures 1–132, by filling in the following chart. The variations that are paired or grouped are indicated in the left column. Portions of the chart have been completed for you.

VARIATIONS	NUMBER OF VARIATIONS IN THE GROUP	PREVALENT DURATION/ RHYTHMIC PATTERN	TEXTURE (MELODY, SCALES, ARPEGGIATION COMPOUND MELODY, BLOCK CHORDS, ETC.)
1–2	2	quarter and half notes	block chords, double theme
3–6		dotted eighth–sixteenth	scalar melody, occasional chords
7–8, 9–10	2 + 2		
11–14			
15–16			
17–19			
20–21			
22			acceleration into the arpeggiation
23–30			
31			
32–33		mostly quarter notes	chords, double theme simplifying variation

Where do you hear the musical climax of the first large section to be? Explain.

D. Larger Form

As indicated in the chapter, this movement is divided into three large parts (**A B A′**), based on the change of mode to D major in Variation 34, and the return to D minor in Variation 53. Based on the total number of variations, however, the change to D major is past the halfway point: 34 of 64.

(1) Without completing a detailed chart tracing the durations, what is the plan for sectional shaping in the **B** section? The **A′** section?

(2) How is the movement brought to a close?

Assignment 25.2

Analysis of variations: Purcell, "Ah, Belinda, I am prest" 🎧

In this early Baroque opera (*Dido and Aeneas*), arias are accompanied by a continuo part (harpsichord playing from a figured bass, with the bass line doubled by a cello or bass viol). The accompaniment provided here is a keyboard realization. Listen to this aria (anthology), then answer the following questions.

A. Ostinato bass and form

(1) The main theme is the repeating bass line in measures 1-4. Trace this bass line throughout the piece, and number the start of each repetition on your score; start by marking measure 5 as statement 2.

 (a) The bass line is stated _____ times (counting mm. 1-4) before the first substantive change.

 (b) The first substantive change to the bass line occurs in what measure? _____
     What is different about it there?

     This changed bass is stated _____ times.

 (c) The bass line from measures 1-4 is reestablished in measure _____ .
     It is stated _____ more times, until the end of the piece.

 (d) What is different about the last two presentations of the bass line in this realization?

(2) This variation set is a (circle one):   continuous variation   sectional variation

B. Upper parts of the accompaniment and the melody, measures 2-17

(1) Listen to the melody for measures 2-17. Draw an arc graph showing the phrase structure of the melody and upper accompaniment parts for these measures. Include measure numbers for each phrase.

(2) Consider each of the melodic phrase endings in measures 2-17. How do they correlate with the bass-line repetitions?

C. Harmonies, melody, and text painting

(1) Write a Roman numeral analysis for these two passages, then compare their harmonies. What elements of the text in the second passage may have inspired the harmonic choices there?

(a) Mm. 1–4

c: i

(b) Mm. 53–56

(2) Identify two features of the melody or harmonies in the whole piece that represent musically the torment addressed in the text. List the measure numbers, and explain how that feature constitutes text painting.

1: mm. _____   Text painting:

2: mm. _____   Text painting:

D. Larger form

(1) Measures 1–17 constitute the first subsection of the piece, which we will call **a**. There are five subsections, based on the text, melody, and accompaniment upper parts. Where are the other subsection divisions? Fill them in here, and assign letters to designate their formal function.

MEASURES	1–17				
SECTION	**a**				

(2) These subsections group into two larger sections, based on the text and the sectional labels. Identify them here.

A: mm. 1–_____ , and **B:** m. _____ to the end.

Assignment 25.3

Analysis: Handel, Chaconne in G Major 🎧

A. Variation procedures: Listen while following the score in your anthology, then complete the following chart. Describe in column 2 the figure, rhythm, or prevalent durations (or insert musical notation). In this variation set, figures often swap hand parts; indicate whether a figure or rhythmic pattern is present in one hand (LH or RH) or both hands. In columns 3 and 4, record any changes of mode or tempo. If a variation pairs or groups with one or more others, indicate which ones in column 5; if it does not, write "none."

VAR.	FIGURE/RHYTHM/DURATIONS	MODE	TEMPO	PAIRS
1	Running eighth-note pattern in RH; three- or four-part block chords in LH.	major	moderate	Var. 2
2	Exchange of hand parts from Var. 1 (block chords RH; running eighth-note pattern in LH).	major	same	Var. 1
3				
4				
5				
6				
7				
8				
9				
10				
11				
12				
13				
14				

VAR.	FIGURE/RHYTHM/DURATIONS	MODE	TEMPO	PAIRS
15				
16				
17				
18				
19				
20				
21				

B. Variation type: This piece contains elements of both continuous and sectional variations. List at least two features that are characteristic of each type.

Sectional variation elements:

(1)

(2)

Continuous variation elements:

(1)

(2)

Assignment 25.3 (*continued*)

C. Harmonic analysis

(1) Theme (mm. 1-8)

Provide Roman numerals below the staves. Label and cadences.

(2) Now compare the harmonies in measures 1-8 with those of Variations 1-8.

    (a) Are the same chords used in each variation? Are the inversions changed?

    (b) How does the texture of the variations and the number of harmonies per measure change as the prevalent durations become shorter?

    (c) Which measure of the theme most often undergoes chord changes in the variations?

(3) Examine the harmonies in the minor variations.

(a) How is the descending bass line (first phrase of each variation) set in Variations 9, 10, 11, and 14? Write in Roman numerals for the opening of Variation 9 (next), and label the intervallic motion for the suspensions. Compare with the other three variations.

Sus:

Key:

(b) Write in Roman numerals for both phrases of Variation 12 (next), and compare with the progressions in the other variations.

Key:

N6*

* Indicates a chromatic harmony we have not studied yet, a Neapolitan 6 (N6 or ♭II6).

How does the second phrase in Variations 9-15 vary?

(c) What is the overall formal organization of these variations as a set? Consider change of mode, harmonic complexity, and tempo, as well as places where the momentum shifts. Add brackets and large section labels (**A**, **B**, etc.) above the variation numbers on the graph to show which variations belong in each large section. Show where there is a rhythmic acceleration (or deceleration) over several variations by using a *crescendo (decrescendo)* symbol under the variation numbers. Be prepared to discuss your decisions in class.

Theme 1 2 3 4 5 6 7 8   9 10 11 12 13 14 15 16   17 18 19 20 21

Assignment 25.4

Analysis of Variation Form: Mozart, Piano Sonata in D major, K. 284, mvt. 3 ∩

Listen while following the score in your anthology, then answer the questions, comparing the variations to the theme and to each other. Additional questions for class discussion are included at the end of this assignment. (There is a detailed analysis of the theme in Chapter 23; we will consider the chromatic harmonies in some of these variations in later chapters.)

A. The theme is in D major; which variations are in a minor key? What is the minor key and what is its relationship with the opening major key?

B. The theme is in cut time (¢); which variations are in a different meter? Which meters?

C. One variation has a different tempo specified—which one? What is the tempo marking, and what features of that variation make the change of marked tempo necessary or appropriate?

D. The last two variations have many more measures than the others (which are the same length in measures as the theme). For each, what accounts for the additional measures?

E. Some of the variations make pairs because of shared rhythms, durations, or figuration. Select two variations that you feel make a pair, and describe what links them together. Describe or write the rhythm or figuration involved.

F. Some of the variations present a distinct mood or character. Select one variation and describe specific elements of the music that help to create that mood or character. Consider dynamic markings, range, and register, as well as rhythmic and melodic figuration.

Question for class discussion (consider this as you listen):

This theme has an "extra measure" of rests in measures 12-13 that makes it a 17-measure-long binary form (instead of the normal 16 measures)—what does Mozart do with that measure in each variation?

Assignment 25.5

Variation Form Analysis: Holst, Second Suite in F Major, mvt. 4, "Fantasia on the 'Dargason'" 🎧

Listen while following the score in your anthology, then answer the questions.

A. Measures 1–56 (first excerpt, with the theme and six variations in full score)

(1) One of the significant factors varied in this movement is the instrumentation—not only which instruments and their timbres, but also the number of instruments, including changes in range and register, and presence of drones (sustained notes mimicking the sound of bagpipes) or countermelodies (melodies with an accompanimental function). Fill in the following chart to trace the changes in range, register, instrumentation, dynamic levels, and texture. For instrumentation, indicate accompanying instruments by putting them in square brackets (e.g., [alto clarinet]). If almost everyone is playing, specify *tutti* (all) then indicate which instruments are omitted. Portions of the chart have been completed for you.

VAR.	MM.	INSTRUMENTATION	LOWEST/ HIGHEST PITCHES	MELODY RANGE	DYNAMIC MARKING	TEXTURE LAYERS
Theme	1–8	solo (one player) alto clarinet, alto sax, tenor sax	F3/G4	F3–G4	*p*	very sparse, melody
Var. 1						melody, drone
Var. 2	17–24					
Var. 3						melody, counter-melody, chords

VAR.	MM.	INSTRUMENTATION	LOWEST/ HIGHEST PITCHES	MELODY RANGE	DYNAMIC MARKING	TEXTURE LAYERS
Var. 4		clarinets, bassoons, alto/tenor saxes; [oboes, E♭ clarinet, bass clarinet, bassoons baritone/bass saxes, 2nd cornets, horns 1–2, trombones, basses; snare drum]				
Var. 5			F1/F7			
Var. 6					dim.	

(2) On the grid provided, use the information you have collected about range, register, instrumentation, and texture to show graphically how this first large section is shaped.

- The rows represent a range of pitches, with each octave divided in half; use row F1 for pitches between F1 and B♭1, row B1 for B1 to E2, and so on.
- Start by lightly shading in the boxes to show which pitches are sounding in the theme and each variation.
- Then darken (or lighten) your shading to represent how thick or thin the texture sounds (based on the number of instruments playing, the dynamic level, and the number of different moving parts) within each variation.

	THEME	VAR. 1	VAR. 2	VAR. 3	VAR. 4	VAR. 5	VAR. 6
F7							
B6							
F6							
B5							
F5							
B4							
F4							
B3							
F3							
B2							
F2							
B1							
F1							

Assignment 25.5 (*continued*)

B. Measures 57-88 (anthology, condensed score)

In measure 57, there is a striking change of mood, marking the beginning of the second large section. A second melodic line, "Greensleeves" (see anthology), enters here. Listen with the condensed score, then describe what is different in this section as compared to the end of the last one. What aspects provide continuity? Consider instrumentation, texture, rhythmic and metrical elements, melody, and accompaniment.

C. Measures 80-end (anthology, condensed score)

(1) We have seen that many of the large variation movements have variations grouped into a large **A B A'** formal design. If we refer to the Theme and Variations 1-6 (mm. 1-56) as the first large section **A**, and the variations with both the Dargason and Greensleeves melodies as large section **B** (measures 57-88), what letter(s) should be applied to the remaining portion of the movement? Is there a coda? If so, which variations/measures? Complete the large-form graph, and explain your choices regarding section labels and section divisions.

SECTION	**A**				
VARIATIONS	Theme, 1–6				
MEASURES	1–56				

(2) This variation movement is based on a melody that is 8 measures long. Though a melody—not a bass line such as continuous variation sets typically employ—the Dargason tune is repeated like a continuous variation bass. Which aspects of this set are like continuous variations, and which are like sectional variations?

Assignment 25.6

I. Writing variations

Choose either a sectional or continuous variation set to compose for performance in class.

A. Sectional variations

Choose a familiar children's, patriotic, or holiday song to serve as the basis for the theme. The variations may be written for keyboard or for any small ensemble that is available in your class. If you like, you may work on this assignment as a group or class project, with each person writing a few variations and then the group arranging the results into a satisfying musical whole.

(1) Harmonize the melody in four-part chordal style to create the theme, keeping your chord choices simple. Check the harmonization and voice-leading carefully before proceeding.

(2) Prepare four or more variations on the theme. One variation should contrast in mode. One should be a figural variation, with melodic embellishment. One should be a "character variation," with rhythms, meter, and figuration characteristic of a specific genre—a march, waltz, minuet, and so on. And one should substitute more complex harmonies or add embellishing secondary dominant or seventh chords.

(3) Arrange your variations in a logical order to make a set. Add a coda if you wish.

(4) Prepare a performance for your class.

B. Continuous variations

Compose a set of continuous variations using the bass line given here, or one of the bass lines provided in the textbook in Example 25.3, part a, b, or e, or Example 25.4, as your teacher assigns. Begin by harmonizing the bass line with a simple progression, then prepare six variations, in three pairs—two with eighth notes, two with triplet eighth notes, and two with sixteenth notes. Keep the bass line identical in each variation, altering only the upper voices. Arrange your settings from the simplest to the most complex, and write a lead-in to connect each variation to the next.

II. Writing about variations

Choose one variation composition to analyze.

Brahms, *Variations on a Theme by Haydn*, Opp. 56a and 56b 🎧
(The theme is provided in your anthology; the score for the complete variation is available from online public-domain score sources.)

Purcell, "When I am laid in earth" 🎧

Begin your study of the piece by listening to the recording while examining the score. On your own paper, write a short essay that addresses the following questions.

Alternately, this assignment could be prepared outside of class for in-class discussion or used as an in-class collaborative learning activity, as your teacher directs.

A. Variation procedures: What musical features help delineate the variations? Describe the theme and each variation. For the Brahms variations, include information about the key, meter, tempo, articulation, prominent rhythmic patterns, mood, instruments, range, character, and any other features that you notice are varied. For the Purcell song, indicate the number of iterations of the ground bass, how its harmonic setting changes, how the vocal line and ground bass interact, and any important text painting.

B. Overall organization: In other variation sets we have considered, there has been an evident strategy for the overall organization—for example, a rhythmic acceleration or **A B A'** form. What seems to be the strategy here?

C. Brahms only: Consider carefully the final variation (Finale): it combines elements of a continuous variation with the overall sectional design. What is happening there?

26 Modal Mixture

Assignment 26.1

I. Identifying mixture chords

A. Write the Roman numeral for each key and chord.

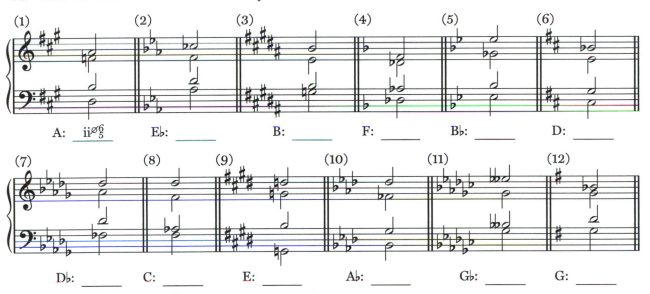

A: ii∅⁶₅   Eb: _____   B: _____   F: _____   Bb: _____   D: _____

Db: _____   C: _____   E: _____   Ab: _____   Gb: _____   G: _____

B. On the following staves, spell each mixture chord in the key and clef specified. First provide the correct key signature, then write the note heads for the correct scale-degree chord, and finally add any necessary accidentals.

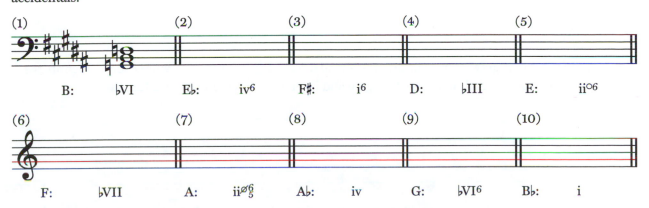

B: bVI   Eb: iv⁶   F#: i⁶   D: bIII   E: ii°⁶

F: bVII   A: ii∅⁶₅   Ab: iv   G: bVI⁶   Bb: i

II. Writing two-chord pairs with mixture

Write the chord pairs specified with SATB voicing. Pay careful attention to accidentals, and watch for parallels when moving between root-position chords.

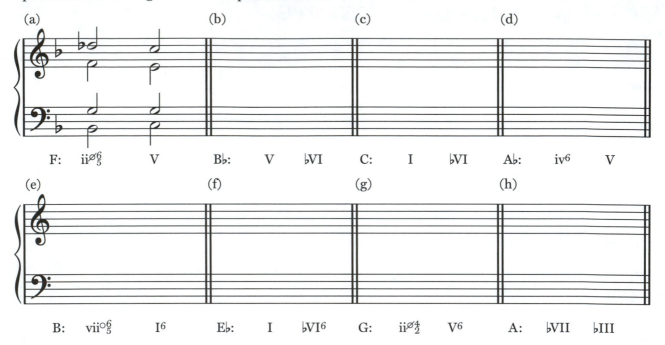

III. Analyzing modal scale degrees: Hensel, "Nachtwanderer," mm. 14-17

Write a Roman numeral analysis under the score. Circle any modal scale degrees.

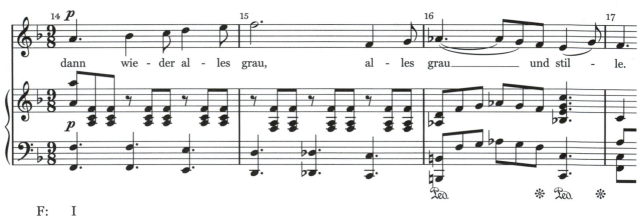

Translation: Then again, all is gray and still.

To color the text "all is gray," Hensel incorporates modal scale degrees but no mixture chords. Identify the scale-degree number for each modal scale degree and its embellishing or harmonic function.

m. 15: _____

m. 16: _____

Assignment 26.2

I. Writing progressions with mixture chords

Write the given diatonic progression on the first grand staff. On the second, rewrite the progression converting at least two of the harmonies into mixture chords (e.g., replace IV with iv). Maintain the same voice-leading where possible. Analyze with Roman numerals, and circle any Roman numeral that represents a mixture chord.

Diatonic progression:

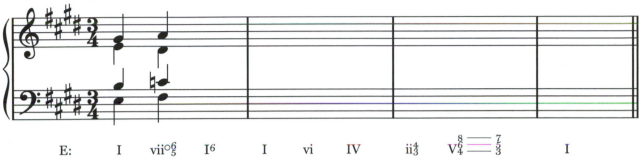

E: I vii°$^6_5$ I^6 I vi IV ii$^4_3$ V$^{8\ -\ 7}_{6\ -\ 5}_{4\ -\ 3}$ I

With mixture chords:

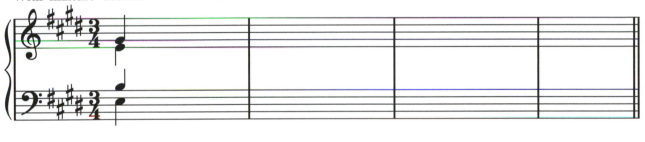

E: I

II. Analysis: Leonard Bernstein and Stephen Sondheim, "One Hand, One Heart," from West Side Story, mm. 1–17 🎧

This love song between Maria and Tony, the two main characters in this updating of the Romeo and Juliet story, includes several mixture chords. Write a Roman numeral analysis beneath the staves, and circle any numeral that represents a mixture chord.

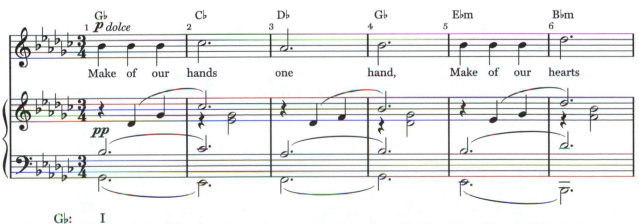

G♭: I

(a) Bernstein uses only two of the three modal scale degrees. Which are they? Where does each one appear?

(b) In what way are the chord symbols above the vocal line misleading when compared with your Roman numeral analysis?

(c) Which phrase of text is set with the most mixture? Why?

Assignment 26.3

I. Spelling chromatic chords

Spell each chromatic chord in the key and clef specified. Chromaticism may indicate a mixture, secondary dominant, or secondary leading-tone chord. First provide the correct key signature, then write the note heads for the correct scale-degree chord, and finally supply any necessary accidentals.

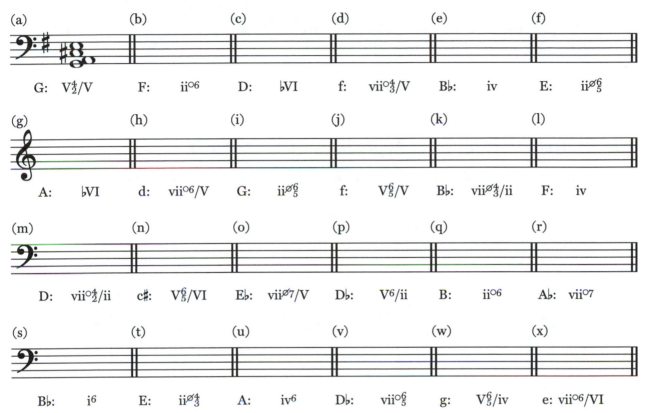

(a)   (b)   (c)   (d)   (e)   (f)

G: V_2^4/V   F: ii°6   D: ♭VI   f: vii°$_3^4$/V   B♭: iv   E: ii∅$_5^6$

(g)   (h)   (i)   (j)   (k)   (l)

A: ♭VI   d: vii°6/V   G: ii∅$_5^6$ f: V$_5^6$/V   B♭: vii∅$_3^4$/ii   F: iv

(m)   (n)   (o)   (p)   (q)   (r)

D: vii°$_2^4$/ii   c#: V$_5^6$/VI   E♭: vii∅7/V   D♭: V6/ii   B: ii°6   A♭: vii°7

(s)   (t)   (u)   (v)   (w)   (x)

B♭: i6   E: ii∅$_3^4$ A: iv6   D♭: vii°$_5^6$ g: V$_5^6$/iv   e: vii°6/VI

II. Writing progressions with mixture chords

Write the following progressions with SATB voicing.

A.

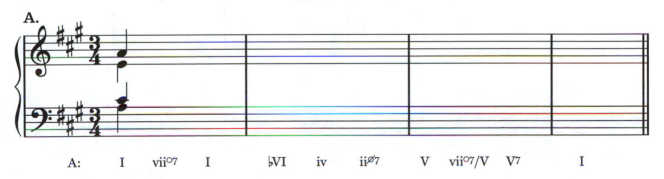

A: I   vii°7   I   ♭VI   iv   ii∅7   V   vii°7/V   V7   I

B.

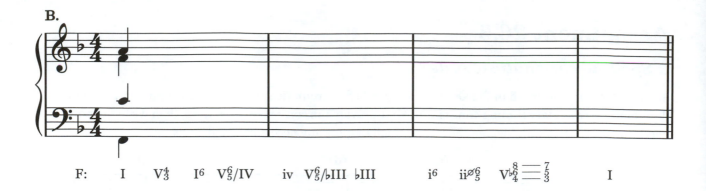

F: I   V$^4_3$ I^6 V$^6_5$/IV   iv   V$^6_5$/♭III ♭III   i^6 ii$^{ø6}_5$ V$^{♭8\,\;7}_{♭6\,\;5}_{4\,\;3}$ I

III. Analysis: Joplin, "Pine Apple Rag," mm. 76–84 🎧

Listen to the concluding strain of this rag, then analyze measures 76–84. There are many embellishing tones in this style; focus on the overall harmonic motion. The harmonic rhythm moves slowly, with one chord per one or two measures for most of the excerpt. Consider the lowest pitch of the measure to be the bass whether it appears on beat 1 or not (don't change the inversion when a chord is arpeggiated). Circle the Roman numeral of any mixture chord.

(a) Describe how the first mixture chord in the passage is foreshadowed.

(b) What is the function of the chord in measure 79? In measure 82?

Assignment 26.4

Analysis: Beethoven, Waldstein *Sonata, mvt. 1, mm. 1-13* 🎧

A. Listen to the opening of this movement. Write the Roman numerals and figures for measures 1-13 beneath the score. Circle any Roman numeral that represents a mixture chord in the context of C major.

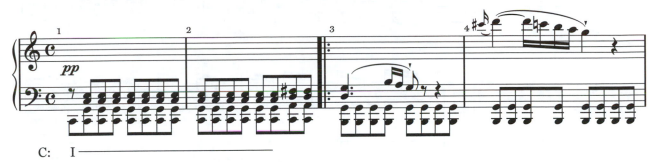

C: I

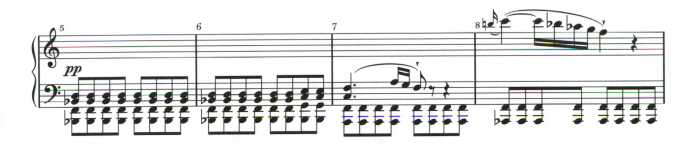

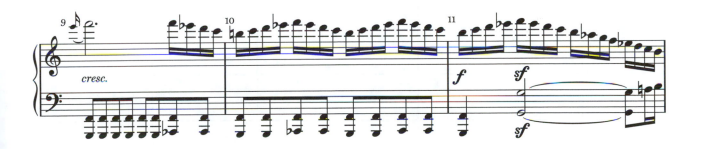

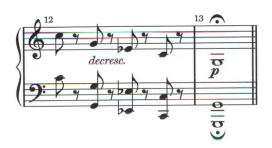

B. Provide Roman numerals for the following measures. Circle any mixture chords. 🎧

C:

C. Locate three mode mixture scale degrees in melodic embellishments in measures 1-13 (refer to your anthology score) that foreshadow their appearance as roots of mixture chords in measures 166-174. Indicate the measure number and context of each embellishment, and also the location and type of mixture chord for which it is later a root.

MEASURE (FROM 1–13)	LETTER NAME	SCALE DEGREE INTRODUCED	CONTEXT	MEASURE (FROM 166–174)	MIXTURE CHORD
4	C♯ (D♭)	♯1̂ (or ♭2̂)	grace note	169	♭II

Using your anthology score, compare the final presentation of this material (mm. 295-302) with measures 1-13 and measures 166-174. How does the final presentation differ in length and use of mixture?

Assignment 26.5

I. Figured bass

Realize the figured bass of each short progression in SATB style, and write a Roman numeral analysis beneath.

A.

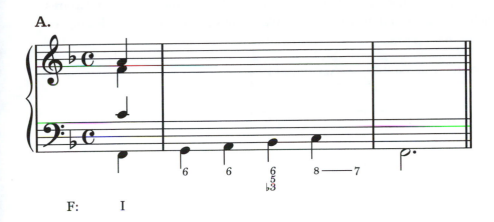

F: I

B.

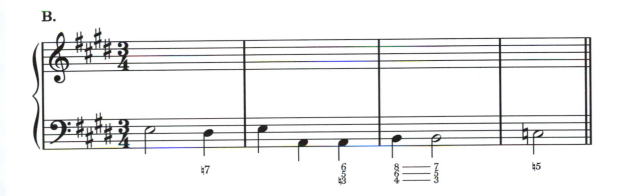

C. Hint: This progression modulates by pivot chord.

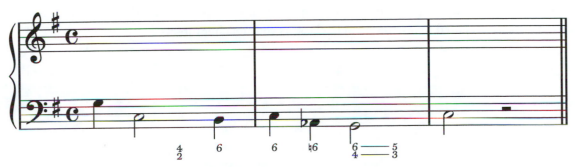

II. Analysis: Hensel, "Neue Liebe, neues Leben," mm. 56-77 🎧 (anthology)

Listen to this song while following your anthology score, paying particular attention to the opening measures and 57-78. Provide a Roman numeral and phrase analysis for these measures in your anthology, then answer the following questions.

A. Compare measures 1-8 with 57-65.

(1) List three chromatic embellishing tones that are added in measures 57-65 as compared with measures 1-8; indicate which measure each appears in, and its scale degree. Watch for these chromatic scale degrees to appear in chromatic chords later in the passage.

CHROMATIC EMBELLISHING TONE	MEASURE	SCALE DEGREE

(2) The Roman numerals for the cadence in measures 64-65 are C: _____ _____ .
The cadence type is   PAC   HC   IAC   DC

(3) How does this surprising harmonic event connect to the text set at that point?

B. Now examine measures 65-74. There are two phrases here; fill in the information, then answer the following questions.

(1) Phrase 1 is measures _____ and ends with a(n) PAC   HC   IAC   DC

(2) Measures 65-67 feature a LIP—which type? _____

(3) Phrase 2 is measures _____ and ends with a(n) PAC   HC   IAC   DC

(4) Write the Roman numerals for phrase 2 here, and circle the mixture chords:

   B♭:

(5) The harmonic sequence in measures 69-71 is a   *Monte*   *Fonte*   *Ponte*

C. Discuss Hensel's use of dissonance from measures 65 to 78. Identify any of the following that you find: accented dissonance, chromatic passing tones that foreshadow mixture chords heard later, suspensions, or diminished seventh chords. How do these elements build to the climax? Which of these dissonances might you single out for special treatment in performance? Give specific measure numbers. Either answer these questions in an essay or be prepared to discuss them in class, as your teacher directs.

27 The Neapolitan Sixth and Augmented-Sixth Chords

NAME _____

Assignment 27.1

I. Spelling Neapolitan sixth chords

For each major or minor key specified, write the key signature and a N⁶ chord.

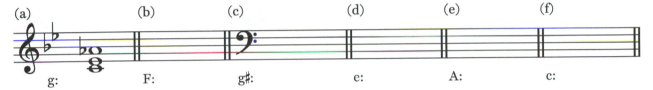

(a)   (b)   (c)   (d)   (e)   (f)

g: F: g♯:   e: A: c:

II. Resolving Neapolitan sixth chords

Write the following progressions, in SATB spacing, in the key and meter indicated. Draw arrows to show the resolution of ♭$\hat{2}$ and ♭$\hat{6}$ downward. The parentheses in (a) show that filling the d3 with a passing tone is optional.

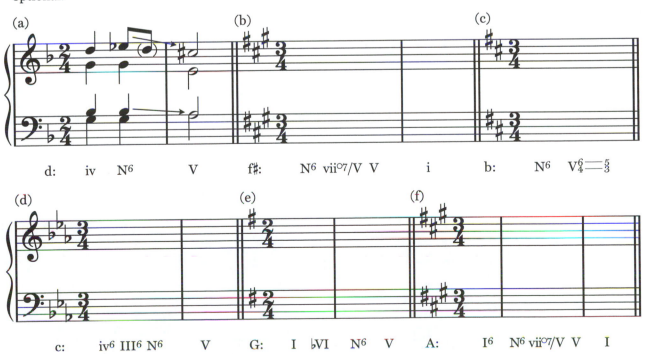

(a)   d: iv   N⁶   V

(b)   f♯:   N⁶   vii°7/V   V   i

(c)   b: N⁶   V$^6_4$—$^5_3$

(d)   c: iv⁶   III⁶   N⁶   V

(e)   G: I   ♭VI   N⁶   V

(f)   A: I⁶   N⁶   vii°7/V   V   I

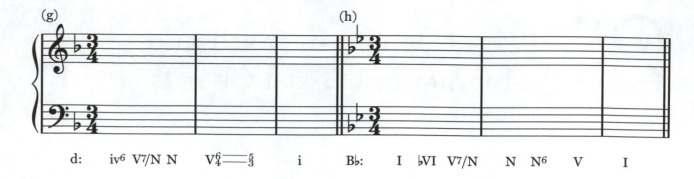

(g)

(h)

d: iv⁶ V₇/N N   V⁶₄═══⁵₃   i   B♭:   I   ♭VI   V₇/N   N   N⁶   V   I

III. Analysis: Mozart, Piano Sonata in C Major, K. 545, mvt. 3, mm. 41–48 🎧

Listen to this movement while following the score in your anthology, then provide a Roman numeral analysis for measures 41–48, with a harmonic rhythm of primarily one or two chords per measure, notating the change of harmony on the downbeat. Although the movement is in C major, this portion is in the relative minor. The exchange of motives between right and left hands produces a $^6_4$ chord in measures 41 and 44.

a: i⁶₄

Is the voice-leading resolution of the chromatic tone(s) in measures 47–48 typical? Briefly explain.

Assignment 27.2

I. Writing progressions with Neapolitan sixth chords

A. Figured bass

Realize the following short progressions from the figured bass in the keys indicated, with SATB spacing.
Provide a Roman numeral analysis below the staff.

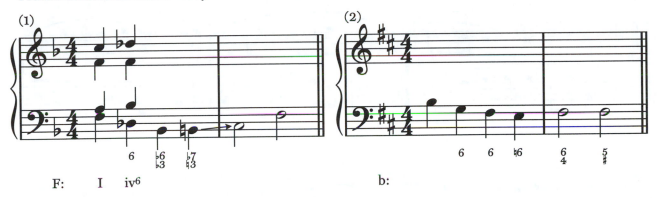

B. From Roman numerals

Write the following progression with SATB spacing.

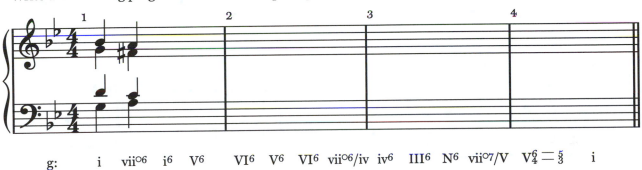

g: i   vii°6 i6 V6   VI6 V6 VI6 vii°6/iv iv6 III6 N6 vii°7/V V6/4 — 5/3 i

II. Analysis: Beethoven, Variations on "God Save the King," Variation V, mm. 1-14

Complete a Roman numeral analysis for this variation, then fill in the chart that follows.

c: i   VI

Find two Neapolitan sixth chords in the variation, then fill in their measure numbers and other items in this chart.

MEASURE	CHORD OF APPROACH	CHORD OF RESOLUTION	DIRECTION IN WHICH $\flat\hat{2}$ RESOLVES

Assignment 27.3

I. Realizing figured bass: Jean Baptiste Loeillet, Sonata in F Major for Flute, Oboe or Violin, and Continuo, Op. 1, No. 2, mvt. 4 (Giga), mm. 1-21

Realize the following figured bass in keyboard spacing. Place a chord on each beat, except

- in measures 1-7, where a rest occupies the second beat of each measure;
- in measure 12, where the figures indicate a faster harmonic rhythm.

Write a Roman numeral analysis underneath the bass staff, then answer the questions that follow. If possible, arrange for performance in class.

(a) The N⁶ is found in measures _____ and _____ .

(b) The N⁶ resolves irregularly to what harmony? _____

(c) What melodic feature implies a regular resolution to the dominant?

_____

(d) Circle the sequence type with which the movement opens (mm. 1-8):

descending thirds   descending fifths   ascending seconds

(e) The excerpt is the **A** section of a binary form. Circle the term that best describes the harmonic design of the form.

sectional   continuous

(f) Be prepared to discuss the phrase structure of this movement in class.

II. Harmonizing a melody: Schubert "Die Krähe" ("The Crow"), from Winterreise, mm. 1–5 (adapted) 🎧

Set the melody with SATB harmonization. The harmonic rhythm is three to four chords per measure. Place a Neapolitan sixth chord in the position marked by an asterisk (*). Optional: Make a piano arrangement, then compare it with Schubert's setting.

c: i   V⁴₃

Assignment 27.4

Analysis

A. Schubert, "Erlkönig," mm. 136–147

You have already analyzed several passages of this piece in earlier chapters. Here, focus on the concluding stanza, in which the child—snatched from life by the Elf King—arrives at the courtyard dead in his father's arms. Write the Roman numerals for the following measures, and be prepared to discuss Schubert's use of the Neapolitan in setting this dramatic conclusion.

Translation: He holds in his arms the moaning child; he reaches the courtyard with effort and distress; in his arms, the child was dead.

B. Mozart, Piano Concerto in A Major, K. 488, mvt. 2, mm. 1-12

Provide a Roman numeral analysis beneath the score, then draw a phrase graph for the passage and be prepared to discuss (1) decisions you made in graphing the passage, and (2) Mozart's use of the Neapolitan chord.

Phrase structure: _____

Graph:

Assignment 27.5

I. Spelling N6 and A6 chords

Write the key signature, then spell a Neapolitan sixth and all three types of augmented-sixth chords in each key specified.

A. G minor

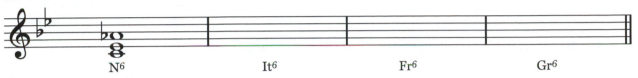

| N6 | It6 | Fr6 | Gr6 |

B. E minor

| N6 | It6 | Fr6 | Gr6 |

C. F major

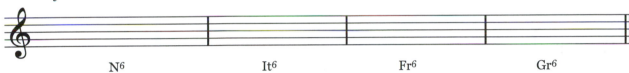

| N6 | It6 | Fr6 | Gr6 |

D. A major

| N6 | It6 | Fr6 | Gr6 |

II. Spelling and identifying augmented-sixth chord types

A. For each major or minor key and augmented-sixth chord, write the key signature and chord.

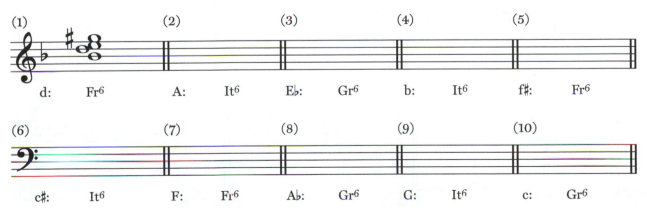

(1)   (2)   (3)   (4)   (5)

d: Fr6   A: It6   Eb: Gr6   b: It6   f#:   Fr6

(6)   (7)   (8)   (9)   (10)

c#:   It6   F: Fr6   Ab: Gr6   G: It6   c: Gr6

B. Label the minor key and chord type in the blanks provided. 🎧

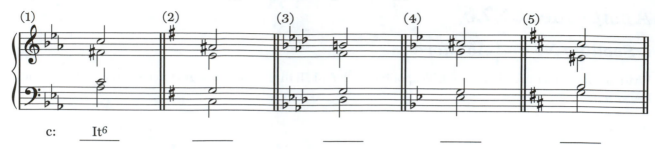

c: It⁶   _____   _____   _____   _____

III. Part-writing with augmented-sixth chords

A. Part-write each set of chords described by the given key and Roman numerals. Write primarily half notes in common time.

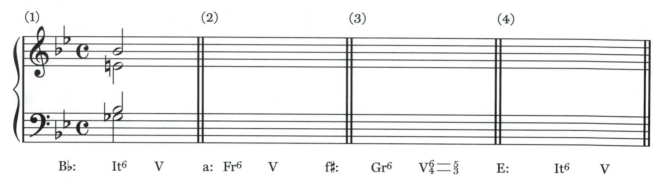

B♭:   It⁶   V   a: Fr⁶   V   f♯:   Gr⁶   V$^6_4$—$^5_3$ E: It⁶   V

B. Part-write each short progression in quarter notes, in the keys specified. Draw arrows to show the resolution of ♭6̂ downward and ♯4̂ upward. Supply an appropriate meter signature.

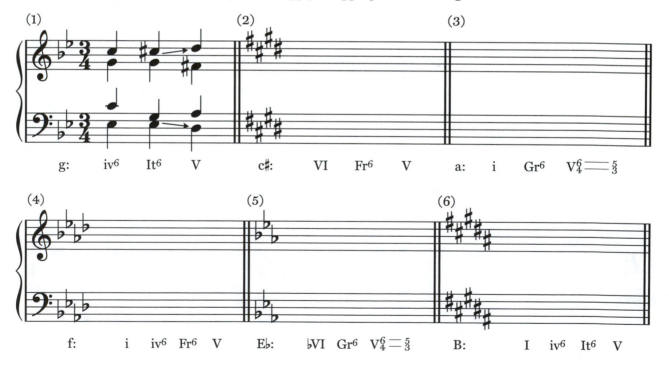

g: iv⁶   It⁶   V   c♯:   VI   Fr⁶   V   a: i   Gr⁶   V$^6_4$—$^5_3$

f: i   iv⁶   Fr⁶   V   E♭:   ♭VI   Gr⁶   V$^6_4$—$^5_3$ B: I   iv⁶   It⁶   V

Assignment 27.6

I. Writing progressions with augmented-sixth chords

A. Figured bass

Part-write the following short progressions from the figured bass given. Analyze with Roman numerals below the staff.

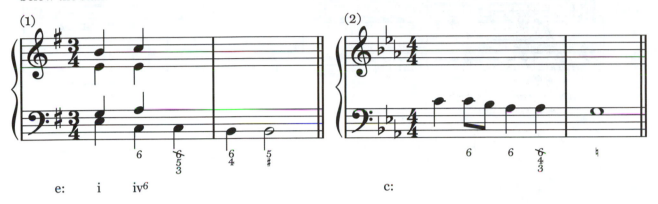

B. From Roman numerals

Write this progression, with SATB spacing.

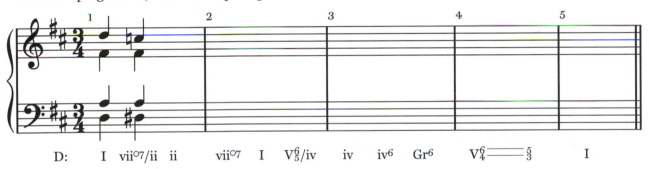

II. Analysis

Provide a Roman numeral analysis for the following passages, where augmented-sixth chords intensify a cadence. Identify each cadence type.

A. Mozart, String Quartet in D Minor, K. 421, mvt. 3, mm. 7-10

d: Cadence: _____

B. Haydn, String Quartet in D Minor, mvt. 1, mm. 1-12

(1) This example has two phrases: measures _____ and measures _____ , and forms a (circle any that apply)

    parallel   contrasting   symmetrical   asymmetrical   period.

(2) The augmented-sixth chord is in measure _____ , beat _____ . It is a   It⁶   Fr⁶   Gr⁶.
What is unusual about its resolution?

Assignment 27.7

I. Analysis: Beethoven, **Pathétique** *Sonata, mvt. 3, mm. 41-51*

A. Listen to this passage, then provide a Roman numeral analysis on the score provided and answer the questions that follow. Although the sonata is in C minor, this passage is in the relative major throughout.

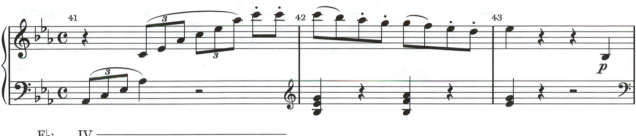

Eb: IV ⎯⎯⎯⎯⎯⎯⎯⎯⎯⎯⎯⎯⎯⎯⎯

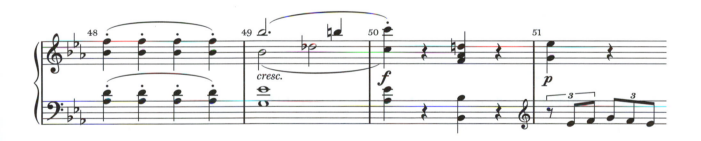

B. Identify an augmented-sixth chord in the passage.

Measure: _____   Type: _____   Preceded by: _____

Voice and resolution of ♯4̂: _____

Voice and resolution of ♭6̂: _____

II. Analysis: Mozart, Piano Sonata in D Major, K. 284, mvt. 3, mm. 246-250

Listen to this passage, then provide a Roman numeral analysis (expect a fast harmonic rhythm in measures 247-248; chord changes on almost every note). Answer the questions that follow.

A. Identify two mixture chords and an augmented-sixth chord by measure number and Roman numeral.

(1) Measure _____   Roman numeral: _____

(2) Measure _____   Roman numeral: _____

(3) Measure _____   Roman numeral: _____

B. Circle the word that best describes the function of the i$^6_4$ chord in measure 249.

   neighbor   cadential   passing

C. What harmonic detail creates a sense of surprise on the downbeat of measure 249?

D. There are several editions of this score, which differ with respect to accidentals in measure 249. What might be the missing accidental? (Hint: It helps to play through the measure.)

28 Vocal Forms

Assignment 28.1

I. Analysis of a recitative-aria pair: Bach, "Soll denn der Pales Opfer" and "Schafe können sicher weiden" 🎧 (anthology)

A. Provide a Roman numeral analysis for measures 4-10 of the recitative. Begin in F major. To which key does this recitative modulate? _____ 🎧

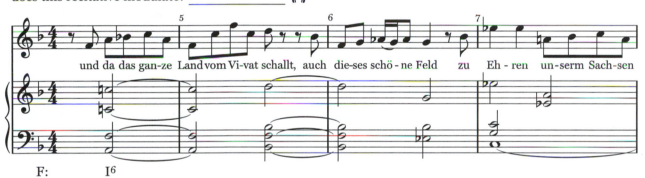

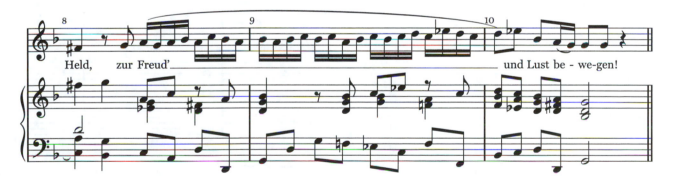

Translation: And since the whole land with "Vivat" echoes—even this beautiful field—to honor our Saxon hero, to stir to joy and passion.

B. Look at the entire recitative in the anthology, along with the text's translation provided there. List two instances of text painting, and indicate how each is set.

C. Listen to the aria, and complete the form graph that follows. In the second row, indicate whether each subsection of **A** or **B** is vocal or ritornello. Which passages are tonally stable and which modulatory? In sections that modulate, mark the Roman numerals for the beginning and ending key (fourth row).

FORM:	A			B				(da capo)
VOCAL/RIT:	rit	vocal	rit					
MEASURES:	1-4	5-17	17-21					
KEY:	B♭	B♭						
ROMAN NUMERAL:	I	I						

II. Analysis of recitative, Handel, "Thy rebuke hath broken his heart," from Messiah, mm. 1–10 🎧

A. Provide a harmonic analysis on the score. Listen to the recording or work through the passage at the piano to hear key changes. Expect direct modulations without a pivot chord; determine changes of key by cadential gestures. Begin in F minor.

B. List three musical factors that help portray the sadness of the text.

Assignment 28.2

Analysis: Schubert, "Der Lindenbaum" 🎧 *(anthology)*

Before listening to the song, read the poem by Wilhelm Müller in the anthology, and number each strophe. Think about imagery that might be reflected in the music. Then listen to the song while following the score to see how Schubert's realization does or does not match what you anticipated.

A. Poetic structure

(1) The poem consists of six strophes, with the same rhyme scheme.

Write the rhyme scheme here, using lowercase letters: _____.

(2) What story does the poem tell?

(3) What shifts of mood in the story might suggest contrasting sections in the musical form?

B. Musical form

(1) In the score, mark the beginning of each strophe, as well as musical phrases, cadences, and sections, then fill in the chart on the back of this page. Trace the progression of keys, and relate any key change to the poem. Use the Comments column for observations on text painting or any other aspect of the setting (texture, repeated phrase, harmony, etc.).

(2) The setting of strophe 5 prolongs a mixture chord—which one? How has this element of mixture been prepared musically by a prominent neighbor-tone motive in the introduction and elsewhere?

POETIC STROPHE	LARGE FORMAL SECTION	PHRASE	MEASURES	KEY/ MODE	CADENCE TYPE	COMMENTS
none	intro		1-8	E major	HC	Rustling figure in piano = leaves on tree
1	A	a	9-12		PAC	Statement of fact (objective)

Assignment 28.3

Analysis: Brahms, "Die Mainacht" 🎧 *(anthology)*

Listen to this piece while following the score in your anthology.

A. Poetry and form

(1) Briefly describe the story of the poem. What do we know about the speaker and where the action takes place? What does he or she hear, see, and do?

(2) Does the poem have a consistent rhyme scheme? Are there any recurrent images that might have implications for the form of the song?

B. Harmonic analysis

(1) One way Brahms depicts the restlessness of the main character is by avoiding the root-position tonic triad on the downbeat. Where is the first downbeat root-position tonic triad?

(2) Find each cadence, then list the measure numbers for each phrase in the chart provided. Identify the cadence type and key area, and include a Roman numeral to show the relationship to the main key of the work. Use the "Comments" column to indicate if the melody and accompaniment cadence in different locations, or other details. Then list the letters for the main sections of the form in column 1.

OVERALL FORM	MEASURES	CADENCE TYPE	KEY	COMMENTS
A	1–8	THC	F♯ major (I)	

(3) Provide a Roman numeral analysis for measures 9-14.

umd die Nach - ti - gall flö - tet, wand - l'ich trau - rig von

f#: V

Busch zu Busch.

Translation: And the nightingale flutes, I wander sadly from bush to bush.

(4) How does mixture in the harmonic progression in measures 9-14 prepare for the key change at 15?

(5) What exotic harmony colors the climax in measure 45? What harmonies and embellishments prepare this chord in the preceding measure? Where has this harmony been foreshadowed (or prepared tonally) earlier in the song?

(6) Choose three specific key words or phrases and be prepared to discuss in class how their harmonic setting, texture, contour, register, and other aspects reflect text painting.

(a)

(b)

(c)

Assignment 28.4

Analysis: Hensel, "Bitte" 🎧

A. Poetic analysis

(1) Read the poem provided below the score on page 342. Analyze the rhyme scheme with lowercase letters, writing the letters beside each line.

(2) List three images that seem essential to setting the scene in this poem, which might influence the composer's musical choices. After you complete part B, explain how each is set using mixture.

B. Harmonic analysis 🎧

Listen to the song while following the score, then provide a Roman numeral analysis in A♭ major for measures 9-16. Circle the Roman numeral of any chord whose quality results from mixture. Hint: Watch for embellishing tones. For example, the first syllable of "süsse" in measure 15 is colored by embellishing tones; analyze the harmony from the eighth-note second syllable. Measure 9 begins with a secondary dominant.

C. Form

(1) Compare the form of the poem's first strophe with the form of its setting. At the end of each line, consider the punctuation and whether Hensel made any changes. Is there a cadence at each line ending? Write "yes" or "no" beside the text to identify where Hensel employed cadences, then identify the cadence type on the score.

(2) The form of this song is (circle one):   **A B A′**   **A A B**   through-composed   strophic

(3) How do the harmonic choices in measures 9 and 13 propel the song forward and correspond with repetitions in the text? How might an understanding of the cadences affect your performance?

"Bitte"   "Please"   Cadence?

Weil' auf mir, du dunkles Auge,   a   Dwell on me, you dark eyes   no

Übe deine ganze Macht,   Exert your entire power,   ____

Ernste milde träumerreiche,   Solemn, tender, dreamy,   ____

Unergründlich süsse Nacht.   Unfathomably sweet night.   ____

Nimm mit deinem Zauberdunkel   ____   Take with your dark magic   ____

Diese Welt von hinnen mir,   ____   This world away from me,   ____

Dass du über meinem Leben   ____   That over my life   ____

Einsam schwebest für und für.   ____   You alone hold sway forever and ever.

Assignment 28.5

Analysis: Schubert, "Der Neugierige" ("Curiosity"), from Die schöne Müllerin ∩

A. Text, musical texture, and form

This song cycle tells the story of a young mill worker who has wandered beside a brook to a mill, where, catching sight of the miller's daughter, he decides to seek work. In this song, he wonders if the beautiful miller maid loves him. Read the poem in the anthology, and consider the rhyme scheme, the speaker, and to whom he is speaking.

(1) The rhyme scheme for each strophe is _____.

(2) In the following chart, indicate for each strophe to whom the miller boy is speaking (including to himself), and any important imagery or ideas. Then decide whether the strophe shares characteristics with another strophe, and what those characteristics are.

STROPHE OF POEM	SPEAKING TO WHOM?	IMAGES/SIGNIFICANT IDEAS	SIMILAR TO STROPHE	CHARACTERISTICS SHARED
1	himself	flower, star, unanswered question	2	
2				
3				
4				
5				

(3) Now listen to the song, and locate the setting for each strophe. For each, provide a formal designation (**A, B, C,** etc.) and measure numbers.

STROPHE:		1	2	3	4	5	
	intro	**A**					
MEASURES:	1–4	5–12					

(4) What "character" is represented by the piano accompaniment figures in strophes 3 and 5?

(5) How does the musical texture of strophe 4 differ from the rest, and what is the significance of this change of texture?

B. Harmonic setting

(1) What aspects of the harmonic motion might represent asking a question? Consider in particular the introduction and the beginning and end of the first two (eight-measure) phrases.

(2) The meter, tempo, and accompaniment patterns change when the singer addresses the brook (from m. 23). Where is there mode mixture in this passage, and what does it indicate?

(3) What key area appears with the word "Nein" (no) in measure 35? How does it relate to the previous key? How is the modulation accomplished?

(4) Provide Roman numerals for measures 40-42, beginning in G major. How does Schubert get back to the tonic key in measure 42 for the question to the brook?

(5) There is one last surprising harmonic twist in this song, in measure 50. What chord represents the answer to "Brook, does she love me?" The singer does not take that answer as the final one, and repeats the ending of the phrase to attain a tonic cadence. What do you think the answer is: "ja" or "nein"?

Assignment 28.6

I. French mélodie: Fauré, "Après un rêve," mm. 24-30 🎧

A. Provide a Roman numeral analysis for the following passage.

Translation: The skies parted their clouds for us, splendors unknown, divine light glimpsed.

B. List three harmonic features that give this passage a characteristic sound quite different from the German Lieder you have studied. Explain what is unusual about each.

II. Analytical writing: Hensel, "Neue Liebe, neues Leben" ⌒

Write a short analytical paper about this song. Begin by reading the poem in your anthology. Think about the structure and meaning of the text, as well as the ways you might interpret them musically if you were the composer. Next, listen to the song while following the score. Apply all the skills you have developed in recent chapters to analyze form, harmony, phrase structure, modulatory schemes, motives, and text painting. Support each point you make by giving measure numbers, reproducing musical examples with analytical markings, or creating charts or graphs.

Your essay should include the following:

- A description of the form of the song and its relation to the form of the text, including rhyme scheme and musical rhyme, poetic and musical strophe structure, objective versus subjective lines of text, characteristics of contrasting sections, and all changes of key.

- A detailed harmonic analysis of at least two sections of your choice, with a discussion of the dramatic and musical function of any mixture or chromaticism and its possible relation to the text.

- Analysis of motives, text painting, and/or embellishment of repeated motives.

- A discussion of the relationship between the vocal line and piano accompaniment, including changes between the two as the song progresses and changes of texture that correspond with form.

- A discussion of the dramatic structure, including comments on how your analysis of this song may have enriched your ideas about its interpretation and how you would shape the large-scale structure of your performance.

29 Popular Music

NAME

Assignment 29.1

Song analysis

A. Stephen Foster, "Jeanie with the Light Brown Hair" 🎧 (anthology)

Listen to this nineteenth-century American song, then complete the analysis as directed.

(1) Draw an arc to represent each phrase. Label the arc with a lowercase letter, and identify each cadence and key change. In the blanks provided, identify the form: quaternary, verse-refrain, strophic, and so forth.

m. 1 ⌢⁴ 4
a
E♭:   HC

Form of each verse: _____

Form of entire song: _____

(2) Identify three ways Foster creates contrast in the bridge section.

(a) _____

(b) _____

(c) _____

(3) Name two ways Foster musically portrays the insubstantial "vapor" of the longed-for Jeanie at the end of the song.

(a) _____

(b) _____

B. Jerome Kern, "Look for the Silver Lining" 🎧 (anthology)

Listen to this 1920 Broadway musical song, then complete the analysis as directed.

(1) At the largest level, this song is divided into two parts. Give the term that is associated with each part, then examine how the two differ.

mm. 1–11: _____   mm. 12–43: _____

(2) Identify three ways that the two parts differ.

    (a) _____

    _____

    (b) _____

    _____

    (c) _____

    _____

(3) For the second part of the song (beginning in m. 12), draw a graph with an arc to represent each phrase. Label each arc with a lowercase letter, and identify each cadence. Watch for a key change and label the cadence in that new key (mark both cadence and key). In the blank provided, identify the form of this part of the song.

Form of the second part: _____

C. Quaternary song form in television theme songs

In the 1960s and 1970s, when television was a relatively new form of entertainment, many of the television shows had theme songs that introduced the show and were composed in quaternary song form. Here are two that you may know—both from cartoons.

- Find a video of each theme song online. Count along while listening to the song (you may wish to conduct to help count the measures), then complete the following graphs. Each song has a brief introduction prior to the main body of the song. Begin counting measure numbers after the introduction ends.

- List measure numbers for each phrase (including any cadential or phrase extension), identify the cadence type, and provide phrase letters. You may find variant versions from different years of the show; you can use this technique to compare them.

(1) Hoyt Curtin, Joseph Barbera, and William Hanna, "Meet the Flintstones" (theme song from *The Flintstones*):

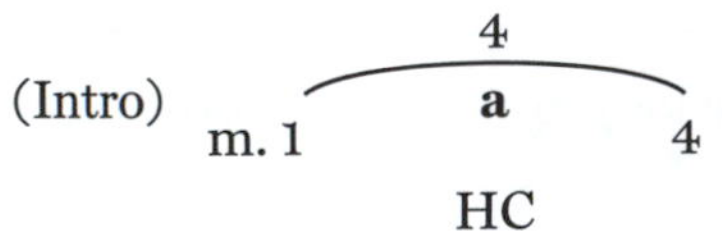

(2) Ben Raleigh, Scooby-Doo Theme Song (1969)

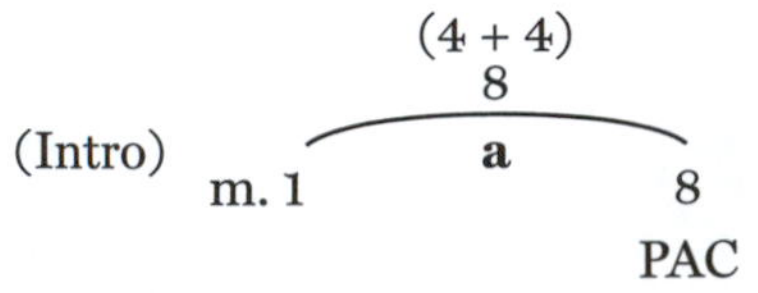

Assignment 29.2

I. Reading chord symbols

In the space provided, notate the root-position chords indicated by the chord symbols above the staff.

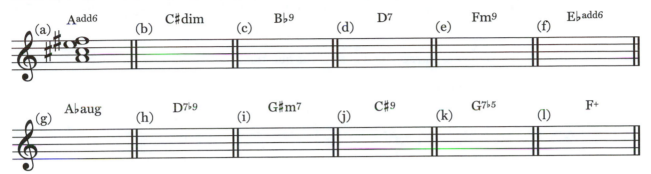

II. Writing blues scales

On the given staves, first write the indicated minor pentatonic scales ascending and descending, then add blue notes (check the spelling on the ascending versus descending form).

A. Begin on E4.

B. Begin on B♭2.

C. Begin on G2.

D. Begin on D4.

E. Begin on F4.

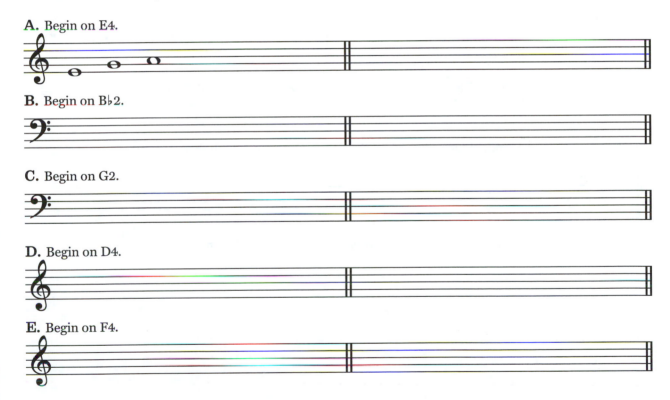

III. Analysis

A. Chord symbols: For each chord, provide the appropriate chord symbol.

(1) <u>Bᵇadd6</u>   (2) _____   (3) _____   (4) _____   (5) _____   (6) _____   (7) _____   (8) _____

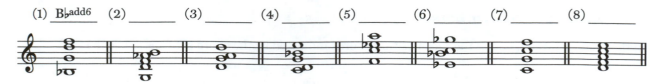

B. Blues: Listen to the following passage, then answer the questions.

Phillips, "Blues for Norton," mm. 20–24

(1) Write out the appropriate blues scale (ascending) that corresponds with this passage.

(2) From what point in the standard blues progression is this passage drawn?

Assignment 29.3

I. Song analysis: Mel Leven, "Cruella de Vil," from 101 Dalmatians 🎧

Listen to this song, then answer the questions.

A. Harmonic analysis: Indicate the key, and write in Roman numerals for measures 5-12; the harmonic rhythm is typically one or two chords per measure. Several chords include sevenths and ninths—indicate them with the Roman numeral.

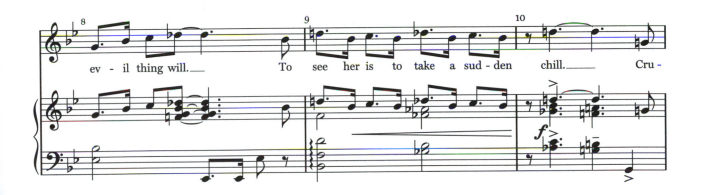

B. Form: Complete the form chart for the entire song. Count along with a recording (starting after the introduction) to determine the measure numbers, formal divisions, and cadences.

MEASURES	FORMAL DIVISION	CADENCE TYPE (OR INDICATE NO CADENCE)
1-4	introduction	authentic cadence in B♭, mm. 3-4

What is the overall form of this song? (circle one)

through-composed   verse-refrain   quaternary   da capo aria

C. Text painting

Give three specific examples of text painting, as requested here. For each, include the measure numbers and a description of how that example represents text painting.

TYPE OF TEXT PAINTING	MEASURE(S)	DESCRIPTION
harmonic quality or chord choice		
the melodic line		
one other example of text painting		

D. Blues style elements

Though this song is not based on the twelve-bar blues harmonic progression, it does feature some blues-related style elements. Listen carefully to the melody, and identify blues elements.

II. Writing a blues melody

Taking "Splanky" and "Blues for Norton" as your models, write three melodic ideas on your own manuscript paper, using a blues scale in the key of your choice. Next to each melodic idea, write at least one variant (for example, change the melodic contour or add, replace, or remove a note). Keep a copy of the one you like best; you may be asked to play it in class and, if you wish, you may use it in Assignment 29.4.

Assignment 29.4

Composition: Twelve-Bar Blues

Compose a blues tune using the twelve-bar blues progression, as shown here and demonstrated in Example 29.6 (MGTA p. 603), transposed to a key other than C. Those familiar with blues or jazz blues style may choose to use a more elaborate version of this progression; students working with the blues progression for the first time are encouraged to keep it simple, as shown here. Chords in parentheses are optional; the chord prior to them can continue through those measures. The progression should be in common time (**C**) as shown.

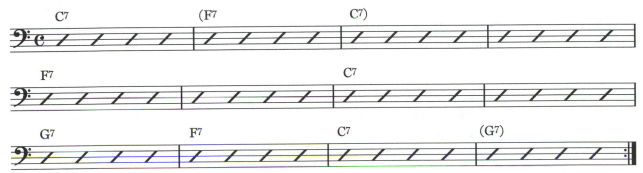

Provide a melodic line for two complete cycles through the twelve-bar progression:

(1) write a blues melody for a solo instrument (or for call-and-response between two instruments) to be played over one cycle through the progression, and

(2) write a different blues melody to be sung, along with your own lyrics, for a second cycle through the progression.

This means your entire composition will be 24 measures long: 12 measures of instrumental melody and 12 measures of vocal melody. In your performance, either the sung melody or the instrumental melody can be played first, followed by the other setting.

Notate your score on your own manuscript paper using two staves: a staff with the melody (instrumental, then voice, or vice versa) aligned above a staff with the accompaniment part (keyboard, guitar, or small combo) in slash notation as shown. Be sure to include the lyrics for the vocal melody. If you are writing your instrumental one for call-and-response between two instruments you can use two staves for the melodic instruments in addition to the one for the keyboard, for a total of four staves.

This type of composition is intended for performance by a jazz or blues combo: accompaniment part, one or two melodic instruments (trumpet, saxophone, flute, or trombone are typical, but don't consider that a limitation), and voice. Practice your song and solo for performance in class, and/or get a friend (or two) to help you perform it. If available in your class, the performance may also include a bass player or percussionist (those parts are normally improvised; you will not notate them).

Getting started

(1) Your composition should model blues style. The style is conveyed through the conflict between the major-key chords in the accompaniment, the minor-inflected melody, characteristic rhythmic patterns including swung rhythms (notated as straight eighth notes, but played swung), melodic motives, lyrics, and other features. Closely observe the compositions you are modeling to create your own composition in that style.

Here are some models to emulate for a blues composition:

"Rock Around the Clock"   "Blues for Norton"
"Hound Dog"   "Splanky"
"Blues in the Night"   "Harlem Nocturne"
"Blue Monk"
"Mustang Sally" (twenty-four bars—each measure of the progression repeated)

(2) Begin by transposing the harmonic progression given to a key than C major, using a major key signature with one to three flats or sharps, and set up the measures for the accompaniment part in common time, using four slashes per measure. If you wish, make this progression more elaborate by modeling a specific blues composition. Write out the harmonic progression twice, to make 24 measures.

(3) Write out the blues "scale" in the key you have chosen, following Example 29.7 (MGTA p. 603) to serve as a collection of notes from which to improvise melodic ideas.

(4) A suggested way to start composing your melodies is by playing the chords of the progression and improvising above the chords. You may use chord tones, but also connect between chord tones using notes of the blues scale. The instrumental solo melodies often feature short motives, as shown in Example 29.6 (MGTA p. 603), that are expanded or elaborated over the course of the solo, and you may choose to feature call-and-response between two instrumental soloists. Choose interesting rhythms, especially for the instrumental melody; it is possible to create a stylistic blues melody using mostly rhythmic motives without a lot of pitch elaboration. Write down your best melodic ideas and work with those to create your melodies.

(5) For the vocal melody, you will need to write lyrics.

Strategies for creating lyrics:

- Keep the language simple and direct.

- Most popular songs are about love—finding love, being in love, losing a love; blues lyrics tend to be about love gone wrong in some way, but are not usually sad overall (singing the blues helps put a better perspective on the problem, perhaps). Blues lyrics may engage other topics, too, including hard times, poor employment, or anything else worth complaining about.

- Blues lyrics often have double meanings or implied subtexts—for example, the "hound dog" in Big Mama Thornton's performance of "Hound Dog" is two-legged (a man), not four-legged.

- Try this model for the lyrics: subphrases 1 and 2 state a "problem" and subphrase 3 reveals a consequence of the problem.

- You can also think of the blues lyrics as a kind of call and response, with a conclusion.

Subphrase 1 (call)	I	I	I	I
Subphrase 2 (response)	IV	IV	I	I
Subphrase 3 (conclusion)	V	IV	I	I (or V7)

The lyrics to W. C. Handy's "St. Louis Blues" are a good example:

I hate to see that evening sun go down,	call
I hate to see that evening sun go down,	response
'Cause, my baby, he's gone left this town.	conclusion
Feelin' tomorrow like I feel today,	call
If I'm feelin' tomorrow like I feel today,	response
I'll pack my truck and make my get away.	conclusion

Assignment 29.5

Song analysis

Listen to each song online or by download, then fill in the form chart and answer the questions that follow. Both of these songs from the 1960s draw on earlier forms—quaternary song form or twelve-bar blues.

Include the section name (intro, verse 1, verse 2, chorus, bridge, instrumental break, outro), the start of the text, and the number of measures in the section (conduct along in $\frac{4}{4}$ and count them). If there is a refrain at the end of a verse, indicate its text and location. For any instrumental breaks, write "no text" and what section the break is based on (if identifiable).

A. John Lennon and Paul McCartney, "Can't Buy Me Love"

SECTION NAME	START OF TEXT	NUMBER OF MEASURES
intro (based on refrain)	Can't buy me . . .	6 (plus anacrusis)
verse 1		

(1) Listen for the harmonic changes and number of measures in each verse. What term best describes the harmonic structure of the verse?

(2) If there is an instrumental section, does its musical material come from elsewhere in the song? If so, where?

B. Lennon and McCartney, "Eight Days a Week"

Complete a form chart for this song, counting measures and writing the appropriate formal designation and beginning lyrics in the space provided.

SECTION NAME	START OF TEXT	NUMBER OF MEASURES
intro	(no text)	4
verse 1	Ooh I need your . . .	16

(1) For the first verse, identify the phrases with letters and arcs, and indicate the number of measures for each.

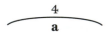

(2) On what form is the verse based?

(3) How is the bridge similar to and different from the verses? (This question refers to the more contemporary meaning of "bridge," which follows the first two verses.)

Assignment 29.6

Song analysis

Listen to each song online, then fill in the form chart. Include the section name (intro, verse 1, verse 2, chorus, bridge, prechorus, postchorus, instrumental verse, outro), the start of the first line of text, and the number of measures in the section (conduct along in $\frac{4}{4}$ and count them). If there is a refrain at the end of a verse, indicate its text and location. For any instrumental breaks, write "no text" and what section the break is based on (if identifiable).

A. Pharrell Williams, "Happy" from *Despicable Me 2*

(1) Counting the measures in this song might be a tricky because of the syncopation in the vocal part. Start counting the verse measures when the voice enters. There is a four-measure harmonic loop under the verse, but there is a stop-time (pause in the accompaniment) measure under the vocal entry, so that the first complete loop begins in the measure with the word "Sunshine"—listening for the loop will help you count. Use the following questions to help you complete the column on "accompanying parts."

SECTION NAME	START OF TEXT	NUMBER OF MEASURES	ACCOMPANYING PARTS
intro	(no text)	1	keyboard
verse 1	It might seem crazy . . .	16 (4+4+4+4)	keyboard, drums
chorus	Because I'm . . .	16 (4+4+4+4)	keyboard, drums, hand claps, backing vocals

(2) Listen again to the verse and chorus sections, and compare the vocal part in these sections. Which has the most continuity in the vocal line and which has more rests between sung lines? Which has more rhythmic repetition? Which has more melodic variety and which stays more on the same few pitches? How does the vocal line (and text) in the bridge differ from both of them?

(3) Now listen to the rhythm section and harmonies. The four-measure harmonic loop under the verse has a sustained chord for two measures then four syncopated chords in the remaining two. How does the harmonic rhythm change in the chorus? How are the sections differentiated by the parts other than the lead vocal?

B. Green Day (Billie Joe Armstrong, Mike Dirnt, and Tré Cool), "Wake Me Up When September Ends"

(1) Identify the sections as before—many are verses—but pay attention to the character of the sections, and consider how the phrases group to help determine whether you hear a bridge or chorus with the verses. If a verse repeats, then repeat that verse number on the chart.

SECTION NAME	START OF TEXT	NUMBER OF MEASURES
intro	(no text)	4
verse 1		

(2) Does a larger section of the form repeat? If so, where?

30 Chromatic Harmony and Voice-Leading

NAME _____

Assignment 30.1

Chromatic sequences

Write an embellished version of each diatonic sequence framework shown. Provide a Roman numeral analysis for each exercise in part A.

A. Descending-fifth sequence with seventh chords, root position

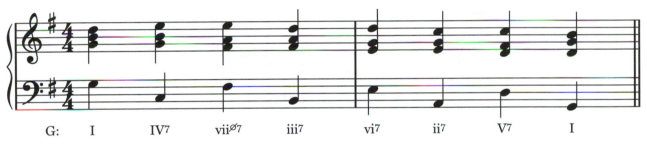

G: I   IV7   vii⌀7   iii7   vi7   ii7   V7   I

(1) With secondary dominants alternating with triads

G: V7/IV   IV

(2) With each chord a secondary dominant. Draw arrows to show leading tones and chordal sevenths both resolving down.

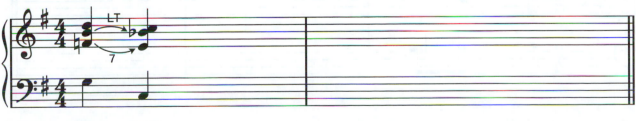

G: V7/C   V7/F

(3) With chromatic passing tones filling in whole steps

G: I   IV7

B. 5-6 ascending sequence

With chromatic passing tones

C. Descending thirds with stepwise bass

With chromatic passing tones

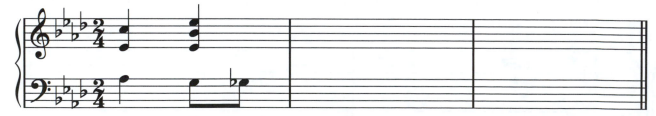

Assignment 30.2

I. Chromatic sequences

Write an embellished version of each diatonic sequence framework provided. Roman numerals are not required.

A. 7-6 descending (parallel sixths)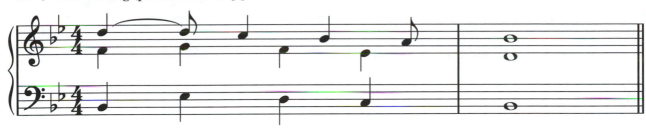

With added chromaticism

B. Descending fifths

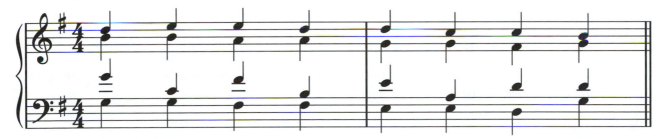

With a descending chromatic bass line

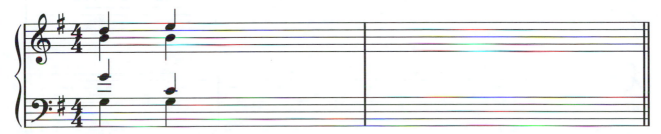

II. Chromatic elaborations of voice exchanges

Write a chromaticized version of each voice-exchange framework. Use durations matching those provided.

A. Fill in the outer-voice exchange with chromatic passing tones (see Example 30.5 in the text).

B. Fill in chromatically with rhythmically staggered chromaticism.

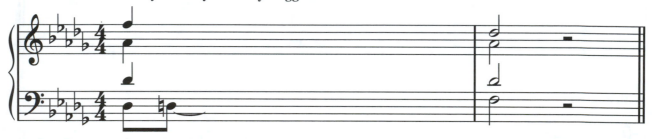

C. Make a harmonized segment of the chromatic scale based on this voice exchange. Use segments of the chromatic scale in the soprano and bass in contrary motion.

III. Writing a chromatic introduction

Write a four-measure chromatic introduction in G major modeled after Joplin's introduction to "Pine Apple Rag" (anthology). Use chromaticism in parallel motion.

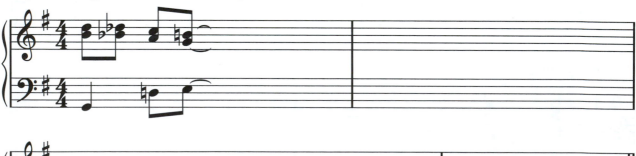

Assignment 30.3

Analysis: Mozart, String Quartet in D Minor, K. 421, mvt. 3 ♫ (anthology)

Begin by listening to this movement while following the score in your anthology.

A. Mm. 1–10 ♫

(1) Examine the first section here. Show how the descending chromatic bass is harmonized by providing Roman numerals and a contextual analysis. Bracket any sequence pattern, and specify the level of transposition within the bracket.

(2) Based on your analysis, explain how this ten-measure phrase is constructed. (Are there internal phrase expansions? Is there a cadential extension?)

B. Mm. 11–22

Examine the beginning of the **B** section given here. Now the descending chromatic line appears in an upper voice. Provide a Roman numeral analysis (except for mm. 14–18); bracket any sequence pattern, and specify the interval of transposition.

a: vii°7

(1) What harmony is prolonged throughout measures 14–19? _____

    How is it prolonged? _____

(2) The upper strings in measures 15–18 are sequential. Mark the pattern and transposition on the score, and write the interval of transposition below.

(3) For class discussion: What constitutes the "harmonic disturbance" that is expected in this passage's position in the binary form (beginning of the **B** section)?

Assignment 30.4

Analysis: Handel, Chaconne in G Major (anthology)

Each of the following passages is taken from an analogous location in different minor-mode variations of the Handel Chaconne. Provide a Roman numeral analysis for each, and consider how Handel varies the basic idea (presented in Variation 9) by introducing chromaticism in subsequent variations.

A. Variation 9, mm. 77–80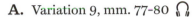

g: i⁶

B. Variation 10, mm. 85–88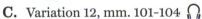

(1) What new chromatic elements are introduced in Variation 10?

(2) What other aspect adds to the intensification of this passage as compared with Variation 9?

C. Variation 12, mm. 101–104

The chord in measure 102, beat 1, is _____ . This chord would normally progress to _____ . What happens here? Explain. (Hint: Write in the contextual analysis.)

D. Variation 14, mm. 117-120

Measures 118 to 119, beat 2, prolong what function in the phrase? _____
Explain.

E. Variation 16, mm. 129-136

You examined mm. 129-132 in the chapter; what happens next? Provide a Roman numeral analysis below the score for mm. 132-136, and answer the questions that follow.

(1) The sequence type in measures 132-134 is _____.

(2) This sequence connects to the previous one by _____.

(3) How does this sequence connect to the cadence?

Assignment 30.5

I. Other chromatic embellishments

Decorate each of the following chords or progressions with the requested embellishment.

A. Common-tone diminished seventh chords (see Example 30.10b and c)

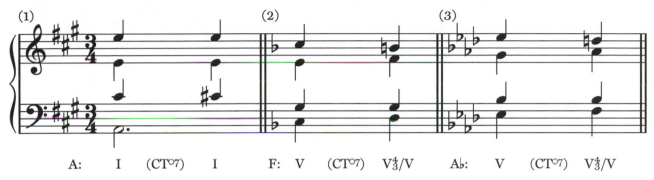

B. Common-tone augmented-sixth chords (see Example 30.12). (Hint: Remember to double the fifth in the tonic triad.)

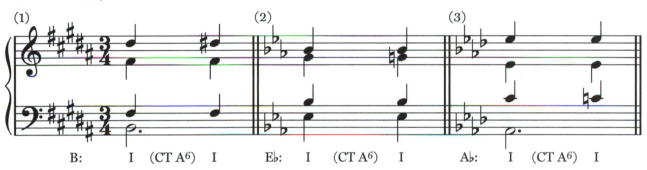

C. Common-tone diminished seventh and augmented-sixth chords. Write an appropriate embellishing chord between the given chords.

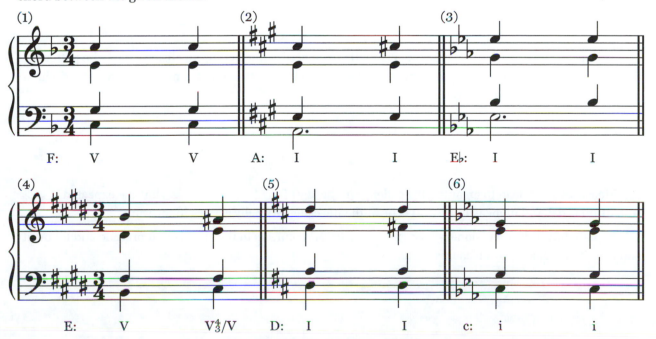

II. Analysis

A. Schubert, Moment Musical No. 6 in A♭ Major, Op. 94, mm. 32-36 🎧

(1) Provide Roman numerals for this short excerpt.

E: V7

(2) What harmonic device creates the chord quality in measure 34?   In measure 35?

B. Beethoven, Piano Sonata in E♭ Major, Op. 7, mvt. 2, mm. 15-24 🎧

Listen to this passage, then provide Roman numerals for measures 15-16 and 19-24 (with anacrusis to m. 19).

(1) Measures 16-18 include two types of chromatic sequences connected by an elision. Mark the patterns of the sequence with brackets, then identify the transposition level between patterns and the type for each. Be prepared to discuss the sequences in class.

(2) Measures 18-19 lead to an authentic cadence in the key of _____, but the expected resolution is delayed in measures 20-21. The authentic cadence finally arrives in measures _____.

(3) Explain how this "diversionary passage" (mm. 20-21) connects to the chords that precede and follow it and how it is prepared by measures 16-18.

Assignment 30.6

Analysis: Beethoven, Piano Sonata in E♭ Major, Op. 7, mvt. 2

Write a Roman numeral analysis under these excerpts; circle and label embellishing tones. Then complete the statements or questions that follow.

A. Mm. 1–14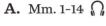

C: I

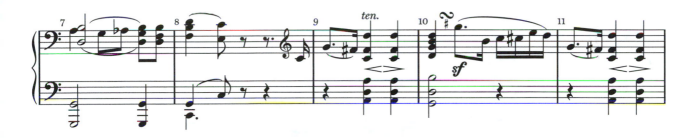

(1) The first phrase ends in measure _____ with a(n) _____ cadence, embellished by _____ .

(2) Measures 9–14 tonicize the _____ .

(3) Describe the quality and function of the chord in measure 13, beat 3.

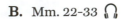

(1) In the key of C major, the Roman numeral for the chord in measure 25 is _____. How are the chromatic pitches of this chord introduced in measure 24?

(2) The chord is tonicized in measure 26. How are the pitches of this new key prepared in the chromaticization of measures 1-14?

(3) The cadence in measures 27-28 is a(n) _____ cadence in the key of _____. This key is a _____ in relation to C major.

31 Chromatic Modulation

NAME _____

Assignment 31.1

Analysis of chromatic modulations: Schumann, "Widmung"

Listen to the entire song while following the score in the anthology before analyzing these two passages. The song is in **A B A′** form, with the middle section in a contrasting key. The following excerpts show the modulation into and out of that contrasting key area.

A. Mm. 10–17

Provide a Roman numeral and contextual analysis for measures 11–17, then answer the questions that follow.

Translation: [O you, my] grave, into which I eternally pour my sorrow! You are rest, you are peace.

(1) The harmony tonicized in measure 11 is _____ (Roman numeral) in the key of A♭ major.

(2) The cadence in measures 12-13 is a (circle one)   PAC   IAC   HC   DC   in the key of A♭ major.

(3) The bass line in measures 14-17 is a (circle one)   tonic pedal   dominant pedal.

(4) The key established in measures 14-17 is _____.

(5) This key may be enharmonically respelled as _____.

(6) Compared with the main key of the song (A), that key is (circle any that apply):

   major   minor   relative   chromatic   mediant   submediant   dominant   tonic

(7) What type of modulation is this? _____

(8) The chord on beat 3 in measure 16 includes elements of two different harmonies. Explain.

B. Mm. 25-30

Provide a Roman numeral analysis for measures 25-29, then answer the questions that follow.

Translation: You lift me lovingly above myself, my good spirit, my better self!

(1) The chord in measure 25 is _____ (fill in Roman numeral) in E major.

(2) The interval in the bass from measure 25 to 26 is a _____.

(3) The bass line in 26-29 is a (circle one)   tonic pedal   dominant pedal.

(4) The cadence in measure 29 is a   PAC   IAC   HC   DC   in the key of _____.

(5) What type of modulation is used in this passage? _____

Assignment 31.2

I. Common-tone or pivot-tone modulations

Given a tonic triad in D major, how many keys can be reached by using D, F♯, or A as a pivot tone? Write each chord as indicated. For some, there are two possibilities (e.g., D as the 3rd). Under the chord, indicate (1) the key for which it would be the tonic and (2) the Roman numeral relationship to D major (e.g., B♭ major would be ♭VI). For the last chord, the seventh of a V7, indicate to which key the V7 would resolve.

A. Keep D as a common tone.

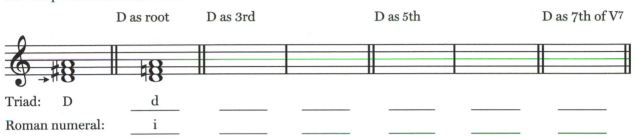

Triad: D   d ____ ____ ____ ____ ____ ____

Roman numeral: i ____ ____ ____ ____ ____ ____

B.

(1) Keep F♯ as a common tone.

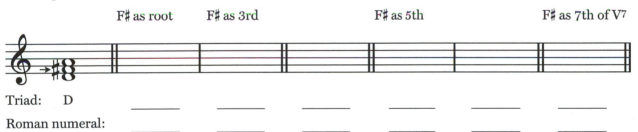

Triad: D ____ ____ ____ ____ ____ ____

Roman numeral: ____ ____ ____ ____ ____ ____

(2) Since F♯ may also be spelled G♭, now spell each chord enharmonically. Roman numerals are not required.

Triad: ____ ____ ____ ____ ____ ____

C. Keep A as a common tone.

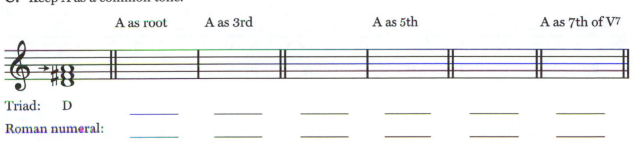

Triad: D ____ ____ ____ ____ ____ ____

Roman numeral: ____ ____ ____ ____ ____ ____

II. Part-writing common-tone modulations

On the following staves, write a melody for a solo instrument of your choice and a keyboard accompaniment.

(1) Begin by deciding whether you need a treble, bass, or alto clef for your solo instrument, and fill in the clefs and key signatures.

(2) Sketch in the bass line and chords, using half notes, whole notes, and dotted whole notes, as indicated by the Roman numerals, in SATB voicing. Be sure to check the doubling, spelling, and voice-leading of the chords.

(3) Now sketch in a melodic framework for the instrumental melody that makes a good counterpoint with the bass, using chord tones. End the first phrase on $\hat{1}$ and begin the melody of the second phrase with the same pitch, which is now $\hat{3}$; this is the common tone. It is stylistic for your melody to double elements of the accompaniment voice-leading.

(4) Embellish your melodic framework with passing tones, neighbor tones, and chordal skips.

Optional: Keeping the bass line simple, write an accompaniment pattern using the voice-leading you have sketched out for the soprano, alto, and tenor parts.

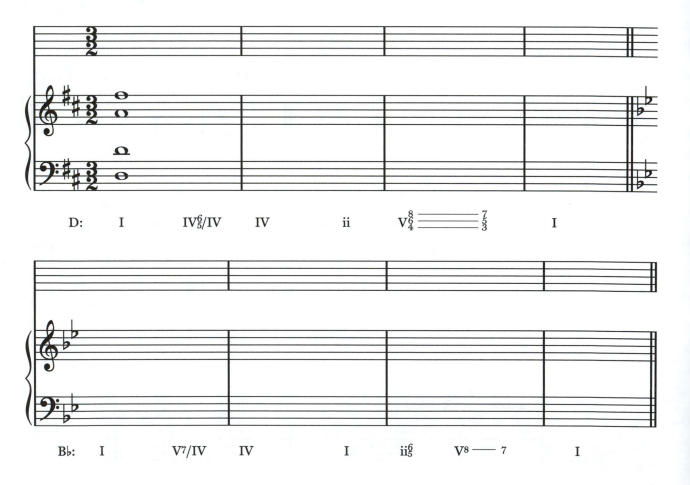

Part III Chromatic Harmony and Form

Assignment 31.3

I. Modulation by enharmonic respelling

A. Using fully diminished seventh chords

Resolve each given diminished seventh chord in (1). Then invert the chord and respell it enharmonically in (2)–(4) so that each note is the root. Resolve each vii°7 chord to its tonic, based on the given Roman numeral (i or I). In the blanks provided, indicate the key of the tonic to which each chord resolves.

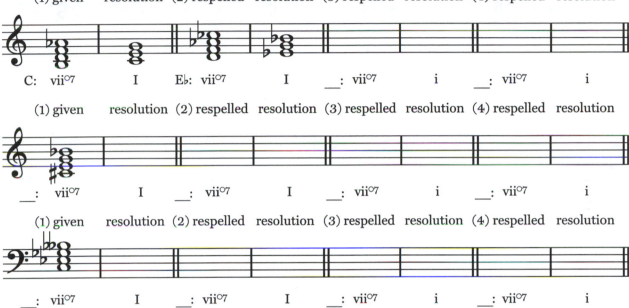

B. Respelling dominant seventh chords and the Gr6

First write the requested chord and resolve it normally. Then respell the chord enharmonically, and resolve it; write a Roman numeral under each chord of resolution. Avoid parallel fifths in resolving the Gr6. Finally, fill in the key name to which the respelled chord resolves. Use half notes and whole notes.

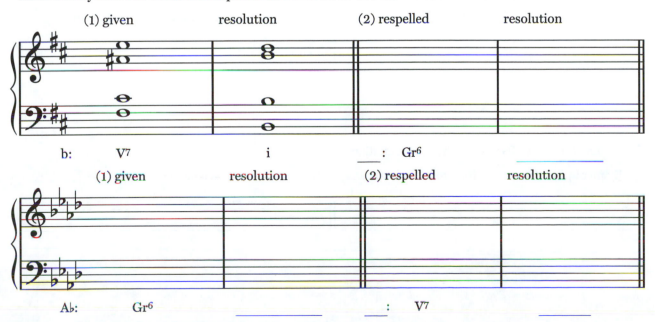

II. Chromatic modulation

For each pair of key areas in A–D, indicate how you would modulate from one to the other, using the two methods specified (no need to provide voice-leading). Write out the chords on the staff, using accidentals rather than key signatures, and provide Roman numerals in each key. Assume that the first key is well established, and that the second key can continue from where the progression leaves off. For example, from F♯ major to C major:

(1) By mixture pivot chord   (2) By enharmonic respelling of vii°7 chord

A. From D major to A♭ minor (tritone relation, plus change of mode)

(1) By mixture pivot chord   (2) By sequence of secondary V7 plus mixture

D:

B. From E major to F major (up a half step)

(1) By enharmonic spelling of a Gr6 to V7   (2) By pivot pitch (common-tone modulation)

C. From C major to B minor (down a half step)

(1) By enharmonic spelling of V7 to Gr6   (2) By pivot pitch (common-tone modulation)

D. From G major to B♭ major (chromatic mediant)

(1) By pivot pitch (common-tone modulation)   (2) By sequence of secondary dominants

Assignment 31.4

Analysis: Beethoven, Waldstein Sonata, mvt. 1, mm. 73–90 🎧

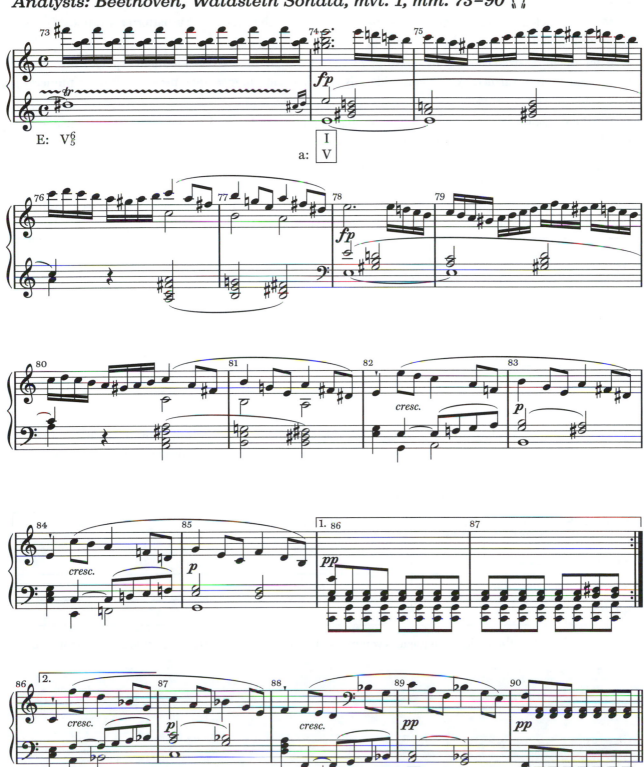

E: V$_5^6$

a: I   V

This modulatory passage is shown with first and second endings. The first ending connects E major to the tonic key of the movement, C major, for the repeat. The second ending moves through C to F to begin the next large section. Both passages make use of a recurring melodic sequence that coincides with the key changes.

A. Mm. 73-87 (first ending) ∩

(1) Mark the melodic sequence patterns in measures 80-86 with brackets. This pattern also appears once earlier in the passage; mark it there as well.

(2) After an emphasized cadence in measures 73-74 in E major, this passage modulates quickly through several keys, each confirmed by a cadence; identify each key and cadence, then provide a Roman numeral analysis for measures 73-86.

(3) For the measures specified in the following chart, identify the key and cadence type. If the passage modulates, specify in the following chart the pivot-chord type; if not, write "none."

MEASURES	KEY/ MODE	CADENCE TYPE	METHOD OF KEY CHANGE
into 74	E major	IAC	Pivot chord (E: I = a: V) or direct modulation by secondary dominant (E: I becomes V7/IV, resolving to iv)
74–76			
76–78			
78–80			
80–82			
82–84			
84–86			

B. Mm. 73-90 (second ending) ∩

(1) Analyze the passage beginning in measure 84; skip over the first ending and examine the harmonies of the second ending. Mark the melodic sequence patterns with brackets, and provide a Roman numeral analysis.

(2) Complete the chart to summarize your analysis of measures 84-90.

MEASURES	KEY/ MODE	CADENCE TYPE	METHOD OF KEY CHANGE
84–86	C major	PAC	
86–88			
88–90			

(3) Now look back at the melodic sequences you marked in both passages. Are the harmonies sequential also?

Assignment 31.5

Analysis of chromatic modulations: Brahms, Neue Liebeslieder, Op. 65, No. 6

A. Provide a Roman numeral analysis in the blanks; the harmonic rhythm (number of chords per measure) is indicated by the number of blanks. Some chord analysis is provided. Then answer the questions that follow.

Translation: Mother pinned roses on me because I am so sad. She is right, the roses wilt as I do, losing their petals.

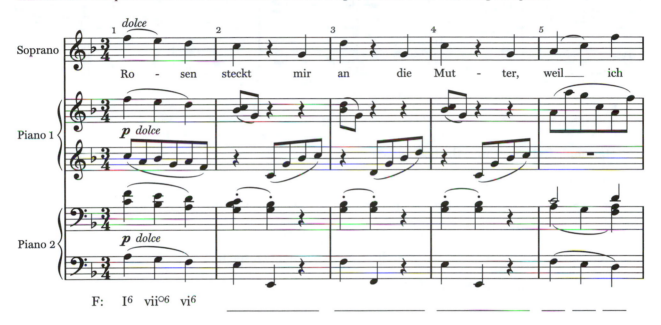

Soprano: Ro - sen steckt mir an die Mut - ter, weil___ ich

Piano 1, *p dolce*

Piano 2, *p dolce*

F: I⁶   vii°⁶   vi⁶   _____   _____

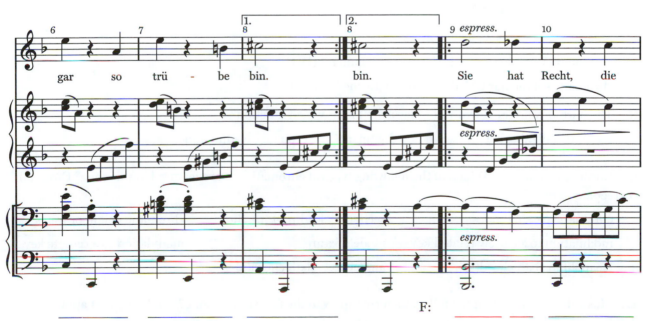

gar   so   trü - be   bin.   bin.   Sie   hat   Recht,   die

9 espress.

espress.

espress.

F:

_____   _____   _____   _____   _____

F: ___ ___ V^9_7 ___ ___ ___ ___ ___ ___ ___ ___ ___ ___

B. Harmonic features: Circle the best answer.

(1) The harmony in measure 3 has which function?

passing   neighboring   secondary dominant   secondary leading tone

(2) The modulation in measure 6 is effected by which method?

pivot note   mode mixture   pivot dyad   enharmonic respelling

(3) The cadence in measure 8 tonicizes the

dominant (V)   supertonic (ii)   subdominant (IV)

chromatic submediant (♭VI)   chromatic mediant (III)

(4) Measure 13 features which harmony?

dominant (V)   supertonic (ii)   subdominant (IV)

chromatic submediant (♭VI)   chromatic mediant (III)

(5) The harmony on the downbeat of measure 14 has which function?

tonic   neighboring   secondary dominant   secondary leading tone

C. Chromatic practices: Which of the following types of chromaticism are featured in this song? Circle all correct answers.

chromatic passing tones   secondary leading-tone chords   chromatic neighbor tones

modulation to a closely related key   mode mixture   modulation to a remote key

Neapolitan sixth chord(s)   augmented-sixth chord(s)

D. Musical form: Which of the following terms apply to the form of this song? Circle any that apply.

ternary   binary   simple   rounded   composite   continuous   sectional

Assignment 31.6

Analysis: Chopin, Mazurka in F Minor, Op. 68, No. 4 🎧 (anthology)

Listen to this piece and determine where new key areas are tonicized; mark them on the score.

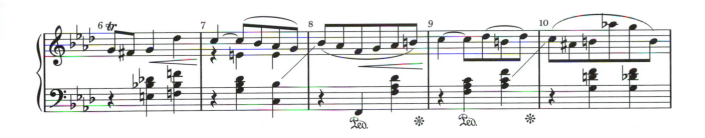

A. Mm. 1-8

Circle and label the embellishing tones of the melody on the score, then examine the harmonies. Where might Roman numerals apply? What else is organizing this passage?

Assignment 31.6 *(continued)*

B. Mm. 9-15

(1) What is the relationship of these measures to the music analyzed in measures 1-8? What is similar? What is changed? Start by comparing the right-hand melodic lines of the two phrases. Circle and label the melodic ornamentations in the melody in measures 9-15.

(2) Examine the harmonies in measures 14-15. What is different about the cadence here as compared with measures 7-8? What type of chromatic modulation technique is used? What is the relationship of the goal of the modulation to the original key?

C. Mm. 15-23

(1) Circle and label the embellishing tones for measures 15-19 in the score, examining the harmonic context carefully, then write in Roman numerals.

The A2 in the left hand is a _____ .

Compared with the previous measures, how chromatic are the harmonic progressions?

(2) Measures 19-23 tonicize several keys in succession; mark keys and Roman numerals for this passage. (Hint: comparing the melodic line of measures 19-20 with 21-22 may help.)

The harmony tonicized in measures 19-20 is _____ .

The key established in measures 20-23 is _____ .

Compared with the main key of the mazurka, the key in measures 20-23 is (circle any that apply):

    major   minor   relative   chromatic   mediant   submediant   dominant   tonic

D. Mm. 24-32

Provide Roman numerals for measures 24-32 and then answer the following questions.

The harmony tonicized in measures 24-25 is _____.

The key established in measures 25-32 is _____.

Compared with the main key of the mazurka, the key in measures 25-32 is (circle any that apply):

major   minor   relative   chromatic   mediant   submediant   dominant   tonic

E. Mm. 32-40

This passage is based on a series of chromatic sequences. Identify the sequence patterns and interval of transposition. You need not provide Roman numerals.

(1) What type of sequence is found in measures 32-36? _____

(2) Examine measures 37-39, and listen carefully. What is the sequence pattern here? Mark it on the score with a bracket, and indicate the level of transposition. How are the chords within the pattern organized?

(3) Find several beats in these measures in which there are two different chromatic notes with the same letter name (for example, E♭ and E♯ on beat 2 in measure 38). Explain the functional meaning of each note.

(4) What is the meaning of "dal segno senza fine"? How might you perform the Mazurka to create an effective ending?

32 Sonata, Sonatina, and Concerto

NAME _____

Assignment 32.1

Form Analysis: Beethoven, Sonata Op. 2, No. 1, mvt. 1 🎧

Listen to this movement in its entirety while following your anthology score. Think about the overall formal organization, and mark where you hear sections beginning or ending. Label any themes or motives that return later in the movement, and indicate with measure numbers where you first heard them. For this analysis, you don't have to label every chord, but do examine the harmony for cadences, sequences, and key changes. Answer questions under parts A–D, then consider the additional questions in part E for class discussion.

A. First theme and transition

(1) The first theme spans measures 1 to _____; it is in the key of _____ (circle one)

      major   minor

(2) The first theme's phrase form is a (circle one)

      contrasting period   parallel period   phrase group   sentence

(3) The transition between the first and second themes first tonicizes the (circle one)

      relative major   minor dominant   subdominant   submediant

     Then it moves to the second key area, which is the (circle one)

      relative major   minor dominant   subdominant   submediant

(4) This transition is a(n) (circle one)   independent transition   dependent transition

B. Second theme and closing theme

(1) The second theme group (part 1) begins with the change in accompaniment pattern in measure _____.

(2) In relation to the key of the second theme group, the pedal in measures 20–25 is a (circle one)

      tonic pedal   dominant pedal

(3) The second key area of the exposition overall is _____ major, but the second theme, part 1, features mode mixture, especially the modal scale degree (circle one)

      $\flat\hat{2}$ $\flat\hat{3}$ $\flat\hat{6}$ $\flat\hat{7}$

(4) The second subsection of the second theme group (second theme, part 2) begins in measure _____, signaled by a change in texture in the left-hand part and regular four-bar phrases.

(5) After a definitive PAC in measures _____, the closing theme begins in measure _____ and extends to measure _____.

C. Development and retransition

(1) The development begins in measure _____ , with material from the (circle one)

first theme   transition   second theme, part 1   second theme, part 2   closing theme

(2) The first key area touched upon in the development is _____ (circle one)   major   minor

Compared to the initial key of the movement, this is (Roman numeral) _____ .

(3) Measures 55-73 develop materials from the (circle one)

first theme   second theme, part 1   second theme, part 2   closing theme

(4) The retransition begins in measure _____ with the entry of a dominant pedal.

D. Recapitulation

(1) The recapitulation begins with the return of the first theme in measure _____ .

(2) Compared to the exposition, there is a change in the transition between the first and second theme in measures _____ to _____ .

(3) The second theme group (part 1) returns in measure _____ in the key of _____ (circle one)   major   minor

(4) The closing theme returns in measure _____ , and there is a cadential extension in measures _____ to _____ .

E. For class discussion

(1) How does the modal degree in the second theme prepare for the return of this theme in the recapitulation?

(2) What is the function of measures 26-32 within the second theme area? Consider the rhythmic and harmonic character of these measures to answer this question.

(3) What characteristics separate the second theme group, part 2, from the closing theme? Discuss, citing measure numbers.

(4) Consider the development and retransition in more detail, and identify as many motives from the exposition as you can, citing measure numbers.

(5) Compare the exposition and recapitulation and identify specific changes between them, citing measure numbers.

Assignment 32.2

Form analysis: Mozart, Piano Sonata in C Major, K. 545, mvt. 1 🎧

Listen to this movement in its entirety while following your anthology score. Think about the overall formal organization, and mark where you hear sections beginning or ending. Label any themes or motives that return later in the movement, and indicate with measure numbers where you first heard them. For this analysis, you don't have to label every chord, but do examine the harmony for cadences, sequences, and key changes. Answer questions under parts A–D, then consider the additional questions in part E for class discussion.

A. First theme and transition

(1) The first theme spans measure 1 to _____ ; this theme is in the key of _____ (circle one)

      major   minor

(2) The first theme's phrase form is a (circle one)

      single phrase   contrasting period   parallel period   sentence structure

(3) The transition between the first and second themes features which compositional technique? (circle one)

      pedal point   melodic sequence   harmonic sequence   augmentation

(4) This transition is a(n) (circle one)   independent transition   dependent transition. Explain.

(5) The accidental indicating the change of key in the transition first appears in measure _____ .

(6) The medial caesura is in measure _____ .

B. Second theme and closing theme

(1) The second theme group begins in measure _____ , after a lead-in.

(2) The second key area of the exposition is _____ (circle one)   major   minor

(3) The closing theme begins in measure _____ .

(4) Between the second and closing themes there is a transition in measures _____ to _____ featuring a sequence. This sequence is best described as

_____

(5) After a definitive PAC in measures _____ , the codetta begins in measure _____ and extends to measure _____ .

C. Development

(1) The development begins in measure _____ , with material from the (circle one)

      first theme   transition   second theme   closing theme   codetta

(2) The first key area touched upon in the development is _____ (circle one)   major   minor.
Compared to the initial key of the movement, this is (Roman numeral) _____ .

(3) Measures 33–35 tonicize _____ (circle one)   major   minor
and develop materials from the (circle one)

     first theme   second theme   closing theme   codetta

(4) There is a long and prominent sequence in measures _____ to _____ . The sequence type is
best described as _____

D. Retransition and recapitulation

(1) There is a very brief retransition in measure _____ , setting up the recapitulation and the
return of the first theme in measure _____ . This theme begins in the unexpected
key of _____ (circle one)   major   minor
Compared to the main key of the movement, this is (Roman numeral) _____ .

(2) In the recapitulation, the transition between the first and second themes is measures _____ to
_____ . Are there changes in the transition in comparison to the exposition? If so, where?

(3) The second theme group returns in measure _____ in the
key of _____ (circle one)   major   minor

(4) The closing theme returns in measure _____ , the codetta theme in measure _____ , and the
movement ends in measure _____ .

E. For class discussion

(1) Consider the phrase form of the theme. What is unusual about it?

(2) In the recapitulation, what does the presence of the unusual key for the first theme change about the
task of the transition between the first and second themes?

(3) Choose one motive that is important in this piece, and briefly describe it. Explain where the motive
appears and how it is developed.

Assignment 32.3

Form analysis: Mozart, String Quartet in D Minor, K. 421, mvt. 1

I. Exposition (mm. 1–41) 🎧

A. Listen to these measures, and locate the first theme, transition, second theme group, closing theme, and codetta. (Hint: Look for a strong cadence in the new key for the beginning of the second theme group.)

- Within each theme, label the phrase structure and cadences.
- Complete the following chart: the questions in part B will help you locate the formal elements.
- Use the optional Comments column to record anything else of interest you notice, such as where a key is tonicized, or what is varied (other than the cadence type) in a phrase that receives a prime (′).

THEME/ SECTION	PHRASES	MEASURES	KEY/MODE	CADENCES	COMMENTS
first theme		1–8	D minor		
	a	1–4	D minor	IAC	

B. Answer the following in a few sentences, or be prepared to answer in class.

(1) The first theme is divided in half after measure 4. How do the first and second halves differ from each other? Consider the melody, bass line, and harmonies.

(2) This movement is in D minor—what is the expected second key area? Where does the modulation occur? Is there another tonicization in the transition to the second key?

(3) In what ways, other than key and mode, do the first and second themes contrast? What is the character of each? How would you perform these themes to bring out their emotional content?

(4) Is the material beginning at measure 35 better labeled a codetta or a closing theme? Defend your choice.

II. Recapitulation (mm. 70–117) 🎧

A. Listen to the whole movement, paying particular attention to measures 1–41 and 70–117.

- Begin by locating the recapitulation, then identify the first theme, transition, second theme, and closing theme or codetta by comparing this passage with measures 1–41.
- Complete the following chart, listing the location of each element. The questions in part B will help you locate the formal elements.
- Use the optional Comments column to include information comparing the phrase here to the comparable one in the exposition.

THEME/ SECTION	PHRASES	MEASURES	KEY/MODE	CADENCES	COMMENTS
first theme		70–77	D minor		
	a	70–73	D minor	IAC	identical to mm. 1–4

Assignment 32.3 *(continued)*

THEME/ SECTION	PHRASES	MEASURES	KEY/MODE	CADENCES	COMMENTS

B. Answer the following in a few sentences, or be prepared to answer in class.

(1) Is the entire recapitulation in the tonic key (D minor)? If so, how is the transition between the first and second themes altered to stay in D minor?

(2) What is unusual about the location of the second theme here as compared with the exposition? What is added here, and how is the shifted location compensated for later in the recapitulation? What does the location of this entry reveal about metrical practices in the Classical era?

(3) In this movement, the second large section is meant to be repeated. How is the end of the recapitulation designed to facilitate the repetition? And how does the movement end?

III. Development (mm. 42-70) 🎧

A. Listen to this movement again in its entirety, now focusing on the development (mm. 42-70). Locate any appearances of musical motives from the first theme, transition, second theme group, closing theme, or codetta.

MEASURES	KEY/MODE	WHAT IS DEVELOPED/COMMENTS
42-58		

B. Answer these questions, or be prepared for discussion in class.

(1) In which key does the development begin? What material is developed there?

(2) Which three motives are developed the most in this section? Identify the origin of each, giving measure numbers.

(3) Where does the retransition begin? What element identifies it as a retransition? What motive appears here?

(4) Considering the movement as a whole, give measure numbers for one passage with each of the following typical string quartet textures.

    (a) One instrument plays a solo part while the others accompany: mm. _____

    (b) Violin 1 and 2 play a duet, while the others accompany: mm. _____

    (c) A motive is passed through the quartet, with each instrument playing it in turn:

        mm. _____

IV. Large essay (optional)

Write an analytical paper of three to four pages that synthesizes your answers in this assignment. Use musical examples, charts, or diagrams to illustrate your analysis. Conclude with a discussion of how this analysis might assist a quartet in shaping their interpretation. Include at least two specific examples (with measure numbers) to support your points.

Assignment 32.4

Analysis: Clementi, Sonatina in C Major, Op. 36, No. 1, mvt. 1 🎧

Listen to this movement while examining the score in your anthology, then provide a complete harmonic analysis with Roman numerals in the score. Since the texture is only two to three voices, you may need to consider some ambiguous chords, determine which pitches are embellishing tones, and draw on your knowledge of progressions to identify them. Label each phrase and cadence.

A. First theme

(1) The first phrase is measures 1 to _____ , and ends with a _____ cadence.

(2) The second phrase is measures _____ to _____ , forming a _____ period with the first phrase.

(3) Write in the Roman numerals and figures for this modulating second phrase.

The cadence at the end of this phrase is a _____ in the key of _____ .

(4) Is there a transition between the first and second themes? If so, indicate which measures; if not, explain how these themes connect, and what takes the place of the transition.

B. Second theme

(1) Write in the Roman numerals and figures for measures 8–15.

(2) How is this passage divided into smaller units? Indicate the length (in measures) for each unit. After the second theme, is there a closing theme or codetta?

C. Development

(1) What themes or motives are explored in the development section? What type of harmonic motion is featured?

(2) Compare measures 16-23 with the Mozart development section reviewed in the chapter, and with the "harmonic disturbance" of rounded binary—which form does this passage most resemble?

D. Recapitulation

(1) What changes when the themes return in the recapitulation? Are the themes all in the tonic key?

(2) How do the changes to the passage between the first and second themes in the recapitulation, when compared with the exposition, confirm that measures 5-8 of the exposition are part of the first theme?

E. Review of overall form

(1) The exposition is measures 1 to _____ .

(2) The development is measures _____ to _____ .

(3) The recapitulation is measures _____ to _____ .

(4) How does this sonatina compare in scope with the Mozart sonata-form movement discussed in the text chapter? What elements are shortened or left out?

Assignment 32.5

Analysis: Mozart, Piano Sonata in F Major, K. 332, mvt. 1 🎧

- Listen to this movement, and begin by identifying the large sections on your anthology score.
- Next, locate the themes, transitions, and key areas in the exposition and recapitulation, and consider the materials used in the development.
- Examine the harmonic progressions in measures 20–40 and 55–67.
- Then use this analytical information to fill in the following blanks.

A. Large sections

(1) The exposition spans measures _____ to _____.

(2) The exposition begins in the key of _____ (circle one)   major   minor

It modulates to _____ (circle one)   major   minor   as the second key area.

(3) The development spans measures _____ to _____.

(4) The recapitulation begin in measure _____.

(5) The coda begins after the PAC in measure _____ and extends to the end of the piece.

B. Exposition

(1) The first theme group spans measures _____ to _____. It has several different melodic ideas, all in the initial key of the movement.

(2) The first PAC of the movement occurs in measure _____. The music from measure 1 to this cadence has two distinct parts. For each, give the measure numbers and a few words that describe the music's style and texture.

Measures _____ to _____ : _____

Measures _____ to _____ : _____

(3) The second PAC of the first theme group occurs in measures _____ to _____, and a cadential extension in measures _____ to _____. Between the first and second PACs are two phrases that form a (circle one)   parallel   contrasting   period

(4) The transition between the first and second theme groups begins in measure _____; it begins with a temporary emphasis on the (circle one)   relative minor   parallel minor   dominant   of the initial key

(5) The fully diminished seventh chord in measure 29 in the transition leads to a tonicization of the (circle one)   minor dominant   dominant minor   subdominant   of the initial key

(6) The medial caesura is in measure _____ with a (circle one)   PAC   HC   DC in the second key area of _____ (circle one)   major   minor

(7) The second theme begins in measure _____. It consists of two phrases. Draw a phrase graph showing the two phrases, indicating the cadence types and the relationship of the phrases to each other (using **a, a′, b**). Then describe the relationship of the phrases.

(8) After the second theme, there is another transitional passage, beginning in measure _____. This transition features (circle one):

      melodic ideas from the first theme group   melodic ideas from the second theme
      a descending-fifth sequence   modulation to a third key area

(9) The closing theme begins in measure _____. It has (circle one)   one   two   three phrases, and ends with a cadential extension, leading to a PAC in measure _____. This cadence marks the beginning of the codetta, which ends the exposition.

C. Development

(1) The first sixteen measures of the development section are surprisingly harmonically stable. They are in the key of _____ (circle one)   major   minor.   Compared to the original tonic key, this is the (circle one)

      relative minor   parallel minor   dominant   subdominant

(2) The melodic ideas in the first part of the development are based on (circle one)
      first theme group   second theme group
      transition between the second and closing themes   codetta

(3) The second part of the development section is sequential, based on musical materials from the (circle one)
      first theme group   second theme group
      transition between the second and closing themes   codetta

(4) The retransition is measures _____ to _____.

D. Recapitulation

(1) The music of the exposition and the recapitulation is identical until measure _____. This first change in musical materials is in the (circle one)
      first theme   transition to the second theme   second theme

(2) Compared to the exposition, the transition to the second theme in the recapitulation is (circle one)
      shorter   the same length   longer

(3) The second theme begins in measure _____ and is presented in the key of _____ (circle one)   major   minor

(4) The closing theme begins in measure _____ and is presented in the key of _____ (circle one)   major   minor

(5) The coda returns in measure _____, and serves as the coda ending the sonata-form movement.

For class discussion

(1) The exposition of this sonata includes some striking changes of texture and mood, which we examined at the beginning of the first theme group. Identify other moments of sudden change of texture by measure number and possible "topic" or style reference (see Chapter 25), and consider how this might impact your performance decisions.

(2) Compare the exposition and the recapitulation. List what is different in the recapitulation as compared to the exposition.

Assignment 32.6

Analyzing a Concerto: Haydn, Concerto for Corno di caccia (Horn), mvt. 1 🎧

Begin by listening to the movement several times while following the score in your anthology.

- Concerto first movements are similar to sonata form, in that they typically have a first theme or first theme group, a transition, a second theme group, and a closing or codetta theme group.

- In Classical-era concertos, some of these are typically repeated by the soloist as a part of a double exposition. The presence of a soloist and the possibility of alternating solo and *tutti* (orchestral) sections provides an added dimension in analyzing a concerto.

- As you are listening, mark in your score the location of themes, transitions, cadences, and other form-identifying features as you would for a sonata-form movement, but also consider where solo and *tutti* passages appear, then use the following questions to refine your analysis.

Note: The horn part is scored for D horn (instead of F horn, which is the most common modern transposition), and is written without accidentals, as if it were in C major. When the horn plays a C, a D sounds; the concert pitch is up a whole step from the notated pitch. Practically speaking, you can look at the first violin part most of the time to help follow what the horn is playing, or think of the scale degree in C, then find that scale degree in D major.

A. Exposition (Part I, orchestra)

(1) Listen to the first 30 measures of the piece (up to the entrance of the solo horn), identify the main key of this work, and locate the cadences in this passage. The key is _____ (circle one)

     major   minor

(2) The first phrase ends in measure _____, beat _____ with a _____ cadence.

(3) Where does the transition between the first and second themes begin? How do you determine that? Is it a dependent or independent transition? Explain.

(4) Is there a medial caesura? If so, where? Explain.

(5) Where does the second theme group begin? What key is it in? Where does it end? (Hint: Listen for a PAC.)

(6) Is there a closing or codetta theme? What type of cadence prepares the entrance of the horn? In which key?

B. Exposition (Part II, with horn)

Now listen to measures 30-60. In a Classical-era concerto with a double exposition, elements of the orchestral exposition are typically repeated, with the melody performed by the soloist and accompanied by the orchestra. Compare these measures to 1-30, noting which aspects are similar and which are different, then answer the following questions.

(1) In which measures does the horn present the first theme and transition? How are these musical materials altered as compared to the orchestra's *tutti* version? What type of cadence ends the transition?

(2) Following the transition considered in question 1, the horn presents new melodic materials in D major (the original tonic key), leading to a cadence in measure 50. What is the cadence type there, and in which key? What happens next, in measures 51-60? (Hint: What would be expected is the orchestral second theme in A major (V), followed by the closing theme that preceded the horn's initial entry.)

C. Development

This movement does not have repeat signs to indicate the end of the exposition or the beginning of the development—since the horn exposition is equivalent to a repeat—but by measure 60, all of the expected exposition elements have been presented (plus a few unexpected ones!). What should happen next is a continuation to the development.

(1) Listen to mm. 60-74. What aspects of the music indicate that this is not a repetition of the exposition, but instead is the beginning of the development? Identify the key and type of cadence in measure 74. Cite specific measures in your explanation.

Assignment 32.6 *(continued)*

(2) Prior to considering which themes appear in the development, it will be useful to locate the end of the development. Listen, following along in the score, to locate the entry of the first theme in tonic that signals the recapitulation. (Hint: This is trickier than it might seem because unusual things can happen in a development section!) When you find a theme entry in D major, check to see that the music continues in the tonic key; explain what you find, citing measure numbers.

(3) Using the starting point of measure 61 and the ending of the recapitulation you located in the previous question, examine the contents of the development section. Locate the following features:

an ascending sequence: measures _____ to _____ pattern length: _____

a descending sequence: measures _____ to _____ pattern length: _____

development of horn closing theme: beginning in measure _____

development of first theme: beginning in measure _____

development of orchestra second theme: beginning in measure _____

(4) Now examine the music just prior to the recapitulation: where is the retransition? Explain, citing measure numbers.

D. Recapitulation

If this were a sonata-form movement, the next step would be simply to locate the reappearance of each of the themes in the tonic key, and note any changes to the transition (to stay in tonic) or other musical materials as compared to the exposition. Because this is a concerto with a double exposition, and different thematic materials in the orchestral and horn expositions, there are more variables.

(1) Start by comparing the presentation of the first theme in the recapitulation with the prior presentations by the orchestra and the horn. Which measures correspond, and where does the similarity break off? How are cadences changed, as compared to the exposition? Explain, citing measure numbers.

(2) Now examine measures 133-154: locate the presentation of the second theme and the closing material. Which is presented—the orchestra version or the horn version? Explain, citing measure numbers to show the correspondence and where there are alterations necessitated to stay in D major.

(3) Measure 154 has two fermata signs, indicating that the orchestra pauses on the first fermata chord for the horn's solo cadenza. The second fermata sign shows the note the horn is to play to signal the end of the cadenza and the return of the orchestra. (The cadenza itself is not notated.) There is a theme that has not yet returned in the recapitulation. Examine the coda, and locate the theme and its source. Does the horn play after the cadenza? Explain, citing measure numbers.

E. For class discussion

(1) Compare the first theme in this concerto with those in Assignments 32.1 and 32.2. How are they alike in harmonic and melodic design?

(2) Thinking back over the Classical sonata forms analyzed in this chapter, what are the primary differences you have observed between sonata first movements and this concerto first movement? What aspects are the same?

33 Rondo, Sonata-Rondo, and Large Ternary

NAME _____

Assignment 33.1

Form Analysis: Mozart, Sonata in C Major, K. 545, mvt. 3 🎧

Listen to the final movement of Mozart's Sonata in C Major, while following the score in your anthology. You will use the information gathered in parts A and B to complete the form chart in part C.

A. A sections (refrain)

(1) The double bar setting off the first eight measures defines the **A** section, or refrain. Graph its phrases using arcs; include key areas, measure numbers, and cadence types. Label the phrase or period type.

Phrase structure type: _____

(2) Where does the **A** section material next return in the tonic key? List the measure numbers and circle the form letter for each return. For now, ignore thematic returns in a non-tonic key.

Measure numbers: _____   (circle one)   **A**   **A′**

Measure numbers: _____   (circle one)   **A**   **A′**   **A″**

B. Episodes and transitions/retransitions

(1) Look at the music between the first and second refrain (**A**) sections, beginning in measure 9. Graph the phrases of the **B** section using arcs; include key areas, measure numbers, and cadence types. Label the phrase or period type.

Phrase structure type: _____

(2) The retransition following the first episode (**B**) is measures _____. Hint: Look after a significant cadence. How does it prepare for the return of the refrain? Explain.

(3) Look at the music between the second and third refrain (**A**) sections. Graph the phrases of the **C** section using arcs; include key areas, measure numbers, and cadence types. Label the phrase or period type.

(4) The retransition in the second episode **C** is measures _____. How does it prepare for the return of the refrain? Explain.

(5) The **B** or **C** sections share material with the **A** section (refrain). Where (give measure numbers) and which materials? Explain.

(6) After the third statement of the refrain, locate the coda, from measures _____ to _____.

C. Using a chart to show rondo form

As you answer the questions in parts A and B, complete this chart then answer the question below.

SECTION	SECTION MEASURES	PHRASE MEASURES	CADENCES	KEY/MODE/RELATIONSHIP TO TONIC
A	1-8			C major (I)
B				

Circle the correct form label: five-part rondo seven-part rondo

Assignment 33.2

Analysis: Beethoven, Für Elise 🎧

Listen to this piece, while following the score in your anthology.

A. Analysis of measures 1-22 (first large section)

(1) Based on both the melodic design and harmonic progressions employed, measures 1-8 are best labeled as a(n) (circle one)

      sentence   constrasting period   parallel period   introduction

(2) Describe two motives introduced in measures 1-8 that are strongly associated with the sound and character of this piece, and that are featured later in the piece. Include the measure numbers, and mention melodic, rhythmic, and contour details.

    (a)

    (b)

(3) Measures 9-12 feature a(n) (circle any that apply)

      upper-neighbor motion in the highest voice-leading strand   melodic sequence

      deceptive resolution of a dominant seventh chord   harmonic sequence

(4) What is the purpose of measures 9-12 in the form of the first section (mm. 1-22)? What is the harmonic progression here? Briefly explain, using appropriate terminology.

(5) What is the purpose of measures 13-14 in the form of the first section (mm. 1-22)? What harmony is prolonged here? Briefly explain, using appropriate terminology.

(6) Though this is the first large section of the piece's overall form, it has a smaller embedded form within it. Draw a form graph that represents the smaller form, with the first and second endings represented by repeat signs. Include the measure numbers, location of phrases, phrase letters, and cadence types.

sections: ||:   **A**
phrases: **a**

measures: mm. 1   4
cadence types: IAC

The overall form of measures 1-22 is best described as (circle any terms that apply):

      binary   ternary   sectional   continuous   rounded   simple   composite

B. Analysis of measures 23-59

(1) To start the second large section, the anacrusis chords in measure 22 (second ending) through measure 23 establish the key of _____ (circle one)   major   minor

    Compared to the key of the **A** section (mm. 1-22), this key is best described as the

        tonic key (i)   parallel major (I)   relative major (III)

        subdominant (iv)   minor dominant (v)   major dominant (V)

        submediant (VI)   subtonic (VII)

(2) The cadence in measures 29-30 is a(n) _____ cadence in the key of _____ (circle one)   major   minor

(3) Compared to the key of the **A** section (mm. 1-22), the key established by the cadence in measures 29-30 is best described as the

        tonic key (i)   parallel major (I)   relative major (III)

        subdominant (iv)   minor dominant (v)   major dominant (V)

        submediant (VI)   subtonic (VII)

    But, compared to the key established at the beginning of this section (mm. 22-23), the cadence in measures 29-30 is to the:

        tonic key (i)   parallel major (I)   relative major (III)

        subdominant (iv)   minor dominant (v)   major dominant (V)

        submediant (VI)   subtonic (VII)

(4) Briefly describe the function of measures 30-37, using appropriate terminology. Indicate where in this passage the key area changes (giving measure numbers), and where the passage leads.

(5) The best sectional label for measures 38-59 (the third large section) is:

    A   **A′**   **A″**   **B**   **B′**   **C**

Briefly explain.

Assignment 33.2 (continued)

C. Analysis of measures 59–103

(1) Now examine the section starting with the lead-in at measure 59. Identify the main key of this section (presence of a pedal point will help with that task!), then provide Roman numerals and figures in each blank for measures 60–67, shown here. (Hint: Where there is a pedal point, identify the chords and inversions above it, ignoring the pedal.)

Key: _____

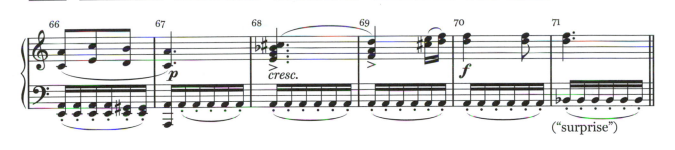

("surprise")

(2) The phrase you just analyzed is repeated beginning in measure 68, but something surprising happens in measure 71 (last measure in the example, labeled "surprise"). Using the key established in the measures you just analyzed, what is this chord? (Roman numeral and figures) _____

What progression follows from this "surprise" chord to conclude the phrase. In what key does this phrase end? Briefly explain how the voice-leading here works to make this connection.

(3) Consider the harmonic motion in measures 76–77. Is there a cadence here? Where? What type? How might this information shape your performance of this passage?

(4) Compared to the main key of this piece, what harmony is prolonged in measures 77–80?

      tonic   dominant   subdominant   relative major

(5) What music is presented in measure 82 to the end? Briefly describe the function of measures 77-81 in this formal location, using appropriate terminology.

(6) Complete the following form chart. Include large sections, retransitions, key areas (including any changes of key within a section), and how the keys are related to the initial tonic.

LARGE SECTION/RETRANSITION	MEASURES	KEY/MODE RELATIONSHIP TO TONIC
A	1-22	A minor (tonic)
B		

(7) The overall form of this movement is:

sonata   composite ternary   five-part rondo   seven-part rondo

Assignment 33.3

Analysis: Schumann, Papillon 𝄐

A. Harmonic analysis: Write in the Roman numerals. Be sure to indicate a change of key anywhere this occurs. (Hint: In mm. 25-32, use the lowest note in the measure as the bass for the figures.)

d: vii°$\frac{4}{2}$

B. Form: Complete the following chart showing the formal organization of this piece. Use the optional Comments column to record any other observation you wish to make about any section.

MEASURES	FORMAL DIVISION	KEY/MODE/ RELATIONSHIP TO TONIC	CADENCE TYPE	COMMENTS
1-6	A			

(1) What is the form of this piece? (circle one)

      ternary   quaternary   five-part rondo

(2) What is unusual about the initial **A** section, based on expectations for this form?

      It does not include any root-position tonic chords.   It does not end in the tonic key.

      It does not have a clear phrase form.   All of the above.

(3) Which of the following terms apply to measures 20-24? (circle any that apply)

      retransition to main key   cadential extension   pedal point

(4) What is the phrase form of measures 25-32, including the repeat with first and second endings?

      contrasting period   parallel period   phrase group   sentence   none of these

(5) What is the relationship of the contrasting-section keys to the main key? (circle any that apply)

      relative major   chromatic mediant   dominant   chromatic submediant

Assignment 33.4

Analysis: Beethoven, Sonatina in F Major, Op. Posth., mvt. 2 🎧 *(anthology)*

Listen to this piece in the anthology to locate the key areas, phrases, and cadences.

A. Rondo form

(1) If measures 1–16 are considered the **A** section, identify where this music returns. Fill in the correct measure numbers for each **A**, **B**, and **C** section in the chart, and add a prime (´) if needed to any of the letters.

(2) Fill in the appropriate information regarding key areas and cadences. List the measure numbers for the retransitions and coda.

SECTION	MEASURES	KEY	CADENCE AT THE END OF SECTION
A	1–16		
B			
retransition			
A´			
C			
retransition			
A			
coda			

B. Analysis of measures 1–36

(1) If you were analyzing only measures 1–36 as a complete piece, what form would this be?

      sectional simple binary   sectional rounded binary

      continuous rounded binary   simple ternary

(2) Draw a form graph for these measures. Show phrases with lowercase letters, draw phrase arcs, and indicate the measure numbers of each phrase. Show sections with uppercase letters. Indicate the key areas, the location of cadences and their type, repeat signs, and any modulations or sequences.

(3) (a) Is the form graph typical in every way of the form you named in B (1)?

YES   NO

(b) Could this section be played as a free-standing piece?   YES   NO

(c) Explain your answers.

C. Analysis of measures 37-66

(1) If you were analyzing these measures as a complete piece, what form would this be?

sectional simple binary   sectional rounded binary

continuous rounded binary   simple ternary

(2) Draw a form graph below for measures 37-66. Show phrases with lowercase letters (beginning with c), draw phrase arcs, and indicate the measure numbers of each phrase. Show sections with uppercase letters (beginning with **C**). Indicate the key areas, the location of cadences and their type, repeat signs, and any modulations or sequences.

(3) (a) Is the form graph typical in every way of the form you circled in (1)?   YES   NO

(b) Could this section be played as a free-standing piece?   YES   NO

(c) Explain your answers.

D. Considering a hybrid form

(1) In a five-part rondo form, the **B** and **C** sections are often about the same length. Is that true of this sonatina? How does this piece deviate from a typical rondo?

(2) If measures 1-36 and 37-66 are analyzed as large sections **A** and **B**, this piece could also be considered to have a composite ternary form. What aspects of the piece are not typical of composite ternary? (Hint: Look at mm. 67-end.)

Assignment 33.5

Analyzing a sonata-rondo: Beethoven, Pathétique *Sonata, mvt. 3* 🎧 *(anthology)*

The final movement of Beethoven's *Pathétique* sonata includes a refrain section that returns like the **A** section of rondo form, but also has sonata-like passages that are transitional or developmental. As you listen, think about which elements are like a rondo and which conform to sonata form. Mark all the sectional divisions in your score as you go, as well as filling in the following information; this will save time on later questions.

A. Analysis of the rondo refrain (**A** sections).

(1) To become familiar with the rondo refrain, start with harmonic and phrase analysis. Provide a Roman numeral analysis for measures 1–17, and label the phrases and cadences. 🎧

(2) In a sonata-rondo (or a seven-part rondo), we expect to hear the **A** section four times in total, each time in the tonic key, alternating with contrasting sections in other keys. Listen to this movement in its entirety while looking at your anthology to locate the places where the refrain returns, mark them on your anthology score, and fill in the information in the following chart.

For now, list the entire span of measures that are "not **A**" for the contrasting sections; we will examine these passages in more detail shortly to determine the key areas, locate transitions, retransitions, or developmental activity, and to apply primes (e.g., **A′**, **B′**) where appropriate.

When you find a return of the refrain, compare it measure by measure with measures 1-17. Confirm that each returns in the tonic key. If an **A** section is shortened, extended, or otherwise altered, indicate that on the chart by adding a prime to the **A** label. There is one place in the form where something unusual happens toward the end of an **A** section; if you are not sure where it ends (or the next section begins), for now write ?? instead of a measure number.

MEASURES	A	NOT A	A	NOT A	A	NOT A	A	CODA
KEY/MODE	C minor (i)		C minor (i)		C minor (i)		C minor (i)	
MEASURES	1-17							

B. First episode (**B**)/sonata second theme group

(1) Now examine the first of the "not **A**" sections. The entire first "not **A**" is measures _____ .

(2) At this point in analysis of a sonata-rondo it is helpful to think about the piece as a sonata. Starting from the end of the **A** section, the sonata's first theme group, listen to determine how long the transition is, where the second key is established, and where the second theme group (rondo **B** section) begins. Now fill in these blanks.

Transition: Measures 18 to _____ . Modulates to the key of _____ (circle one)

major   minor

This key is _____ (Roman numeral) compared to the original tonic key.

The second theme group/rondo **B** section begins in measure _____ .

(3) Now determine for the remaining portion of this "not **A**" section (a) where the second theme group ends, (b) whether there is a closing or codetta theme, and (c) where the retransition to the original tonic and return of section **A** begins.

The first two of these tasks are handled the same way as they would be in a sonata analysis: listen for cadences and changes of melodic material, texture, or other form-defining features. The last of these (retransition) is specific to sonata-rondo, as there is not normally a return to the tonic key in sonatas prior to the development section. Here, consider where the modulation back to the original tonic takes place. You can work on this in either "direction": beginning with the start of the second theme, or by moving ahead to the second **A** section (see your chart) and working backward.

(a) The definitive PACs in this section are in measures _____ and _____ , both in the key of _____ . These cadences may be used to divide the **B** section into subsections.

(b) Compared to the beginning of the **B** section (the sonata's second theme group), significantly different textures appear in measures _____ - _____ , _____ - _____ , and _____ - _____ .

Assignment 33.5 (*continued*)

(c) Based on these cadences and changes in texture, the sonata-form's closing theme group would best be placed at measures _____ - _____ .

(d) The retransition to **A** (modulatory to V7 of C minor) is measures _____ - _____ .

In considering the movement as a rondo, group together the second theme and closing theme as section **B** (both are in the same key), and mark the transition and retransition on your score or form chart separately from **A** and **B**.

C. Rondo second episode/sonata development

(1) Now examine the lengthy second of the "not **A**" sections. The entire second "not **A**" (from your chart in part A of this assignment) is measures _____ - _____ .

(2) In a sonata-rondo, this part of the form emulates the development and retransition of a sonata form. There may be at transition at the beginning of this portion from the immediately previous statement of the refrain, though that is less common.

   Following our procedure for analyzing a sonata form, begin by locating the recapitulation (the third **A** in the rondo chart in part A); then identify the location of the retransition that leads to it. Recall that the retransition of a sonata normally features a dominant pedal (V or V7), and there may be a change of texture also.

(a) A dominant pedal extends from measure _____ to _____ .

(b) Look at the beginning of this "not **A**," which we will now label the rondo's **C** section (or the sonata's development). Is there a transition that leads to it?   YES   NO

(3) What melodic material is developed at the beginning of **C**? Look back at the first, second, and closing theme areas to decide. How is the material developed? It may be helpful to describe this section in terms of a musical "topic" (Chapter 25). Explain.

(4) Consider the tonal structure of the **C** section.

(a) What is the main key area? (Consider the key signature plus the most frequent recurring accidentals.) _____

(b) Is it stable or unstable, with changes of accidentals indicating modulatory activity?

        stable   unstable

Explain:

(c) How does the key or keys relate to the main key of the movement?

D. Recapitulation and coda

In a sonata form, we expect the materials of the exposition to return in the recapitulation with one significant change: the music that was in the second key in the exposition (the second theme and any subsequent materials) returns in the tonic. For a sonata-rondo, the **A** sections are already in the tonic; no change is necessary for the last return of **A**. However, there are often changes between the first **A** of the recapitulation (the third **A** overall) and the return of the **B** section, because of the need to transpose it to tonic.

(1) Start by comparing the beginning of the recapitulation to the first **A** section of the piece. (You may have noted something unusual about this **A** section when you completed part A of this assignment.) Which measures have been changed? Explain.

(2) What key and mode are employed in the return of the second theme and closing theme materials? What is the relationship of that key to the original tonic? (Because there are changes in this section, we will label it **B′**.)

(3) What additional feature is changed in the recapitulation as compared to the analogous locations in the exposition? Why is this change made?

(4) What musical material is included in the coda? Identify the sources earlier in the movement of as many of the coda's motives and themes as you can. List specific measures to which they correspond.

E. Movement as a whole

Looking back through this sonata-rondo, where are passages that might reflect musical topics? List them by section, measures, and topic; you need only list each section once, where sections recur in the form.

Assignment 33.6

Analysis of large ternary form: Brahms, Intermezzo in A Major, Op. 118, No. 2 ♫ (anthology)

Use this worksheet to locate the large sections and subsections of this ternary form piece. Discover how Brahms created its lush, Romantic sound through close harmonic analysis of selected passages, and investigate the procedures of motivic development—called "developing variation"—that are characteristic of this piece.

A. Ternary form

First, listen to the Intermezzo all the way through with the score in the anthology, then locate the three large sections (notated in boxes). The **B** section should contrast in key (sometimes in mode as well) and in melodic, rhythmic, or harmonic material. The third large section features a return of the music from the opening.

(1) The first large section, **A**, is measures 1 to _____ .

(2) The second large section, **B**, is measures _____ - _____ .

(3) The third large section, **A** or **A′**, is measures _____ –115.

(4) The main key and mode of **A** is _____ .

(5) The main key and mode of **B** is _____ .

(6) The key of **B** is the (circle one) of **A** .

　　　　supertonic　　relative major　　subdominant　　dominant　　relative minor

(7) List two specific ways other than key that **B** contrasts with **A** .

　　(a)

　　(b)

(8) Should the last section take a prime (′) to indicate that the content is somewhat different from **A** ? Why or why not?

B. Section **A** and developing variation

The term "developing variation" is applied to pieces where musical ideas, instead of being repeated exactly, begin to mutate (or be developed). For this process to be audible, there has to be a connection between the original version of the musical idea (or motive) and the varied versions. Sometimes two individual ideas will combine to make variants. Use this concept to think about the relationships between motives in **A** .

　　Begin by examining the two opening phrases. The first spans from the anacrusis to measure 4, ending on beat 2. Write a Roman numeral and contextual analysis below the score, then answer the questions that follow. (Hint: There are some elisions where a chord arpeggiation is completed at the same time another chord enters. For example, the D3 of measure 1, beat 3, belongs to the same chord as beats 1–2, while the bass note A2 and the right-hand parts constitute the entrance of a new chord. You can indicate this by a curved line as shown.)

First phrase, mm. 1-4

A: I
      T ———

(1) There are two $^6_4$ chords in measures 1-3: a(n) _____ $^6_4$ in measure _____,
and a(n) _____ $^6_4$ in measure _____.

These both function as (circle one):

       tonic expansion   predominant harmonies   dominant expansion   cadential embellishment

(2) The chord on the downbeat of measure 3 is a (Roman numeral) _____. It connects to the previous
and following chords as a part of a

       tonic expansion   predominant area   strong dominant making a cadence

(3) A third $^6_4$ in measure 4 is a(n) _____ $^6_4$.

(4) This phrase ends with which type of cadence?

       PAC   IAC   HC   Phrygian

(5) The second phrase (mm. 5-8) is shown next. Write a Roman numeral and contextual analysis.

A:

(6) Consider the anacrusis to this phrase. Which terms describe the quality and function of the anacrusis
chord (m. 4, beat 3)? (circle any that apply)

      secondary dominant   secondary leading-tone chord   fully diminished seventh chord

      half-diminished seventh chord   dominant seventh chord   root position

      first inversion   second inversion   third inversion

Assignment 33.6 (*continued*)

(7) What is the role of the F♯3 in measure 4 on the "and" of beat 2? How is the G♮ introduced?

(8) To which closely related key does this phrase modulate?

       supertonic   subdominant   dominant   relative minor

(9) This phrase ends with which type of cadence?

       PAC   IAC   HC   Phrygian

(10) These two phrases (mm. 1–8) form a modulating

       contrasting period   parallel period   phrase group

     The phrases can be labeled (lowercase letters) _____ .

C. Section B

The second large section constitutes a small ternary form embedded within the larger ternary. Locate the three sections by their contrast in key and mode.

(1) The first section (**A**) is measures _____ – _____ ; its key is _____ .

(2) The second section (**B**) is measures _____ – _____ ; its key is _____ .

(3) Other than key and mode, list two ways that this **B** section contrasts with **A**.

    (a)

    (b)

(4) Name one way that it is similar to the **A** section.

(5) The third section (**A′**) is mm. _____ – _____ .

(6) List two ways that this **A′** differs from the **A** section.

    (a)

    (b)

D. For class discussion

(1) Measures 9–16 constitute a written-out repeat of the first two phrases, and with measures 1–8 form an **A** section. Why were these written out instead of using repeat signs? What is changed? Compare each measure to the corresponding measure of 1–8, and circle on your score each note that is changed.

(2) Listen to measures 16-48. Beginning in measures 17-20, Brahms presents musical ideas that contrast with the opening phrases. This portion of the **A** section is similar in function to the contrasting section of a binary or ternary form. Is there a sequence? A pedal point? Does the music of measures 1-8 return? Where? Does the music of 17-20 return? Where? Where is the initial key of this section reestablished?

(3) How does the **B** section employ the idea of developing variation?

The Twentieth Century and Beyond

34 Modes, Scales, and Sets

NAME _____

Assignment 34.1

I. Identifying diatonic modes 🎧

For each given scale, identify the tonic note and scale type (e.g., B Lydian).

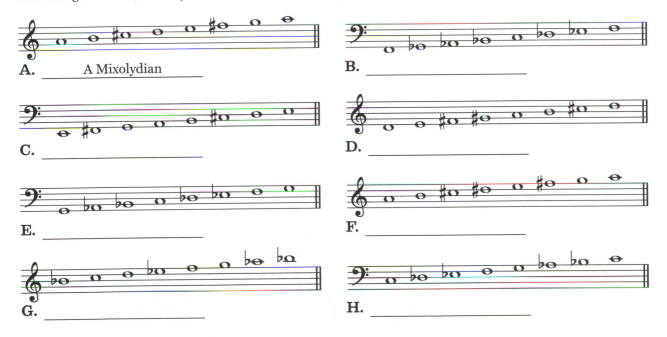

A. _____A Mixolydian_____

B. _____

C. _____

D. _____

E. _____

F. _____

G. _____

H. _____

II. Mode and scale identification in musical contexts

The following excerpts are drawn from music by Béla Bartók. Play each, then: (1) Identify the pc center. (2) List the pcs in ascending order beginning with the pc center, using letter names. (3) Name the diatonic mode. If a particular subset of the scale is featured (e.g., Phrygian tetrachord), specify it. Then, (4) briefly explain how the pc center is established (repetition, register, etc.).

A. Bartók, *Mikrokosmos*, No. 37, mm. 1–8 🎧

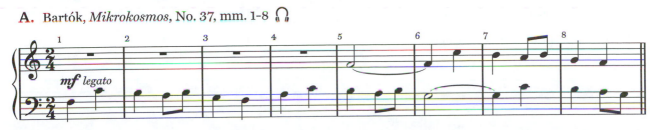

(1) Pc center(s): _____

(2) Pc list: _____

(3) Mode(s) or scale(s): _____

(4) How is the pc center established?

B. Bartók, *Mikrokosmos*, No. 41, mm. 1-4

(1) Pc center(s): _____

(2) Pc list: _____

(3) Mode(s) or scale(s): _____

(4) How is the pc center established?

C. Bartók, *Mikrokosmos*, No. 59, mm. 1-6

This excerpt may be considered bimodal. First, identify the mode or scale in each hand separately. If the pc center is unclear, discuss this ambiguity in your answer to the last question.

(1) Pc center(s): RH = _____ LH = _____

(2) Pc list: RH = _____ LH = _____

(3) Mode(s) or scale(s): RH = _____ LH = _____

(4) How is the pc center established?

Assignment 34.2

I. Writing diatonic modes

On the following staves, write the diatonic mode requested.

A. F Dorian

B. A Lydian

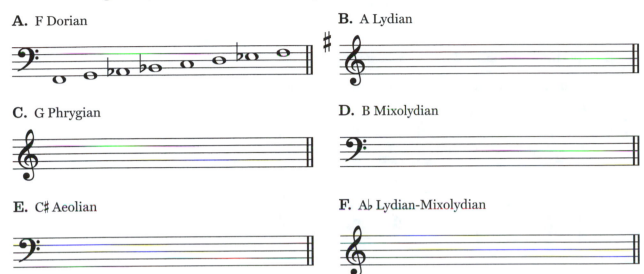

C. G Phrygian

D. B Mixolydian

E. C♯ Aeolian

F. A♭ Lydian-Mixolydian

II. Identifying modes and compositional techniques in context

A. Britten, "In Freezing Winter Night," from *Ceremony of Carols*, mm. 3-6

Listen to the excerpt or sing through it with your class.

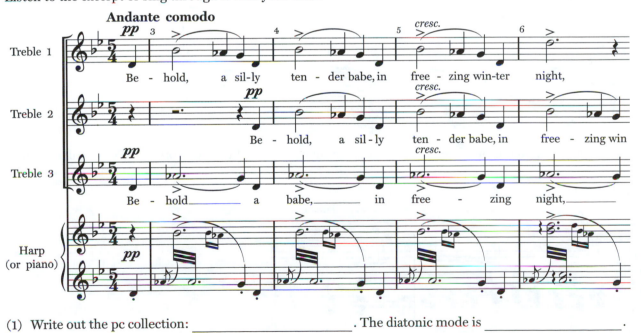

(1) Write out the pc collection: _____. The diatonic mode is _____.

(2) List two musical cues that support your conclusion.

    (a) _____

    (b) _____

(3) How does Britten emphasize the distinctive scale degree that differentiates this mode from natural minor?

(4) Briefly describe the relationship(s) between the melodies in trebles 1 and 2 and in trebles 1 and 3.

B. Excerpts from Stravinsky, *Three Movements from Petrouchka*

(1) Mvt. 1, mm. 22-23 (Hint: Use C, the lowest note, to build the scale.)

The mode used is (circle one)   Lydian-Mixolydian   whole tone   hexatonic

(2) Mvt. 2, mm. 33-36

The harmonic materials used are (circle one)   hexatonic   split-third chord   Petrouchka chord

(3) Mvt. 1, mm. 106-107

The compositional technique used is (circle one)   parallel 9th chords   planing   bimodality

Assignment 34.3

I. Pitch-class integer notation

A. Provide the pc integer notation for each melody. Write the pcs in ascending order, beginning with the lowest number.

(1) Varèse, *Density 21.5*, mm. 1-3 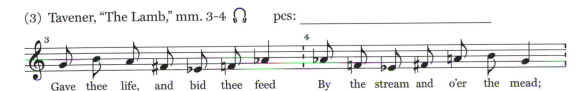   pcs: _____

(2) Webern, "Dies ist ein Lied," mm. 1-2 (voice)    pcs: _____

(3) Tavener, "The Lamb," mm. 3-4    pcs: _____

B. In the following table, fill in the blanks for the chords and scales specified. In the Chord columns, either provide integers for the given chord type or name the chord type. Then combine the two chords to form a scale or mode, taking the root of chord #1 as the tonic pitch. In the last column, list the pcs in the mode or scale you have created, without repeating any pcs. Then give the scale its correct name.

	Chord 1	Chord 2	Scale type when combined
(1) Integer notation:	2 6 9 0	4 7 e	2 4 6 7 9 e 0
Chord/scale type:	D Mm7	E minor triad	D Mixolydian
(2) Integer notation:	_____	_____	0 1 3 5 7 8 t
Chord/scale type:	C mm7	D♭ major triad	_____
(3) Integer notation:	4 8 0	6 t 2	_____
Chord/scale type:	_____	_____	_____
(4) Integer notation:	_____	0 4 7	t 0 2 4 5 7 8
Chord/scale type:	B♭ Mm7	_____	_____
(5) Integer notation:	2 6 9 0	_____	_____
Chord/scale type:	_____	F∅7	_____

II. Writing scales

Write the scale requested on the following staves, beginning on the pc indicated. Then write out the pcs of the scale in integer notation (in the same order as notated, but excluding any repeated pc). Use the integer notation to check that what you have written matches the scale name.

A. F octatonic 23 (OCT 23)

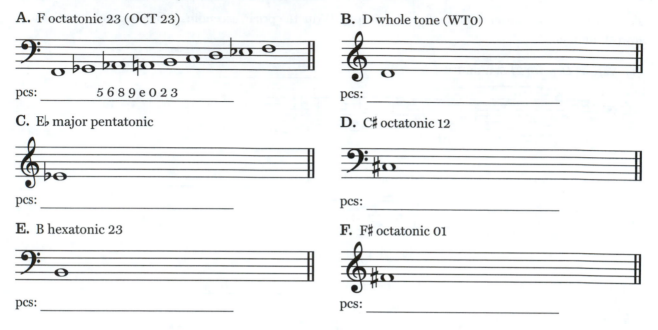

pcs: _____ 5 6 8 9 e 0 2 3 _____

B. D whole tone (WT0)

pcs: _____

C. E♭ major pentatonic

pcs: _____

D. C♯ octatonic 12

pcs: _____

E. B hexatonic 23

pcs: _____

F. F♯ octatonic 01

pcs: _____

III. Analysis: Charles Ives, "The Cage" 🎧

Listen to this work while following the score in your anthology, then answer the questions. The composer note at the bottom of the score instructs you to read all notes not marked with a sharp or flat as natural (no accidentals carry across from beat to beat).

A. The chords of the piano introduction are (circle one):

whole tone   quartal   quintal   octatonic

B. The piano accompaniment relies on the same type of chordal construction for most of the song, with only a few exceptions.

(1) In the last line, what type of chords accompany the words "three hours"?

whole tone   quartal   quintal   octatonic

(2) The dotted-half-note chord accompanying "wonder" contains all possible pcs except

(list the pcs missing from the aggregate) _____

C. The singer's line rocks back and forth between the even and odd whole-tone collections, much as a leopard might pace back and forth in his cage. On the vocal line excerpted here, write "even" or "odd" and write an arrow above the staff each time the collection changes.

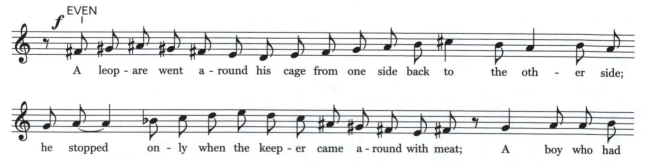

Assignment 34.4

I. Analysis: Debussy, "Fantoches," from Fêtes galantes, mm. 10-13 🎧

In this short passage, the characters Scaramouche and Pulcinella gesticulate to the moon while contriving an evil plan. Debussy emphasizes the difference between that gesture and the simplicity of song ("la-la-la") by a change of mode. Write the pc collection for each two-measure unit in integer notation, then identify the mode.

Translation: Gesticulate, black, to the moon; la, la, la.

Mm. 10-11 pc collection: _____   Mm. 12-13 pc collection: _____

Subset of which octatonic: _____   Mode (tonic E): _____

II. Analysis: Bartók, Mikrokosmos, "Whole-Tone Scale" (No. 136) 🎧

Listen to this short piano piece in its entirety, following the score in your anthology. Then answer the questions.

A. Measures 1-6

(1) List the pcs in ascending order.

Letter names: _____   Integers: _____

(2) Of which mode or scale is this pitch collection a subset? _____

(3) The focal pitch of this section is _____ . Briefly explain how is it established.

B. Measures 7-12

(1) For these measures, consider each hand a separate layer. How do the hand parts relate to each other and to the opening phrase?

(2) List the pcs in each hand part, in ascending order beginning with the pc center.

Letter names: RH: _____   LH: _____

Integers: RH: _____   LH: _____

(3) List the collections of which these are subsets.

RH: _____ LH: _____

(4) Are there focal pitches or pcs? If so, what are they, and how are they established?

C. Measures 13-19

(1) List the pcs in each hand part, in ascending order beginning with the pc center.

Letter names: RH: _____ LH: _____

Integers: RH: _____ LH: _____

(2) List the collections of which these are subsets.

RH: _____ LH: _____

(3) What motivic similarities and differences do you find when comparing the final phrase with the first two?

D. Measures 20-27

(1) List the pcs in each hand part, in ascending order beginning with the pc center.

Letter names: RH: _____ LH: _____

Integers: RH: _____ LH: _____

(2) List the collections of which these are subsets.

RH: _____ LH: _____

(3) List two ways in which this section differs from those that preceded it.

  (a) _____ (b) _____

E. Remainder of the piece

The work continues juxtaposing the two whole-tone scales. It builds to a climax in measures 55-61, where reiterated chords likewise come from different whole-tone scales.

(1) What striking change in texture occurs at the Tempo I, measure 62?

_____

  Do the hands belong to the same collection here, or different collections?   same   different

(2) Describe the pitch material of the closing section (m. 74 to the end).

Assignment 34.5

I. Analysis: Bartók, Mikrokosmos, "From the Isle of Bali," (No. 109) 🎧

Listen to this work while following your anthology score, then answer the following questions.

A. Mode and scale

(1) The primary mode or scale of this composition is: _____.

Pcs in letter names: G♯ A B C D E♭ F G♭   Integers: _____

(2) Where does Bartók introduce a noncollection pc, and as what type of embellishment?

Measure: _____   Embellishment type: _____

B. Change of scale

(1) Where does the pc collection begin to change? (Hint: Look for a pc that falls outside of the scale.)

New pc: _____

Introduced in measures _____

Octatonic?   YES   NO

(2) Speculate on compositional reasons why Bartók may have made this departure from the scale of the opening passage.

C. Motivic development: List at least one aspect that is the same and one that is different in the passages specified.

(1) Compare measures 5–10 with measures 1–4.

Same:

Different:

(2) Compare measures 12–30 (*risoluto*) with measures 1–4.

Same:

Different:

D. How do the two hands relate to each other in measures 31–39 and 40–43? (Both are notated in the treble clef in measures 31–35 over a sustained dyad in the bass clef.)

II. Style composition

On your own manuscript paper, write a short duo (12-16 measures) in the style of Bartók or Stravinsky. The goal of this project is to write a piece you will be proud to have performed in class and, in the process, to learn more about early twentieth-century styles.

- Style is conveyed through texture, scales or modes used, pitch materials, meter, rhythm and durations, melodic design, range and register, sizes of intervals employed, and other features.
- Closely observe the compositions you are modeling—Bartók's "Isle of Bali" and other *Mikrokosmos* movements, "Song of the Harvest" violin duo, and Stravinsky "Lento" (*For the Five Fingers*)—to create your own composition in that style.
- This composition will be scored as a duet—either for two instruments each playing one part, or for two separate hands on a piano (can be played by one or two people).
- Include all expressive markings (tempo, dynamic levels, articulation, etc.) needed by the performers to reflect the mood or attitude your piece is intended to convey.

Choose one of the following designs for your composition:

(1) *Modal in an* **A B A′** *form.* The **A** sections should have a lyrical, folk-inspired melody in $\frac{5}{8}$ meter, in Dorian mode, with a counterpoint. The **B** section should be syncopated and aggressive, in $\frac{2}{4}$ meter, using Lydian mode. Choose different pitch-class centers for the **A** and **B** sections (e.g., if the **A** section has a center of D, the **B** section might focus on A♭).

(2) *Octatonic* **A B** *or* **A B A′**. Write a piece employing two of the three octatonic collections using changing meter (several different meters in the piece). The form may be **A B A′** or simply **A B**, with one of the octatonic collections associated with the **A** section, and the other with the **B** section. Choose a different pitch-class center for each section. The **A** and **B** sections should contrast in several ways—in motives used, rhythm, texture, dynamics, and/or mood—as well as pc center and colleciton.

Getting started

(1) Decide which of the options you are going to work with and choose your instrumentation. Prepare your score with the correct clefs and meter signature, and with enough systems for the required number of measures.

(2) On a scratch sheet of paper, write out the scale(s) that form the foundation of your composition. Then play with melodic ideas or motives using those materials. What sorts of pitch intervals and contours do you wish to use? How are you going to make the melodic elements coherent, yet varied?

(3) Consider the meter(s) that you will be using. Write out some rhythmic patterns that work within that meter, keeping in mind how the meter and rhythms are employed in the models you are studying. How will the parts relate to each other rhythmically?

(4) Think about the musical texture(s) you wish to use. Do you want contrapuntal imitation between the parts? Or a melody and accompaniment? Or some other texture? How can texture provide variety or coherence in your composition?

(5) What moods or attitudes do you wish each section of your composition to convey? How can you create them using musical materials? Consider expressive markings, as well as change of tempo, articulation, and dynamic levels.

(6) Now consider the form of the piece. Sketch in the number of measures you will need, and mark where you will need to express beginnings and endings of phrases. Label the sections **A**, **B**, and (if needed) **A′**.

When these steps are completed, you will be well on your way to writing the composition.

Assignment 34.6

I. Scale review

On the following staves, write the scale or mode requested.

A. G minor pentatonic

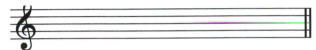

B. B hexatonic 23

C. F♯ whole tone 0

D. E Lydian-Mixolydian

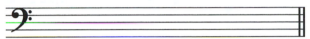

E. A octatonic 23

F. B major pentatonic

G. E♭ whole tone 1

H. D Phrygian

I. C♯ octatonic 01

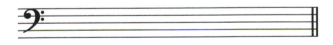

J. D♭ major pentatonic

II. Analysis: Compositional techniques

For each given passage, circle the term that identifies a prominent compositional feature. (For class discussion, consider other compositional techniques operating in each passage.)

A. Stravinsky, *Three Movements from Petrouchka*, mvt. 1, mm. 9-12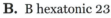

Petrouchka chord   planing   stratification   bimodality

B. Barber, "Sea Snatch," from *Hermit Songs*, mm. 29-31 🎧

planing   split-third chord   aggregate   ostinato

C. Ligeti, "Désordre," mm. 1-3 🎧

Petrouchka chord   quintal chords   bimodality   planing

D. Bartók, *Bagatelle*, mm. 4-7 🎧

planing   quartal chords   ostinato   split-third chord

35 Rhythm, Meter, and Form in Music after 1900

NAME _____

Assignment 35.1

Changing meter, asymmetrical meter, ostinato, and polymeter

In each of the following examples, identify at least one rhythmic or metric compositional technique, and explain your choice.

- If the excerpt features polymeter, which type is it?
- If it features asymmetrical meter, how is the measure divided into beat units?
- If it features ostinato, mark the content and length of the pattern on the score.

A. Stravinsky, "Triumphant March of the Devil," from *L'histoire du soldat*, mm. 7-11 🎧

Technique(s): _____

Explanation: _____

B. Stravinsky, *The Rite of Spring*, rehearsal number 31 (mm. 216-223) (two-piano score)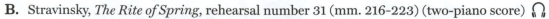

Technique(s): _____

Explanation:

C. Modest Mussorgsky, "Promenade," from *Pictures at an Exhibition*, mm. 1-8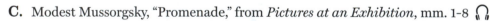

Technique(s): _____

Explanation:

Assignment 35.2

I. Rhythmic composition

On the rhythm staves provided, write a short rhythmic composition in one part. Before beginning each exercise, study the relevant examples in the chapter. Write the meter signature(s), measure lines, and durations (no pitches), with optional dynamic and tempo markings. Be prepared to perform your patterns in class and explain how each fits the specified criteria.

A. Ametric

Write a four-measure rhythmic composition that is notated with a meter signature but sounds ametric. Above your example, mark where all the beats fall, and circle rhythmic patterns that work against the perception of those beats.

B. Changing meter

Write an eight-measure rhythmic composition that features changing meter. Each measure should include rhythmic patterns characteristic of that measure's notated meter.

C. Perceived meter vs. notated meter

Write a rhythm that is notated in one meter but sounds like it is in another. When you perform this rhythm in class, ask your classmates to conduct along, first in the meter they hear, then in the notated meter.

II. Form Analysis: Debussy, "La cathédrale engloutie," mm. 1–43 🎧

(1) Listen to this movement, keeping in mind its programmatic and evocative title. Describe at least two musical elements that paint the image of a Gothic cathedral shrouded in fog, or rising out of the ocean.

(2) Form: This prelude does not easily fit into any established formal design. One possible division of the opening large section (mm. 1-43) is shown next.

(a) Fill in the missing elements in the chart. If the pc center is too ambiguous to determine the mode, write N/A for that section. If a section includes more than one mode, specify each.

	Theme group 1			"Transition"		Closing theme	
	a¹	b	a²	c¹	c²	c³	tran-sition
MEASURES	1-6	7-13	14-15	16-22	22-27	28-42	42-43
PC CENTER	G						
MODE/SCALE							

(b) Briefly discuss how you identified the pc centers and modes for each section. Specify measure numbers and/or pcs as needed. If the pc center was too ambiguous to determine the mode, describe the musical elements that created the ambiguity.

Section a¹:

Section b:

Section a²:

Section c¹:

Section c²:

Section c³:

(3) Trace the descent of the long sustained bass line—expressed by dotted-whole notes, pedal points, or the lowest pitch of each bar—that extends through much of measures 1-43. Indicate when and where the bass note changes, and where it sustains the same pitch. How does it help establish formal units, stability, and mode?

(4) Trace reappearances of the opening D-E-B motive. How is this motive developed?

Assignment 35.3

I. Rhythm and form analysis: Alan Hovhaness, "Sicut locutus est," from Magnificat, mm. 44-45

Perform this passage with your class, then complete the exercise that follows.

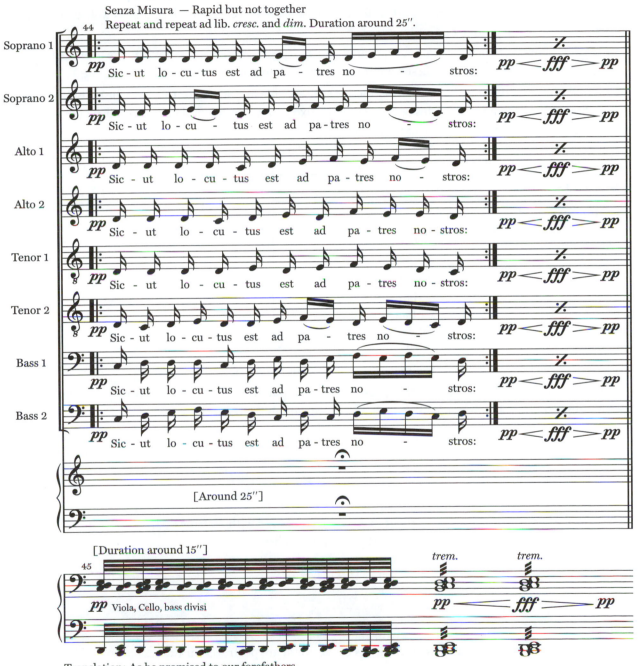

Translation: As he promised to our forefathers.

In the space on the reverse side, write a paragraph that addresses these questions.

- How is sectional form created in this example?
- Which musical elements take the lead in shaping the passage?
- What type of rhythmic/metric structure is shown here?

II. Form analysis: Ravel, "Aoua!," from Chansons madécasses 🎧

A. Listen to the movement, read the text and translation, then complete the following chart. "Refrain" refers to the "Aoua!" motive. Sections are indicated in the score by rehearsal numbers, as well as by changes in text, texture, pedal points, and/or tempo.

- Pedal points may be dyads rather than single notes (specify both pcs) or may change every few measures in less tonally stable sections (specify each change).
- Modes may be diatonic but with a distinctive scale-degree alteration; or they may be combinations of tetrachords from two modes (e.g., D Lydian-Mixolydian), or incomplete (e.g., F Phrygian subset). Write "subset" if there are five or fewer pcs.

SECTION	Intro/refrain	A				
MEASURES	1-5	6-17				
REHEARSAL		1				
PEDAL POINTS	A-G♯ dyad	G-F♯ dyad				
MODE IN VOICE (PC CENTER AND TYPE)	E Aeolian	D♯ Aeolian-Locrian (Aeolian with ♭5̂)				

B. Prepare the following questions for class discussion, or write a short paragraph for each, as assigned.

(1) In sections where the pedal points change, discuss any patterns you see in their transpositions. Where pedal points are doubled by some interval, how does this doubling color the section?

(2) Describe how the musical layers differ in **A′** when compared with **A**. How do they differ in **A″**? Discuss how the layers differ in their pc collections, rhythm, and timbre.

(3) Comment on at least three ways the images of the poem are portrayed in Ravel's setting.

Assignment 35.4

I. Pitch-time graphic analysis

Play through this excerpt at a keyboard, then make a pitch-time graph (like that in the chapter) on the grid provided. The pitch axis (y) is divided into semitones; divide the time axis (x) into eighth notes.

Bartók, *Mikrokosmos*, No. 141, "Subject and Reflection," mm. 1–6

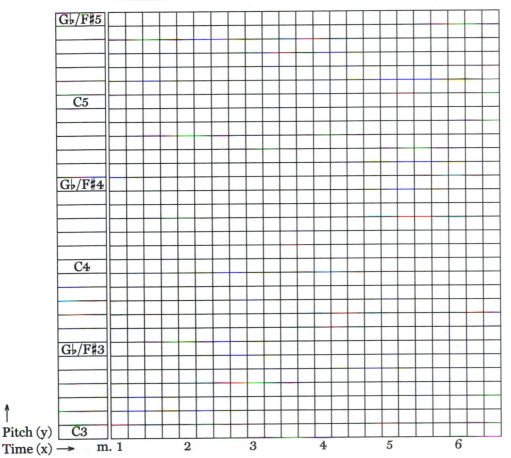

A. The center of the pitch symmetry is _____.

Is that pitch emphasized in this segment?   YES   NO

Explain.

B. The pitch class emphasized most in this passage is _____.

How is it emphasized?

C. Metrical procedures demonstrated in this example include (circle all that apply):

changing meter   ametrical   polymeter   symmetrical meter

D. How is the structure of this work indicated by its title?

II. Composition: Two-part rhythmic exercises

On the rhythm staves provided, write the following rhythmic compositions in two parts. Before beginning each exercise, study the relevant examples in the chapter. Write the meter signature(s), measure lines, and durations (no pitches), with optional dynamic and tempo markings, and one part aligned above the other. Choose a partner and perform one or more of your duets in class. Afterward, ask your classmates to name the combination of rhythmic or metric techniques you were performing.

A. Polymeter, with one part in ¾ and the other in ²⁄₄. Each part should include rhythmic patterns that strongly imply its notated meter, while combining well with the other part.

B. Ostinato in one part, changing meter in the other. Both parts may be notated in the same or a different meter.

C. Polymeter, with one part in ¾ and the other in ⁹⁄₈. Each part should include rhythmic patterns that strongly imply its notated meter, while combining well with the other part.

D. In a meter, write one part in a rhythm that sounds ametric. Add a second part that emphasizes the beats of the notated meter. Does your example sound syncopated? Or polymetric?

Assignment 35.5

Analysis

A. Corigliano, "Come now, my darling," from *The Ghosts of Versailles*, mm. 23-26 🎧

This passage shows an interchange between soprano Rosina, and mezzo-soprano Cherubino—characters drawn from Mozart but given a contemporary setting here.

(1) What rhythmic/metric compositional technique is shown? _____

(2) How does the composer use rhythm to portray the differing emotions and characters of the two singers?

B. Webern, "Dies ist ein Lied," Op. 3, No. 1 🎧

Listen to this song while following the score in your anthology.

(1) Counterpoint: Play through the vocal line of measures 1-4 several times, then play the vocal line along with the upper line of the accompaniment. Consider the counterpoint used between the vocal line in measures 1-2 and the upper line of the piano part in measures 1-3. Comment on the exact or inexact nature of this counterpoint, as well as the rhythmic relationship between the two voices.

(2) Overall form: This song falls into a ternary (**A B A′**) form, largely generated by the text. Indicate the measures for each section in the following chart, and list the primary images in the text in the right column.

SECTION	MEASURES	TEXT
A	1-4	song for you, childish beliefs, pious tears
B		
A′		

(3) List three musical features that link the **A** and **A′** sections; specify which measures are involved.

(4) List three musical elements in the **B** section that contrast with the **A** and **A′** sections; specify which measures and features are involved.

(5) What other musical cues separate one section from the next?

Assignment 35.6

Analysis

A. Barber, "Sea-Snatch" 🎧

Listen to this song while following the score in your anthology, and then answer the questions.

(1) Complete the following form graph. Then write a few sentences that explain how the form is articulated by text, mode or scale, vocal range, and accompaniment.

SECTION	intro	A	interlude			
MEASURES	1-4					

Explanation:

(2) Discuss the pitch collections of the song, and how they align with its form.

(a) How is the pentatonic scale hinted at in the opening? What pcs are missing from the diatonic collection? How are these missing pcs specially treated later in the song?

(b) Where are the diatonic sections? Are they written in major or minor or some other mode? Does the harmonization support a modal interpretation or a tonal one?

B. Bartók, *Bagatelle*, Op. 6, No. 2 🎧

(1) Using the score in your anthology and the graph paper on the following pages, make a pitch-time graph for measures 19-30 of this piece, like that in the text. (Note: The lowest notes in measure 29 will not fit on the graph; draw arrows downward to show where they belong.)

(2) Compared with measures 1-7, what has changed about the registral placement of the hand parts (the wedge figure and repeated dyad) in measures 19-21? Does each hand play the same musical figure?

(3) Now consider measures 24-29. How do these differ from measures 1-7 and measures 19-21?

(4) Where in the piece are the hand parts in the lowest register? How does that placement contribute to sectional shaping and closure?

(5) Consider the cadence at the end of the work. It sounds definitive—why? What elements come into play? Consider both pitch and rhythmic elements.

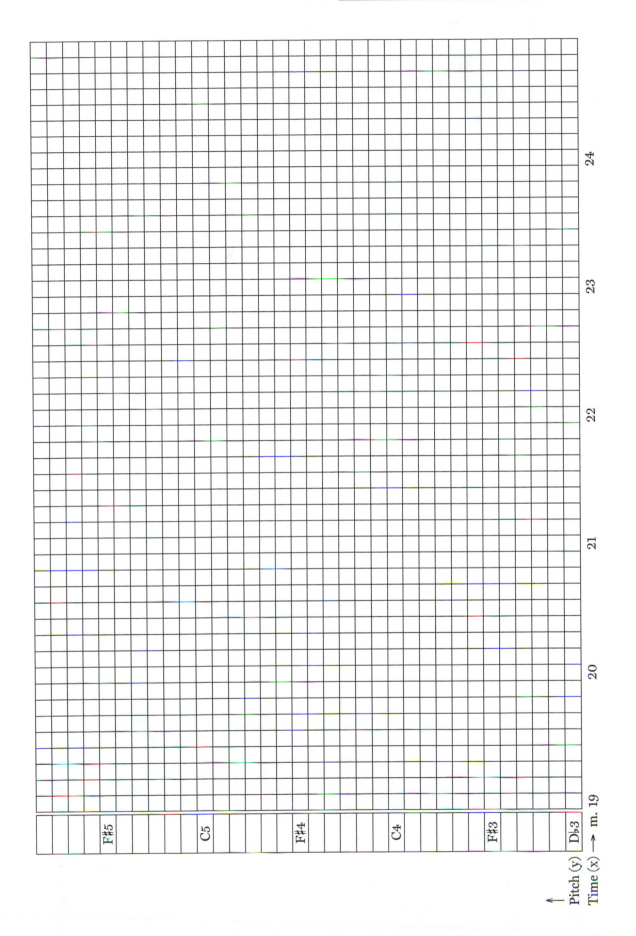

Pitch (y) ←

Time (x) → m. 19   20   21   22   23   24

Db3   F♯3   C4   F♯4   C5   F♯5

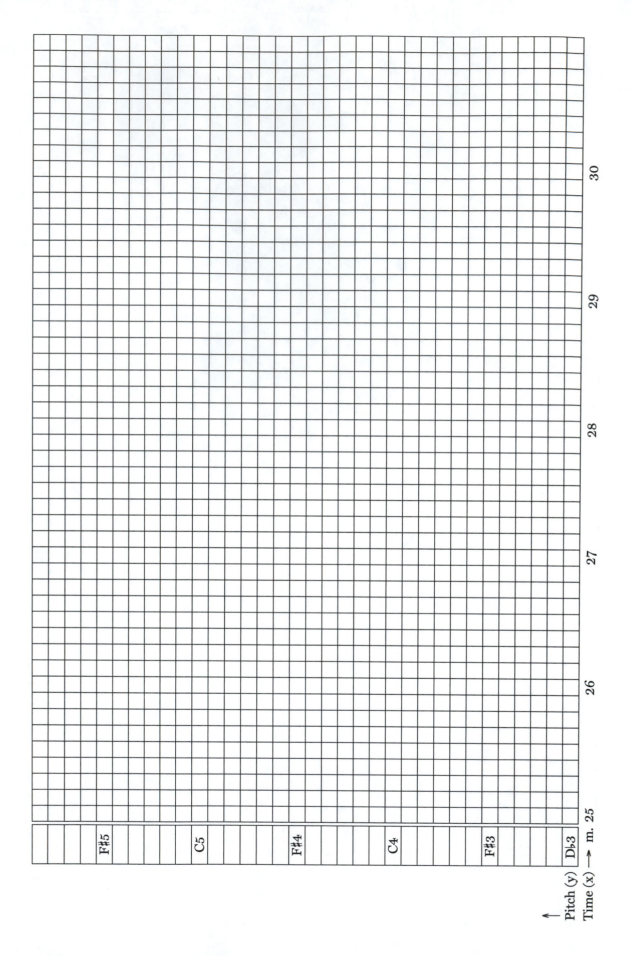

36 Music Analysis with Sets

NAME _____

Assignment 36.1

I. Pitch-class sets in integer notation

For each given pcset, circle the pcs on the clock face to determine the most compact form. Then write the pc integers in normal order in the blank provided.

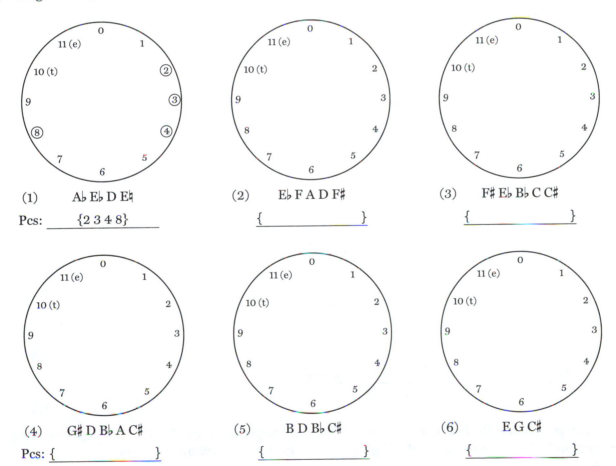

(1)   Ab Eb D E♮

Pcs: {2 3 4 8}

(2)   Eb F A D F♯

{   }

(3)   F♯ Eb Bb C C♯

{   }

(4)   G♯ D Bb A C♯

Pcs: {   }

(5)   B D Bb C♯

{   }

(6)   E G C♯

{   }

II. Ordered pitch and pitch-class intervals

For the following melody, provide the pc integers, ordered pitch intervals, and ordered pcs intervals. The excerpt begins in treble clef and changes to bass clef. For the chord in measure 32, provide the (unordered) harmonic interval; you need not calculate an interval between measures 32-33. Ignore octave doublings.

Schoenberg, Three Piano Pieces, Op. 11, No. 1, mm. 30-33 (left hand)

Pcs: 8   9   __   __   __   __   __   __   __
Ordered pitch intervals: +1 -6   __ __   __   __   __
Ordered pc intervals: 1   6   __ __   __   __   __   __

III. Transposing pitch and pitch-class sets

A. Transpose Segment A as indicated, maintaining the contour, rhythm, and pitch intervals of the original. On the right, rewrite in integer notation as a pitch-class set, in normal order.

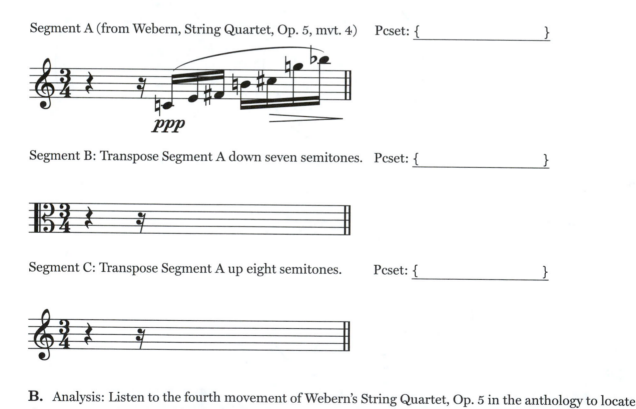

Segment A (from Webern, String Quartet, Op. 5, mvt. 4)   Pcset: {_____}

Segment B: Transpose Segment A down seven semitones.   Pcset: {_____}

Segment C: Transpose Segment A up eight semitones.   Pcset: {_____}

B. Analysis: Listen to the fourth movement of Webern's String Quartet, Op. 5 in the anthology to locate the segments of part A in the score (rhythms may differ). Provide the measure numbers.

Segment A: _____   Segment B: _____   Segment C: _____

Assignment 36.2

I. Transposing pcsets with mod12 arithmetic

For each given pcset, provide integer notation in normal order. Then transpose the pcset by the given pc interval and write the result. (If it's helpful, use the clock faces on pages 359–460 to determine the normal order.)

Pcset	Integer notation	Transpose by	Transposed set
(1) C♯ A D A♭	{8 9 1 2}	T_9	{5 6 t e}
(2) C A D F♯ A♭	{ }	T_3	{ }
(3) A B A♭ D	{ }	T_5	{ }
(4) G C♯ E♭	{ }	T_e	{ }
(5) B A D A♭ E	{ }	T_2	{ }
(6) G♯ G A B♭	{ }	T_4	{ }

II. Interval-class vectors

Write the pc integers in ascending order and most compact form for the following excerpts. Calculate the ic vector for the pentachord from these pcs.

A. Bartók, *Music for Strings, Percussion, and Celesta*, mvt. 1, m. 1

pc integers: { } ic vector: [ ]

B. Webern, "Dies ist ein Lied," m. 4 (vocal part)

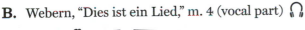

von from - men Trä - nen . . .

pc integers: { } ic vector: [ ]

C. Messiaen, *Méditations sur le mystère de la Sainte Trinité* (Meditations on the Mystery of the Holy Trinity), for organ, mvt. 4, m. 76

pc integers: { } ic vector: [ ]

D. Webern, String Quartet, Op. 5, mvt. 3, mm. 18–19 🎧

pc integers: { _____ }   ic vector: [_____]

E. Bartók, *Mikrokosmos*, No. 136, mm. 1–3 🎧

pc integers: { _____ }   ic vector: [_____]

F. Steve Reich, *Piano Phase*, pattern 1 🎧

pc integers: { _____ }   ic vector: [_____]

III. Analysis

Compare the pentachords in part II (A–F) to answer the following questions.

A. How many ics are in a five-element set? _____

B. Which two pentachords share the same ic vector? _____

C. Which one has the most ic 3? _____

D. Which one has the most ic 4? _____

E. Which one has the most ic 5? _____

F. Which one has the fewest ic 1? _____

G. Which three have the fewest ic 5? _____

Assignment 36.3

I. Inverting pitch and pitch-class sets

A. Write the ordered pitch intervals for Segment A on the blank provided; below it, write its ordered pitch intervals. Then for Segments B and C, beginning on the pitch specified, write its inversion by reversing the contour (from − to +) and notating the pitches that result. On the right, provide integer notation for each new pcset, in normal order.

Segment A: Pcset: { _____ }

Ordered pitch intervals: _____

Segment B: Inversion beginning on B3   Pcset: { _____ }

Ordered pitch intervals: _____

Segment C: Inversion beginning on C2   Pcset: { _____ }

Ordered pitch intervals: _____

B. Analysis 🎧

Listen to the third movement of Webern's String Quartet, Op. 5 (in the anthology). Locate Segments A and C by measure number.

Segment A: _____   Segment C: _____

II. Inverting pcsets from integer notation

A. For each set, first write the pcs in normal order, then calculate the inversion and write it in the blank. If using clock faces (optional) to complete the task, circle the pcs on the clock face and write the normal order in the blank. Then invert the set (around the 0/6 axis) by drawing arrows across to the complementary pcs; put a box around these pcs. Write these boxed pcs in the most compact ascending order in the inversion blank.

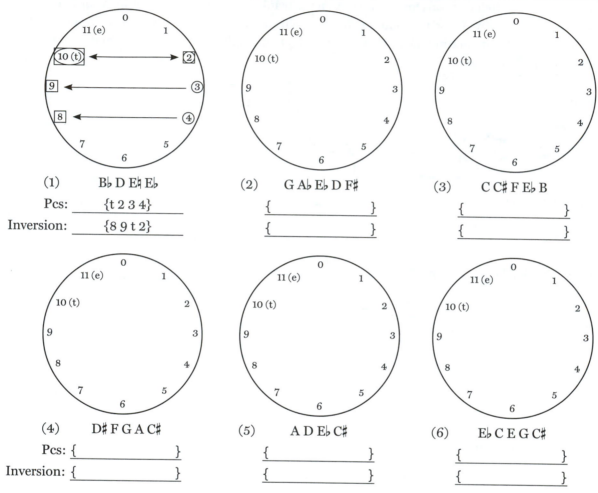

(1)	Bb D E♮ Eb	(2)	G Ab Eb D F#	(3)	C C# F Eb B
Pcs:	{t 2 3 4}	{ }		{ }	
Inversion:	{8 9 t 2}	{ }		{ }	

(4)	D# F G A C#	(5)	A D Eb C#	(6)	Eb C E G C#
Pcs: { }		{ }		{ }	
Inversion: { }		{ }		{ }	

B. Invert each pcset by T_0I and place in ascending order, then transpose by the integer given. Use mod12 arithmetic or clock faces. Check your work by making sure the pcset and its transposed inversion (in reverse order) add up to a consistent index number.

	Pcset	Invert by	T_0I (clock) inversion	Transposition
(1)	{9 t 0 1 3}	T_3I	{9 e 0 2 3}	{0 2 3 5 6}
(2)	{e 1 2 5 6 8}	T_7I	{ }	{ }
(3)	{3 6 8 t}	T_2I	{ }	{ }
(4)	{2 4 5 9}	T_eI	{ }	{ }
(5)	{e 0 1 5 6}	T_6I	{ }	{ }
(6)	{1 2 3 4 7 8}	T_1I	{ }	{ }
(7)	{3 6 9 e}	T_4I	{ }	{ }
(8)	{1 2 4 6 8}	T_8I	{ }	{ }

Assignment 36.4

I. T_n/T_nI relationships

Most pcsets identified in the following excerpts are related by T_n or T_nI. In the blanks provided, write the pcs of each set in normal order, then calculate the relationship requested between specific segments. (For example: B = T_7A means that if you transpose set A by 7, the result is set B.)

A. Bartók, *Bagatelle*, mm. 10-11

Right-hand part

Segment A pcs: {4 6 8 t e}   Segment B pcs: {   }   Segment C pcs: {   }

B = _____ of A   C = _____ of

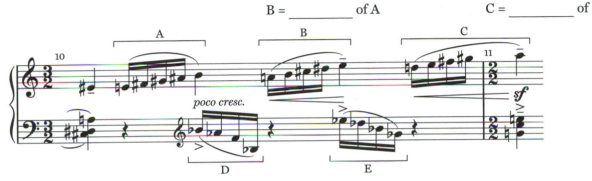

Left-hand part

Segment D pcs: {   }   Segment E pcs: {   }

Which pc in Segment E does not match an exact transposition between D and E? Which note would need to be changed in Segment E to create an exact transposition of D?

B. Stravinsky, *Three Pieces for String Quartet*, mvt. 3, mm. 10-11

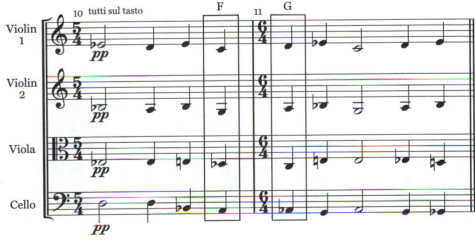

Segment F pcs: {   }   Segment G pcs: {   }   G = _____ of F

C. Stravinsky, *Three Pieces for String Quartet*, mvt. 3, mm. 15-18
(Accidentals continue to bar line.)

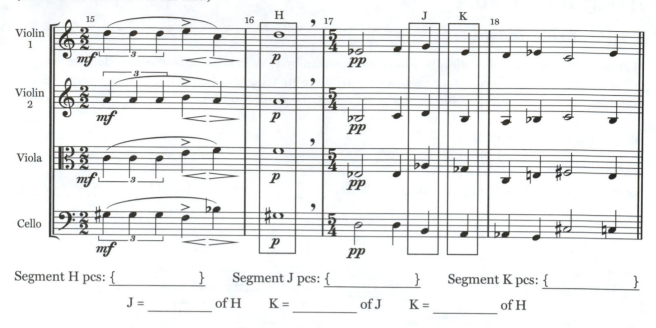

Segment H pcs: { _____ }   Segment J pcs: { _____ }   Segment K pcs: { _____ }

J = _____ of H   K = _____ of J   K = _____ of H

II. Melody writing

Write a phrase in $\frac{5}{8}$ meter, in a dance-like folk style, using the unordered pcset {0 1 3 4 6 7}. Then write a second phrase whose unordered pcset content is related by T_5I. As always when composing, include expressive and tempo markings, dynamic markings, and so on.

Assignment 36.5

I. Transposing pcsets with mod12 arithmetic

For each given pcset, provide integer notation in normal order. Then transpose and invert the pcset as requested and write the result.

- For transpositions (T_n), add n (mod12) to each pc.
- For inversions (T_nI), take the inverse of each pc in the original pcset, then add n to each pc and write in normal order.
- Shortcut for inversion: subtract each pc from the index number, n, and write in normal order.

A. Stravinsky, "Chez Petrouchka," m. 16

Normal order: { 6, 8, 9, 0, 3 } T_7: { _____ } T_5I: { _____ }

B. Ravel, *Pavane pour une infante défunte*, m. 13

Normal order: { _____ } T_3: { _____ } T_4I: { _____ }

C. Ives, "The Cage," m. 2

A   leop - ard   went   a - round

Normal order: { _____ } T_8: { _____ } T_6I: { _____ }

D. Schoenberg, *Klavierstück*, Op. 19, No. 2, m. 4

Normal order: { _____ } T_t: { _____ } T_1I: { _____ }

II. Trichordal Analysis: Schoenberg, Drei Klavierstücke, Op. 11, No. 1

Listen to these passages from the beginning and middle of the piece. Identify the circled trichords by writing their normal order in the corresponding blank. Finally, answer the questions that follow.

A. Measures 1-3

Trichords

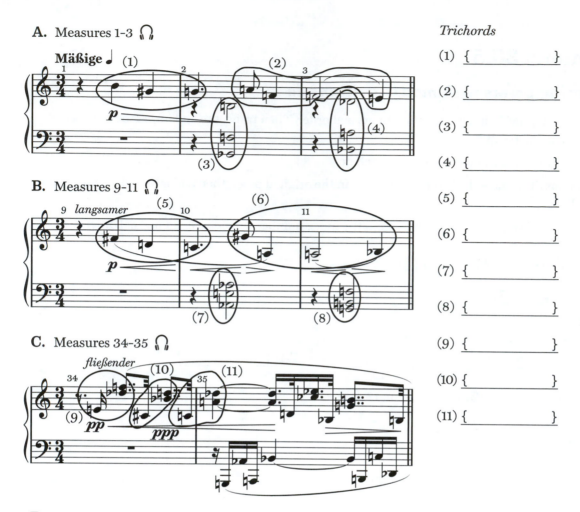

(1) { _____ }

(2) { _____ }

(3) { _____ }

(4) { _____ }

B. Measures 9-11

(5) { _____ }

(6) { _____ }

(7) { _____ }

(8) { _____ }

C. Measures 34-35

(9) { _____ }

(10) { _____ }

(11) { _____ }

D. Passages A and B seem, on first hearing, to be quite similar, yet their trichordal structures differ. Explain both the similarities and differences. Include rhythm, contour, set types, and intervallic structure.

E. Passages A and C seem, on first hearing, to be quite different, yet their trichordal structures are similar. Explain both the similarities and differences. Include rhythm, contour, set types, and intervallic structure.

F. In passages A and C, what are the T_n and T_nI relationships between the trichords specified below?

Trichord (9) is _____ of trichord (1).

Trichord (10) is _____ of trichord (1).

Trichord (11) is _____ of trichord (10).

Assignment 36.6

Analysis: Alban Berg, "Sahst du nach dem Gewitterregen" ("Did You See, After the Summer Rain"), from Altenberg-Lieder (Five Orchestral Songs), Op. 4 (reduction) 🎧

We discussed the opening of this song in Chapter 36; now look at the entire movement. Listen to this song with piano accompaniment in the recording provided, or locate an orchestral performance online or in your library. Listen to the recording or play through the vocal line at the piano while thinking about the text. Where possible, play portions of the accompaniment as well.

Translation: Did you see, after the summer rain, the forest?
         All is quiet, sparkling, and more beautiful than before.
         See, woman, you too need summer rainstorms!

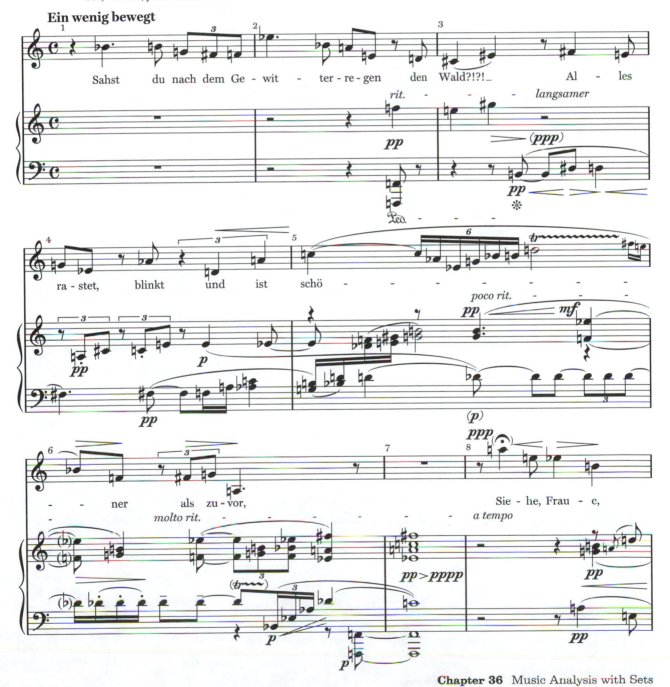

Write an extended essay that analyzes this song, using the following questions as springboards. Organize the essay as you see fit (don't simply answer the questions in a list). Support your ideas with specific examples, citing measure numbers. Turn in an annotated copy of the score with your essay.

A. As always when dealing with text, consider the poetry and the relationship of its form and content to the music. Does the song draw on elements of any standard formal schemes, or is it through-composed? Support your answer by discussing pcsets used as melodies and harmonies. If appropriate, give instances of imitation or other contrapuntal procedures.

B. Several of the important pcsets are presented in the opening vocal phrase (the first two and a half measures). Divide the phrase into distinct motives, and identify the pcsets for each motive. How do these motives return later in the song? How are they developed? If the pcsets return transposed or inverted, label them with letters and give the T_n and T_nI relationships.

C. This song is filled with thirds, which often occur in the context of the split-third chord: a major-minor triad, such as {0 3 4 7}. It also features transpositions and inversions of {0 1 4}. Find as many examples of these sonorities as possible, including transposed or inverted forms.

D. Is this music centric? Is there a focal pitch class? Support your answer, pro or con, with examples from the music.

Optional: Clock-face "scratch" paper

37

Sets and Set Classes

NAME _____

Assignment 37.1

I. Finding prime form

For each given pcset, find the normal order and prime form by one of the methods described in the chapter. Clock faces are provided if you choose to use them. Fill in the SC or Forte number (found in Appendix 6).

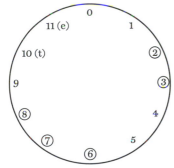

A.   G♭ E♭ D G A♭

N.O.:   {2 3 6 7 8}

Prime form: [0 1 2 5 6]

SC: 5-6

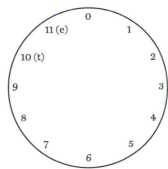

B.   E G D F♯

N.O.:   { _____ }

Prime form: [_____]

_____

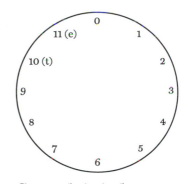

C.   F♯ E♭ A♭ C♯ C

N.O.:   { _____ }

Prime form: [_____]

_____

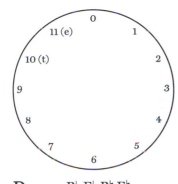

D.   B♭ E♭ B♮ E♮

N.O.:   { _____ }

Prime form: [_____]

SC: _____

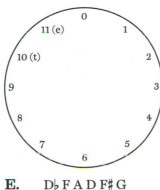

E.   D♭ F A D F♯ G

N.O.:   { _____ }

Prime form: [_____]

_____

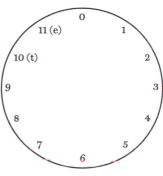

F.   F B D

N.O.:   { _____ }

Prime form: [_____]

_____

II. Melodic analysis

Here are the six pentachords analyzed in Assignment 36.2. Calculate the prime form and SC (Forte) number for each.

A. Béla Bartók, *Music for Strings, Percussion, and Celesta*, mvt. 1, m. 1

Prime form: [   ]

SC: _____

B. Webern, "Dies ist ein Lied," m. 4 (vocal part)

Prime form: [   ]

SC: _____

C. Messiaen, *Méditations sur le mystère de la Sainte Trinité*, for organ, mvt. 4, m. 76

Prime form: [   ]

SC: _____

D. Webern, String Quartet, Op. 5, mvt. 3, mm. 18–19

Prime form: [   ]

SC: _____

E. Bartók, *Mikrokosmos*, No. 137, mm. 1–3

Prime form: [   ]

SC: _____

F. Steve Reich, *Piano Phase*, pattern 1

Prime form: [   ]

SC: _____

Assignment 37.2

I. Trichord identification

In each of the following excerpts, identify the two specified trichords. Circle the first specified trichord with a solid line; circle the second with a dotted line (or different color). Circles may overlap by one or two pcs. Hints: Look for different transpositions or inversions of the trichords—not just the prime form. It may be helpful to identify the potential pitch interval successions for that trichord, and scan the excerpts for those intervals.

A. Messiaen, *Méditations sur le mystère de la Sainte Trinité*, mvt. 4, mm. 72-76

Find at least three SC 3-4s [0 1 5] and six SC 3-5s [0 1 6].

B. Berg, "Sahst du nach dem Gewitterregen," mm. 1-4

Find at least five SC 3-3s [0 1 4] and four SC 3-5s [0 1 6].

Translation: Did you see, after the summer rain, the forest? All is quiet, sparkling, and is [more beautiful than before].

II. Trichord analysis: Webern, String Quartet, Op. 5, mvt. 3, mm. 1-8 🎧

Listen to this passage, then analyze the set classes of its melodies and chords.

A. Find at least eight SC 3-3s [0 1 4] and eight SC 3-4s [0 1 5]. Circle 3-3 with a solid line and 3-4 with a dotted line (or different color).

B. Which trichord appears primarily as staccato chords? _____

Which as melodies? _____

Where does the "chord" motive appear instead as a melody?

C. In measure 6, how are the melodic lines (violin 1, 2, viola) related to the staccato pizzicato trichords?

D. In measure 7, how are the violin and cello related? _____

Examine each trichord within these melodies (overlapping). How are these trichords related?

Assignment 37.3

Analysis

A. Stravinsky, Kyrie, from *Mass*, mm. 1-5

With your class, sing through the opening measures of Stravinsky's *Mass*, then answer the following questions.

Translation: Lord have mercy upon us.

(1) The movement opens with three statements of the same set class.

Identify them here. What is their SC label and prime form? _____

   (a) piano accompaniment, normal order: { _____ }

   (b) bass melody, measures 2-3, normal order: { _____ }

   (c) bass melody, measure 4, normal order: { _____ }; T___ of the previous statement.

(2) The SC sung by the tenors in their initial "Kyrie eleison" is repeated by the sopranos in their second "Kyrie eleison." What is the relationship between the two?

   (a) SC label and prime form: _____

   (b) tenor melody, measures 2-3, normal order: { _____ }

   (c) soprano melody, measures 4-5, normal order: { _____ }; T___I of tenor statement.

(3) The altos' two statements of "Kyrie eleison" belong to the same set class.

   (a) SC label and prime form: _____

   (b) alto melody, measures 2-3, normal order: { _____ }

   (c) alto melody, measures 4-5, normal order: { _____ }; T___I of previous statement.

(4) If we consider the single B♭ in measure 5 (tenors) to function as a chromatic passing tone (and therefore eliminate it from our set), to what set class would the pitches of the entire excerpt (voices and piano reduction) belong? What scale or mode is this?

Normal order: { _____ }   SC and prime form: _____

Mode or scale: _____

B. Bartók, *Bagatelle*, Op. 6, No. 2, mm. 7–8 and 14–16

Listen to this piece in the anthology, then consider the melodic motives x (first three notes) and y (last three notes) from measures 7–8. Calculate the ic vector, and listen for the difference in sound between the two trichords.

Mm. 7–8

Trichord x pcs: { _____ }   Trichord y pcs: { _____ }

Trichord x ic vector: [_____]   Trichord y ic vector: [_____]

In a few words, describe how the trichords differ in intervallic content, based on examining their ic vectors.

For the following labeled segments, compare the first three pcs with trichord x and the last three pcs with trichord y. Specify the precise relationships using T_n and/or T_nI notation. Because trichord x has symmetrical properties, it will always have multiple correct answers, including both T_n and T_nI relations; you need give only one of each. (For unrelated trichords, write NE for "not equivalent.")

Mm. 15–16

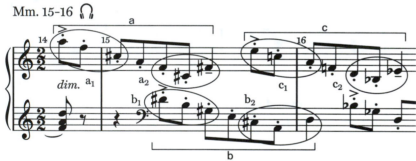

(1) Measures 14–15 right hand (set a)

pcs in a_1: { _____ }

Relationship between set a_1 and x trichord: $a_1 = T\underline{\ 0\ }x$

$a_1 = T\underline{\quad}Ix$

pcs in a_2: { _____ }

Relationship between set a_2 and y trichord: $a_2 = T\underline{\quad}y$

(2) Measures 15–16 left hand (set b)

pcs in b_1: { _____ }

Relationship between set b_1 and x trichord: $b_1 = T\underline{\quad}x$

pcs in b_2: { _____ }

Relationship between set b_2 and y trichord: $b_2 = T\underline{\quad}y$

(3) Measures 15–16 right hand (set c)

pcs in c_1: { _____ }

Relationship between set c_1 and x trichord: $c_1 = T\underline{\quad}x$

pcs in c_2: { _____ }

Relationship between set c_2 and y trichord: $c_2 = T\underline{\quad}y$

Assignment 37.4

Analysis: Benjamin Britten, "That yongë child," from Ceremony of Carols, mm. 1-8

Listen to this passage. Britten features sonorities made of a triad plus a half step, which create several different types of tetrachords. Identify the tetrachords circled in the score, copy your answers onto the chart that follows the score, then answer the questions that follow.

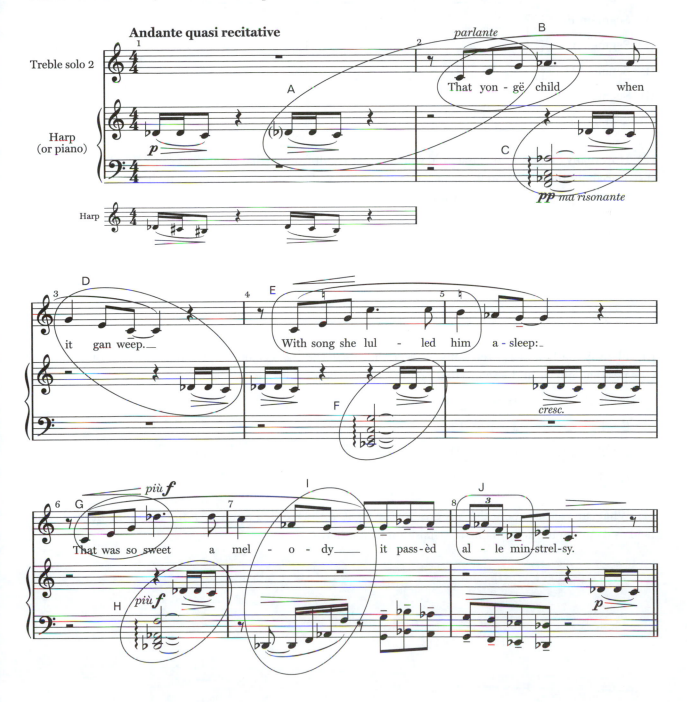

(1) Set-class identification

		Normal order	Prime form	SC (Forte) number
(a)	Segment A:	{ _____ }	[_____]	_____
(b)	Segment B:	{ _____ }	[_____]	_____
(c)	Segment C:	{ _____ }	[_____]	_____
(d)	Segment D:	{ _____ }	[_____]	_____
(e)	Segment E:	{ _____ }	[_____]	_____
(f)	Segment F:	{ _____ }	[_____]	_____
(g)	Segment G:	{ _____ }	[_____]	_____
(h)	Segment H:	{ _____ }	[_____]	_____
(i)	Segment I:	{ _____ }	[_____]	_____
(j)	Segment J:	{ _____ }	[_____]	_____

(2) How many different set classes did you find that result from a triad plus a half step? What can you discover about their location in Forte's table of sets? How does this location reflect their intervallic structure? (Hint: Check the ic vector.)

(3) Identify the T_n and $T_n I$ relations between the sets in the given chart. Use the normal order of each set (the pcs that appear in the score) to determine these relationships.

$D = T_0 A$ $\qquad$ $H = T\_\_\_ I\,E$

$E = T\_\_\_ C$ $\qquad$ $J = T\_\_\_ I\,F$

$E = T\_\_\_ I\,C$ $\qquad$ $G = T\_\_\_ D$

$H = T\_\_\_ E$

(4) What can you say about the "progression" from SC A to D to G? From C to E to H? Comment on the pcs held as common tones from one transposition to another.

Assignment 37.5

I. Analysis

A. Schoenberg, *Drei Klavierstücke*, Op. 11, No. 1, mm. 1-5 🎧

Listen to this passage, then complete the exercises that follow.

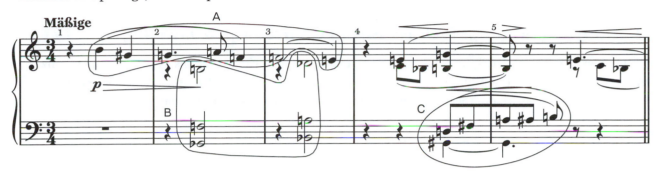

(1) Identify the prime form, ic vector, and SC (Forte) label for each of the three hexachords circled in the example.

A: Prime form: [_____]   ic vector: [_____]   SC: _____

B: Prime form: [_____]   ic vector: [_____]   SC: _____

C: Prime form: [_____]   ic vector: [_____]   SC: _____

(2) What can you say about two of the ic vectors? How do the set-class labels reflect this relationship?

B. Webern, String Quartet, Op. 5, mvt. 4, mm. 3-5 🎧

Begin by listening to this excerpt. Find the normal order for each circled segment, then write the prime form and T_n/T_nI relations requested.

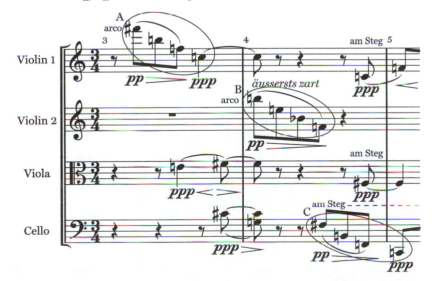

(1) Normal order   Segment A: { _____ }   Segment B: { _____ }   Segment C: { _____ }

(2) Prime form: [_____]

(3) Because this set is symmetrical, more than one operation transforms one member of the set class into another. For each relation, provide two possible T_n and T_nI values in the blanks.

Comparing A and B (by T_n):

B = T___ A   B = T___ A

Comparing A and B (by T_nI):

B = T___ I A   B = T___ I A

Comparing B and C:

C = T___ B   C = T___ B

Comparing B and C (by T_nI):

C = T___ I B   C = T___ I B

II. Analytical writing: Webern, String Quartet, Op. 5, mvt. 3 ♫

Write an extended essay analyzing this movement, taking the following questions as guidelines. Organize the essay as you see fit (don't simply answer the questions in a list). Support your ideas with specific examples, citing measure numbers. Turn in an annotated copy of the score with your essay.

A. Listen to the movement a few times without a score. What makes the work "hang together," and what elements help you divide it into formal sections? What type of mood does this music convey? What musical elements contribute to the mood?

B. If the presence of ostinatos in the bass divides the composition into sections, there are three parts: measures 1-6 (C♯ ostinato), 9-14, and 15-21 (B-G-A♯ ostinato). How would you characterize these sections? What elements are different (or the same) between sections? How would you characterize measures 7-8 and 22-23?

C. You have already identified SCs 3-3 and 3-4 in the opening section (Assignment 37.3). Do these set classes continue to play a prominent role in the remainder of the movement? Discuss.

D. There are a few places in the movement where whole-tone subsets may be found. Identify these by measure number and set-class type.

E. Find at least three canonic passages (including canon by inversion). Give measure numbers and instruments.

Assignment 37.6

Analysis: Stravinsky, "Bransle gay," from Agon

Find a recording of this piece in your library, online, or listen in class, while following the score on pages 473–474. Complete the form chart, using the following instructions.

(1) Column 3: For each group of measures shown in the chart, write the complete pitch-classes and content in normal order with pc integers (leave the Phrase Letter column blank for now). If there are no pitches in a measure, write "none."

(2) For each normal order you have written, calculate the prime form and look up the Forte number in Appendix 5. Write this number in the Set Class column.

(3) Now study the rhythmic and metrical aspects of each section identified on the chart. In the Meter column, write the meter if it is consistent (in instruments other than the castanet), or write "changing" if it is not consistent. In the Comments column, note where rhythmic patterns from one section recur (exactly or varied) in another.

MEASURES	PHRASE LETTER	PITCH CLASSES	SET CLASS (FORTE NUMBER)	METER OR MARK AS CHANGING	OPTIONAL COMMENTS (REPEATED PATTERNS, TEXTURE CHANGE, AGGREGATE COMPLETION)
1–8		none		$\frac{3}{8}$	castanet only
2–5	a				
6					
7–10					
11					
12–20					
21–22					
23–25					
26					

(4) How do rhythmic motives help define the groupings?

(5) What musical aspect partitions off measures 2-5, 7-10, and 12-20 from the other parts of the piece? Refer to the score and your chart to decide.

(6) What musical aspects help establish a new phrase in measure 21? What aspects divide up measures 21-25 into the groupings shown in the chart (mm. 21-22 and 23-25)?

(7) Comment on the rhythmic/metric role of the castanet in this movement.

(8) Look back at the aspects of the music you have examined, and provide phrase letters (**a**, **a′**, **b**, etc.) for measures 2-5, 7-10, 12-20, 21-22, and 23-25 in the second column of the chart.

(9) Examine the pitch-class content of measures 21-22. How does this pc set relate to the sets in other sections? How do the Forte numbers reflect this relationship?

(10) What is the formal design of this movement—binary? ternary? quaternary? Which aspects of the music contribute to the perception of form? Write several sentences that defend your choice of form with analytical evidence.

Score: Stravinsky, "Bransle Gay" from Agon

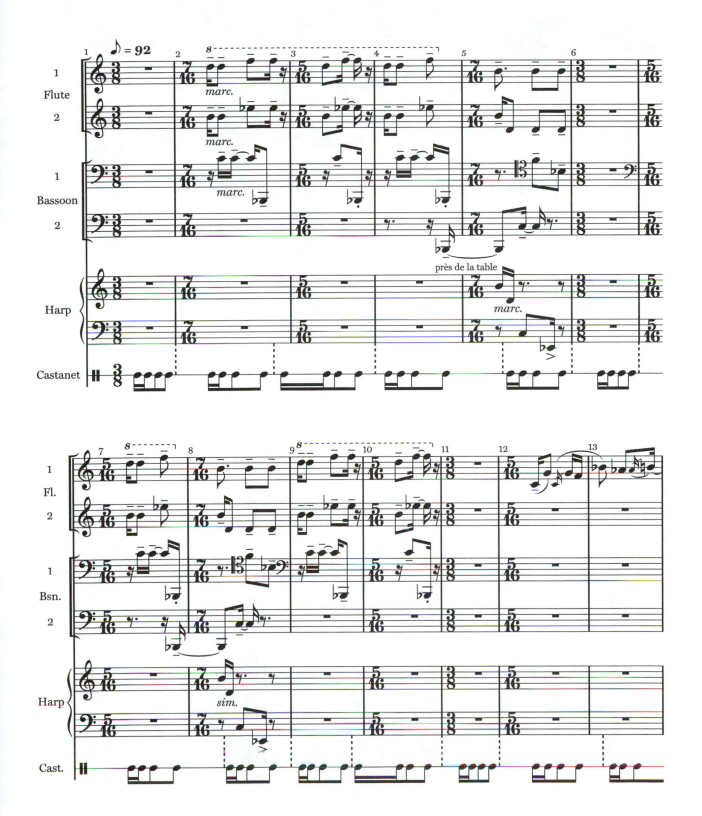

Optional: Clock-face "scratch" paper

38 Ordered Segments and Serialism

NAME _____

Assignment 38.1

I. Identifying serial operations on ordered pitch segments

For each of the given ordered pitch segments A and B, the segments (1), (2), and (3) are transpositions of the prime (P), inversion (I), retrograde (R), or retrograde inversion (RI).

- First write the ordered pitch intervals below each segment (using + and – signs).
- Then use the information from the interval succession to label the segments as P, I, R, or RI.

A. Based on Stravinsky's "Full Fadom Five," from *Three Songs from William Shakespeare* 🎧

Prime segment:

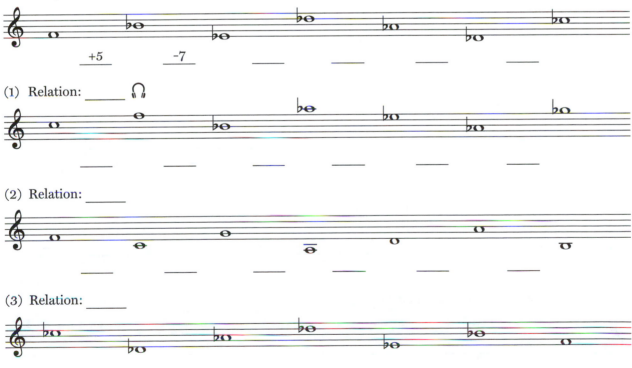

+5   -7   ___   ___   ___   ___

(1) Relation: _____ 🎧

___   ___   ___   ___   ___

(2) Relation: _____

___   ___   ___   ___   ___

(3) Relation: _____

___   ___   ___   ___   ___

B.

Prime segment:

_____   _____   _____   _____   _____   _____

(1) Relation: _____

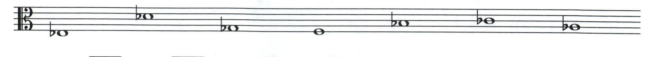

_____   _____   _____   _____   _____   _____

(2) Relation: _____

_____   _____   _____   _____   _____   _____

(3) Relation: _____

_____   _____   _____   _____   _____   _____

II. Writing serial operations on ordered pitch segments

Taking the following pitch segment as a starting point, transform the segment in the following ways. (Reminder: You are working with pitches, not pitch classes, in this exercise. Use ordered pitch intervals to complete the tasks.)

A. Transpose up ten semitones.

B. Invert with the same starting pitch as the original.

C. Retrograde the original series of pitches.

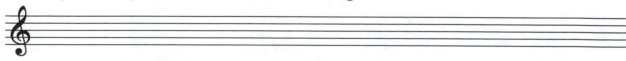

D. Transpose the original down three semitones and retrograde.

Assignment 38.2

I. Identifying serial operations on ordered pitch-class segments

For each of the ordered pitch-class segments A and B, segments (1), (2), and (3) are transpositions of the prime (P), inversion (I), retrograde (R), or retrograde inversion (RI).

- Write the ordered pitch-class intervals (0 to 11, calculated clockwise around the clock face) under each segment, then compare the segments.
- Use the information from the interval succession to label the segments as P, I, R, or RI.

For P or I segments, include the pc integer of the first note in the label (e.g., I_6); for R or RI, include the pc integer of the last note in the label.

A. From Stravinsky, "Full Fadom Five"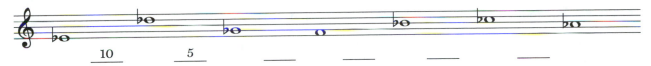

Prime segment: P_3

10 _____ 5 _____ _____ _____ _____ _____

(1) Relation: _____

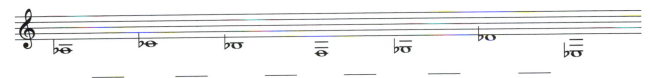

_____ _____ _____ _____ _____ _____

(2) Relation: _____

_____ _____ _____ _____ _____ _____

(3) Relation: _____

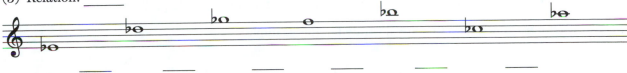

_____ _____ _____ _____ _____ _____

II. Analysis

A. Tavener, "The Lamb" (anthology)

Listen again to this piece while following the score in your anthology, and examine measures 13-16. Find one example of the work's prime segment in each of its four forms (P, I, R, and RI). On the staves provided on page 480, write each form, and give its location (measure number and voice part) and its label (for example, I_7).

SEGMENT	MEASURE NUMBER (MM. 13-16)	S, A, T, B	LABEL

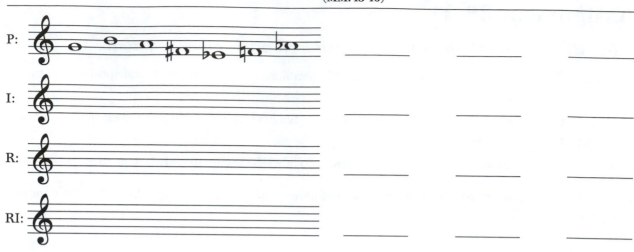

P:	___ ___	___ ___	___
I:	___ ___	___ ___	___
R:	___ ___	___ ___	___
RI:	___ ___	___ ___	___

B. Stravinsky, "Four Duos," from *Agon*, mm. 1-7 (score on p. 481)

(1) How are the pitches organized? The following questions will help you discover the answer.

   (a) Consider the intervals between instruments. What is the relationship between the three parts?

   (b) List the first twelve pcs that sound in this excerpt: < _____ >

   (c) List the second twelve pcs that sound in this excerpt: < _____ >

   (d) What is the relationship of the pitch classes in measures 1-3 to those of 4-7? Examine the ordered pc intervals to answer this question.

   (e) Is this row symmetrical?

   (f) If the first twelve pcs are labeled P_0, what is the label for the second 12 pcs? _____

(2) List two metrical practices that are illustrated in this example.

   (a)

   (b)

(3) The passage includes only quarter notes, and could have been notated in $\frac{4}{4}$ (or some other meter with a quarter-note beat) throughout. What effect might Stravinsky's metric choices make in performance?

Score: Stravinsky, "Four Duos" from Agon, mm. 1–7

Assignment 38.3

Analysis: Milton Babbitt, "Play on Notes," mm. 1–16

This composition, written for a children's music textbook, was intended for performance by children's voices and bells. Sing and play this piece in class or with a friend playing the other part. Consider the first two measures of the voice part to be the segment P_0. The remaining segments are also two measures each.

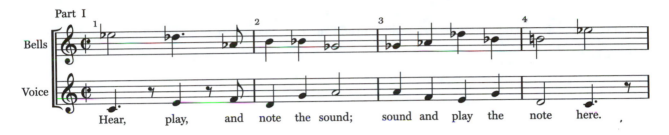

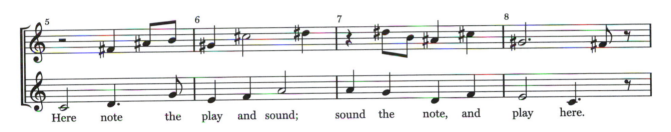

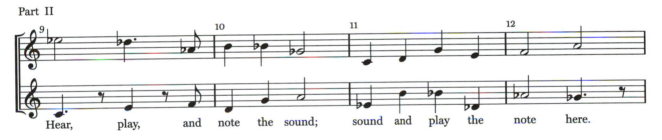

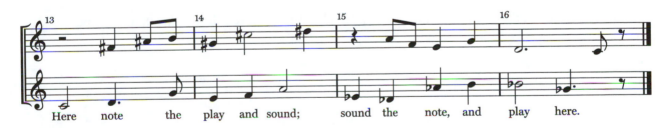

A. Label each segment on the score (e.g., P_0, R_6), then copy the row labels onto the table.

Part I	mm. 1-2	3-4	5-6	7-8
Bells:	R_6	_____	_____	_____
Voice:	P_0	_____	_____	_____

Part II	mm. 9-10	11-12	13-14	15-16
Bells:	_____	_____	_____	_____
Voice:	_____	_____	_____	_____

B. Compare the first hexachord in each part.

(1) List the pc collection for each part in measures 1-2 in normal order, then calculate the ordered pitch-class interval sequence for each.

Bells: { _____ }   pci sequence: _____

Voice: { _____ }   pci sequence: _____

(2) What property does the pci sequence display?

(3) If you consider each hexachord as a scale, played from its lowest pitch, to which keys do they belong?

Bells scale type: _____

Voice scale type: _____

C. Consider the pcs of measures 1-2 when both parts are combined.

(1) What type of collection results?

(2) Compare this collection with that of measures 5-6.

(3) Where is this collection found elsewhere in the piece?

D. Babbitt divides the piece into two parts. What musical features support this division? Consider phrase structure, rhythms, and patterns of repeated segments.

E. List each word of the text with its particular pitch class (in measure 1 "hear" = pc 0, "play" = pc 4, and so on).

(1) hear or here   pcs: ____ and ____

(2) play   pcs: ____ and ____

(3) and   pcs: ____ and ____

(4) note   pcs: ____ and ____

(5) the   pcs: ____ and ____

(6) sound   pcs: ____ and ____

(7) Use these pitch classes to describe the structure of the song's lyrics.

Assignment 38.4

Analysis: Stravinsky, "Full Fadom Five"

A score to this song is given on pages 489–490 of this workbook. Find a recording online; listen to the movement and then answer the following questions.

- Following the initial introductory measure, this passage is based on a seven-tone row and its serial transformations. The row is first presented in the voice part in measures 2–3.
- Important to your analysis is the fact that Stravinsky was a self-taught serialist who did not follow Schoenberg's conventions for row transformations.
- Stravinsky used IR (inversion of the retrograde), rather than RI (retrograde of the inversion). To analyze these row forms, write out the retrograde first, then invert it.

A. Analysis of measure 1

(1) The pitches of the vocal melody are drawn from what scale type? (Hint: On your own paper, write the pitches of the melody as a scale, beginning with the last pitch class.)

Scale type: _____

(2) The pitches of the viola line are drawn from what scale type? Scale type: _____

(3) How are the flute and clarinet lines related?

(4) By what serial operation do the flute/clarinet lines relate to the vocal line? What invariant pitches do they share with the voice as a result of this operation?

(5) Write out the vocal melody of measure 1, without rhythm, on the staff provided. Then label the ordered pitch intervals and interval classes between adjacent pitches, as shown. What observations can you make about the construction of this melody? (Hint: Look for symmetries or repetitions of interval patterns.)

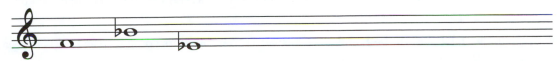

Pitch intervals: +5   −7   ____   ____   ____   ____

Interval classes: 5   5   ____   ____   ____   ____

Observations about melodic construction:

B. Supply the following information for the seven-note row (voice part, mm. 2–3), which you will use to complete the analysis. (Remember Stravinsky's idiosyncratic "IR.")

Row form	Pitch classes	Ordered pc intervals
(1) Prime row (P_3)	_____	_____
(2) Retrograde of prime (R_3)	_____	_____
(3) I_3 (inversion of P, beginning with pc 3)	_____	_____
(4) IR_3 (inversion of R, beginning with its first pitch class)	_____	_____

(5) List the pitch classes of line (3) in retrograde order, and compare them with line (4).

　　$R(I_3)$—line (3) retrograded: _____

　　IR_3—line (4): _____

(6) Is the inversion of the retrograde (IR_3) the same as the retrograde inversion (RI_3) of the prime row?

　　　　YES　　　NO

C. Now write out the pitch classes of other row forms that will be helpful in this analysis. You may transpose the basic forms above, or use the ordered pc intervals to generate the elements.

(1) P_0 _____　　　(2) R_8 _____　　　(3) R_1 _____

(4) P_8 _____　　　(5) R_t _____

D. Analyze the row forms for measures 2–15 by marking them in your score. Enter all the completed row forms from your score into the chart on p. 487, in the order that the rows appear in the music. The first three row labels are given.

Hints:

- Some rows may be completed in a different instrumental part from the one in which they began.
- The first two pitches of the flute part complete the clarinet row of measures 2–3.
- Throughout, pairs of row pitches may be repeated before going on.
- Some rows are elided. When a row is completed, check the next series of pitch classes to see if it matches one of the rows listed above. If not, back up to check for row elision (that is, whether the last pitch[es] of one row also serve as the first of the next).
- Finally, the rows break off (wherever they were in the series) as soon as the voice sings "knell" at the end of measure 15.
- For this analysis, label both the R and IR forms with order numbers going forward. This is because the IR is not the same as the retrograde of I.

In the Comments column, note any relationships among the voices. Indicate if a row form is completed in a different part from the one in which it began, if notes are added or left out, or if there are serial connections between rows in two different parts (e.g., same row form but different durations or contour).

MEASURES	PART	ROW FORM	COMMENTS
2-3	voice	P_3	
2-4	viola	P_3	Same row as voice down an octave
2-4	clarinet	IR_3	Order no. 6 in flute also; order no. 7 only in flute

For class discussion: Are measures 16 and 17 of the song serial? Discuss their pitch structure in comparison with the previous portions of the song you have already analyzed. How do the pitch and rhythmic materials here invoke the images of the text?

Score: Stravinsky, "Full Fadom Five," mm. 1–17

Assignment 38.5

Making and reading a row matrix

Make a row matrix for each of the following twelve-tone rows on the grids provided, using integers to represent the pitch classes.

- Begin by writing the pitch classes below the staff for each pitch.
- Transpose the row to begin with 0.
- Write the integer representation of the series beginning with 0 on the top row of the matrix, and the inversion down the first column.
- Complete the rest of the matrix.

A. Webern, "Das dunkle Herz" ("The Dark Heart"), Op. 23, No. 1, mm. 2-6 (row)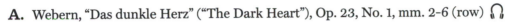

Das dunk - le Herz,   das   in   sich lauscht,   er - schaut den Früh - [ling]

Translation: The dark heart, which listens to itself, recognizes spring.

pcs: ___ ___ ___ ___   ___ ___ ___ ___   ___ ___ ___ ___

P_0: ___ ___ ___ ___   ___ ___ ___ ___   ___ ___ ___ ___

Using the matrix you have created for this row in part C, write out the following row forms:

(1) I_5 < _____ >

(2) R_e < _____ >

(3) P_7 < _____ >

(4) RI_6 < _____ >

B. Webern, *Symphonie*, Op. 21, mvt. 2, mm. 12-17 (cello)

pcs: ___ ___ ___ ___   ___ ___ ___   ___ ___ ___   ___ ___ ___

P_0: ___ ___ ___ ___   ___ ___ ___   ___ ___ ___   ___ ___ ___

As discussed in the chapter, this row has symmetric properties that make two row labels possible for each row. Using the matrix in part D, provide two labels that correctly identify each of these rows.

(1) <   2 e 0 1 9 t 4 3 7 6 5 8   >   Row form: _____ or _____

(2) <   t 1 0 e 3 2 8 9 5 6 7 4   >   Row form: _____ or _____

(3) <   t 7 8 9 5 6 0 e 3 2 1 4   >   Row form: _____ or _____

(4) <   5 8 7 6 t 9 3 4 0 1 2 e   >   Row form: _____ or _____

C. "Das dunkle Herz"

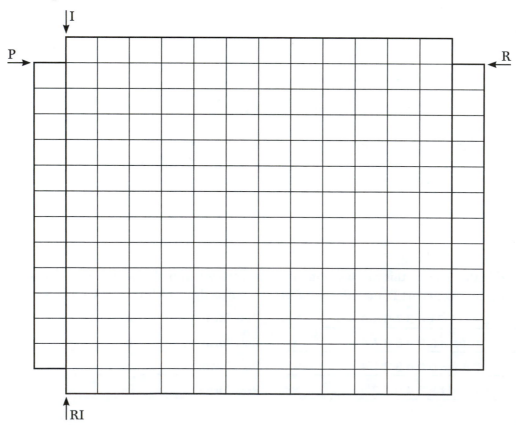

	I	I_0	I_2	I_e										
P →	P_0	0	2	e									R_0	← **R**
	P_t	t	0	9									R_t	
	P_1	1	3	0									R_1	
		RI_0	RI_2	RI_e										

↑ RI

D. *Symphonie*, Op. 21, mvt. 2

↓ I

P →   ← **R**

↑ RI

Assignment 38.6

Analysis: Webern "Das dunkle Herz," Op. 23, No. 1, mm. 1–11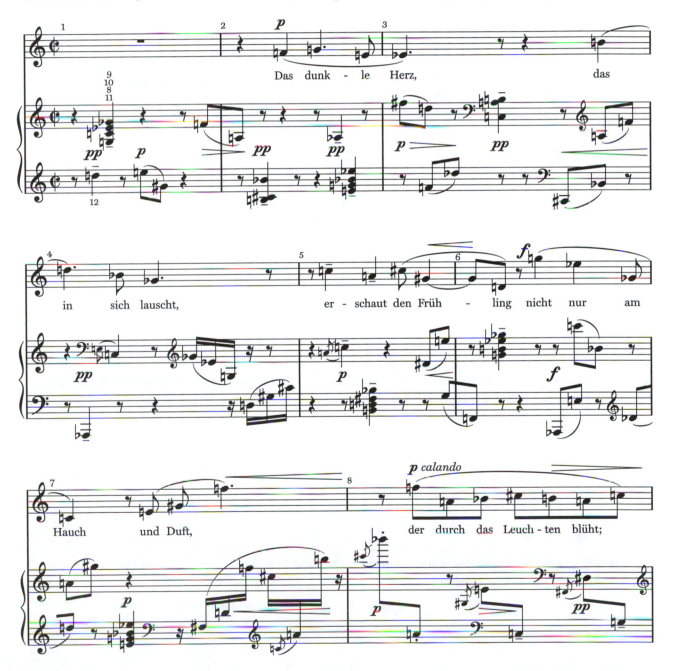

Listen to the passage twice: once while following the text and translation, and again while following the score. Using the matrix you constructed in Assignment 38.5, label the row forms, then answer the questions. Begin with the vocal line: write the row's name (e.g., P_6, RI_4) at its beginning, then label row members with order numbers (1 to 12 for P and I forms, and 12 to 1 for R and RI forms). Analysis of the keyboard part takes some detective work because of its chords. As you identify row forms and trace them through, write order numbers to show the correspondence of row ordering to chord pitches. There are several row elisions, where the end of one row shares pitches with the beginning of the next.

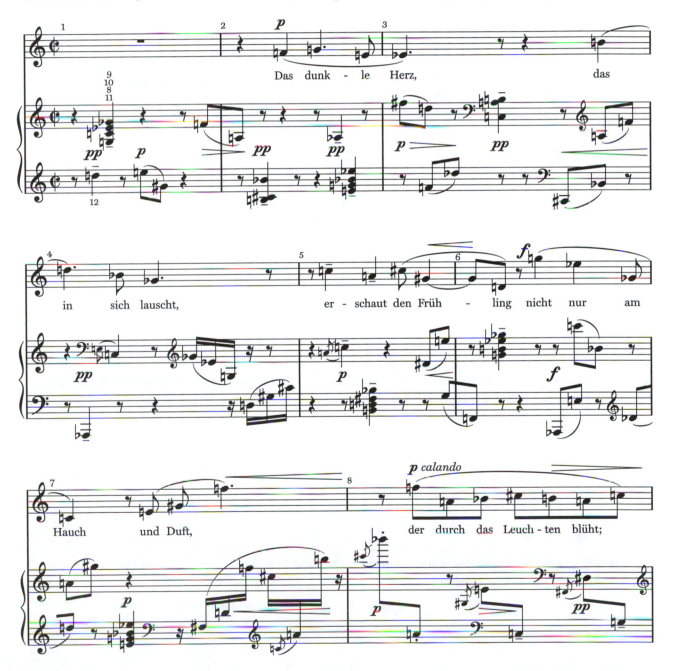

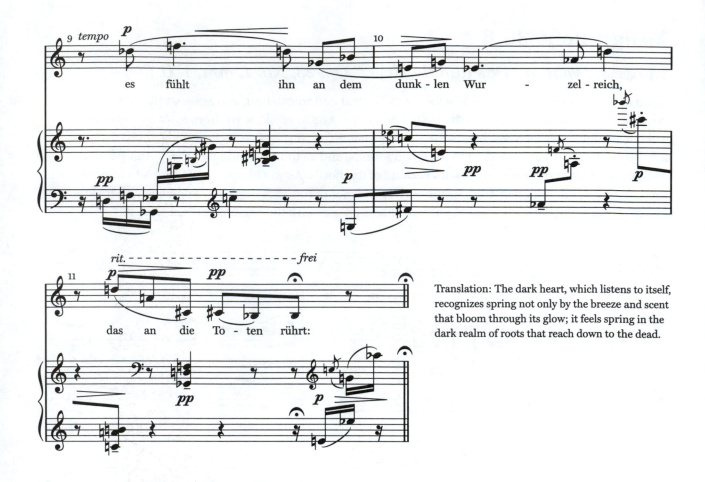

Translation: The dark heart, which listens to itself, recognizes spring not only by the breeze and scent that bloom through its glow; it feels spring in the dark realm of roots that reach down to the dead.

A. Consider the harmonic dimension. Which intervals or harmonies are featured as chords? Name them with set-class or pitch-class interval names.

B. Consider the singer's strategies for finding and tuning pitches with the accompaniment. Cite at least three places where the piano part provides a pitch in advance, doubles a pitch in the vocal line, or plays a vocal pitch immediately after it is sung.

m. _____ :

m. _____ :

m. _____ :

C. Identify at least two examples of text painting in the vocal part. (It may help to write the translation below the German text in your score.)

Measures   *German text*   *English translation*   *Describe setting*

Assignment 38.7

I. Analysis: Webern, Symphonie, Op. 21, mvt. 2 ♫

A score with excerpts from this movement is given on pages 497–499 of this workbook. This is a C score: transposing instruments sound as notated. Listen to the movement, and then answer the following questions.

A. Theme, winds and harp, mm. 1–11 ♫

(1) Begin by labeling the row forms, referring to the row matrix you constructed in Assignment 38.5.

- Because of special properties of this row, each R is identical to a P form, and each RI is identical to an I form. When labeling rows, use the P and I labels (rather than the retrograde labels).

The clarinet melody has one row form, the accompaniment has another. Identify these forms.

Clarinet row: _____   Horn/Harp row: _____

(2) Label the row members on the score. Then take a close look at the ways the pcs are realized in terms of pitch register. What registral technique discussed in the chapter is used here? Explain.

Technique used: _____

Explanation:

(3) Look at the pitches, rhythm, and contour centered around measures 5–7 and extending in either direction. What compositional technique characterizes the structure centered around these measures? (Hint: The symmetry of the row is reflected in other types of symmetries.)

Pitch:

Rhythm:

Contour:

B. Variation I, string parts, mm. 11–23 ♫

Use the row matrix you constructed in Assignment 38.5 to label the row forms in measures 11–23 (using P and I labels), then answer the following questions.

(1) In this passage, the instruments are paired. Look closely at the pitch intervals, rhythms, and articulation to determine the pairing.

Which instruments are paired? _____

How are the paired instruments related to each other? _____

(2) Beginning in measure 11, for each pair of instruments, one row is an I form and the other is a P form. Write the two row labels for each instrument pair.

Pair 1: _____

Pair 2: _____

(3) How are the paired rows related to each other (hint: how are the subscripts of their labels related)?

(4) In which measure does the first set of rows end and the second set begin? _____

What happens in this passage when any part gets to the end of its row?

How do the rhythms, dynamics, and articulations relate to this change of rows (if at all)?

C. Coda, harp and strings, mm. 89-99 🎧

In this variation, two rows cross back and forth between instruments: as you label the rows in the score, it might be helpful to circle the numbers of one of the rows to distinguish between them.

(1) The harp plays the first note of each row, before the rows begin crossing among instruments. The two rows in this passage are: _____

(2) Is there a palindrome here in pitch, contour, and rhythm—as in the previous sections you analyzed from this movement? If so, where is the center of the mirror?

(3) Compare these measures with the opening of this movement (part A). List at least two differences and two similarities.

Differences:

Similarities:

(4) Is there registral invariance in this passage?

Score excerpts: Webern, Symphonie, Op. 21, mvt. 2

A. Theme, winds and harp, mm. 1–11 (C score: transposing instruments sound as notated.)

B. Variation I, string parts, mm. 11-23

C. Coda, harp and strings, mm. 89-99

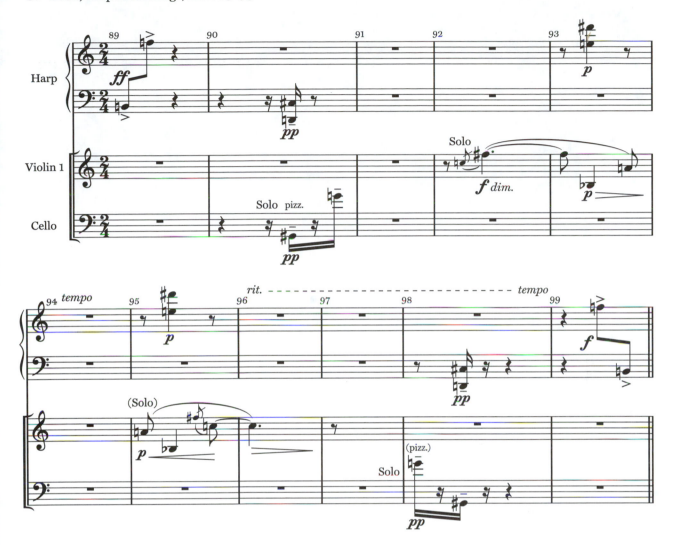

NAME _____

Assignment 38.8

I. Finding combinatorial row pairs

A row matrix for Schoenberg's Violin Concerto is given. Circle the appropriate hexachords in the matrix to find combinatorial rows for: (1) P_0, (2) R_9, and (3) R_7. Then write out the combinatorial pairs below the matrix, with the same hexachords circled.

	I_0	I_1	I_6	I_2	I_7	I_9	I_3	I_4	I_t	I_e	I_5	I_8	
P_0	0	1	6	2	7	9	3	4	t	e	5	8	R_0
P_e	e	0	5	1	6	8	2	3	9	t	4	7	R_e
P_6	6	7	0	8	1	3	9	t	4	5	e	2	R_6
P_t	t	e	4	0	5	7	1	2	8	9	3	6	R_t
P_5	5	6	e	7	0	2	8	9	3	4	t	1	R_5
P_3	3	4	9	5	t	0	6	7	1	2	8	e	R_3
P_9	9	t	3	e	4	6	0	1	7	8	2	5	R_9
P_8	8	9	2	t	3	5	e	0	6	7	1	4	R_8
P_2	2	3	8	4	9	e	5	6	0	1	7	t	R_2
P_1	1	2	7	3	8	t	4	5	e	0	6	9	R_1
P_7	7	8	1	9	2	4	t	e	5	6	0	3	R_7
P_4	4	5	t	6	e	1	7	8	2	3	9	0	R_4

RI_0 RI_1 RI_6 RI_2 RI_7 RI_9 RI_3 RI_4 RI_t RI_e RI_5 RI_8

(1) P_0 is combinatorial with which I row? _____

P_0: < _____ >

___ : < _____ >

(2) R_9 is combinatorial with which RI row? _____

R_9: < _____ >

___ : < _____ >

(3) P_7 is combinatorial with which R row? _____

P_7: < _____ >

___ : < _____ >

II. Integral (or total) serialism

In the following passage, start by identifying the duration of each pitch (counted in thirty-second notes) combined with the rest that follows. Write the durations below each pitch in the score, then answer the questions that follow.

Pierre Boulez, *Structures Ia*, mm. 73–81 (piano 2, left hand)

(1) Write out the pitch names, adding the durations (counted in thirty-seconds) above and the pc integers below.

Durations: <   4   5   2   8   >

Note names: <   F♯   C   F   G   >

Pc integers: <   6   0   5   7   >

(2) Name two rhythmic techniques seen here: _____

Assignment 38.9

Style composition

On your own manuscript paper or music-notation program, write a serial composition in the style of (1) Schoenberg or Webern (twelve-tone) or (2) Tavener, Babbitt, or Stravinsky (serial but not twelve-tone). The goal of this project is to write a piece you will be proud to have performed in class and, in the process, to learn more about twentieth-century styles.

- Style is conveyed through texture, scales or modes used, pitch materials, meter, rhythm and durations, melodic design, range and register, sizes of intervals employed, and other features.

- Choose one of the following works as your model (from the chapter text or other homework assignments): Schoenberg's Op. 33a, Webern's *Piano Variations* or "Das dunkle Herz," Tavener's "The Lamb," Babbitt's "Play on Notes," or Stravinsky's "Full Fadom Five." Closely observe the composition you are modeling to create your own composition in that style.

- Score your composition as one of the following: a piano piece, an SATB choral piece (provide a piano reduction or accompaniment), or a song for voice and piano.

- The length of your composition should be 12 to 16 measures.

- Include all expressive markings (tempo, dynamic levels, articulation, etc.) needed by the performers to reflect the mood or attitude your piece is intended to convey.

Choose one of the following designs for your composition:

A. A twelve-tone composition that uses one or more of the following: a palindrome in pitch and rhythm, hexachordal combinatoriality, a derived row, or registral invariance. Label the composition as to which option(s) you have chosen.

B. A serial composition with a prime segment of 6-7 pitches, and at least four transformations of your row (P, I, R, or RI). Use one or more of the following: pitch or pitch-class invariances between voices or hands (or between piano and voice), row elision, row combinations that produce aggregates, or rows constructed of primarily diatonic pc collections.

Instructions and getting started:

(1) Write a melody that features 12 different pcs (Choice A: a twelve-tone composition) or 6-7 pcs (Choice B: a serial composition); this will be your ordered segment and the foundation of your serial composition. Each pitch class will not be repeated (other than an immediate restatement of one or two of the pitch classes in order) when the melody is presented in the composition.

(2) Explore the transformations of your melody: write out the retrograde, inversion, and retrograde inversion, and see what happens when you transpose these transformations up or down to different pitch levels. Construct a row matrix, if this is helpful.

(3) Look for transformations that can be used for row elisions, that have potential pc invariances to be explored in your realization, or that may be used to create palindromes or other features you are planning.

(4) Consider your row transformations in pitch-class space, but also in pitch space, preserving contour and/or the rhythmic character of the melody. The parts should work together in an interesting way in regard to both pitch and rhythm.

(5) Prepare a composition for two to four performers based on the musical materials you have developed. If you compose for singer or choir, write words or choose a preexisting text for your composition. If you write for choir, prepare a piano reduction or accompaniment, to assist with performance in class (if class performances are planned).

(6) Your assignment should include the score—analyzed with all rows and their transformations—and a short paragraph with information about the row and how it was constructed, as well as the special features you chose to realize in your composition.

If possible, rehearse your composition for performance in class. (Another option: prepare your composition in a music-notation software program that will allow for playback possibilities, and prepare a recording.)

Sketch your ideas here:

39 Rhythm, Meter, and Form after 1945

NAME _____

Assignment 39.1

Analysis: John Tavener, "The Lamb" 🎧

We analyzed portions of this choral piece in Chapter 38 in the chapter and homework; now we will look at the piece as a whole. Begin by listening to this work while following the score in your anthology.

A. "The Lamb" has a sectional form. The end of each section is marked by a fermata followed by a tempo indication. The large formal divisions are given in the following chart; fill out the remainder of the chart.

- For serial passages, include the voice part and segment labels—soprano (or S): P_7, alto (or A): I_7, and so on. Use subsections to show where the seven-note row segments change. If no row is present, write "none."

- For modal passages, determine the pc center and mode or scale type. If no scale is present, write "none."

MEASURES	COMPOSITIONAL TECHNIQUE	MODE (IF PRESENT)	SUBSECTIONS (FOR ROW CHANGES)	ROWS (IF PRESENT) BY VOICE PART, SATB:
1-6	serial	none	1-2	S: P_7, then S: P_7 and A: I_7
		none	3-4	S: P_7, then R$_7$
7-10				
11-16				
17-20				

B. Describe the pc structure of the opening:

(1) The opening measure suggests what key or mode and pc center? _____

(2) What is the total pc content of measure 2?

Letter names: _____   pcs: { _____ }

(3) Write out the ordered letter names of the seven-note row segment:

Letter names: _____ pcs: { _____ }

(4) How is the row's pc content related to the pcs of measures 1-2?

(5) What is true about the (unordered) pc content of P_7 as compared with I_7?

C. Given the tonal implications of measure 1, what is surprising about the tonal structure of measures 5-6, and of measures 7-10?

D. Measures 7-10 feature a pattern of pitch and rhythmic repetition that gives this passage a timeless character.

(1) Write a few sentences to explain how the rhythm is structured, what is repeated, how each measure is changed on its repetition, and how a sense of closure is attained.

(2) What strategy might you use to count measures 9-10? What term applies to this strategy (Chapter 35)?

E. How do the closing measures (mm. 17-20) relate to measures 7-10? What is the same and what is different?

Assignment 39.2

George Crumb, "Los muertos llevan alas de musgo" ("The dead wear mossy wings"), from Madrigals, Book I, mm. 1–8

Find a recording of this work in your library, online, or listen to it as a class, while following the score on the back of this page. Then answer the following questions.

A. There are examples of changing meter in measures _____.

Will the notated changing meters be audible to the listener?   YES   NO

Why or why not?

B. Based on the tempo, notated rhythms, and performance instructions, will any sort of regular beat be perceptible in a performance following those instructions?

      YES   NO

If so, where? What element creates the sense of a pulse?

C. The pitch intervals featured in the bass part are primarily _____.

D. Look back at the notation of pitch, durations, articulations, and timbres. List at least three elements that indicate this work was composed after 1945.

(1)

(2)

(3)

(4)

Write a few sentences about how these elements contribute to the overall aural effect of the piece. Be prepared to discuss in class.

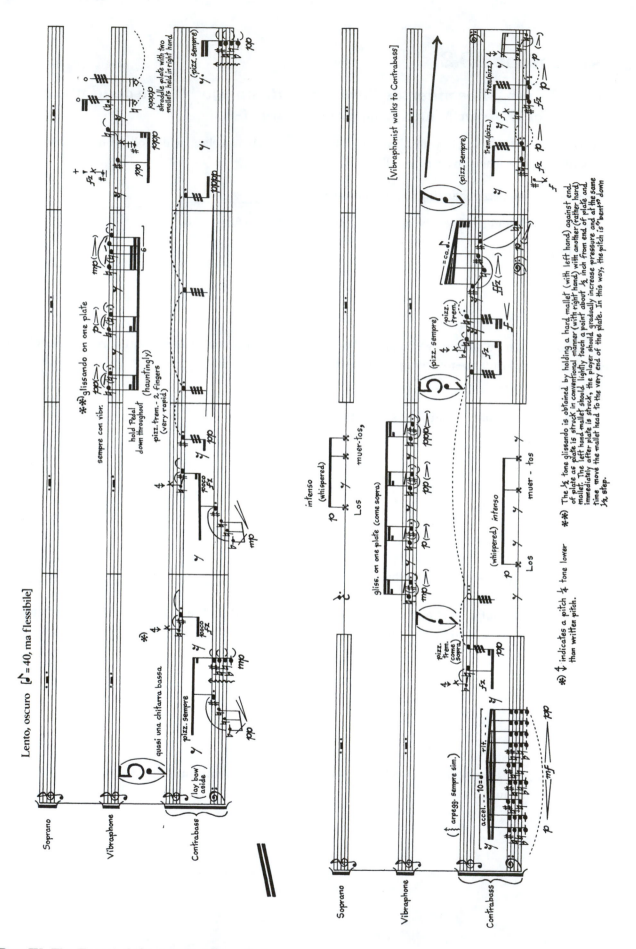

Assignment 39.3

Analysis

In each example given, identify the rhythmic or metric techniques shown. In the discussion section, write a few sentences that answer the following questions:

- If the excerpt features metric modulation, how is the tempo change made?
- If it features time-line notation, what is the length of time in each unit of measurement?
- What other rhythmic techniques (review Chapter 35) can you find in each example?

A. Elliott Carter, "Canaries," from *Eight Pieces for Four Timpani*, mm. 1–16 🎧 (mm. 9–16)

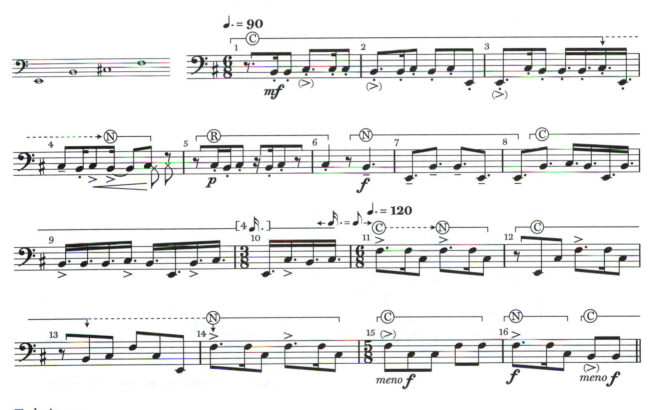

Techniques: _____

Discussion:

B. Krzysztof Penderecki, *Threnody for the Victims of Hiroshima*, rehearsal numbers 64–66 🎧

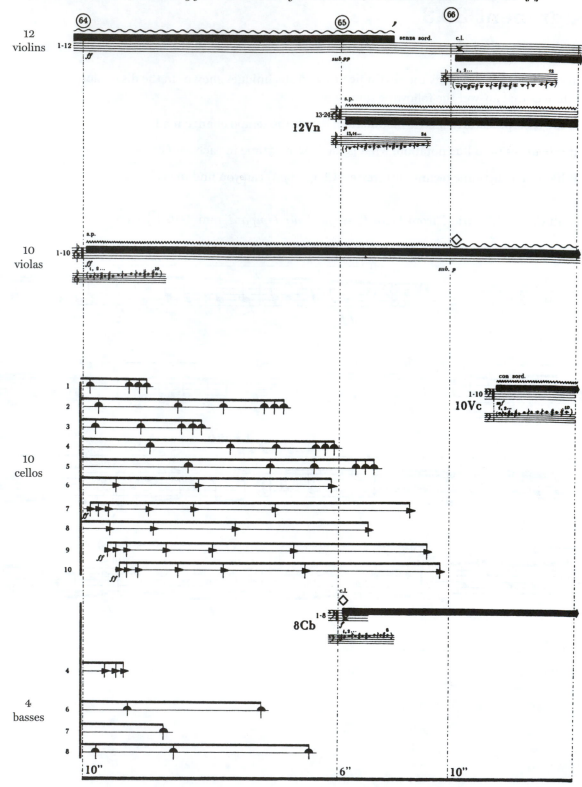

Techniques: _____

Discussion: _____

Assignment 39.3 *(continued)*

C. Carter, String Quartet No. 2, mvt. 1, mm. 54–60

Techniques: _____

Discussion: _____

D. Luciano Berio, *Sequenza I*, for solo flute, first two staves

Play through this excerpt at the keyboard or on your own instrument (or listen to a recording online), then answer the questions that follow.

(1) The tempo is indicated as ♩ = 70. At that rate, this passage lasts about _____ seconds. How did you compute the duration?

(2) Is there a strong sense of beat or meter in this passage?

(3) Are there any repeated rhythmic patterns here? What effect does the lack of repetition of patterns have on the sound of the passage?

Assignment 39.4

I. Analysis: Cathy Berberian, Stripsody, pages 10-11

Examine the score that follows. Its layout, in strips (like comic strips), may be the source of the composition's title. The spacing of the sounds on the strips shows how close in time they should be performed. Page 10 of the score includes two scenes (we could informally call them "grunts, etc." and "baby"). Page 11 includes one continuous scene that begins with barnyard sounds and ends with a baby crying. After studying the score, answer these questions.

A. Describe the rhythmic character of these pages. Is there a beat or meter? If so, where? How does the performer know when to make the sounds illustrated?

B. Where is the most rhythmically active portion of this passage? Where is the least rhythmically active portion?

C. Examine the sound content of each scene. Describe the "story line" or "characters" in each scene. How will the listener distinguish one scene from another?

Extra challenge: Try to perform this piece—it is much harder than it looks!

II. Composition or Essay

Complete one of the following creative exercises (your choice): a composition or essay.

A. On the following page, write a "scene" of your own, using graphic notation like Berberian's.
- Choose a scenario (like the "barnyard sounds" and "baby").
- Prepare a performance, making the representation of the sounds as artistic as possible.
- Plan to display the score while you perform the scene in class.

B. On the following page, write a paragraph or two that answers the question *What is music?*
- Make sure your definition includes any sounds or activities that you associate with music and excludes those that you don't.
- Consider Maue's *In the Woods* and Cage's *4′33″* in your essay. Are they or are they not music? Mention at least one other composition of your choice from this chapter (or another recent work you know).
- Defend your ideas. Be prepared to discuss your essay in class.

Write your graphic score or essay in this space.

Score: Berberian, Stripsody, pages 10 and 11

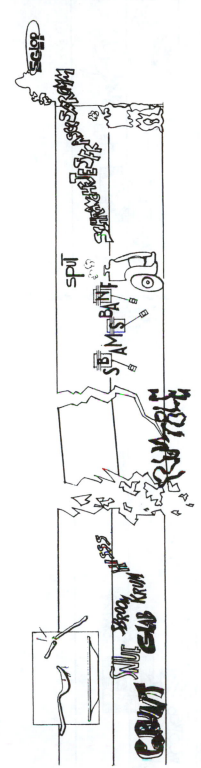

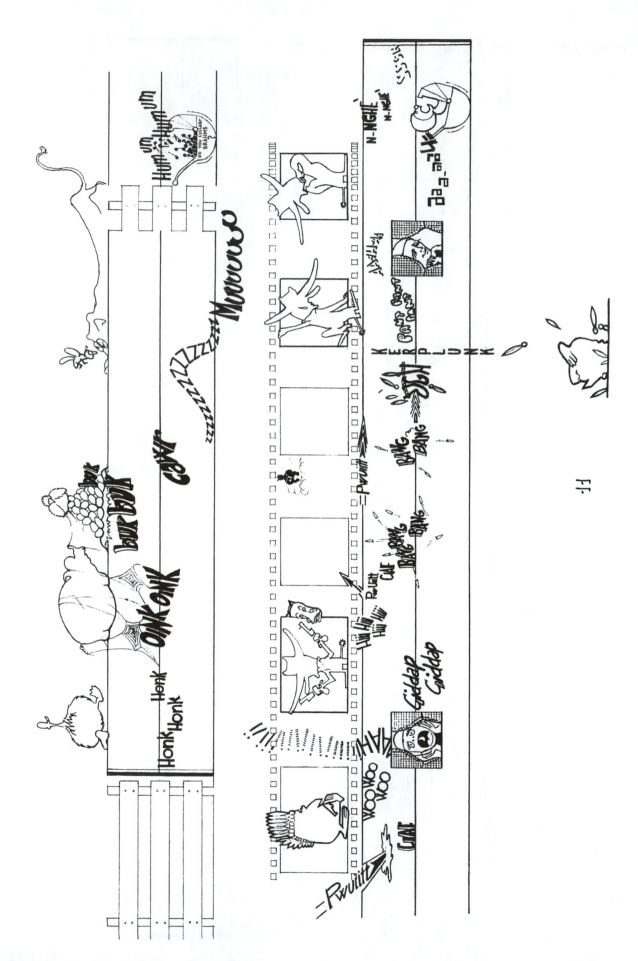

Assignment 39.5

Analysis

A. La Monte Young, *Composition 1960*, No. 2

Read the following score, then write a paragraph in the space provided that discusses the form of this piece. Like many pieces using text notation, this one may vary in the details from performance to performance, but it will show consistent elements, too, if the score is followed precisely.

> *Build a fire in front of the audience. Preferably, use wood,*
> *although other combustibles may be used as necessary for*
> *starting the fire or controlling the smoke. The fire may be*
> *of any size, but it should not be the kind which is associated*
> *with another object, such as a candle or a cigarette lighter.*
> *The lights may be turned out.*
> *After the fire is burning, the builder(s) may sit by and*
> *watch it for the duration of the composition; however, he*
> *(they) should not sit between the fire and the audience*
> *in order that its members will be able to see and enjoy*
> *the fire.*
> *The composition may be of any duration.*
> *In the event that the performance is broadcast, the*
> *microphone may be brought up close to the fire.*

What is the form of this piece? In your answer, consider which elements are variable and which will be the same in every performance. Also consider your aesthetic response to the piece—which aspects appeal to you and which do not, and why?

B. John Cage, *Two*

This work is the first of a series of so-called "number" works that Cage wrote at the end of his life (from 1987 until his death in 1992) that are titled by the number of performers; *Two* is for flute and piano.

All of the "number" pieces employ time brackets, which are interpreted as follows: the time bracket at the beginning of a staff line indicates the span of time within which the note must begin; the time bracket at the end of the staff indicates the span of time within which the note must end.

Following are the instructions given the performers of *Two*, along with the first two time brackets:

Each part has ten time brackets, nine which are flexible with respect to beginning and ending, and one, the eighth, which is fixed. No sound is to be repeated within a bracket. In the piano part each ictus in a single staff is to be played in the order given, but can be played in any relation to the sounds in the other staff. Some notes are held from one ictus to the next. A tone in parentheses is not to be played if it is already sounding. One hand may assist the other.

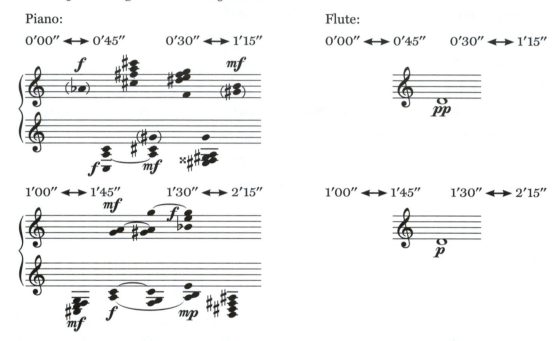

Write a paragraph answering the following questions or prepare these questions for class discussion, as your teacher directs.

(1) Consider the score's notation. What about the notation is traditional? What is unusual? Is the score indeterminate? In what ways?

(2) In what ways would performances of this score be the same? In what ways might they differ?

(3) How would one analyze this work? What can be determined about it? What elements of the music seem to be interesting for analysis?

Assignment 39.6

Analysis: Steve Reich, Piano Phase, *patterns 1-32*

A. Analytical graphing

Listen to this work while following the score in your anthology.

- In the alignment graphs on the following pages, the squares along the horizontal (or x) axis represent sixteenth-note durations; the squares up the vertical (or y) axis represent semitones. The pattern played by piano 1 is marked with Xs.

- Begin your study of the piece by graphing the pattern shifts played by piano 2, using Os, to contrast with the Xs. (When pianos 1 and 2 play the same note simultaneously, place the X within the O.) For alignment 1, piano 2 is tacet (silent); for alignment 2, it is playing in unison with piano 1.

- In each of the other alignments, piano 2's part shifts forward one sixteenth note (represented here by one square). Alignments 3 and 4 have been completed for you.

- Complete the graphs for alignments 5-13, then listen carefully to the piece. When you hear the parts "click" into each alignment, circle (on the graphs) the rhythmic patterns that emerge—sometimes the lower pitches stand out, sometimes the upper ones. When you hear the piano parts beginning to shift, listen for the next alignment. When you have finished circling the emerging rhythmic patterns, below each graph write in rhythmic notation (with the sixteenth note as the basic unit) the rhythmic pattern you heard.

B. What scale is implied by the pitch content of this section (patterns 1-32)? Does it sound major or minor?

C. Which melodic and harmonic intervals are formed as the patterns realign?

D. The close of this section sounds like a cadence, but there are no traditional cadential elements—harmonic or intervallic resolution, longer note values, falling melodic shape, and so on. How is the close created?

Alignments 1, 2, and 14

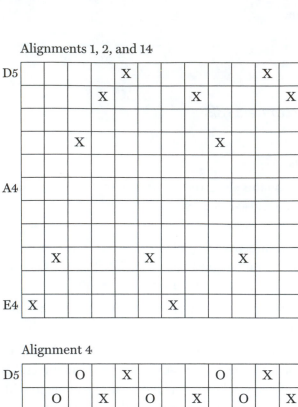

Alignment 3

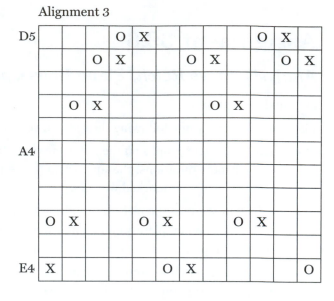

Alignment 4

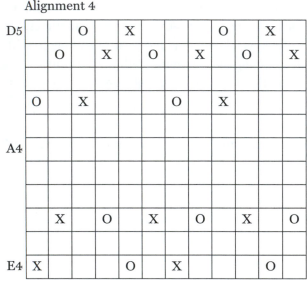

Alignment 5

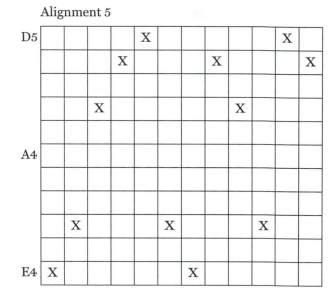

Alignment 6

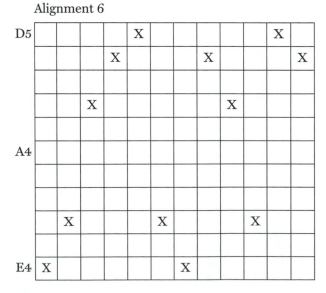

Alignment 7

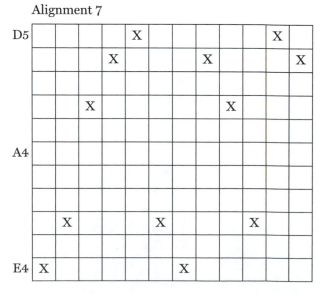

Alignment 8

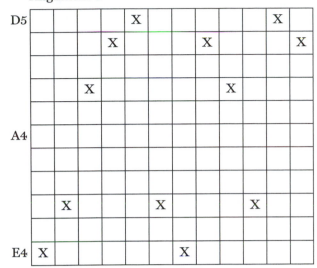

Alignment 9

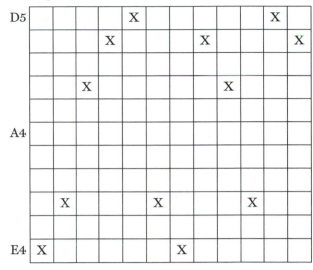

Alignment 10

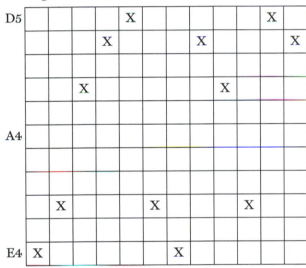

Alignment 11

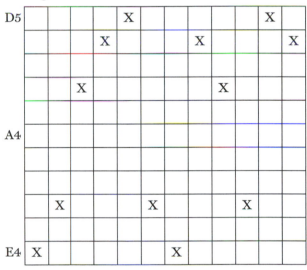

Alignment 12

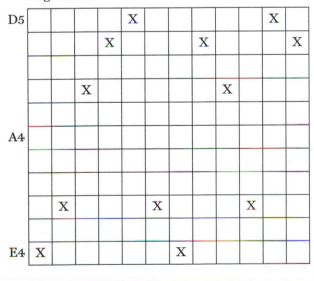

Alignment 13

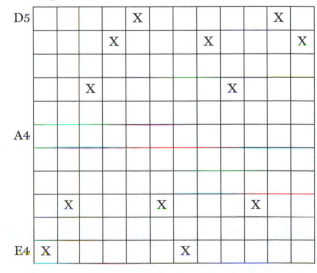

40 Recent Trends

NAME _____

Assignment 40.1

Analysis: Arvo Pärt, Magnificat, *first four phrases*

Listen to a recording or perform this passage with your class (use a keyboard to accompany, if necessary), then answer the following questions. The circled rehearsal numbers mark the phrases.

Translation: My soul doth magnify the Lord, and my spirit hath rejoiced in God my Savior. For he hath regarded the lowliness of his handmaiden. Behold, from henceforth all generations shall call me blessed.

A. Which voice in each phrase has the melody (that is, the moving part) and which has the accompaniment? (Hint: for phrase 4, consider which part has notes outside of the accompanying harmony F-A♭-C-E♭.)

B. How do the phrases correspond to the text? What marks the end of each phrase? Consider register, durations, and the text.

C. How is the ametric rhythm structured? What determines the placement of the dashed measure divisions?

D. What aspects of the excerpt evoke the musical traditions of church music? Consider the pitch collection used, rhythm, and text setting.

Assignment 40.2

Analysis: Corigliano, "Come now, my darling," mm. 1-72 🎧

Listen to this passage while following the score in your anthology.

A. Measures 1-37. This passage is divided into short units by change of key signature. Which key areas are implied in measures 1-37? Using the key signatures of the accompaniment as your guide, complete the following chart. Trace the presence of each key signature (columns 1 and 2), determine what key is represented in those measures (column 3), and identify the character who is singing (4). In column 5, indicate significant harmonic motion, important lines of text, changes of texture, and how the keys relate to the emotional state of each character.

MEASURES	KEY SIGNATURE (PIANO PART)	KEY/MODE	CHARACTER SINGING	INTERPRETATION/COMMENTS
1-3	one flat	F major? D minor?	Rosina	The section starts ambiguously; "where are you taking me?"
4-10	one sharp	G major	Cherubino	Diatonic in G major except for tonicization of ii in mm. 8-9; relative tonal stability
11-13	three sharps	A major	Rosina	"I'm not acquainted with these parts"

B. Measures 38–72. Use change of key signature as before to fill in the chart, but also indicate a division when the character singing, or the relationship of the parts, changes.

MEASURES	KEY SIGNATURE (PIANO PART)	KEY/MODE	CHARACTER SINGING	INTERPRETATION/COMMENTS
38–49	none	C major	Cherubino	Sings uninterrupted in key that is IV of Cherubino's G major; more tuneful, like an aria

C. List four characteristics of the music that are Mozartean, and specify measure numbers where that characteristic appears.

(1)

(2)

(3)

(4)

D. Now list four characteristics, with measure numbers, that indicate that the music was not composed in the eighteenth century.

(1)

(2)

(3)

(4)

Assignment 40.3

Analysis: Kurtág, "Invocatio," from 6 Moments musicaux, mvt. 1, mm. 17-23

A. Analytical graphing

Using the score from Example 40.6 in the textbook, complete the following pitch-time graph. Each square on the pitch (x) axis equals an eighth note, and each square on the time (y) axis equals a semitone (as labeled). For two-beat triplets and other divisions of time smaller than the eighth note, you can "round up" to the nearest eighth note and fill any boxes where that pitch is present during that eighth note. If possible, use a different color or type of shading for each instrument, to see how the individual parts contribute to the full texture.

B. Using the graph you have created, examine the registral space filled by the sustained chords. Answer each question with a few sentences.

(1) What is the overall registral shape created by the pitches in this excerpt? How does it compare to the graphs we have examined previously, of works by Ligeti and Bartók (both also Hungarian composers) and to Penderecki's graphic score notation?

(2) What types of simultaneities are created?

(3) What span of registral space is occupied by each string part? How does this compare to the register employed in other string quartets we have studied, such as Mozart's K. 421?

C. Now consider the "melody" that is created from the accented entries traced by the dotted lines using the composer's representation of the melody at the bottom of each system in Example 40.6.

(1) On the following staff write out the pitches in this melody as a scale, beginning with the lowest note.

What is the collection type (circle one):   diatonic   octatonic   chromatic

(2) Now examine segments of the melody. How is it structured? Are there any motives that are repeated?

(3) Listen to this work while following the melody line. Can you hear it within the string-quartet texture of sustained tones? Based on your answer to that question, in what sense is this melody a part of the audible texture of the work? Is it hidden, like some of Ligeti's canonic lines? Or does it create some other effect?

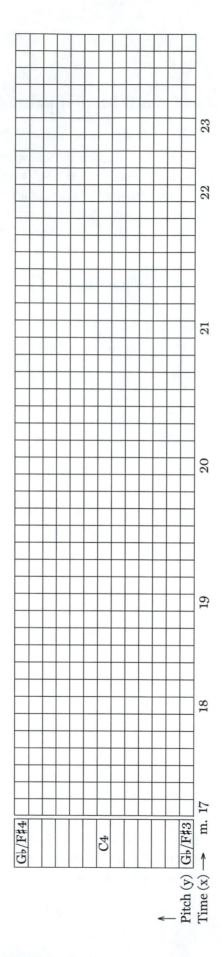

Assignment 40.4

I. Analysis: György Ligeti, "Désordre," from Piano Etudes, Book I, mm. 1–9

Using the score from Example 40.8 in the textbook, answer the questions that follow.

A. What changing meters are implied by the accents and groupings in measures 1–3?

B. Composite rhythm: In the following grid, consider the top row as the right-hand part and the bottom row as the left-hand part; one box equals an eighth note. Shade in the box for each accented eighth note, to show the placement of the accents in the composite rhythm (as in m. 1).

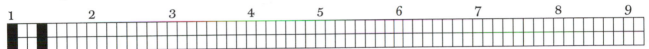

C. What does the grid illustrate about the rhythmic structure of this excerpt?

D. Describe what changes in the audible rhythm and meter as indicated by the accent patterns in measures 4–9. What feature of the left-hand part sets this change in motion?

E. Collections

(1) Describe the collection (mode or scale) that appears in the right-hand part. Give the SC label, and list the pcs in normal order.

Collection: _____

SC and normal order: _____

(2) Describe the collection (mode or scale) that appears in the left-hand part. Give the SC label, and list the pcs in normal order.

Collection: _____

SC and normal order: _____

(3) Which collection is formed when the left- and right-hand parts are combined?

Collection: _____

II. Composition

Carefully inspect the first four measures to Pärt's *Magnificat* in Example 40.2 and Assignment 40.1. Using the D Dorian scale, set syllabically (one pitch to each syllable) the text "Gloria in excelsis Deo, et in terra pax hominibus bonae voluntatis" (Glory to God in the highest, and on earth peace to men of good will) or a brief text of your choosing, after the style of Pärt. Choose longer durations for important words or syllables of the text. Then write a counterpoint above the melody with the closest chord members of the D minor triad. Your composition should be set for choir in 2–3 voice parts. Perform your composition in class.

Assignment 40.5

Analysis: Toru Takemitsu, "Rain Tree Sketch," mm. 1-13 (for piano)

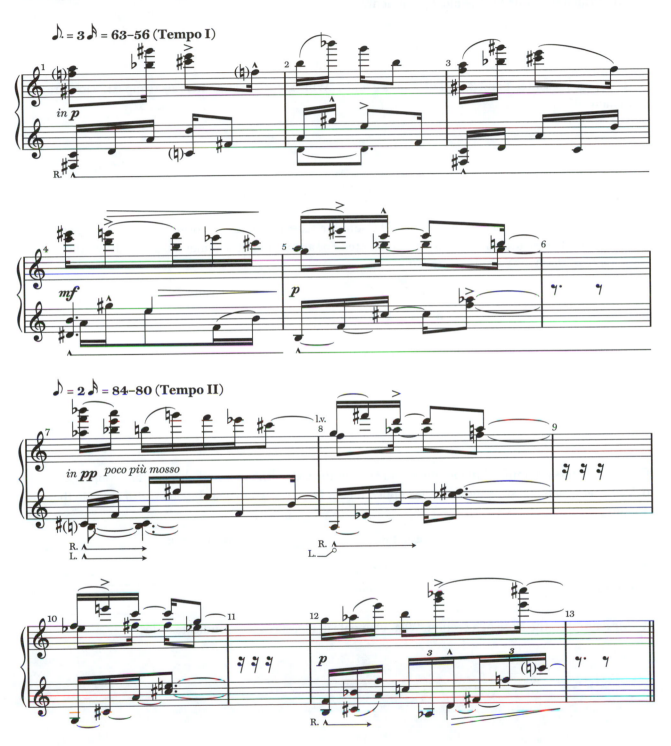

A. Pitch and interval analysis

(1) In measure 1, examine the pcs and intervals used.

    (a) How many pcs of the aggregate are present? _____   Which are missing? _____

    (b) Which intervals are the most prominent?

B. Compare measures 1 and 3, and measures 2 and 4. Which motives and intervals reappear? How are they changed?

C. What meters are implied in measures 1-6? Count the sixteenth notes and observe the groupings to decide. For each measure, indicate the implied meter. For any asymmetrical meters, also indicate the grouping (e.g., 2 + 3 + 2) within the meter.

measure 1: _____   measure 2: _____   measure 3: _____

measure 4: _____   measure 5: _____   measure 6: _____

D. Which previous measure(s) do 8 and 10 resemble?

E. What meters are implied in measures 7-13? Count the sixteenth notes and observe the groupings to decide. For each measure, indicate the implied meter. For any asymmetrical meters, also indicate the grouping within the meter.

measure 7: _____   measure 8: _____   measure 9: _____

measure 10: _____   measure 11: _____   measure 12: _____

measure 13: _____

F. Measure 13 is the close of a section. What elements in measures 12-13 indicate a close?

Assignment 40.6

Exploring contemporary counterpoint

A. Write a modal melody on these staves, leaving space beneath it to write a counterpoint. Keep it simple, with no more than three different durations and a range of an octave or less. Then set your melody against itself to make counterpoint, like that of Steve Reich's *Proverb* (Example 40.1 in the text). Begin by trying several alignments, then select the one you like best. Label the intervals between the voices. For class, prepare a performance with a friend.

B. Many of the melodic motives from Reich's *City Life* were drawn from spoken phrases. With your smartphone, tablet, or other digital recorder, record several brief segments of spoken language that you think have musical characteristics. Then transcribe these into musical notation, making melodic motives that mimic your recorded samples. Copy both the contour or pitch content and the rhythm of speech. Combine the motives you have composed and, if desired, the recorded segments to make a short passage of counterpoint. You can incorporate transposition, imitation, inversion, canon, other contrapuntal techniques, or phasing (as in *Piano Phase*, from Chapter 39). Arrange for a performance of your work in class.

Credits

Index of Music Examples